The Mobility Imperative

The Mobility Imperative

A Global Evolutionary Perspective of Human Migration

Augustin F. C. Holl

LEXINGTON BOOKS
Lanham • Boulder • New York • London

Published by Lexington Books
An imprint of The Rowman & Littlefield Publishing Group, Inc.
4501 Forbes Boulevard, Suite 200, Lanham, Maryland 20706
www.rowman.com

86-90 Paul Street, London EC2A 4NE

British Library Cataloguing in Publication Information Available

Library of Congress Cataloging-in-Publication Data

Names: Holl, Augustin, author.
  Title: The mobility imperative : a global evolutionary perspective of human migration / Augustin F. C. Holl.
  Description: Lanham, Maryland : Lexington Books, [2022] | Includes bibliographical references and index.
  Identifiers: LCCN 2022033554 (print) | LCCN 2022033555 (ebook) | ISBN 9781666903799 (Cloth) | ISBN 9781666903812 (Pbk.) | ISBN 9781666903805 (epub)
  Subjects: LCSH: Human beings--Migrations. | Human evolution.
  Classification: LCC GN370 .H65 2022 (print) | LCC GN370 (ebook) | DDC 304.8--dc23/eng/20220812
  LC record available at https://lccn.loc.gov/2022033554
  LC ebook record available at https://lccn.loc.gov/2022033555

Contents

List of Tables and Figures

TABLES

FIGURES

Preface

Two series of totally independent events inspired "the Mobility hypothesis" formulated and tested in this book. According to this hypothesis, "mobility is one of the overarching processes driving long-term human biological and cultural evolution."

The first series of events consists of the tragedies of migrants' crises triggered by combinations of different factors ranging from extreme poverty to political violence, one of the dominant aspects of the beginning of this twenty-first century. People from Western Asia and Africa try to reach Europe and Australia. Those from South and Central America move north trying to access the United States. It is however not the moral or ethical dimension—important indeed—of these crises that is addressed in this work but its long-term evolutionary implication, as will be shown later.

The lockdowns imposed in different parts of the world to fight against the COVID-19 pandemic, provisionally implemented a ban on mobility, for public health reasons. Paradoxically, these dramatic moves bring to the fore the foundational nature of mobility for human societies and individual well-being.

It may have started with the series of random mutations that led, via natural selection, to the adoption of bipedal gait by some hominin species some 7–6 million years ago. Hominids and later human population movements became a constant of human history, a constitutive aspect of the very existence of the human species. The theory of "mobility transition" developed to address patterns of rural exodus from countryside to cities, very limited in scope, as rightly pointed out by Lucassen and Lucassen (2009), is but a restricted case of a much broader and extensive mobility phenomenon.

The SArFe [S=speciation; Ar=adaptive radiation; Fe=founder effect] model formulated in the introductory section is tested through five situations (case studies) ranging from the emergence of hominins and dispersal of the *Homo* genus to the emergence and expansion of cattle pastoralism in Africa. Environmental, ancient DNA (aDNA), genomic, archaeological, linguistic, historical, and cultural anthropological data are weaved into coherent and integrated narratives to highlight the foundational and overarching role of mobility as a paramount evolutionary force. The mobility of human beings can be channeled, slowed down, countered, resisted for a short time, but is, in the long run, unstoppable.

Mobility under its different guises has always been part of explicit and implicit archaeological discourses in different academic traditions, at different times, in different part of the world (Ashley et al. 2016). It is, however, the concept of mobility viewed as an imperative in global evolutionary perspective that sets this work apart as an exercise in global and comparative archaeology.

Acknowledgments

Archaeological and ethnoarchaeological projects carried out in the Houlouf region from 1981 to 1991 were funded grants from the National Geographic Society Exploration and Research committee, the French Ministry of Cooperation, the French Ministry of Foreign Affairs, and the National Center for Scientific Research (CNRS, France).

Introduction

The Mobility Imperative

A GLOBAL EVOLUTIONARY PERSPECTIVE

The hypothesis positing that mobility plays a foundational role in human's biological and cultural evolution formulated in this book is tested through five case studies ranging from the emergence and expansion of humans to cattle domestication and the spread of pastoralism in Africa.

The first case study focuses on human origins from its early manifestations in Africa to the expansion of modern humans all over the planet. The process clearly involved successive SArFe iterations in the successive and/or overlapping stages, shifting from the Ardipithecines to the Australopithecines, the early Homo-species to modern humans, operating at ever-increasing territorial scales. Climate change, expansionary dynamics, as well as natural and cultural selection assist in shaping material cultures, genes flows, and language emergence as well as human territorial expansion in long-term evolutionary perspective.

Case studies 2 to 4, selected from different linguistic families and arranged along a chronological cline, are variants of SArFe iterations in Holocene population dynamics. Case study 2 addresses the origin and expansion of speakers of Austronesian languages from Southeast China to the Eastern Pacific on the one hand and East Africa on the other hand, with however a dominant emphasis on the Indian Ocean side of the phenomenon. Unique in the annals of human history, the "Austronesian expansion" is clearly one of the most extraordinary human cultural adaptations to maritime environments and the only case of connected recent populations spread across two-thirds of the globe.

Case studies 3, 4, and 5 are continental from Africa. Case study 3, selected from the Afroasiatic linguistic family, examines the origin and expansion of speakers of Chadic languages from East Africa to the Chad basin in

1

north-central Africa. Case study 4, selected from the Niger-Congo linguistic family, discusses the origin and expansion of speakers of Bantu languages from Northwest Central Africa to Eastern and Southern Africa. And finally, case study 5 explores the multiple implications of cattle domestication and the genesis of Africa pastoralism with emphasis on the spread of zoonoses, particularly bovine tuberculosis (bTB) in this case.

Environmental, genomic, archaeological, anthropological, linguistic, and historical data are relied upon to craft a global evolutionary archaeology narrative. There are strong similarities in the evolutionary pathways featured in the four Holocene case studies.

1. There is initially the formation of a small colonist group, equivalent to a "speciation event": Proto-Austronesians in Northwest Taiwan, Proto-Chadic in the Mid-Holocene Lake Chad delta, Proto-Bantu along the Cameroon-Nigeria Border Area, and areas of pristine cattle domestication in Northeast Africa and the Near-East.
2. The expansion to new territories is equivalent to "adaptive radiation." Adaptation and expansion with admixture and linguistic drift all over Taiwan for the Early Austronesian–speaking communities; the Chad basin for the Early Chadic–speaking groups; the southern Cameroon for Early Bantu–speaking collectivities; and finally, the Eastern Sahara and Northeast Africa for the initial expansion of domesticated cattle.
3. The successful adaptation to and colonization of new territories are equivalent to the "founder effect," with the cycle starting again and again at each expansion phase.

Evidence for population admixture is robust. Technological innovation and diffusion were the rule. All four case studies involve food-producing collectivities: rice farming for Proto-Austronesians; livestock herding for Proto-Chadic, and finger-millet farming for Proto-Bantu, and the spread of cattle herding and the emergence of pastoralist societies all over the continent. And finally, all four situations, starting likely with small pioneer group–based communities along a moving frontier, developed into diverse social formations ranging from self-sustaining agricultural and mixed farming autonomous villages, pastoral-nomadic communities to hierarchical and centralized chiefdoms and kingdoms. The parallel evolution outlined above is very likely dependent on mobility. It can be conceptualized as a derivative from the fractal nature of the evolutionary process itself.

FROM BIPEDAL GAIT TO INTERPLANETARY TRAVELS

For 99.99 percent of their relatively short evolutionary history, protohuman and human communities were integrally mobile. Mobility was, and still is multi-scalar, embedded in subsistence as well as global social systems (Munoz-Moreno and Crawford 2021). Its manifestations range from the rounds of daily-life activities to planned and unplanned changes of localities, as well as exploration and settlement in new places.

Human history can be read from the perspective of mobility and its derived technologies. Transportability was a critical bottleneck in human history for a very long time, particularly when human locomotion and muscular energy were the unique mobility engines. Carrying raw material, collected resources, and infants required the invention of different devices and containers, all initially made of perishable materials (Holl 1989).

The manufacture of early high-sea watercrafts is indirectly indicated by Modern humans' settlement in Sahul (North Australia) some 65,000 years ago; this exploit required a 90–100 kilometer sea-crossing from the Wallacea to North Sahul. Objects geared to water bodies crossing, at different spatial scales, came to be the first significant artifacts of human mobility engineering. Direct and indirect evidence of high sea navigation are indicated by the circulation of raw material like obsidian from Melos Island to continental Greece, the presence of tuna bones—suggesting high sea fishing—and remains of domesticated sheep/goats in the Eastern Mediterranean islands. Early Holocene dugouts are found farther inland, as is the case for the eight thousand years BP Dufuna specimen in Northeastern Nigeria (Breunig 1996) and the six thousand years BP one on the ancient shore of the Seine River in Paris-Bercy, France (Arnold 1998).

With the domestication of plants and animals, animal power was progressively harnessed for mobility purposes in different parts of the world from the Middle Holocene onward. Within a process summed up under the concept of "Secondary Product Revolution" (Sherratt 1981), cattle, horses, donkeys, camels, dromedaries, and llamas opened the era of animal-based transportation systems. The invention of the wheel in Mesopotamia around 3500 BCE, coupled with animal power, assisted in the construction of the earliest transportation and agricultural machines.

The European industrial revolution led to the invention of the steamboat in 1812, the steam-train in 1825, the automobile internal combustion engine in 1886, and the first heavier-than-air flying machine of Orville and Wilbur Wright at Kitty Hawk, North Carolina, on December 17, 1903. All these inventions facilitated, amplified, and accelerated humans and goods mobility. Today, mobility machines move people in the air, on land, and on and underwater. The implication of this long-term perspective is fundamentally that every human, every community, every nation, is the product of deep-time multi-scalar mobility.

MULTI-SCALAR MOBILITY

Humans with their commensals are the only sets of species to have expanded in virtually all the world's ecosystems, from the equatorial to the periglacial zones. This expansion operated at different space-time scales. It started some 7–6 Ma ago, with pulls and pushes followed by relatively long adaptive stasis, and keeps going on today. Much of the initial human expansion took place within the context of hunting-gathering lifeways, with two kinds of mobility dominant in the Initial History of humanity: routine subsistence mobility on the one hand and push for territorial expansion on the other hand. Agroecological systems generated their own mobility pattern with settlement relocation following fallow systems (Boserup 1965). Urbanization and contemporary societies are sustained by the constant transfer, in and out, of people, information, and goods via mobility technologies.

As demonstrated by the Time-Geography school (Carlstein 1982, Corbett 2001), mobility research brought to light some profound implications generally taken for granted. In his paper "What about People in Regional Science," Hagerstrand (1970) shows that human spatial activity is not carried out after independent decisions made by temporally or spatially autonomous individuals but is instead constrained by limitations. Three such constraints, visualized in the space-time prism, were identified: (1) capability: the physical limitation that does not allow an individual to be in more than one place at the same time; (2) coupling: one's space-time path must temporarily link up with that of another individual to accomplish a particular task; and finally, and (3) authority: the access or lack of access to a place or locality (Corbett 2001). Social spatial behavior thus requires either presence or representation, simple or multiple coupling, and accessibility or its alternative. Time is intrinsically embedded in any spatial activity, in the daily routine of foragers food gathering to city commuters shifts from home to work and back.

Routine hunter-gatherers' subsistence operates at two embedded territorial scales: the local band daily foraging range and the annual territory. The former consists of a subsistence space around the foragers' camping site also called "site catchment" (Vita-Finzi and Higgs 1970), visited on a daily basis for the gathering of the necessary food and subsistence resources. Hunting may require larger territorial range, but on the average small mammals and other sources of animal proteins can be accessible through the gathering of mollusks, insects, birds, and larvae. The camp is moved to another locale of the band's territory when daily foraging trips returns drop.

Resource availability and distribution are controlled by seasonality. Hunter-gatherers' annual territories generally consist of two complementary components: one settled in the "lean" season (dry season territory) and the other visited during the "plenty" season (rainy season). It is the sum total of these distinct territorial units visited during a whole year that delineates a forager's band annual territory. Hunter-gatherers' territoriality thus consists above all of networks of places and resources patches, not bounded territorial units. Distinct contemporary foragers' bands annual territories can overlap and/or crisscross. Depending on the demography, different foragers bands can use the same space for different purposes at different times, with social mechanisms—exchange, matrimonial alliances, conflict—forged to deal with actual circumstances.

The carrying capacity—the sum-total of animal and plant biomass per space unit (km^2)—of foragers' annual territory is relatively inelastic. The adjustable variable therefore is foragers' population density. In circumstances of sustained population growth, foragers' groups will expand in new territories to maintain a sustainable population/carrying-capacity balance. In situation of population crises, previously settled territories can be abandoned, only to be resettled in the next growth phase.

Humans move with their "cultural package": their ideas, worldviews, and "know-how." They do not reinvent the world anew at each new step. Edgar Anderson (1952) studying the dynamics of weeds unintentionally spread by humans coined the concept of "transported landscape." He intended to emphasize human's colonization impacts on natural ecosystems (Chang et al. 2015, Kirch 1982, Matisoo-Smith 2015, Penailillo et al. 2016).

> In the colonization of new lands . . . humans do more than act as the means of transport for a group of adventives. They carry with them a cultural concept of landscape, which causes them to actively shape a new environment in that mold. (Kirch 1982: 2)

Individuals, families, corporations, cities, states, and nations operate at different but nested temporalities that range from cosmological to individual time. F. Braudel's 1949 systematics

"Event—Conjuncture—*Longue durée*" capture the most relevant dimensions of human activity. The commonsense definition of "Event"—something that happen—seems obvious enough, but in fact requires multiple qualifications to be intelligible. Conjuncture—a combination of events—singles out a time segment with particularly well delineated characteristics. And finally, the *longue durée*—or long-term perspective—focuses on slowly changing connections between people, institutions, and the world that constitute the most fundamental aspects of social life, generally in a multidisciplinary perspective. The *longue durée* approach, initially formulated by Lucien Febvre and Marc Bloch, the founding figures of the Annales school of social and economic history in 1929, was re-elaborated and popularized by F. Braudel in his 1947 doctoral thesis published in 1949 as *La Méditerranée et le Monde Méditerranéen a l'Epoque de Philippe II*. The world-systems approach developed by I. Wallerstein (1976, 2004) is explicitly derived from the Annales school and F. Braudel works. Following Wallerstein (1976: 229), "a world system . . . has boundaries, structures, member groups, rules of legitimation, and coherence. Its life is made up of the conflicting forces which hold it together by tension and tear it apart as each group seeks eternally to remold it to its advantage." The core-periphery rationale derived from Wallerstein analysis of the emergence of European capitalism had to be reconsidered for the model to be used by archaeologists (Algaze 1993, Peregrine 1996). It was done through a redefinition of the characteristics of intra-world-system geographic differentiation and the reexamination of the kind of economic interdependence among connected regions. Consequently, it is the concept of a world system without core-periphery dichotomy and dependency, but one with multiple cores connected by flows of people, goods, ideas, cultures, and religions that is relied upon in this book.

LARGE-SCALE POPULATION MOVEMENTS
AND THEIR IMPACTS IN WORLD HISTORY

Beside the emergence and expansion of humans all over the planet, a panoramic and longitudinal look at the last ten thousand years of human history attests to the ubiquity and profound cultural as well as biological impact of large-scale population movements. A few examples will be relied upon to make this assertion obvious.

The Expansion of Farming

In different parts of the world, the spread of farming led to the expansion of human populations, cultivars, and domesticated animals. Neolithic expansion from the Near-East to Europe is one of the best-known cases of farming population expansion with admixture with late Mesolithic hunter-gatherers (Shennan 2018). The area of origins is the Anatolian plateau and the northern portion of the Near East. From 8000 to 5000 BCE, Neolithic farmers cultivating wheat, barley, and lentils and rearing cattle, sheep, goats, and pigs, spread all over Europe following two axes: the continental axis, termed Danubian, and the coastal Mediterranean axis, called Cardial or "Impressed Ware" culture in Italy.

Early Anatolian farmers moved north and formed the Initial Danubian current called Starcevo-Koros (6500–6000 BCE) in the south-central Europe Danube River catchment. In their north-northwest expansion between 5400 and 4500 BCE, these farming communities formed the Linear Band Ceramic cultures in the Central Europe plains with their characteristic longhouses and pottery decoration design and syntax. A further move west resulted in the formation of the Rossen culture (4500–4000 BCE) in Western Germany, Northern France, Belgium, and the Netherlands. England was reached around 4000 BCE, and Scandinavia between 3500 and 500 BCE.

The Cardial axis developed from Eastern Mediterranean islands around 6000 BCE and reached the Iberic peninsula and northern Morocco around 5600 BCE, via the coastal Balkans, Italy, France, and the Mediterranean islands. The Chalcolithic, Bronze Age, and Iron Age cultures that followed all feature significant material culture and population redistribution and expansion.

The Formation of World-Empires

Starting from the Macedonian kingdom, Alexander the Great conquered the Achaemenid—Persian—empire, reached Afghanistan and India in the east and Egypt in the south from 334 to 323 BCE, resulting in what is known as the "Alexander the Great Empire" (Liebert 2011).

The formation of the Roman Republic and Empire started sometime around 218 BCE, with Italy, Corsica, Sardinia, and Sicily as core territory. It expanded from there to Iberia, Tunisia, the coastal Balkans, and coastal Turkey around 133 BCE. The Gaul region, North Africa, Turkey, and Syria were added around 44 BCE, with the Roman world reaching its maximum expansion in 115–117 CE (Heather 2005). Constantly battling with restive groups along its borders, especially with the Germanic groups along its northern borders, the Western Roman Empire collapsed around 300 CE. The Eastern Roman Empire, then called the Byzantine Empire with its capital at Byzantium—later changed to Constantinople and Istanbul—lasted from 330 to 1453 CE when it was conquered by Moslem troops.

The collapse of the Western Roman empire resulted in social and political fragmentation of Western Europe. A process triggered by "the Great invasions" by Angles, Saxons, Vandals, Burgunds, Goths, Ostrogoths, Wisigoths, Sueve, Alamans, Huns, etc. (Heather 2005). From 100 to 500 CE, these communities carved new territories and created new rival and competing kingdoms. A new round of political centralization, supported by the powerful Catholic Church and the Vatican, succeeded with the coronation of

Carolus Magnus—Charlemagne—by the Pope and established the Holy Romano-Germanic Empire that lasted from 753 to 1806 CE.

The Arab and Islam expansion from 633 to 1453, started with the success of Islam in the Arabic peninsula. This first success was followed by the conquest of Syria and Egypt, North Africa, Spain and southwestern France in the West, Inner Asia, Pakistan, parts of India and Island Southeast Asia in the East, up to the conquest of Constantinople in 1453 (Kennedy 2007).

Similar sociopolitical cycling processes articulated on successive steps including: emergence and consolidation, centralization, expansion through conquest, political domination, and fragmentation and collapse, can be documented in the dynamics of every large-social formation in all continents.

The cycling of China dynasties is a good example (Loewe and Shaughnessy 1999). Chinese civilization is considered to have been shaped by three initial dynasties, Xia (2100–1600 BCE), Shang (1600–1050 BCE), and Zhou (1046–256 BCE), divided into Northern and Southern Zhou.

The Qin dynasty (221–206 BCE), even if comparatively short-lived, unified the political leadership and formed the first China Empire but also ruined the country. Consolidation and expansion were carried out by the Han dynasty (206 BCE–220 CE) for almost four centuries, followed by fragmentation and the rise of competing regional kingdoms from 220 to 589 CE.

A new cycle of consolidation and centralization was initiated by the short-lived Sui dynasty (581–618), expanded under the Tang dynasty (618–906), and ended with a new phase of regional fragmentation from 907 to 960 CE.

The Song (Sung) dynasty (960–1279) divided into Northern and Southern Song, presided over a cycle of consolidation and centralization, interrupted by the short-lived Yuan dynasty (1279–1368) but expanded by the Ming dynasty (1368–1644 CE) and part of the Qing dynasty (1644–1912).

Population Movements from 1500 to 1900

Large-scale population movements are well documented for the modern period from 1500 to the present (Castles et al. 2014). The provided figures are approximations that are very likely underestimations. This having been said, these data are clear indications of the crucial impact of population movements in the construction of the modern and present world (O'Brien 1999: 211).

Figures on the number of Africans displaced through enslavement are disputed. Some 12 million are estimated to have been shipped from Africa through the Atlantic to the Caribbean, North America, and South America from 1530 to 1860, and 4.3 million to the Near East from 1500 to 1900.

Europeans spread to the Americas, Australia, South Africa, and North Africa (Algeria), colonizing other peoples' lands. Some 32 million are estimated to have flocked to North America between 1620 and 1914, 10 million to Siberia and East Asia from 1880 to 1914, 7.4 million to South America from 1530 to 1914, 3 million to Australia and New Zealand from 1790 and 1914, and finally, 1.5 million to Algeria between 1850 and 1914.

As far as Asia is concerned, 3 million Indians spread to the Indian Ocean Islands, East and South Africa, and the Caribbean from 1850 to 1914. Twenty-two million Chinese spread to Island Southeast Asia and 1 million to the Pacific islands and Americas between 1820 and 1914. And finally, 8 million Japanese spread to Island Southeast Asia, Northeastern China (Mandchouria), the Pacific islands, and the Americas from 1900 to 1914.

In total, over a period of five hundred years and less, 103.2 million people moved, and brought their language, culture, and genes in different parts of the world. 16.3 million were Africans, 53.9 million were Europeans, and 33 million were Asians (Castles et al. 2014).

A GLOBAL EVOLUTIONARY PERSPECTIVE

While philosophy and theology were dominant in Post-Renaissance Europe humanities, the scientific quest for understanding human origins, part of a broader coalition of ideas looking for explanation of the history and diversity of life on earth, was rooted in the natural history research field. That emerging research field blended a broad range of natural science disciplines in the eighteenth and nineteenth centuries (Pigliucci 2007). Some towering scientists set the stage for the phenomenal development of natural history in the twentieth century. Carl von Linné published his groundbreaking eleven-page *Systema naturae* in 1735, later called Linnean taxonomy. It is a hierarchical classification with three kingdoms: stones, plants, and animals, each partitioned into classes, orders, genera, species, and varieties.

Charles Lyell popularized the concept of "uniformitarianism." He asserted that there are natural explanations for all visible geological phenomena still in operation today—erosion, aggradation, accumulation—but effective in the buildup of geological formation only in very long timescales. His *"Principles of Geology,"* published in 1830 laid the foundation for earth and soils sciences.

Charles Darwin published his magnum opus *"The Origin of Species by means of Natural selection"* in November 1859. The work frames the theory of evolution and laid the foundation of evolutionary biology. It sent shock waves through Western cultures that are still palpable in some parts of the world today. Evolution is defined as change, over successive generations, in the heritable characteristics of biological populations. The theory of evolution states that all life-forms are related and emerged from nonlife. In its initial formulation, known as classical Darwinism, change, through the operation of natural processes, was viewed as effected via small, gradual, and cumulative modifications. Relying on Lyell's principle of "uniformitarianism" and Malthus's observations on the relationship between population and resources, Darwin crafted "the first two conceptual pillars of modern evolutionary theory: 1—descent with modification . . . the pattern that accounts for life's history and diversity, . . . [and], 2—natural selection, the mechanism that explains the form-function dilemma" (Pigliucci 2007: 2743). The core of initial classical Darwinism thus focuses on variation, inheritance, and natural selection.

The fusion of Darwinian evolution and Mendelian genetics during the first half of the twentieth century with its concentration on genetics and adaptive variations in populations led to the "modern synthesis" (MS). While never an all-encompassing synthesis, the MS brought together the basic neo-Darwinian principles of variation, inheritance, differential reproduction, and natural selection with Mendelian experimental and population genetics, as well as concepts and data from paleontology, botany, and systematics (Laland et al. 2015, Muller 2017, Pugliucci and Muller 2010). Gradualism, externalism, and gene-centrism are considered the general hallmarks of the MS. In a paper entitled "Punctuated equilibria: An alternative to phyletic gradualism" published in 1972, Niles Elredge and Stephen Jay Gould mounted a frontal challenge to Darwinian gradualism. They argued that evolutionary development is made of limited episodes of rapid speciation (punctuations) between long periods of stability (equilibrium), also known as "stasis."

There are a number of research fields with important evolutionary potentials that are either tangential to or completely absent from the MS that triggered calls for a bold conceptual extension (Baedke et al. 2020, Bartlett 2017, Buskell 2019, Laland et al. 2015, Muller 2017, Murray et al. 2020, Pigliucci 2007, Pigliucci and Muller 2010, Richard and Pigliucci 2021, Smith et al. 2018, Zeder 2018). The extended framework, called for by number of researchers and termed extended evolutionary synthesis (EES), is one of a number of current attempts to put in place a new evolutionary conceptualization. It includes inputs derived from evolutionary development biology (evo-devo), phenotypic plasticity, genomics, multilevel selection, reciprocal causation, inclusive inheritance, epigenetics, niche construction, and complexity theory, as well as evolution on adaptive landscapes. "EES can provide information about cultural niche construction, social learning, source of variability, directionality, causality, modes of inheritance, targets of selection and tempo of evolution. . . . Humans and plants are treated as reactive developmental systems undergoing plastic changes on multiple levels of organization, through non-linear pathways and various causes" (Baedke et al. 2020: 10).

Directionality provided by variation derived from genetic and constructive developmental processes manifests itself in phenotypic plasticity. Causality operates as a reciprocal process. Organisms are not only shaped by selective environment but also shape it. In the niche construction process, acquired characteristics and phenotypic changes do not invariably follow genetic changes but may lead it. "Advances at the interface of ecology, behavior and culture have shown that populations of organisms are . . . actively involved in the formation of their environment that constitutes the selective conditions for the later populations" (Muller 2017). Targets of selection vary considerably. They can be genomes, genes cells, tissues, organisms, regulatory processes, groups of organisms, or populations. Inheritance is the transmission from one generation to the next. There are multiple systems that shape trans-generational inheritance, both internal and external to the organism. Acquired traits can be inherited with trans-generational epigenetic inheritance.

And finally, the tempo and pace of evolutionary change is very variable depending on organisms and systems under consideration. In all the cases however, evolution proceeds at an uneven pace with periods of stasis punctuated by periods of rapid macroevolutionary change. In summary, the EES is a theoretical framework that takes into account the plurality of factors and causal relations in evolutionary process (Muller 2017).

The theoretical developments derived from the EES are particularly suitable and effective for evolutionary anthropology and global archaeology research (Anton and Kuzawa 2017, Murray et al. 2020, Smith et al. 2018). They can be operationalized and visualized in three successive steps based on the nature and characteristics of the processes involved:

1. variation has to be generated to initiate the process;
2. selection operates on the generated variation via developmental bias and/or niche construction; and finally
3. heritable variations are sieved and distributed through a number of processes, all resulting in phenotypic evolution.

As shown above, biological evolution operates along much more complex pathways than the standard sequence of random mutations, natural selection, and adaptation. It is this larger scope of evolutionary processes involving biological and cultural dimension that is adopted in this work. The evolutionary scenario can be spelled out in a series of successive steps encapsulating biological and cultural aspects that may operate at different timescales:

1. speciation event;
2. adaptive radiation; and
3. founder effect.

The invention of tools and the ensuing cultural transmission added to the biological dynamics that is always in operation. The challenge at this juncture is to frame a pragmatic and applicable methodology, delineating some core principles. "Unifying principles are used to provide simplifying assumptions to complex problems, which allows them to be effectively tackled by tools at hand. "the primary goal of a unifying principle is to provide a mental map to researchers as to the territory . . . they are exploring" (Bratlett 2017: 1). What is being explored in this book, is the profound implication of mobility in the shaping of humanity, biologically and culturally. The core dimension of mobility relied upon are spelled out below and used to formulate a model. The crafted model is then tested on five case studies.

Speciation Event

"Speciation" is a biological lineage-splitting event that result in the emergence of two or more separate species. "Divergent selection may generate barriers to gene flow and ultimately lead to the evolution of distinct species— a process referred to as ecological speciation. Partial reproductive isolation can arise as a by-product of local adaptation within dozens to a few hundred generations, suggesting that divergent selection may initiate speciation over ecological timescales; more uncertain, however, is how often and at what pace divergence proceeds along the speciation continuum until strong reproductive isolation is established" (Momigliano et al. 2017).

Adaptive Radiation

Newly formed species emerge following different adaptations, each a response to an opportunity. Adaptive radiation is characterized by great ecological and morphological diversity, the driving force behind it being the adaptation of organisms to new ecological contexts (Neige 2015, Parsons 2016). Expansion in new territories without competitors, such as new environmental settings and/or islands, offers optimal condition for adaptive radiations.

Founder Effect

Founder effect is a special case of genetic drift. The latter is an evolution mechanism in which allele frequencies of a given population change randomly over generations. The former applies to a small group that split from the main population and established a colony. Having separated from its initial larger population, the new group may contain different allele frequencies and as such represent narrower genetic diversity. Founder speciation has been suggested to be a potent force in the generation of new species. However, "the relative frequency of changes in the genetic and the phenotypic composition of a population due to founder effects, and the importance of these changes, remain a contentious issue on the nature of the evolutionary process" (Matute 2013: 229–30).

In their schematic range expansion model, Peter and Slatkin (2015: 3) formulate the issues involved as follows: "We assume that the population starts from a single deme in a one-dimensional (1D) array of empty locations and evolves in discrete generations. Every generation, the population expands to occupy a previously vacant location. The new deme is colonized by the offspring of individuals in the most recently founded deme. We assume that the colonizing process results in a founder event that temporarily reduces the effective population size. During the same time step, all other demes experience genetic drift at a rate determined by their effective population size, which is larger than the size of the colonizing group."

As shown in the above discussion, mobility at different pace and scale is a core dimension of evolutionary change and the construction of Humanity. The evolutionary model outlined above, labeled SArFe—(S for Speciation, Ar for Adaptive Radiation, and Fe for Founder Effect) is applicable to virtually all aspects of human biological and social evolution.

Miocene hominids, Gigantopithecus, Sivapithecus, and Dryopithecus branched off and cannot be considered as remote human ancestors. The current human phylogenetic tree thus started with SArFe 1, ranging from 7 to 4.5 Ma in Africa with the Ardipithecines: *Sahelanthropus tchadensis* (7 Ma) in Chad Republic, North Central Africa, *Orrorin tugenensis* (6 Ma) in Kenya, East Africa, *Ardipithecus kadabba* (5.8–5.2 Ma) and *Ar. ramidus* (4.4 Ma) in Ethiopia, with a territorial range limited to Chad-Ethiopia-Kenya in Africa.

SArFe 2 consists of two branches, one with gracile—Australopithecines—and the other with robust forms, known as Paranthropus. The gracile australopithecines with *Au. anamensis* (4.2–3.8 Ma), *Au. afarensis* (3.9–2.9 Ma), *Au. africanus* (3.6–2 Ma), *Au. garhi* (2.6–2.5 Ma), *Au. bahrelghazali* (3.5 Ma), and *Au. sediba* (1.9–1.7 Ma), range from 4.2 to 1.7 Ma. They were spread over a more extensive territory from North Central Africa to the southern tip of the continent. The Paranthropus branch limited to eastern and southern Africa includes *P. aethiopicus* (2.7–2.3 Ma), *P. bosei* (2.3–1.34 Ma), and *P. robustus* (2–0.6 Ma). The production of hominin made objects started in SArFe 2.

Without going further into details at this stage, SArFe 3 (also known as Out of Africa 1) includes all early *Homo* species with stone knapping skills who spread all over the old-world middle latitudes, reaching western and eastern Eurasia and well as Island Southeast Asia from 2.5 to 3/200,000 years ago.

SArFe 4 (Out of Africa 2), the "human cognitive revolution," witnessed the expansion of modern humans all over the planet during the last 300,000 years, resulting in the extinction of three and partial absorption of two of five other contemporary species. SArFe 5 will very likely take place via interplanetary travels if there is successful human colonization of the moon or another planet.

Contemporary human genetic makeup (Duda and Zrzavy 2019) and languages (Atkinson 2011, Atkinson et al. 2008, Dunn et al. 2011, Greenhill et al. 2018, Perreault and Mathew 2012) feature the same evolutionary dynamics. It can even be said that, provided necessary adjustments, the SArFe theoretical approach can help understand the evolution of many other aspects of human cultural developments, ancient and contemporaneous. Human mobility cannot be stopped. It is the engine of human biology and cultural creativity.

The model outlined above is global and incorporate aspects of most of the disciplinary fields involved in research on the human past. Explicit and coherent approaches to evolutionary archaeology have been in the making within the last three decades. Cochrane and Gardner (2011), for example, initiate a conversation between evolutionary and interpretive approaches in archaeology, featuring an uneasy mix of divergent theoretical and methodological approaches. Hart (2002), O'Brien (1996), O'Brien and Lyman (2000), Prentiss (2009, 2019), and Telster (1994) work on the formulation of archaeological theory and methods based on Darwinian principles, with special focus on material culture. Artifacts are viewed as human phenotypes, with analyses targeting variation in the archaeological record. Material culture is however a dependent variable of population, a tool among many, and as such cannot be the main locus of global evolutionary archaeology development. The SArFe model outlined above offers a more parsimonious and effective approach.

CONCLUSION

Fractal geometry (Mandelbrot 1982) is the mathematical branch of Measure Theory. A fractal is generally "a rough or fragmented geometric shape that can be subdivided in parts, each of which is (at least approximately) a reduced-size copy of the whole." This property is called self-similarity. The term, derived from the Latin *fractus*, meaning "broken" or "fractured," was coined by Benoit Mandelbrot in 1975 (Chandra et al. 2012: 251). A fractal is accordingly made by repeating a simple process again and again—iteration. It exhibits similar patterns at different scales—self-similarity, as expanding or unfolding symmetry. The SArFe model outlined in this introduction has all the properties of fractals, in time however instead of space. It provides a parsimonious model for the analysis of the foundational effect of mobility in the making of humanity.

Chapter 1

Human Origins and Expansion

IN THE BEGINNINGS

Introduction

The acceleration of paleoanthropological research during the last two decades in Africa and other parts of the tropical world, particularly midlatitude Europe and South Asia, has resulted in many important discoveries that are changing our understanding of the emergence and expansion of humankind. This section features the major recent discoveries and their implications for the understanding of the origin and evolution of the human phenomenon. The roots of "humanity" are pushed deeper back in the past, around 7–4 Ma ago with the "Ardipithecines," including *Sahelanthropus tchadensis* and *Orrorin tugenensis*, followed by *Ardipithecus ramidus* and *Ar. Kadabba*. The "Australopithecines" speciation, radiation, and diversification followed between 4–1.5 Ma. And finally, the *Homo* genus (*Homo habilis*) emerged around 2.8 Ma ago, diversified, and expanded out of Africa to reach midlatitude Europe and Southern and Eastern Asia between 2.5 and 1.8 Ma ago. Regional diversification through evolutionary drift led to *Homo heidelbergensis*, and later to Denisovans, Neanderthals, *Homo sapiens sapiens*, *H. naledi, H. floresiensis*, and *H. luzonensis.* during the last 300,000 years. The latest global expansion of *H. sapiens sapiens*, the only surviving species that spread to Australia 65,000 years ago, the Americas, the Pacific, and the whole world, is one of the greatest breakthrough of ongoing paleoanthropological research. Archaeological sites, genomic explorations, mitochondrial DNA mapping, and human languages are permanent reminder of the unity of humankind.

Initial Research on the Cradle of Humankind

At the very end of the nineteenth century, Abbot Henri Breuil, Jesuit priest and professor of prehistory at the Paris Institute of Human Paleontology is claimed to have said: "*Le berceau de l'Humanite est un berceau a roulette*" (The cradle of humankind is a wheeled one). He was clearly alluding to the rising competition and rivalry between European nations to "own" the cradle of humankind or to contribute to its discovery (table 1). The foundation of prestigious natural history museums in all European countries and the Americas, and the creation of wide-ranging networks of learned societies fueled research on human origins. Avocational archaeologists and prehistorians initiated systematic surveys and excavation of sites located in their respective regions. News on significant discoveries were spreading fast through learned societies networks.

Charles Darwin dealt directly with humans in "*The Descent of Man and selection in relation to sex*," published in 1871. Humans were then firmly inserted in the ape family, and all aspects of human's evolution including language, ideas, etc. were asserted to be explainable in terms of the operations of natural processes. E. Lartet (1837) published the first discovery of a fossil ape in 1837. Archival research carried out by Kennedy and Ciochon (1999) shows that it was in fact Hugh Falconer and associates who made the first discovery of a fossil ape in the Siwalik, India, in the 1830s (Falconer 1832). The first human fossils discovered between 1829 and 1888 were concentrated in Western Europe (table 1.1). Remains later assigned to *Homo neanderthalensis* were found at Engis Cave in Belgium in1829, Forbes Quarry in Gibraltar

Table 1.1: Chronology of the discovery of human fossils in the nineteenth and early twentieth century

Date	Fossil Name	lace	Country
1829	*Homo neandertalensis*	Engis Cave	Belgium
1830	Ape tooth	Siwalik Hills	India
1848	*Homo neandertalensis*	Forbes Quarry	Gibraltar
1856	*Homo neandertalensis*	Neander valley	Germany
1868	*Homo sapiens sapiens*	Cro-Magnon Cave	France
1888	*Homo sapiens sapiens*	Chancelade	France
1891	*Pithecanthropus erectus*	Trinil	Java
1901	*Homo sapiens sapiens*	Grimaldi	Italy
1907	*Homo heidelbergensis*	Mauer	Germany
1907–1912	*Eoanthropus dawsoni*	Piltdown	England
1921	*Homo rhodesiensis*	Kabwe	Zambia
1921	*Sinanthropus pekinensis*	Chou Kou Tien	China
1925	*Australopithecus africanus*	Taung	South Africa
1959	*Zinjanthropus bosei*	Olduvai	Tanzania

in 1848, and finally at Neander Valley in Germany in 1856. In the remaining part of the nineteenth century *Homo sapiens sapiens* [*H. sapiens sapiens*] fossils were discovered in Southwestern France, at Cro-Magnon in March 1868 and Chancelade on October 1st, 1888. With the significant exception of Hugh Falconer and associates' research in the Siwalik hills and Eugene Dubois's discovery of a fossil skull cap, femur, and teeth, assigned to *Pithecanthropus erectus* at Trinil (Java) in 1891, most nineteenth-century investigations on early human origins took place in Western Europe.

The search of human origins was expanded to different areas of the Old World—Africa and Asia—in the first half of the twentieth century (table 1.1) in the context of increasing European nations rivalry and competition. Additional *Homo sapiens sapiens* fossils were found at Grimaldi in Italy in 1901. Fossils of *Homo heidelbergensis* were discovered at Mauer in Germany in 1907. Charles Dawson, referring explicitly to the Mauer discovery launched an excavation program at Piltdown in Sussex (England), in the same year with the collaboration of A. Smith Woodward, paleontologist and curator at the Natural History Museum. The project failed to produce the expected results, leading C. Dawson to "fabricate" the fake *Eoanthropus dawsoni* known in paleoanthropology history as the "Piltdown fake" (Price 2016, Szalay 2016):

Scientists in Belgium, France and Germany uncovered early human fossils that shined light on human evolution. Among these findings was the highly significant jaw fossil from Homo heidelbergensis, found in Germany in 1907. Geopolitical ties between the United Kingdom and the continent were relatively weak; the tensions that would come to light in World War 1 were already brewing. The British were jealous of these findings and wanted to find their own "early man" to bring glory to England. Hancock wrote that the French teased the British about their lack of fossils, calling them "pebble hunters." (Szalay 2016).

The twists in the search for humankind cradle did not stop there. The bitter European rivalry spilled on the Old-World scene. A human's skull found at Kabwe in Zambia—then known as Broken Hill in Northern Rhodesia—in 1921 was assigned to *Homo rhodesiensis* by A. S. Woodward—reassigned today to *H. heidelbergensis*. The same year, research was launched at a rich fossiliferous deposit of Chou Kou Tien at 40 kilometers southwest of Beijing by Dr J. G. Anderson and Dr. O. Zdansky. The first scientific report was published in March 1923 in the *Memoirs of the Geological Survey of China* (Black 1926). The remains of 20 to 40 individuals were collected from Chou Kou Tien deposit, the site of Beijing Man—*Sinanthropus pekinensis*—(table 1.1).

It is however the discovery from South Africa that was met with scorn, rejected and ignored by European scientists for almost a quarter century in stark contrast with the "Piltdown Fake" that was accepted as evidence of the Darwinian "missing link" for more than half a century. In 1925, Raymond Dart's "discovery" stole the "show" and shifted the focus to Southern Africa. The words, expressions, and sentences Dart used in his 1925 paper in *Nature* were probably irritating for his European colleagues.

Summarizing the implications of the recent Zambian and South African discoveries, Dart writes: "for these discoveries lend promise to the expectation that a tolerably complete story of higher primate evolution in Africa will yet be wrested from our rocks." (Dart 1925: 195). Reasserting along the way that the six-year-old Taung child's specimen described in the paper is "an anthropoid and not cercopithecid ape" (ibid.). The material he describes "constitutes a specimen of unusual value in fossil anthropoid discovery. . . . Here as in *Homo rhodesiensis* Southern Africa has provided documents of higher primate evolution that are amongst the most complete extant" (ibid.). It was probably his strong emphasis on Africa as the cradle of humankind at the peak of European Colonial domination that displeased his colleagues, as he suggested the specimen to

> be designated *Australopithecus africanus*, in commemoration first, of the extreme southern and unexpected horizon of its discovery, and secondly of the continent in which so many new and important discoveries connected with early history of man have recently been made, thus vindicating the Darwinian claim that Africa would prove to be the cradle of humankind. (Dart 1925: 198)

Finally, Louis Seymour Leakey, born in Kenya and educated at Cambridge University, started his archaeological research in East Africa in 1924. In 1931 he launched the Olduvai Gorge project in Tanzania with Mary Leakey and discovered the fossil of *Zinjanthropus bosei* in 1959. This episode marks the beginning of a profound transformation of methods and techniques of paleoanthropological research.

Revolution in Paleoanthropology

There has been a profound change in paleoanthropological research during the last four decades. The territorial ranges of the earliest hominins were extended considerably to include North-Central Africa. Research was intensified in Eastern Africa—Ethiopia, Kenya, and Tanzania—and South Africa. Paleoanthropology is a multidisciplinary endeavor by definition (Picq 2020). It brings together scientific expertise across the whole spectrum of natural and social sciences, in fieldwork as well as laboratory research: geology and soils sciences to locate, survey, and unlock the secrets of fossil-bearing sedimentary formations such as the Omo Shungura formation or the Olduvai gorge; paleozoologists and paleobotanists to identify animal and plants remains and assist in the reconstruction of past environmental changes; trained paleontologists to search, spot, collect, and analyze fossils; weak radio-activity physicists to run radiometric dating of the collected samples; archaeologists to collect and analyze material culture; etc. . . . and the addition of the relatively new research field of paleo-genomics, a welcome derivative of the Human Genome Project (1990–2003), that allows new probes into human history through genes.

Field methods were tested and improved through practice from the early days of pioneer avocational archaeologists. They are much more rigorous backed by increasing scientific instrumentation. Some areas, like the Rift Valley in East Africa, and limestone caves in Southern Africa, China, Europe, Indonesia, etc. are more favorable for the preservation and retrieval of fossils and archaeological evidence.

The geographic extension and distribution area of the earliest hominin specimens was expanded significantly northwestward during the last two decades (Brunet et al. 2002). Important early hominin fossils series were found at 1,500 kilometers as the crow flies west of the East African Rift valley in North Central Africa, in the Chad basin and the Djourab desert in the northern Chad Republic.

The size of the equatorial rainforest, the habitat of present-day great apes—gorilla and chimpanzees—has fluctuated significantly through time, shrinking to the verge of disappearance during dry and cold circumstances like the Late Glacial Maximum and expanding during warm and humid climate episodes. Sustained and more intensive paleoanthropological field research has produced more exciting and challenging data. The resulting human phylogenetic arborescence that can be reconstructed is bushier than ever. The direct correlation between any particular hominin genus and early stone tools complexes is less and less reliable.

The Human Phylogenetic Arborescence

The Human phylogenetic arborescence is made of successive and/or partially overlapping sets stretched over 7 Ma. Hominin fossils are partitioned into an initial set of Ardipithecines dated from 7 to 4.5 Ma, followed by a large and diverse set of Australopithecines stretched chronologically from 4.2 to 1–1.5 Ma. And the genus *Homo,* the largest and most diverse set that emerges around 2.8 Ma, is stretched up to the present.

SArFe 1: The Ardipithecines

The Ardipithecines group is made of four genus, *Sahelanthropus tchadensis*, *Orrorin tugenensis*, *Ardipithecus ramidus*, and *Ar. kadabba*. *S. tchadensis*, the oldest hominin genus fossils on record—also called Toumai, "hope of Life" in Goran language—is dated to 7 Ma. A nearly complete but deformed skull was found in the Djourab desert in Northern Chad Republic by M. Brunet research team (Brunet et al. 2002). The skull, jaw, and teeth, despite their primitive character, present some hominin traits. *S. tchadensis* is claimed to have bipedal gait and an erect posture. The hominin fossils were associated with a fauna including rodents, monkeys, freshwater fish, and crocodiles suggesting a habitat in a humid wooded environment, in swamps or not far from a lake (Vignaud et al. 2002). Some researchers disagree with the hominin status assigned to *S. tchadensis* and consider it to be a kind of ape unable of bipedal walk (Wolpoff et al. 2006).

M. Pickford and B. Senut found a series of hominin fossils in four localities of the Lukeino formation in the Tugen Hills, Kenya (Pickford and Senut 2001, Senut and Pickford 2001, Senut et al. 2001). The finds, thirteen fossils belonging to at least five individuals, including a jaw with teeth, isolated teeth, arm bones, finger bones, and a left femur dated to 6.2–5.6 Ma, were assigned to a new genus named *Orrorin tugenensis*. The femur indicates bipedal gait on the ground and the phalanx point to arboreal locomotion adaptation. While contributing scientists agree with the factual consistency of the finds, it is Pickford and Senut (2001) radical phylogenetic tree reconstruction that is debatable (Aiello and Collard 2001, Balter 2001). The critics remark that cranial and dental anatomy does not necessary reflect molecularly constructed phylogenies in modern primates. It can therefore not be relied on to reconstruct evolutionary trees.

Dated to 5.8–5.2 Ma, *Ardipithecus kadabba*—"oldest ancestor" in the Afar language—is the third member of the Ardipithecines group. Its remains, made of eleven specimens representing some five individuals were discovered by Yohannes Haile-Selassie in 1997 and 2002 at Asa Koma and other localities in the Middle Awash in Ethiopia. They consist of a clavicle, partial arm bones, hand bones, and foot bones. *Ar. Kadabba* featured a bipedal gait and lived in humid woodlands and grasslands (Haile-Selassie et al. 2004).

Finally, *Ardipithecus ramidus*, the fourth and last member of the Ardipithecines group, is dated to 4.4 Ma. Its remains found in the Middle Awash and Gona in Ethiopia amounting to some one hundred specimens. The discovery was made in 1994 by Tim White and his team (White et al. 1994). *Ar. ramidus* combine arboreal adaptation and bipedal gait. The average stature for an adult female is 1.20 m for fifty kilograms average weight. The fauna associated with the fossils point to humid wooded habitat (White et al. 2009, Lovejoy et al. 2009).

Ardipithecines' fossils are distributed over an extensive territory stretching from the Tugen Hills in Kenya in the southeast, to the Middle Awash and Gona in Ethiopia in the east and finally the Djourab desert in northern Chad in the northwest. That delineated space can be considered as the territorial range of the Ardipithecines. The finds are however very widely scattered and localized, pointing to distinct and independent speciation events. These genus appear to have favored humid habitat, either marshlands, grasslands, or wooded humid environments. Despite the *Orrorin tugenensis* femur pointing to bipedal gait, Ardipithecines locomotion is still highly debated. They probably relied on occasional bipedalism, with more or less semi-erect postures with arboreal lifeways predominant.

SArFe 2: The Australopithecines

The time segment between 4 and 2 Ma witnessed a significant diversification of hominin populations. The australopithecines group includes three genera with partially to completely overlapping ages and areal distribution. The genus *Australopithecus* spp. is not only the earliest but also the most diverse with the largest territorial extension. The genus *Paranthropus* spp. is the youngest with the second-largest territorial extension. And finally, the genus *Kenyanthropus* spp. is strictly confined to the Lake Turkana Basin in Kenya.

Australopithecus spp, fossils recorded so far belong to six species documented in North Central, Eastern, and Southern Africa. *Au. anamensis* is dated from 4.2 to 3.9 Ma. The fossil specimens consist of an arm bone found in 1965, and numerous teeth and bone fragments collected by Meave Leakey and her team in 1994 at Kanapoi in northern Kenya (Leakey et al. 1995). Additional specimens were found later, in 2006 by Tim White in the Middle Awash in Ethiopia, and particularly, an almost complete skull collected at Woranso-Mille, Ethiopia in 2019 by Y. Haile-Selassie (Haile-Selassie et al. 2019). *Au. anamensis* presents a combination of ape and human traits, with however regular bipedal gait and tree-climbing aptitude. It fed on hard and abrasive food and lived in humid forested and woodland environments.

Au. Afarensis, also called "Lucy species" dated to 3.58–2.95 Ma is represented by more than four hundred fossils found in Ethiopia, Kenya, and Tanzania. (Johanson et al. 1978, Johanson and Edey 1981). The Hadar fossil was found on November 1974 by Donald Johanson and Tom Gray in the context of the International Afar Research Expedition (Corvinus 1976, Johanson and Taieb 1976). The fame of the Hadar specimen "Lucy" is partly derived from the fact that she offered about 40 percent of the skeleton of a single person. It is also one of the rare cases with independent supporting evidence of bipedalism and "parental care"—an adult walking with a child.

Combining ape and human traits, this species had bipedal gait and tree-climbing adaptation. Predominantly vegetarian, it fed on leaves, seeds, fruits, insects, and sometimes meat from small animals or scavenged carcasses. The average stature ranges from 1.51 meters for males and 1.05 meters for female, with weight fluctuating from forty-two kilograms for the former to twenty-nine kilograms for the latter.

Au. bahrelghazali (3.4–3.0 Ma) was found in the Chad Basin in North Central Africa in 1995 by M. Brunet and his team. If the Chad research team favors the idea of a new species, the majority of paleoanthropologists considers it a regional variant of *Au. afarensis* located at some 1,500 kilometers northwest in north central Africa.

The *Au. africanus* species found at Taung in South Africa in 1924 was described and published by R. Dart in 1925. It lived in the southern part of Africa 3.3 to 2.1 Ma ago and has strong similarities and minor differences with *Au. afarensis*. It was not the killer ape as portrayed in the literature in the first half of the twentieth century but a vegetarian, feeding on fruits, leaves, seeds, nuts, occasionally insects, and eggs. Sometimes it was hunted by predators.

The two remaining Australopithecus species, *Au. garhi* and *Au. sediba*, are strictly localized at a single site in Ethiopia and South Africa. *Au. garhi* fossil specimens are very few, found at Bouri in the Middle Awash, Ethiopia, dated to 3–2 Ma (Asfaw et al. 1999). The first *Au. sediba* specimen was found in August 2008 at Malapa in South Africa (Berger et al. 2010). It lived between 2 and 1.9 Ma ago, is a fully bipedal species, small in size, with a small brain, and long arms, presenting a mixture of *Australopithecus* and *Homo* genus traits. It is too late in the sequence and can be ruled out as potential ancestor of the genus *Homo.*

The *Paranthropus* spp. genus consists of thick-boned species with strong masticatory apparatus. Three main species have been recorded. *P. aethiopicus* is the earliest of all the Paranthropus genus. It lived in the Omo valley, southern Ethiopia, and the Turkana Basin, Northern Kenya, 2.7 to 2.3 Ma ago. It was initially discovered in 1967 in the Omo Valley by a team led by C. Arambourg (Arambourg et al. 1968). An additional new discovery was made in the Turkana Basin (Walker et al. 1986). *P. bosei* found in East Africa (Tanzania, Kenya, Ethiopia, Malawi) is considered to have descended from *P. aethiopicus.* Its skull was discovered at Olduvai by Mary Leakey in 1959 and named *Zinjanthropus bosei* (Leakey 1959). It lived between 2.3 and 1.2 Ma, and fed on coarse food requiring strong chewing. Average stature and weight range from 1.37 meters and forty-nine kilograms for males to 1.24 meters and thirty-four kilograms for females. Finally, *P. robustus*, the third and last of the genus, lived in Southern Africa 1.8 to 1.2 Ma ago. The specimen was found by Robert Broom at Kromdraai, South Africa, in 1938 (Broom 1938). The males are on average 1.2 meters tall, for fifty-four kilograms in weight, and females 1 meter tall for forty kilograms. All three Paranthropus species reviewed are generally understood to have branched off from *Au. afarensis.*

Kenyanthropus spp. genus, comprised of species *K. platyops*—flat-faced human from Kenya—and *K. rudolfensis*, is confined to the Lake Turkana basin in northern Kenya. The former lived in that area some 3.5 Ma ago. Its fossil specimens were found in 1998 and 1999 by M. Leakey's team at Lomekwi (Leakey et al. 2001). The fossilized skull was significantly distorted by postdepositional taphonomic processes. Some researchers consider *K. platyops* to be a regional variant of *Au. afarensis* and expect additional material to assess the status of the named species (White 2003).

K. rudolfensis, initially assigned to *Homo rudolfensis* species, did not really fit well in the *Homo* genus. It lived in northern Kenya, northern Tanzania and Malawi 1.9–1.8 Ma ago and has a larger brain, some 775 cubic centimeters. The princeps specimens was found at Kobi Fora, East Turkana, in Kenya by Richard Leakey team in 1972 (Wood and Collard 1999). *K. rudolfensis* is considered by some scientists to be a better candidate for the ancestry of *Homo erectus*, with *H. habilis* considered as a dead end.

As shown by a broader range of evidence including leg bones and footprints, full bipedalism definitely developed with the Australopithecines, but they still present features of adaptation to life in the trees.

All the hominin fossils reviewed above are confined to Africa. It is this rich and diverse body of data that sets Africa as the cradle of humankind (Toth and Schick 2005). Much depends on the defining criteria of humankind one relies on. There is no final word in historical research, each synthesis being provisional, to be constantly scrutinized, sustained with supporting data, or falsified if better evidence is available. New discoveries can shift the focus elsewhere in the Old World. Some may feel uncomfortable with this fundamental characteristic of historical science conclusions. It is however what make all kinds of historical research exciting and fascinating, a "wonderful life!" to borrow the title of Stephen J. Gould's 1989 book.

EMERGENCE AND EXPANSION OF THE *HOMO* GENUS

The speciation events that presided over the emergence of the *Homo* genus and the ensuing adaptive radiation reached the east and west confines of the Old World. The evolutionary stage then shifted to Africa and Eurasia with early *Homo* expansion out of Africa—also called "Out of Africa 1." The *Homo* genus presents the greatest diversity with very complex branching history. The many and growing number of represented species will not be reviewed in detail in here. The ongoing debate is interesting, with an increasing body of data challenging the "Out-of-Africa-I" scenario (Bechly 2018).

SArFe 3: The Genus *Homo*

The emergence of the genus *Homo* is a hotly debated topic, in taxonomic as well as environmental terms. What are the environmental conditions that led to the emergence of the genus *Homo*? And how many early *Homo* species are represented in the fossil record? New fossils attest to the presence of multiple groups of early *Homo* with overlapping body, brain, and tooth size. The data available do not support the traditional interpretation of *H. habilis* and *H. rudolfensis* as representing respectively small and large morphs (Anton et al. 2014, Sahnouni et al. 2018). New finds from Ethiopia shed new light on the origins of the *Homo* genus. "The identification of the 2.80 to 2.75 Ma Ledi Geraru mandible as representing a likely phyletic predecessor to early Pleistocene *Homo* implies that phylogenetic schemes positing the origin of the *Homo* lineage from *Au. sediba* as late as 1.98 Ma are likely to be incorrect" (Villmoare et al. 2015: 1354). Early *Homo* remains can be arranged into four groups, all found exclusively in East Africa: the new nonspecific early *Homo* sp. from Ledi-Geraru (2.75–2.8 Ma), *Kenyanthropus rudolfensis* and an African *Homo erectus* are today the most plausible ancestors to all remaining Plio-Pleistocene hominins, with possible input from *Homo habilis* (Argue et al. 2017).

In contrast to the model of steady and sustained increase in aridity that led to the formation of savanna and grasslands, new evidence shows the environment to have been highly variable in East Africa, with unpredictable fluctuations during the time of emergence of the genus *Homo*. "In the face of a dynamic and fluctuating environment . . . the unique combination of larger brain size, the potential for diverse body sizes, inferred dietary flexibility, and cooperation enabled *H. erectus* to attain a level of niche construction and adaptive versatility that allowed this species to outpace its congeners" (Anton et al. 2014: 1236828–9) and expand in different parts of Eurasia.

Instead of a simple linear reading of the paleoanthropological evidence that envisions *H. erectus* speciation event and radiation all over Eurasia, available fossils suggest the possibility of more diverse and flexible scenarios. Distinct hominin cohorts related to *Homo* spp.—var. Ledi-Geraru, *K. rudolfensis*, and African *H. erectus* could have spread at different times in different parts of the Eurasian landmass as early as 3 Ma ago, and through genetic introgression triggered the adaptive radiation of the *Homo* genus in the Old World. *H. erectus*– related specimens dated from 1.8–1 Ma are documented in east Asia—Chou Kou Tien, South Asia—Java, Indonesia—, and midlatitude

Europe—Dmanisi, Georgia. Genetic drift combined with the relative geographic isolation of these small populations led to series of punctuated speciation events in Europe, East Asia, and Africa.

New evidence from Drimolen Cave in South Africa shows that "between 2.3 million and 1.8 million years ago, there were major climatic changes and faunal turnovers in the region including the last occurrence of the genus *Australopithecus*, and the first occurrence of *Paranthropus* and *Homo*, as well as the first occurrence of stone and bone tools" (Herries et al. 2020: 1). The DNH 134 crania, deposited 2.04 Ma ago, shares affinities with *H. erectus* and predates all known specimens of that species.

There is however a dearth of fossil evidence for the time period stretching from ca. 1.3 to 700,000 BP. *Homo mauritanicus/antecessor* remains, probably derived from *Homo erectus,* are recorded in Morocco and Spain. *Homo heidelbergensis*, the last common ancestors of modern humans, Neanderthals, and Denisovans is dated to 700,000–200,000 BP (Rightmire 1998). Its remains have been recorded at Jebel Irhoud in North Africa, Bodo, Kibish, Ndutu, Eyasi, Ngaloba, and Kabwe in East Africa, Florisbad and Elandsfontein in South Africa, and Atapuerca, Terra Amata, and Schoningen in West Eurasia.

The emergence of modern humans, *Homo sapiens sapiens,* initially considered to have taken place in Eastern Africa and followed by a second "out of Africa" is accepted as the most parsimonious explanation of the latest phases of human expansion all over the planet (Scerry et al. 2014, Smith et al. 2007). However, recent works show the scenarios to be much more complex. New evidence of *Homo sapiens sapiens* skull and jaw from Jebel Irhoud dated to 315,000 years ago points to a complex evolutionary history of *H. sapiens* involving the whole African continent. The analysis of the whole-genome sequence of "3 Stone Age hunter-gatherers [without admixture] coupled with the high-quality ancient DNA (aDNA) coverage obtained from the boy from Balito Bay, provide with the unique opportunity to recalculate the genetic time depth for our species *Homo sapiens* to between 350,000 and 260,000 years ago" (Lombard et al. 2018: 2). This new estimate covers the time range of the Jebel Irhoud (ca. 315,000) fossils from Morocco (North Africa), Florisbad (ca. 260,000) in South Africa, as well as *Homo heidelbergensis* from Hoedjiespunt (300–200,000), also in South Africa.

At the southern end of the continent, L. R. Berger and his team of forty-five researchers discovered a new species of small-bodied hominin with *Australopihecines* brain size in the Dinaledi chamber of the Rising Star Cave system near Swartkrans in Gauteng province, South Africa. Bones—1,550 in all—belonging to some fifteen individuals were recorded. *Homo naledi*, dated to 335–236,000 years ago, buried the dead (Berger et al. 2015). *Homo sapiens sapiens*, *H. heidelbergensis*, and *H. naledi* thus coexisted in the southern part of the continent for several millennia.

Early *Homo sapiens* remains were excavated at different sites distributed all over the continent. It is the case at Rabat, Sale, and Jebel Irhoud in north Africa; Bodo, Omo Kibbish, and Herto in Ethiopia; Kabwe in East Africa; Florisbad, Cave of Hearths, Border Cave, Klasies River Mouth, Blombos, Saldanha, and Elandsfontein in South Africa. The earliest *H. sapiens sapiens* specimens are dated from 315,000 to 259,000 years ago, respectively at Jebel Irhoud in North Africa and Florisbad in South Africa. The Ethiopian specimens are dated to 195,000–160,000 years ago (Hublin et al. 2017, Berger et al. 2015, Stringer and Galway-Whitam 2018).

The earliest *H. sapiens sapiens* remains found so far out of Africa, at Skhul and Qafseh in Southern Levant, are dated to 120,000–90,000 years ago. However, genetic analyses of Denisova cave (Siberia, Russia) and Hollenstein-Stadel (Germany) Neanderthal remains suggest "at least one earlier phase of introgression from *H. sapiens* into Neanderthals. This event has been estimated at 219,000 to 460,000 years ago." (Stringer and Galway-Whitam 2018: 390). *Homo sapiens sapiens'* exit from Africa was accordingly a much earlier event. I. Herkovitz's (2018) team's recent discovery of *H. sapiens sapiens* remains dated to 180,000 years ago at Misliya (Israel) points to an earlier but still relatively recent presence in the Near East. Older and earlier *H. sapiens sapiens* remains are therefore expected to be found in the Levantine corridor in the future.

Thanks to the significant intensification of paleoanthropological research in the last three decades, the last 300,000 years of the human phylogenetic tree are filled with at least six distinct species: *H. neanderthalensis* in Europe and the Middle East, Denisovans in Eastern Asia (Chen et al. 2019), *H. floresiensis* in Indonesian archipelago (Argue et al. 2017), *H. luzoniensis* in the Phillipines (Detroit 2019), *H. naledi* in South Africa (Berger et al. 2015), and finally, *H. sapiens sapiens* (Hublin et al. 2017), the only surviving species. The state of research is exciting and fascinating. Denisovans are derived from *H. Neanderthalensis* with the oldest specimen from the Tibet plateau dated to 170,000 years ago (Chen et al. 2019). *H. floresiensis* is not derived from the continental *H. erectus* as initially thought but connected to *H. habilis* who lived 1.75 Ma ago in East Africa (Argue et al. 2017).

CULTURAL BEGINNINGS: EARLY HUMAN
SITES, TECHNOLOGIES, AND LIFEWAYS

From *K. platyops* on some 3.3 Ma ago, intermittently or permanently, hominins relied on artificially made objects to fulfill their subsistence needs. The
investigation of human origins involves many fields of inquiry, all part of
paleoanthropology (Holl 2005). The archaeological part focuses on the analysis of hominin/human-made artifacts collected from early hominin/human
sites. The idea of cultural beginnings is relatively easy to grasp: culture
begins with the manufacture of artifacts. This beginning is however difficult
to pin down in the archaeological record. Does the selection of a specific kind
of unmodified pebble indicative of "cultural drive"? Does the use of slightly
modified nature-facts qualify for inclusion in the "cultural universe"? Setting
the demarcation line is tricky, as the selection, use, and manufacture of tools
are part of a continuum at the interface between the hominins/humans and
the world they live in. The systematic use and production of artificially made
tools put the emerging humanity in a peculiar evolutionary path, away from
"animal-hood."

Early Hominin Sites: Taphonomic Characterizations

Early hominin sites are found on riverbanks and lakeshores, encased in fine
sandy to silty sediment. Postdepositional disturbances vary but tend to be
moderate to low in the "higher resolution" excavated localities. None of the
sites is totally isolated. Instead, they are nodes in a more extensive protohuman territory, generally partitioned into three broad categories depending on
their "taphonomic integrity."

1. "Occupation floors" are the less disturbed sites. The cultural deposit is
   generally thin, 0.10 to 0.30 m, and the archaeological remains are more
   often than not clustered in high-density patches. Such sites were used
   frequently by groups of protohumans, but the construction of a shelter as
   suggested at DK IA in Lower Bed I, Olduvai Gorge, is still controversial.
2. Slightly modified sites have thicker deposits, 0.40 to 1.00 m, with moderate to high density of cultural remains. They result from short-distance
   remobilization of archaeological remains from their original locations.
   The spatial relationship between artifacts is disrupted but their preservation is generally good.
3. Hydraulic jumbles are not strictly speaking archaeological sites but
   "finds spots." The sedimentary matrix is generally a few meters thick
   and the density of finds very low. The artifacts as well as animal bones

were generally dragged on considerable distance within a river drainage and trapped here and there in the riverbed.

Early Human Sites as Scatters of Stones and Bones

The earliest traces of protohuman culture consist of scatters of stones and bones. Some of the stones are unshaped nature-facts; others are utilized; and others again are shaped into cores-tools and sharp-edge flakes. Some animal bones were dropped by protohumans; others were redeposited by natural agencies; and others again came from in situ dead animals. How and why did these two distinct categories of material remains came to be intricately mixed in protohuman sites? The distribution of protohuman sites across the landscape and the differential frequencies of stone pieces and animal bones have been used to draft what Glynn Isaac (1981) called "Stone-Age Visiting Card." Special purpose sites display a narrower range of "cultural by-products." A single animal species site with a small amount of stones pieces signals a butchering or meat-procurement locale. A dense concentration of debitage by-products with very few formal tools points to a workshop. The occurrence of a handful of bones and stones pieces indicates a short stop, a bivouac. A large concentration of bones and stones pieces suggests a frequently visited spot used as "base camp," "home base," or "central place foraging." The Stone Age sites systematic outlined above was derived from contemporary hunter-gatherers ethnographies, is thought-provoking and good for model-building. Its heuristic value is however severely limited if the aim of the investigation is to understand and explain early protohuman sites. How did protohumans access resources to sustain their lives? Several competing hypotheses formulated since the beginning of the twentieth century are briefly reviewed and assessed below.

Early Hominin Lifeways

The Hunting Hypothesis

Hunting performed by protohumans was the obvious explanation for the co-occurrence of stone and bones in the archaeological record. Bones found in association with stone tools were accepted ipso facto as the product of protohuman behavior, the leftover of their meals. The influential "hunting hypothesis," formulated in the first decades of the twentieth century, dominated paleoanthropology debates up to the early 1970s (Ardrey 1966, 1976). According to that theory, hunting is the driving force behind human social evolution (Lee and DeVore 1966). It explains the need for efficient tools as well as their constant improvement. It generates and structures the social division of labor between "man-the-hunter" and "woman-the-gatherer." It makes senses, justifies the territorial imperative, and provides an outlet for the violent instincts of protohumans and later humans.

Accordingly, hunting provided protohumans with the much-needed high-grade food and alleviated in-group tensions. The hunters not only hunted and brought meat back to be shared among women, children, and elder individuals, but also protected the group from dangerous predators and competitors. Social and cultural evolution was consequently viewed as driven by male competition for resources and mates. Fundamentally, the hunting hypothesis was based more on a series of assumptions than supported by facts. Long-term participant-observation-research on hunter-gatherers lifeways that started after World War II challenged the hunting hypothesis. Meat is a desirable food item, but its supply is uncertain. People thus rely more often on gathered plant products. Plant resources offer the certainty and predictability crucial in the maintenance and reproduction of protohumans/ humans groups.

The Gathering Hypothesis

The "gathering hypothesis" was a reaction against the "man-the-hunter" approach to human evolution. Its main claims were, in fact, more supported by the empirical evidence marshaled to strengthen its criticism of the then dominant point of view. The proponents of the "woman, the gatherer" (Dalberg 1983) theory questioned the importance assigned to meat in proto-human/early human diets and the prominent role attributed to males in the procurement and supply of meat to the rest of the community. Ethnographic research among intertropical hunter-gatherers has shown meat to be a highly desired food item, of variable availability, and most of the time unreliable. Tropical forager diets were shown to include more than 80 percent plant products with minor if fluctuating proportion of meat. Accordingly, with protohumans living in the tropics, their diet is expected to include more plants than meat. In addition, the access to plants resources is more reliable and less stressful. The gathering of plant resources carried out by women thus provided more reliable and sustainable food sources to proto- and early human groups. The ideas of exclusive pair-bonding between mother and child as well as mate selection are other crucial dimensions of the "woman-the-gatherer" hypothesis. In both cases, male presence is peripheral and dependent upon the will and decision of the female. In social evolutionary terms, most of the reliable food resources are provided by women. Women carry the babies during their pregnancy and develop strong if exclusive relationship with them once they are born. Women make decisions and select their mates following their preferences. Considering these interwoven crucial social roles, the "woman-the-gatherer" hypothesis suggests that women were likely the driving force in the emergence of human social characteristics.

The Sharing Hypothesis

The "man-the-hunter" and "woman-the-gatherer" hypotheses are antithetic mirror-images. The polarized debate of the 1960s–1970s had more to do with contemporary social issues than early human evolution. In the late 1970s, the "sharing hypothesis" was developed, with wide-ranging implications for the emergence of human characteristic behaviors. According to this hypothesis, the members of any distinct hominin group characteristically cooperate, support each other, and share information and resources. This cooperation and sharing triggered the development of elaborate communication that ultimately led to spoken languages. It generated the characteristic division of labor along gender lines to ensure the procurement of much-needed resources. Information on the distribution and timing of resources, as well as potential dangers, collected by each member of the group is pooled and shared. The home base or central place foraging (CPF) was the main locus where the hominin group was supposed to enact the different facets of the sharing hypothesis. In simple terms, the sharing hypothesis tried to reconcile the "man-the-hunter" and "woman-the-gatherer" hypotheses into one more encompassing model. Men hunt, women gather, and share the products of their respective subsistence forays out of the home base. The sharing hypothesis was widely adopted as the most "parsimonious" explanation for the emergence of human social systems. It was however anachronistic, plagued by the reliance upon Homo sapiens analogues to understand and explain protohuman behavioral characteristics. A devastating critique was launched against the home base sharing and hunting hypotheses (Binford 1981). It suggested that protohumans were more or less skilled scavengers, triggering a new round of debate on the origins of human behavioral patterns.

The Scavenging Hypothesis

As indicated by the archaeological record from Koobi-Fora and Olduvay, protohumans' access to potentially large supply of meat from big-size mammals is compelling. Sharp flakes with "meat" polish and cut marks on long bones are clear indications of both the procurement and consumption of meat. How did such a system operate? According to the "scavenging hypothesis," initially formulated by Lewis R. Binford (1981), protohumans relied on scavenging strategies to acquire meat. They were often secondary feeders exploiting marrowbones and the leftovers of effective and specialized predators. Scavenging is nonetheless a complex procurement system. It involves spotting animal carcasses across the landscape, avoiding and/or driving away competitors, collecting pieces of the kills, and moving to safer locations. However, while scavenging is likely the best explanation for protohuman access to large animals' carcasses, it does not completely rule out the possibility for hunting of small game. In summary, the period running from ca. 2.7 to 1.65 Ma was characterized by diversification in protohuman species. The "bushy pattern" of interspecies evolution ended with *Homo ergaster* emergence at the 1.7–1.6 Ma boundary. Based on the most recent discussions of the issues pertaining to protohuman patterns of behavior, plant gathering was likely the most reliable component of their food procurement strategies. Meat was accessed from time to time, and its overall availability may have been strongly seasonal. Protohumans may have developed ways of conveying and communicating information and emotions to fellows within and outside their respective groups. It was certainly a kind of language; spoken language—speech—was a much later development.

In summary, the hominins, not at the top of the trophic chain, were part of a more comprehensive community ecology, relying more on scavenging strategies than hunting for access to meat and predators' avoidance tactics. Nesting in trees was very likely the optimal option for groups safety. The development of technical skills that resulted in the manufacture of stone tools is now firmly dated to 3.3 Ma with the Lomekwian complex of West Turkana (Harmand et al. 2015). It is not yet known if this early shift to stone tool production and use lasted to be transmitted to other groups or was an isolated punctuated episode. The Oldowan complex that followed emerged some 700,000 years later. This chronological gap may be filled in future research. But it may also have been real and confirmed as a genuine singularity before the routine steady succession of early stone tools traditions. The latter, arranged in five successive modes (I to V), shifting from core-tools to microliths, are characteristically the toolboxes of Pleistocene hunter-gatherers (Clark 1969). Without inserting the new Lomekwi complex, Mode 1 corresponds to the Oldowan with choppers and chopping tools; Mode 2 to the Acheulean with hand ax and some flake tools; Mode 3 to the Middle Stone Age/Middle Paleolithic flake tools assemblages; Mode 4 to the Upper/Terminal Paleolithic blade complex, and finally, Mode 5 to Mesolithic/Epi-Paleolithic microlithic assemblages. The more than century-old taxonomy of African prehistory, with Early Stone Age (ESA), Middle Stone Age (MSA), and Late Stone Age (LSA), simple, robust, and resilient is perfectly adequate for the description of long-term Stone Age technological evolution.

Early Hominin Technologies

The Lomekwian (3.3 Ma)

The earliest protohuman-made artifacts were found in a number of localities distributed along the Rift Valley in Eastern Africa. A recent discovery at Lomekwi 3 in West Turkana in Kenya singles out one case and put the earliest production and use of stone tools much earlier in time, around 3.33 Ma (Harmand et al. 2015).

In 2011, S. Harmand and J. Lewis from Stony Brook University launched the West Turkana Archaeological Project with a systematic exploration and excavation of the Lomekwi member of the Nachukui formation on the left shore of Lake Turkana. At Lomekwi 3, surface probing revealed the presence of some thirty stone artifacts, exposed or partially buried on a low hill partly eroded by water runoff. Artifacts, not heavily disturbed despite a minor rearrangement by erosional agencies, were deposited 3.31 Ma ago in an arboreal savanna environment.

An assemblage combining surface and excavated 149 stone tool specimens was collected after the 2011 and 2012 field seasons. It includes eighty-three cores, thirty-five flakes (complete and fragmented), seven anvils, seven hammerstones, three used and two split pebbles, and finally twelve undetermined fragments. The selected stone raw materials include basalt, phonolite (a fine-grained volcanic rock), and trachyphonolite (lava pebble). Two complementary approaches were relied upon to assess the technical skills that presided over the production of these stone artifacts. The experimental approach was used to replicate—make the same object—the stone artifacts collected from the site. It was backed by a detailed technological analysis aimed at the reconstitution of the number of short *"chaines operatoires"*— sequence of successive technical gestures—represented in the assemblage under investigation. The "stone-and-anvil" was by far the most frequently used knapping method. It consists of striking a selected cobble or stone block laid on an anvil—larger flat stone—with a hammerstone to remove sharp flakes. The Lomekwian tool kit was used in hominin daily cutting, pounding, cracking, and breaking subsistence activities. The insertion of intentionally made items in the hominin adaptive package set these ancestral lineages on a quasi-revolutionary evolutionary pathway. Even if there is no direct correlation, it is worth mentioning that *K. platyops* is the only hominin genus represented in the Turkana basin during the 3.5–3.0 Ma time period.

The Oldowan (2.7–1.7 Ma)

The Oldowan tradition emerged some 700,000 years after the Lomekwian. It is named after the famous site of Olduvai Gorge even if its earliest manifestations were found along the Gona River in the Kada Hadar Member of the Hadar Formation in Ethiopia. The recovered material, consisting of stone artifacts as well as a small amount of animal bones, is dated from 2.7 to 2.4 Ma. The density is low but the clustering is unmistakable. The artifact repertoire consists of two basic categories: cores and flakes. Each category is divided into two classes: core-tools/chopper and core fragments, and whole flake and flake fragments. Some cores and flakes show traces of intentional modification from their use in subsistence activities. In general, the stone pieces are irregular in shape and small in size. The faunal material, highly fragmented, presents spiral and longitudinal fractures but no cut marks. At least six mammal species are represented, including hippopotamus, elephant, equid, and several bovids. Comparable artifacts associated with animal bones and dating from 2.4 to 1.6 Ma were recorded elsewhere along the Rift Valley and North Africa. It is the case in member E and F of the Shungura Formation (Omo valley) in southern Ethiopia, KBS Industry in the Koobi Fora Formation, and Bed I in Olduvai Gorge, and Oued Boucherit in Algeria (North Africa) (Sahnouni et al. 2018, Toth and Schick 2009). The Oldowan complex spread at both the west and east ends of Eurasia as early as 2.5 Ma ago.

The Acheulean Complex (1.7–200,000 Years)

The Acheulean complex is named after the site of Saint-Acheul in the Somme Valley in northern France where prehistoric hand axes were documented for the first time in the middle of the nineteenth century. It emerged in East Africa around 1.7 Ma ago and seems to have spread along with the expansion of *Homo erectus*, as far east as India and Indonesia and as far west as the United Kingdom. The flakes, pebbles, and core-tools tradition spread in the eastern part of Asia. The Acheulean combining core and flake tools represents a significant cognitive development in human mental capacity. Bilateral symmetry, soft-hammer technique, and the use of fire in assisting stone tools production are some key innovations from the Acheulean period. The hand ax, very likely the longest-used tool ever—some 1.5 Ma—was the first multifunctional tool (fig. 1.1). The tip can be used to pierce and crack bones and wood. The sinuous sides, re-sharpened as much as needed, could be for cutting and sawing. And finally, through its mass and weight could be used for hammering and breaking hard tissue and crushing materials. There are three main core tools of the Acheulean tradition. 1) the classic hand ax— also called biface because of two more or less similar sides; 2) the cleaver, with a straight chopping edge; and finally, 3) the pick, a heavy-duty piercing tool. Flake are modified through retouching to make more specialized tools like front-scrapers and side-scrapers, borers, etc.

Figure 1.1. The Acheulean hand ax, the first multifunctional tool with bilateral symmetry. *José-Manuel Benito Álvarez (España)*

Solid, durable, and convincing evidence of hunting date from the Acheulean
period is documented at Olorgesailie in East Africa and Torralba-Ambrona in
Spain. Data from the latter site point to coordinate group hunting strategies,
from tracking the migrating elephants' herds to butchering in a marshland.

Tempo and Patterns of Early Human Expansion

Ecosystems are dynamic entities. All their key components—geological,
botanical, and zoological—are in constant interactions and change at different timescales. Landforms change more slowly than vegetation and animal
communities. Biological populations as constitutive parts of ecosystems are
either in a steady state, contraction, or expansion. Expansion is accordingly
one of a range of adaptive response to natural selection.

When looked at from the perspective of community ecology, one is entitled
to assert that change is the rule and stability the exception. Aristotle defined
humans as "zoon politikon," "political animals" living in herds and following rules enforced by leaders. At a more fundamental level however, humans
are better defined as "curious apes." It is those special characteristics that
set humankind apart in the long-term evolutionary process of life-forms on
earth. It is therefore the intersection of that cognitive disposition—called

curiosity—with the dynamics of social and biological systems that constantly tip the balance toward novelty and change. 99.99 percent of human history took place with hunting-gathering as the sole subsistence systems. Grasping the principles, structures, and dynamics of hunting-gathering systems is necessary to understand the evolutionary pathways followed by hominins and humans.

The Dynamics of Hunting-Gathering Systems

Hunter-gatherers, put in the category of savagery in nineteenth-century evolutionist discourse, were viewed as the antithesis of the ideal sedentary urban life. They had no homes. They did not own property. They had no government. It took several decades of dedicated research through participant observations among Australian Aborigines and Southern Africa Khoisan hunter-gatherers to bring to light key aspects of hunter-gatherers' lives and social organization (Hiatt 1996, Lee and DeVore 1966, 1976, Sahlins 1972). Contemporary hunter-gatherers are *Homo sapiens sapiens* and not facsimile of Paleolithic foragers or hominins. In addition, the aborigines and Khoisan communities studied by anthropologists were under siege. Their original lands were grabbed by British convicts in Australia. In Africa, and in successive and overlapping waves, people of Khoisan descent were first impacted by the expansion of Bantu farmers and herders, and from the seventeenth century on by European settlers as well. Consequently, and contrary to what is generally asserted, anthropologists did not study pristine societies out of time, but communities in crisis that developed adaptive mechanisms to cope with actual situations of territorial encroachment.

In general, with variations from nation to nation, "simple" hunter-gatherers are mobile, and rely on a network of places instead of bounded territorial units. The have fluid social organization with the band as basic social unit. They have an overarching sharing ethic and lack private ownership. Decisions are made by consensus in small face-to-face communities—the band—of twenty-five to thirty individuals, including elders, parents, and children. Population growth is kept in check by the long birth spacing enhanced by long periods of breastfeeding. Their diet is generally well balanced. They have short work hours on average and enjoy plenty of leisure time. Impressed by all these particularities, M. Sahlins (1972) ended up dubbing them as "the first affluent society."

Mobility is one of the key characteristics of hunting-gathering systems. It is however not an endless pursuit of animals as initially understood but articulated on seasonality and intragroup dynamics. Seasons preside over the availability and distribution of subsistence resources. Through residential mobility, hunter-gatherers tailor their moves to be at the right place at the right time. Via logistic mobility, they do also use a central location, and bring back resources collected within the daily territorial range. Population grows exponentially and resources grow arithmetically. Bands' territorial range having an inelastic carrying capacity, there is a constant fluctuating but unstable balance between population and resources. Such instability generates pulls or pushes depending on circumstances. In favorable environmental circumstances with sustained population growth—fertility rate> Mortality rate—new bands are formed and settle in their own new territory. Such processes generate moving frontiers on the peripheries of all pristine hunter-gatherer bands.

Primatology—the systematic study of nonhuman primates in their natural environments—provides additional data for modelling hominin behavior and groups dynamics (Anapol et al. 2004, McGrew 1992). The optimal hunter-gatherer daily territorial range is estimated to be "two hours' walk" or a ten-kilometer radius around the home base or central place foraging. The optimal simple hunter-gatherer band's size is twenty-five to thirty individuals (Lee and DeVore 1966). These data factored with varying growth rates can be used to run multi-iterated simulations of hominin and human expansion, in and out of Africa. A very simple operation will show that hominin expansion can be relatively rapid.

A thought experiment: How long would it take for the descendants of a hominin group to spread from the Middle Awash in Ethiopia to the Nihewan basin in China, some 11,000 kilometers apart?

1. Hypothesizing conservatively that new bands are formed five kilometers away from their "mother band annual territory," along a moving frontier in each generation.
2. with twenty-five years for a generation.
3. Starting from the Middle Awash in Ethiopia, it will take some 2,200 generations to reach the Nihewan basin in China
4. or—2,200 x 25 = 55,000 years.
5. If the generation is shortened to, say twenty years, it will take 2.200 x 20 = 44,000 years.
6. The expansion of hominins and early human hunter-gatherers bands does not have to be framed in geological time perspective. It can be relatively rapid. Can be accelerated and/or slowed down by natural and cultural phenomena.

Out of Africa I: The Expansion of Early Humans

The hypothesis of an initial expansion of *Homo* genus out of Africa is based on converging bodies of paleontological, environmental, and geological data. In the present state of research, Ardipithecines, Australopithecines, and Kenyanthropes are confined to the African landmass. The last two are considered the most plausible ancestors of the genus *Homo*. *H. erectus*, in possible tandem with *H. habilis*, are considered as the principal agents of the initial and classic formulation of "Out of Africa 1" scenario. These early hominins drifted north from East Africa, then west, east, and south, with the Olduwan tool kit.

They reached southern Europe and the southwestern confines of Eurasia 1.8 to 1.4 Ma ago with evidence found at such sites as 1.8 million-year-old Dmanisi (Georgia), Fuentes Nova and Rarranco Leon 1.3 Ma in Andalusia (Spain), and 1.5–1.4 Ma old Pirro Nord (Italy).

The scenario presented above does not apply to most of the Asian continent (Scardia et 2019, 2020, Zhu et al. 2018), where hominin expansion took place much earlier as indicated by 2.5–1.5 Ma old Longgupo Cave (Chongqing Municipality, China), 2 Ma old Renzidong (Anhui province, China), Shangchen, 2.12–1.26 Ma (Shanxi Province), Nihewan basin 1.7–1 Ma, Majuangou III 1.66 Ma, Xiaochangliang 1.4 Ma, Donggutuo 1.1 Ma, Riwat (Potwar plateau, Pakistan), 1 million year old Isampur (Hungsi valley, India), and possibly Liang Bua cave (Indonesia).

Research proceeds forward with challenging new data in the western and Eastern components of the "Out of Africa I" hypothesis. Bechly (2018) discusses a series of publications that according to his understanding requires "rewriting human origins." These interesting data (Dambricourt Malasse et al. 2016, Han et al. 2017, Scardia et al. 2019, 2020, Zhu et al. 2018) deserve serious consideration, in strict Popperian conjecture and refutation terms (Popper 2002, 1963).

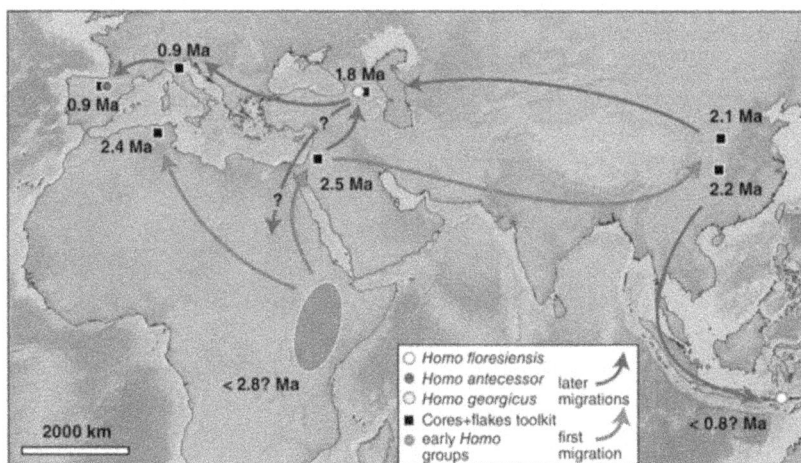

Figure 1.2. Out of Africa I distribution map. *Created by the author.*

Han et al. (2017) provides a recent update on research carried out at Longgupo Cave, in Chongqing autonomous municipality in China. The paper focuses essentially on the re-dating of mammalian remains—teeth in this case—from secure stratigraphic positions. A series of "three teeth from CIII of the south wall give an average age of ca. 2.48 Ma.," making this locality one of the earliest instances of hominin presence in East Asia. In fact, Longgggupo Cave was visited intermittently for a very long time from the beginning of the Pleistocene, resulting in the formation of a long stratigraphic sequence divided by researchers into two main components: a Lower Member dated to 2.5–2.2 Ma, and an Upper Member accumulated after a 400,000-year hiatus and dated to 1.8–1.5 Ma.

Dambricourt-Malasse et al. (2016) discuss the implications of early cutmarks found on three bones in the faunal assemblages from the Siwalik hills in India dated to ca. 2.6 Ma. Experimental replications with the same stone raw material confirmed that "the profiles are typical of the sharp edge of a flake or cobble in quartzite; their size and spatial organization testify to energetic and intentional gestures from an agile wrist acting with precision, and to a good knowledge of the bovid anatomy" (Dambricourt-Malasse et al. 2016: 317).

For Bechly (2018), "these two findings are remarkable because they not only predate the previous oldest fossil remains of the genus *Homo* outside of Africa (from Dmanisi in Georgia about 1.85 Ma ago), but even predate most of the oldest *Homo* fossils from Africa, except for a recently described single jawbone from Ledi-Geraru in Ethiopia (Villmoare et al. 2015), dated to 2.8 Ma ago. The new set of discoveries suggests either an earlier origin and migration of the genus *Homo* to Asia, or a prior migration of australopithecine hominins into Asia still to be discovered, or even an independent development of non-hominin tool-using apes (Bechly 2018. EN Nov. 28, 4.12 AM).

Zhu et al. (2018) document hominins presence at Shangchen in North China loess plateau dated from 2.12 to 1.26 Ma ago. The loess deposits accumulated during the last 2.6 million years contain pebble and cobble-sized stone tools dated from 2.1 to 1.3 Ma, supporting the 2.2 Ma old Longgupo cave finds (Scardia et al. 2020).

And finally, Scardia et al. (2019, 2020) present the consistent presence of stone tools in the Dawqara formation in the Zarqa valley in Jordan. The recorded evidence made of core and flakes, was found above the basalt layer in sediment dated between 2.52 and 1.95 Ma.

All these new contributions require a reconsideration of "the timing of initial dispersal of early hominins in the Old World" (Barras 2018, Kappelman 2018) but certainly not the rewriting of Out of Africa I. The taxonomy and chronology of Plio-Pleistocene hominins has changed considerably during the last few years. The discovery of the unspecified *Homo* jawbone from

Ledi-Geraru dated to 2.8 Ma referred to above by Bechly (2018) is one important variable among many backing the "Out of Africa I" hypothesis. The others are: 1) the discovery in West Turkana, Kenya, of the Lomekwian early stone tools tradition dated to 3.3 Ma, very likely made by *K. platyops*; 2) the re-assignment of *H. rudolfensis* fossils to *K. rudolfensis* making the Kenyanthropus genus—with *K. platyops* dated to 3.5 Ma—the most plausible ancestral branch of the *Homo* genus; and finally, 3) *H. floresiensis* was initially thought to derive from either Asian *H. erectus* or Denisovans. It is not the case anymore. Its ancestry is traced back to australopithecines or *H. habilis* (Argue et al. 2017). In summary, the most parsimonious explanation for the presence of early Pleistocene hominins in East Asia is an earlier expansion of an "Early Homo" (Scardia et al. 2020) or more than one earlier still unknown hominin genus.

EMERGENCE AND EXPANSION OF MODERN HUMANS

Cann, Stoneking, and Wilson's 1987 paper "Mitochondrial DNA and Human Evolution" published in the journal *Nature* triggered a paradigm shift and a genuine revolution in paleoanthropology. They sampled 147 individuals selected from five different geographic populations in Africa, Asia, Australia, Europe, and New Guinea, and analyzed their mitochondrial (mt) DNA—transmitted through female line. They used mtDNA sequences to track genetic differences and migration patterns of the human population and found that "all human populations had a common ancestor in Africa around 200,000 years ago" (Haskett 2014).[1] This extraordinary claim sent all involved paleoanthropologists back to the "drawing board." *H. sapiens sapiens* was understood to have emerged around 45,000 years ago in western Eurasia. A new exciting and interesting debate was launched, along with the accelerated pace of discovery of early *H. sapiens sapiens* fossils in Africa.

The Fossil Record

Early *H. sapiens sapiens* remains have been recorded in North, East, and South Africa. The oldest and most complete skull found at Jebel Irhoud in Morocco is dated to 315,000 years ago (Hublin et al. 2017). The Rabat-Kebibat remains of a teenager, also in Morocco, are dated to more than 200,000 years (Ouja et al. 2017). Wade Dagadie (Djibouti) and Florisbad (South Africa) fossils are dated to the same 260–250,000 years time range. The former is a maxilla and the latter part of the sides and front of the face. The Omo-Kibish formation in Ethiopia has provided three early *H. sapiens sapiens* fossils, the earliest specimen dated to 195,000 years ago. Herto, also in Ethiopia, contained human remains dated to 160,000 years ago; the Ngaloba cranium in Tanzania, also called "Laetoli 18," is dated to 129,000 ago.

Comparatively, the oldest non-African *H. sapiens sapiens* remains are found at Misliya cave, Israel, dated to 180,000 years ago (Herkovitz et al. 2018); Qafzeh, also in Israel and dated to 120,000 years ago; Liujiang in Guangxi province, South China, dated to 139–111,000 years ago (Rosenberg 2002), Daoxian in Hunan province, China, dated to 120–80,000 years ago (Liu et al. 2015), and finally, Skhul cave, in Israel, dated to 90,000 years. Africa has the oldest specimens of *H. sapiens sapiens*, but it is not yet clear where this ancestry emerged from in the continent and what the last common ancestor of modern and archaic humans looks like.

> Fossils from around 200–700 Ka have revealed many anatomically distinct humans' groups, and the period has been dubbed the 'muddle in the middle' of human evolution. It is still extremely difficult to identify any early Middle Pleistocene fossils as definitively representing the common ancestral population for *H. sapiens*, Neanderthals and Denisovans. (Bergstrom et al. 2021: 235).

Technological Traditions

The Post-Acheulean time—the Middle Stone Age (MSA)/Middle Paleolithic— is marked by strong regional diversification of stone tools complexes and the development of radically new stone knapping method—the *Levallois* method. It overlaps in some areas with the Late Acheulean complexes. Mousterian-like assemblages are well represented in Western Eurasia, North Africa, the Nile Valley, and the Horn of Africa. Depending on areas, the MSA started around 450–400,000 years ago and lasted in some places up to 40–35,000 years. Despite the assertion by Akhilesh et al. (2018), there is no direct correlation between the invention of the Levallois debitage method and the expansion of modern humans. The invention, which is above all a cognitive breakthrough, occurred independently in Africa, Europe, the Middle East, and South Asia and was also invented and used by Western Eurasian Neanderthals.

The Levallois method, also called the "predetermined knapping method" requires forethought and planning. An adequate source of raw material, generally fine-grained rocks like flint or obsidian, has to be available. The stone-tool maker has to have a precise mental image of kind of artifact to obtain and all the technical process to be implemented, the "*chaine opera-toire*," geared to achieve that goal. A pebble or stone block is selected from a rock outcrop or quarry. A hard rock piece, the hammerstone, is used to strike the selected cobble. The next steps are part of the preparation of the striking platform, through successive flake removals along the core perimeter and one of its side, resulting in a tortoise-shell-like Levallois core. A decisive stroke produces a Levallois flake, a blank with sharp edge, that can be used immediately. The core can be rejuvenated, retrimmed to remove another Levallois flake, and so on so forth, up to the exhaustion of the core. The Levallois method, particularly wasteful of raw material, has as a main objective the production of blanks—Levallois flakes—used for the production of a broad range of formal stone tools—points, denticulated, scrapers, borers, burins, etc.—through adequate kinds of retouch.

The repertoire of Middle Stone Age (MSA)/Middle Paleolithic (MP) lithic assemblages is rich and diverse, presenting patterns of intra-regional differentiation brought to light by F. Bordes (1961). He identified five facies—variants—of the Mousterian in Southwest France: the Mousterian of Acheulean Tradition (MTA), the Quina A and B Mousterian, the La Ferrassie Mousterian, and the Charentian Mousterian. For L. R. Binford (1973), the documented Mousterian interassemblage variability was essentially functional, showing flexible long-term use of ancient landscapes and resources by mobile hunter-gatherer groups, and in this case Neanderthals. The Bordes-Binford debate was one of the foundational moments in the rise of anthropological archaeology in the 1960s (Canadi Wargo 2009).

> the Bordes-Binford debate is emblematic of the differing traditions within the discipline of archaeology as it was practiced by American and French scholars and that an understanding of the debate furthers understanding of how archaeology developed and is practiced and conceptualized in those countries today. To that extent, the Bordes-Binford debate is best understood in its transatlantic context; that is, it grew out of an encounter and exchange between protagonists who were profoundly influenced by their respective national and cultural experiences. The debate and its aftermath changed the practice of Paleolithic archaeology on both sides of the Atlantic. (Canadi Wargo 2009: iv–v)

Patterns of interassemblage variability brought to light in southwestern Europe were later shown to be present in the Middle East, the Nile Valley, and Southern Africa in different past time segments. Combined with the development of hafting techniques and the increasing use of bones, MSA/MP lithic technologies acquired more versatility and flexibility. Africa witnessed two additional innovations in lithic tools production with the development of the Aterian and Howieson Poort complexes. The former, the Aterian, dated from 145,000 to 20,000 years ago and spread from the Morocco Atlantic coast to the Nile Valley emerged in North Africa and the Sahara. It is singled out by the production of stemmed tools, enhancing and facilitating their hafting. The latter, the Howieson Poort complex dated to c. 66,000–59,500 and limited to the southern end of the continent, features a precocious microlithization of stone tools production, suggesting an early invention of the bow and arrow.

Composite tools and probably bows and arrows were very likely part of Howieson Poort hunter-gatherer toolkits. Blade debitage techniques were invented during the latter part of the MSA but expanded and were generalized during the Upper Palaeolithic/Late Stone Age (LSA). Microlith complexes, pointing to the generalization of the use of the bow and arrow, emerged at the end of the Pleistocene and lasted up to the Middle Holocene.

A stunning bone craftsmanship was brought to light in three archaeological sites at Katanda in the Semliki Valley in eastern Democratic Republic of Congo (Yellen et al. 1995). The uncovered artifacts consist of several harpoons, barbed and unbarbed, as well as knifelike objects. They were clearly part of the MSA fishing communities' tool kit, used to spear and process relatively large catfish. Initially thought to be contemporary with the Western European Upper Paleolithic specimens dating to c. 40,000 years ago, they happened to be much older, dated by different techniques to 90,000 years ago, contemporary with early Aterian bone tools (Bouzouggar et al. 2018).

Cultural and technological change as well as and regional diversification did amplify significantly during the latter part of the Pleistocene. *H. sapiens sapiens* populations expanded in all major landmasses: along the Malaysian archipelago to Sahul and Australia between 70,000 and 50,000 years ago; and Northeastern Asia and the Americas between 35,000 and 15,000 years ago. It is very challenging to do justice to the constitutive diversity of the late Pleistocene technological situation.

A new blade debitage method, already represented in some regions during the MSA/MP, expanded and became mainstream. Blade are relatively narrow elongated flakes obtained through an elaborate technical protocol, variations of the "punch-debitage." Following the initial steps of the striking platform preparation, the selected stone block or pebble is shaped into a prismatic core with parallel faceted scars. The blades are then removed one after another, up to the exhaustion of the core. The obtained blades are blanks and parts used later for the production of formal tools. Thanks to better preservation in general, wood, plants fiber, and bone tools are constitutive parts of later Pleistocene hunter-gatherer groups' material culture.

By the time of the final Pleistocene/Early Holocene global warming, 10,000–9,000 years ago, hunter-gatherer communities were settled in almost every portion of the world, with the exception of the Pacific islands and New Zealand. Mesolithic or Epi-paleolithic communities of the Old World invented the bow and arrow, indirectly represented by geometric microliths. These small flaked pieces were used as parts for arrow tips. Such a tool was unknown in Australia, where ancestral Aborigines relied on clubs and spears as standard hunting gear. Pottery was also invented in the same time frame with the oldest specimens found at Xianrendong Cave (Jiangxi province) and Yuchanyan Cave (Hunan province) in China, dated respectively to 20,000 and

18,300–15,430 years ago (Boaretto et al. 2009, Wu et al. 2012). The domestication of plants and animals kicked off later during the Holocene and shifted the evolutionary trajectory of humankind in another direction, away from the million- year-old hunting and gathering traditions.

Models of Modern Humans Expansion

Genomic explorations, aDNA, and archaeological research converge and present a picture of significant regional variations and chronological differences in the worldwide expansion of modern humans. It is the meaning and interpretation of these variations that led to the formulation of competing explanations of the emergence and expansion of *H. sapiens sapiens*. Two contrasted scenarios were crafted in the initial phase of the debate on the origins of modern humans: expansion with replacement on the one hand, and regional continuity of the other hand. Continuous theoretical developments and the sustained refinement of evolutionary processes have shown both views to be extreme and implausible, resulting in the formulation of more nuanced scenarios.

Skeletal morphology is of paramount importance in the theoretical elaborations of the regional continuity model. Different contemporary populations of different parts of the world present clusters of morphological characteristics that single them out. According to the regional continuity model, also called "Multiregional evolution model," there was an initial expansion of *H. erectus* that resulted in the colonization of most of Africa and Eurasia. Modern humans emerged more or less simultaneously from regional populations in different parts of the world, partly because interregional gene flow was never interrupted (Wolpoff and Caspari 1997). Biologically speaking, the probability for distant populations to generate the emergence of the same species— *H. sapiens sapiens*—more or less simultaneously along their independent evolutionary trajectories is almost nil, making the regional continuity model hardly plausible.

For the replacement model (Stringer and Andrews 2005), a new speciation event took place in Africa around 200,000 years ago, leading to the emergence of modern humans—*H. sapiens sapiens*. The new species initiated a new process of expansion, Out of Africa 2. It outcompeted all previous populations of the Old World—Neanderthals in Western Eurasia and the Middle East, Denisovans in Central and East Asia, and epi–*H. erectus* groups in Southeast Asia—and drove them all to total extinction. However, the presence of a small but consistent proportion of Neanderthal and Denisovan genes in contemporary *H. sapiens sapiens* populations point to early introgression and admixtures, falsifying the "strong" replacement model.

The assimilation model, also known as "replacement with hybridation" was crafted by Smith et al. (1989), adopted and expanded by Gunter Brauer (1992), as an intermediate between the regional continuity and the replacement models. It considers that modern humans—*H. sapiens sapiens*—emerged exclusively in Africa and expanded later in Eurasia, where they met other populations, Neanderthals in the Middle East and Europe, Denisovans in continental, Central, and East Asia, and post-*H. erectus* in Southeast Asia. They interbred with all these distinct populations with modest admixture levels represented in small proportion of modern humans' genes. Assimilation is an ambiguous term to be used in this context. It evocates the equal mutual "fusion," one population absorbing the other. The fact that Neanderthals, Denisovans, *H. naledi*, *H. floresiensis*, and *H. lusonensis* are all extinct suggests that replacement was, after all, the dominant process at work in interspecies interaction, with minute degree of hybridation.

"Out of Asia" 1: From Sundaland to Sahul

The expansion of modern humans to Sahul and the southern sea was channeled through the southern Asia mosaic landscape, known as Sunda during the Late Glacial Period (Florin et al. 2020, Wurster and Bird 2014). Sahul is the name given to New Guinea, Australia, and Tasmania when they formed a single landmass during the glacial period.

"The favoured hypothesis for the initial dispersal of AMH [Anatomically Modern Human] from Africa to Asia was along a 'southern coastal route' (Highamet et al. 2009, Oppenheimer 2009). It is thought that this route had available coastal ecotones with high-ranked food resources that were easily exploited and accessible, thus encouraging continued rapid dispersals along coastal India, into Sundaland and Sahul. . . . Genetic dating suggests that founding populations in equatorial SE Asia may have arrived as early as about 65–79 ka" (Wurster and Bird 2014).

The expansion process involved many distinct dispersal episodes from different source populations that converged in Sundaland. An early dispersal to Australia from an African source population took place around 70,000 years ago (Florin et al. 2020, Wurster and Bird 2014). Another later dispersal event took place around 30,000, with the East Asian source population carrying Denisovan genes found today in modern Aboriginal Australians, Polynesians, Fijians, and East Indonesians. How did the dispersal processes work and what were the key variables in the successful adaptation of early modern humans (EMH) to their new environments?

Modern humans' expansion to Sahul involved settlement across Sundaland, hoping from island to island in the Wallacea Archipelago, a sea crossing of at least 90–100 kilometers, and finally landing either in Australian or New

Guinean parts of Sahul. It is generally assumed that expanding hunter-gatherer groups have a narrow diet, tending to favor coastal habitats with high-calorie, low-handling-cost food—meat, fish, seafood—with secondary consideration for food plants. Florin et al. (2020) challenge that assumption with new data from a north Australia early site, Madjedbebe rock-shelter, dated between 65,000 and 53,000 years.

The excavated rock shelter is located in Western Arnhemland at the foot of the Djuwanba massif. The recorded archaeological record includes charcoal, abundant ground ochre, grinding stones, a dense assemblage of unique flaked-stone artifact types and raw materials (Florin et al. 2020: 2). The archaeobotanical assemblage, the earliest evidence of an early modern human (EMH) diet in Sahul, features the exploitation of a relatively broad range of plant foods, some requiring significant processing:

> The evidence for a broad plant food diet at Madjedbebe 65–53 kya [kya =1000 years] is consistent with later Pleistocene archaeobotanical studies conducted in Island Southeast Asia and Sahul, and evidence for EMH diets in Africa and the Middle East. As such, it indicates that plant exploitation was a fundamental aspect of EMH diets globally. Culturally transmitted botanical knowledge, and the cognitive ability to perform multi-step and intensive processing sequences likely contributed to the adaptability and flexibility required by EMH populations to traverse continents and colonize new environments around the world. (Florin et al. 2020: 6)

"Out of Asia" 2: From North East Asia to the Americas

The "Out of Asia 2" expansion includes two distinct geographic and temporal series of events. One and the earliest is the expansion of modern humans from Asia to the Americas. The other and latest concern the colonization of the Southern Pacific islands from Sahul, reaching the Hawaii archipelago in the north, Easter Island in the East, and New Zealand in the south around 900–1000 CE.

The focus will be on the expansion in the Americas as it was the last massive landmass to be reached by modern humans. The baseline chronology for the initial access to the Americas is subject of passionate debate with competing scenarios. It is however not disputed that East Asians were the source population that expanded at different times and places in the Americas via Beringia during the Late Glacial maximum.

Fagundes et al. (2018) study confirms "a late Pleistocene split between Siberians and Native Americans, with Asian populations splitting off some thousand years earlier." It also corroborates the idea that the Native American founder population, which may have ranged in size from 200 to 400 individuals, underwent a strong bottleneck, though less extreme than previously suggested. The expansion of modern humans in the Americas was an interconnected three-step process. 1) The first step was articulated around the sustained divergence from ancestral Asian populations in Far Northeast Siberia. 2) The second step was a period of Arctic hunter-gatherers settlement consolidation in Beringia, along with genetic diversification and relative isolation from the source population. And finally, 3) the third step was the relative rapid expansion, faster along the Pacific coast, and slower in the hinterlands because of the presence of Laurentide glaciers (Mulligan and Szathmary 2017).

The expansion of modern humans was clearly an expansion with hybridation. Regional continuity and multiregional evolution hypotheses were relevant scientific hypotheses at the beginning of the debate in the 1980s. New data from aDNA, genomics, archaeology, paleontology, paleoclimatology, and environmental research overwhelmingly support the "Out of Africa 2" scenario.

COGNITION, GENES, AND LANGUAGES

With the expansion of the single modern human species—*Homo sapiens sapiens*—all over the globe during the last 20,000 years, natural selection, adaptive radiation, and the founder effect operated and manifested themselves under phenotypic variations, along with cultural selection. "Speciation" event per se is no more relevant as analytical concept. Accordingly, all the ensuing evolutionary developments of *Homo sapiens sapiens* populations are distinct, sometime parallel aspects of SArFe 4.

The Global mapping of humans' genetic makeup and languages features strong similarities between processes of historical inference in biology and linguistics (Atkinson 2011, Atkinson et al. 2008, Botha and Knight 2009, Crevels and Muysken 2020, Duda and Zrzavy 2019, Dunn et al 2011, Fan et al. 2019, Ferretti et al. 2018, Greenhill et al. 2018, Hellenthal et al. 2014, Janson 2011, Lopez et al. 2016, Perreault and Mathew 2012, Pipek et al. 2019, Speidel et al. 2021). Baker et al. (2017) provide strong evidence for correlations between languages and patterns of modern humans' ancestries. They compiled genome-wide data on 5,966 individuals, from 282 samples representing thirty primary language families in order to investigate early humans' genetic differentiation, human admixture, migration events, relationships among ancestries, and language groups. They identified twenty-one ancestries delineating the genetic structure of present-day population, with the vast majority (97.3%) of individuals on all continents having mixed ancestry:

- Genetic differentiation of human ancestries largely occurred subsequent to the Out-of-Africa migrations. The vast majority of present-day humans have mixed ancestry.
- Furthermore, the group labels continent, sample, race, and ethnicity are all imperfect descriptors of ancestry, such that ancestry is the preferred genomic classifier. We also find moderate to strong correlations between ancestries and languages at the family or branch levels (Baker et al. 2017: 7).

Genes

> Genetic variation is shaped through evolutionary processes acting on our genomes over hundreds of millennia, including past migrations, isolation by distance, mutation or recombination rate changes, and natural selection. Such events are reflected in the genealogical trees that relate individuals back in time. While these are unobserved, recent advances have made their reconstruction from genetic variation data feasible for many thousands of individuals and have enabled powerful inferences of our genetic past. (Speidel et al. 2021: 2)

aDNA and genomics thus provide reliable entries into past population histories and genealogies (Hellenthal et al. 2014).

Duda and Zrzavy (2019: 332–33) advocate efforts to increase representation of diverse world populations in human population genetics research and single out some of the limitations of current research. They particularly emphasize the overreliance on the same narrow data sets, "such as the HGDP-CEPH Human Genome Diversity Cell Line Panel, the International Hap Map Project, or the HUGO Pan Asian SNP Consortium." To help correct this distortion, they launched a new project and carried out an analysis of a "revised, and expanded data set, both in terms of number of populations, from 186 to 1,962, and number of source trees, from 257 to 388" (Duda and Zrzavy 2019: 335). As a result, they documented an "Out-of-Africa" superclade that supports a single dispersal of modern humans from Africa. Accordingly, a treelike model of human population allows to assess the congruence between genetic and linguistic data in research on cultural evolution.

Fan et al. (2019) focus on the African side of modern humans' evolution. Their analysis, based on high coverage (>30x) whole genome sequences of ninety-two individuals from forty-four indigenous African populations from all four main language families shows the San lineage to be the basal of all modern humans. It diverged from the rest of humans between 300 and 260,000 years ago. The split with Central African forest foragers occurred next.

Speakers of Africa's four major languages families went through a population bottleneck between 200,000 and 60,000 years (Fan et al. 2019: 6). Based
on the earliest evidence of population divergence, the ancestors of San hunter-
gatherers and ancestors of Niger-Congo, Nilo-Saharan, and Afroasiatic speakers may have diverged around 200,000 years ago. Niger-Congo, Nilo-Saharan
and Afroasiatic speakers' last common ancestor is dated around 34,000 years
ago. Niger-Congo diverge from Nilo-Saharan and Afroasiatic, and finally,
Nilo-saharan split with Afroasiatic around 16,000 years ago.

Migration and admixture events do occur at multiple times and/or involve
many groups. An analysis of 1,490 individuals from 95 worldwide human
groups carried out by Hellenthal et al. (2014) effectively shows "that it is
possible to elucidate the effect of ancient and modern migration events and
to provide fine scale details of the sources involved, the complexity of the
events, and the timing of mixing of groups by using genetic information
alone" (Hellenthal et al. 2014: 751).

However, there are limitations on genomic data's ability to accurately
reflect intricate ancient population histories relying only on modern individuals' DNA to study the Out of Africa migrations. There is strong evidence of
genes' backflow to Africa. "The first indicators of what is termed the 'back
to Africa' migrations were obtained from phylogeny of mt DNA haplogroups
U6 and M1, which have an origin outside Africa and are currently largely
distributed within North and East Africa" (Lopez et al. 2016: 64). The current uptake of aDNA research in Africa provides empirically sound addition to genomic based inferences. The potential of the new methodologies
to further unlock human genetic history is even brighter in the near future.
"Future improvements in whole-genome sequencing, greater sample size, and
incorporation of aDNA, together with additional methodological extension
are likely to allow better understanding of ancient events, to infer sex biases,
and to provide more precise event characterization then currently possible"
(Hellenthal et al. 2014: 751).

Languages

Research on language origin considered wildly speculative in the nineteenth
century was banned by the influential Societe de Linguistique de Paris in
1866 and the Philological Society of London in 1872. Languages, "spoken
words," are one of the most extraordinary developments in human evolution. "Language itself is rather difficult to define, existing as it does both
as transitory utterances that leave no trace, and as patterns of neural con-
nectivity in the natural world's most complex brains. It is never stationary,
changing over time and within populations which themselves are dynamic.
It is infinitely flexible and (almost) universally present. It is by far the most

complex behavior we know of—the mammoth efforts of 20th century language research across a multitude of disciplines only serve to remind us just how much about language we still have to discover" (Christiansen and Kirby 2003: 305). It can nonetheless be defined as "the full suite of abilities to map sound to meaning, including the infrastructure that supports it," ranging from vocal anatomy to neurocognition and the ethology of communication (Ferretti et al. 2018: 222).

There are many attempts at tracking anatomic and genetic clues suggesting hominins' capacity for speech (Ceolin et al. 2020, Ferretti et al. 2018, Perreault and Mathew 2012). Language very likely emerged within the context of *Homo sapiens sapiens*'s "cognitive revolution." "The human mind [is] a system of symbolic computations, instantiated by rules of natural language syntax" (Ceolin et al. 2020). Since language does not fossilize, Ferretti et al. (2018: 219) suggest the investigation of its origins does not rely on empirical evidence but instead has a mainly theoretical character in a multidisciplinary conceptual space. Fisher (2017: 34) asserts the opposite and indicates that language sciences are witnessing a paradigm shift, away from speculative models, with human cognitive traits "transformed into empirically addressable questions, generating specific hypotheses that can be explicitly tested using data collected both in the natural world and experimental settings."

Research on the origin of language is conducted along a multiplicity of paths, ranging from anatomy, neurobiology, and genomics to evolutionary psychology and linguistics. Mounier et al. (2020) explore the potential of paleoneurology to address the complex issue of the origin of language, through new interpretations of endocranial phenotypic data from fossils. Relying on the globularity hypothesis that highlights neurobiological properties that would have set anatomical and physiological preconditions for the emergence of language, they point to "the expansion of the parietal region [as] part of the globularization process within the hominin lineage that may have played a role in the formation of a language network" (Mounier et al. 2020: 150). Their suggestion that Neanderthal and *H. sapiens sapiens* would have had similar language faculties is difficult to reconcile with their explanation of brain structure anatomical differences.

> Early and extant *H. sapiens* presented a larger cerebellum than Neandertals. The cerebellum is linked to higher cognition, including language, and the morphological differences identified between the two species may indicate distinct language faculties. (Mounier et al. 2020: 150)

Fisher (2017) analyzes the implications of the revolutionary identification of a mutation in the gene FOXP2, a slightly altered version of a gene found in apes that appears to reach its present form between 200,000 and 100,000 years ago, erroneously dubbed the "language gene." "The identification of a gene like FOXP2 opens up unique molecular windows into both the neural bases and the evolutionary origins of speech and language" (Fisher 2017: 35). There are however important limitations as FOXP2 represents a hub in a genetic network. 1) A gene in itself does not specify a particular neural circuit or behavior output; 2) it contributes to more than one process and does not have a single restricted function; 3) genes and proteins interact in networks and complexes and do not operate in isolation. The observed genetic changes—ninety-six amino-acid changes, in eighty-seven protein-coding genes—"have become fixed on the human lineage after splitting from our common ancestor with Neandertals" (Fisher 2017: 38).

The study of the evolutionary history of genes and human anatomy connected to speech production is an important contribution. However, "the anatomical and genetic data lack the resolution necessary to differentiate proto-language from modern human language" (Perreault and Mathew 2012: 1).

Current research on the origin and evolution of languages is strongly anchored on linguistic data themselves, and relied upon to test alternative theories (Greenhill et al. 2018). Atkinson et al. (2008: 588) formulated a hypothesis according to which punctuational or rapid burst of change associated with the emergence of new languages, or at later language contact are an important feature of language evolution. The hypothesis was tested with data from Austronesian, Indo-European, and Niger-Congo, three of the world's largest language families, totaling a third of the world's languages. It was found that "the punctuational effects account for a surprising amount of the total lexical divergence among the languages: 31% of vocabulary difference among Bantu language speakers arose at or around the time of language splitting events; 21% among Indo-European languages, and 9.5% in Austronesian" (Atkinson 2008: 588). The initial foundation burst producing new language is followed by a longer time of gradual and slower divergence.

A decisive step in empirically sound research on language origins was laid by Atkinson (2011) and Dunn et al. (2011). Dunn et al. made two important findings: (1) that cultural evolution is the determining factor of linguistic structure, with the current state of a linguistic system shaping and constraining future ones; and (2), that linguistic diversity is not tightly constrained by universal cognitive factors specialized for language but the product of cultural evolution via diversification. Atkinson (2011) crafted the theory and designed the methodology allowing to track language expansion. His methodology is anchored on phoneme frequency and diversity across languages. Phonemes are distinct sound units, word building blocks, that are continuously gained and lost because of a stochastic process homologous to random mutations in genes. Phonemic diversity is correlated to population size.

Atkinson (2011: 346) looked at the geographic variation in phoneme inventory size from 504 languages along with speakers' demography, language location, and affiliation. His study shows the distribution of phoneme number to be clinal. "The single major cline in phonemic diversity is consistent with a linguistic founder effect operating under conditions of rapid expansion from a most likely origin in Africa. This supports a picture congruent with similar analysis of human genetic and phenotypic diversity" (Atkinson 2011: 348). Complex languages are suggested to have emerged in the context of modern human "cognitive revolution" marked by the earliest archaeological evidence of symbolic culture in Africa 80,000 to 160,000 years ago.

Building on Atkinson hypothesis, Perreault and Mathew (2012), in the first appraisal of the time line of language origin based on direct linguistic data, relied on language phonemic diversity to derive a minimum date for its origin. As human populations expanded all over the globe, they went through a series of bottlenecks. The process resulted in a serial founder effect resulting in clinal loss of phonemic, phenotypic, and genetic diversity observable in present-day world populations. "African languages today have some of the largest phonemic inventories in the world, while the smallest inventories are found in South America and Oceania (Perreault and Mathew 2012: 1). Phoneme change is slow, and phonemic diversity is driven exclusively by cultural transmission, allowing us to craft a "slow clock" to date the origin of language. It is estimated to coincide with the chronological range of the emergence of *Homo sapiens sapiens* around 300–250 000 years ago (Perreault and Mathew 2012: 5). Once formed, initial languages spread and diversified, or better, diversified through human dispersals. Accordingly, languages are the product of long-term cumulative cultural evolution. As the product of social learning, transmission, and use, they respond to selection pressures posed by local communication contexts derived from physical, social, and cognitive environments (Padilla-Iglesias et al. 2020: 1).

The formation of new languages is structurally connected to mobility, population size, and distribution. The rate of language change may be accelerated by serial founder effects as new languages are started from relatively small populations (Atkinson et al. 2008). Greenhill et al. (2018) launched a project to test the consistency and generalizability of the association between population size and rates of word gain and loss. They relied on 153 pairs of closely related sister languages from the Austronesian, Indo-European, and Niger-Congo languages families to conduct their test. They found on the one hand that smaller Indo-European languages have greater rates of words loss from the basic vocabulary, and, on the other hand, a lack of evidence for a negative relationship between population and words loss rates in Austronesian and Bantu groups. The study concludes with a note of caution according to which the "population size" effect may be another example of a pattern featuring superficial similarity between linguistic and biological evolution, that may in fact be driven by different mechanisms. They however added that despite differences in the processes underlying linguistic and biological change, the same analytical tools can be applied to both research domains.

The Cognitive Revolution: Adornment, Empathy, and Representations

The "cognitive revolution" essentially revolves around the emergent symbolic ability of the human mind. It is manifest via the creation of mental realities. Beside language, personal adornment of the body, empathy, and representations are distinct but complementary dimensions of the "cognitive revolution" kicked off and amplified by *H. sapiens sapiens*.

Personal Adornment ˙

Personal adornment of the body can be looked at from two complementary dimensions: the use of selected modified/unmodified mollusks shells on the one hand, and the production and use of pigments on the other hand. "There is general agreement among researchers that modern humans, *Homo sapiens*, are the one responsible for the surge of the use of shell beads, but Neanderthals also exploited mollusks shells, and also decorated themselves (Bar-Yosef Mayer 2020: 12). The earliest shell specimens selected for personal adornment and made of selected unmodified and latter strung beads have been recorded at the Middle Stone Age sites of Pinnacle Point in South Africa and Misliya Cave in Israel. They consist of a few unmodified shells of *Glycymeris nummaria* (Israel) and *G. connollyi* (South Africa), likely picked on the beach and brought to the respective caves around 180,000 and 160,000 years ago (Bar-Yosef-Mayer 2020, Bar-Yosef-Mayer et al, 2009, 2020). Naturally and artificially perforated shells use expanded between 120,000 and 115,000 years ago. They are documented in Moroccan Mousterian and Aterian sites of Taforalt, Grotte des Contrebandiers, El Manasra, and El Harhoura 2, in Algeria at Rhafas, Ifri n'Ammar, Oued Djebbana, and Bizmoune, in Israel at Es-Skhul and Qafseh caves. A similar but latter development took place at the end of the Middle Stone Age in South Africa, with shells beads documented around 78–72,000 years ago at Blombos Cave, *ca*. 74,000 years ago at Border Cave, and finally, 69–72,000 years ago at Sibudu Cave in Lesotho. According to Bar-Yosef-Mayer et al. (2020: 1), "between 160 and 120 ka [ka = 1000 years] BP there was a shift from collecting complete bi-valves to perforated ones, which reflects both the desire and the technological ability to suspend the shell beads in string to be displayed on the human body."

The use of pigments, particularly red ochre, but also other colors touch on aspects of personal adornment, and as such is generally linked to the symbolic implications of body painting (Bar-Yosef-Mayer et al. 2009, Geggel 2018, Henshilwood et al. 2011, 2018, Roebroeks et al. 2012). The earliest indication of the human use of ochre dated to 285,000 years ago has been recorded at the MSA site of GnJh-03 in Kenya, East Africa, where seventy pieces of red ochre weighing some 5 kgs were collected (Geggel 2018). Neanderthals also "imported" red ochre some 200–250,000 years ago as documented in the archaeological record from Maastricht-Belvedere Middle Palaeolithic site in the Nertherlands (Roebroeks et al. 2012). Eighty-four lumps of ochre were recovered from layers dated to 100–90,000 years ago at Qafseh in Israel.

It is however at Blombos Cave in coastal South Africa that the versatility of early ochre use is manifest in its different aspects (Henshilwood et al. 2011, 2018). The earliest instance, recorded in Sequence BBC (for BlomBos Cave) M3, dated to 100,000 years ago, was found in a "processing workshop where liquefied ochre-rich mixture was stored in two abalone shells," containing a production tool kit including hammerstones, grinding stones, charcoal, bone, and ochre (Henshilwood et al. 2011: 219). The Sequence BBC M1 and M2 Upper dated from 77,000 to 73,000 years ago, provided eight pieces of ochre engraved with geometric patterns, sixty-seven *Nassarius krausianus* shell beads stained with ochre, and a "cross-hatched pattern drawn with an ochre crayon on a ground silcrete flake" (Henshilwood et al. 2018: 115), precisely dated to 73,000 years ago. By the end of the Middle Paleolithic period, ochre is represented in Neanderthal sites ranging from 60,000 to 40,000 years ago, with its use ranging from symbolic to practical.

Burial Practices

Deciphering the ultimate origin of human burial practices is a difficult exercise. It is however not controversial to considered them as collateral consequences of empathy, the capacity of intersubjective understanding, at cognitive, emotional, and somatic levels (Preston and de Waal 2002). It is therefore, not a surprise that the earliest human burials dated to the same time range, 110,000–90,000 years ago, are all found virtually in the same area, at Es-Skhul (Mount Carmel) and Qafseh (Lower Galilee) in Israel (Stringer et al. 1989, Vandermeersch and Bar-Yosef 2019).

The remains of ten individuals—seven adults and three children—were excavated at Es-Skhul, three of them considered to have been deliberate burials. The remains of twenty-five individuals were excavated from the Terrasse, most of them from the Middle Palaeolithic layers XVII–XXII. Only a few of them, as is the case for Qafzeh (Q-) 8, Q-9, Q-10, Q-11, and Q-15, were buried intentionally (Vandermeersch and Bar-Yosef 2019).

Q-8 found in layer XVII and partially preserved is an adult of unknown sex and age, laid on the right side and oriented east-west. For postdepositional taphonomic reasons, the outline of the burial was undetectable.

Q-9 and Q-10 are part of a double burial found in layer XVII. The former is the skeleton of a twenty- or twenty-one-year-old female, laid to the left side and oriented north-south. The latter is a six-year-old child, buried south and perpendicular to the female adult, oriented east-west, laid on the back and compressed in a small pit. The twin burial is interpreted as the inhumation of a mother and child (Vandermeersch and Bar-Yosef 2019: 264).

Q-11, found in layer XXII, displays a well-delineated burial pit containing the remains of a twelve- to thirteen-year-old adolescent, laid on the back, oriented north-south, and buried with the skull of a large deer—*Dama dama*—as offering. He/she had a severe but healed skull injury that was probably not the direct cause of death.

And finally, Q-15 in layer XVII was a three- or four-year-old infant, laid on the back. The unburied human remains could have resulted from the abandonment of deceased bodies on the cave's terrasse where they may have been affected by scavengers.

Burial appears to have been highly selective during the initial phase of the emergence of the practice. Qafseh burial orientation appears to have followed cardinal directions, north-south and east-west, without a preferential position of the deceased body (three times on the back, one left and one right side). At the end of the Middle Stone Age, burial practices were adopted by Neanderthals and *H. sapiens sapiens* and spread in different regions of the Old World between 60,000 and 50,000 years ago. In Africa, the earliest modern human burials all dated to the Middle Stone Age have been recorded at Taramsa Hill in southern Egypt, Border Cave in southern South Africa, and Panga Ya Saidi in coastal southeast Kenya. Taramsa Hill contains the remains of an eight- to ten-year-old child dated to 69,000 years ago, buried in a sitting position, "the body . . . laid down against the side of the extraction pit and covered up by the dumped material" (Vermeersch et al. 1998: 478). A four- to six-month-old infant wearing seashell beads (D'Errico and Backwell 2016) was buried at Border Cave 74,000 years ago. And finally, a 2.5- to 3-year-old child was buried in a flexed position in a pit 39.8 centimeters long, 36.7 centimeters wide, and 12.5 centimeters deep at Panga ya Saidi cave in Kenya some 78,000 years ago (Martinon-Torres et al. 2021). These earliest African *H. sapiens sapiens* burials belong to infant-children. "The PYS [Panga ya Saidi] child, in combination with the infant burial from Border Cave and the 'Funerary Caching' of a juvenile at Taramsa, suggests that the *H. sapiens* populations were intentionally preserving the corpses of young members of their groups between about 78 and 69 ka [ka = 1000 years]" (Martinon-Torres et al. 2021: 99).

Representations

Representations can be partitioned into two main categories: visual on the one hand, made of a wide array of sign and motifs made on a surface, and sculptural on the other hand, consisting of the production of volumetric artifacts of variable bulk and size. Visual representations—usually referred to as rock art—and the exclusive prerogative of modern humans—*Homo sapiens sapiens*—are the earliest manifestations of human pictorial forms of expression. They emerged at different times and places during the Late Pleistocene in the Old World, in Southern African (Blombos Cave), Southeast Asia (Leang Tedongnge Cave in Sulawezi, Indonesia), and Westernmost Eurasia/Southwestern Europe (Chauvet Cave).

So far, the oldest cave paintings have been recorded in Sulawezi (Indonesia) in Island Southeast Asia (Aubert et al. 2018, 2019, Brumm et al. 2021) at Leang Tedongnge cave (45,500 years ago), Leang Bulu Sipong 4 cave (43,900 years ago), and Leang Balangajia 1 (32,000 years ago). These pre-Austronesian visual representations are made of figurative animal paintings associated with hand stencils. The animal outlines, depicted in profile, "are filled with irregular patterns of lines and dots, predominantly representing swine (*Sus celebensis*) and dwarf bovids (*Bubalus sp*) called anoas locally (Brum et al. 2021: 1).

The earliest painted scene from Leang Tedongnge features four pigs arranged in face-to-face pairs. Pig 1, 136 centimeters long and 54 centimeters wide, associated with two hand stencils, is oriented right, facing Pig 4 which is unfortunately extensively worn out. Pig 2 and 3 are face to face. The narrative is suggested to depict male pigs' confrontation (Brumm et al. 2021).

The second oldest painting recorded at Leang Bulu Sipong 4 and dated to 43,900 years ago is a 4- to 5-meter wide panel featuring 6 animals—2 pigs and 4 dwarf buffaloes—and 8 human-like figures with spears in a representation of hunting strategy, either game drive or communal hunt (Aubert et al. 2019: 443). The structure of the painting is particularly interesting. It is articulated on two parallel oblique lines combining humans and different animal species. The front line, that of pigs, includes from left to right: (1) hand stencils, (2) human (Ther 1), (3) Pig 1 and hand stencils, and finally, (4) Pig 2, all staged at almost equal distance from one to the next. A similar pattern is implemented in the rear line, that of dwarf buffaloes (anoa), but this time with discrete equidistant scenes: (1) a relatively isolated "Animal figure," (2) a human figure facing Anoa 1, (3) a human (Ther 2) flanking Anoa 2, and finally, (4) a series of humans facing Anoa 3 and 4. The structure and balance of the composition attest to high mastery of the "canvas space" and movement. All depicted animals are oriented left, with humans oriented in the opposite direction.

These early cave paintings are thoughtful creative achievements, not unsteady initial graffiti. So far, they "represent the oldest reported indication for the presence of AMH—Anatomically Modern Human—on the island and perhaps in the wider Wallacea region" (Brumm et al. 2021: 9).

Noncontroversial and securely dated sculptures appear to have emerged after 40,000 years ago, as is the case for the Lion Man of Hohlenstein Stadel (38,000 years ago), the Hohle Fels Venus (38,000–33,000 years ago), the Brassempouy Venus (25,000 years ago) (Lobell 2012), and a wide array of portable artworks in different parts of the world after 20,000 years ago (Li et al. 2020). Large works like the bisons from Tuc d'Audoubert, dated to 13,000 years ago during the Magdalenian Period, are latter developments.

CONCLUSION

Humankind is a relatively young biological population. Its contemporary version, *Homo sapiens sapiens* or modern humans, presents a broad range of phenotypic diversity—skin color, hair, facial traits, etc.—as a consequence of natural selection and somatic adaptation to different environments. Fossils, material culture, languages, genes, representations, and the very scientific reconstruction of the human career from its ardipithecines roots emphasize the unity and diversity of humankind. Evolutionary forces are blind, with no goals, but humans have the potential of shaping their destiny.

NOTE

1. https://embryo.asu.edu

Chapter 2

Origins and Expansion of Speakers of Austronesian Languages and the Formation of the Indian Ocean World System

AUSTRONESIAN ORIGINS AND EXPANSION

Introduction

Mobility, at different spatiotemporal scales and its derived technologies, has shaped human phenotypic and cultural similarities and differences. From the emergence of Modern humans in Africa some >300,000 years ago to their final expansion all over the world, Southeast Asia, both mainland and islands, have played a key role in the colonization of the Southern Seas along the east flank of the Indian Ocean. It is this complex and intricate set of processes involving sustained adaptation to climate change, expansion in new biomes, and the formation of new cultural identities that is addressed in this chapter through a multidisciplinary lens. Archaeological, genomic, linguistic, as well as cultural anthropology data are harnessed to unveil and understand the patterns of human mobility that brought *Homo sapiens sapiens* hunter-gatherers to Sundaland and Sahul, cultivated plants first from New Guinea to Asia and Africa, and from China to Island Southeast Asia and Madagascar, resulting in the formation of the multi-cores Indian Ocean world system. The availability of higher resolution and more precise paleoenvironmental data allows to formulate for the first time an integrated but differentiated model of Austronesian expansion, in its "out-of-Taiwan" and "Go-West" components. The ensuing Trans-Indian Ocean connections boosted the linkages with multiple Coastal Asian trade networks, from China to East Africa, generating the first Land and Sea dynamic world systems.

The Indian Ocean is the third largest water body of the planet, after the Pacific and the Atlantic. It has an inverted U-shape, bounded by Africa in the west, mainland Asia in the north, Southeast Asia archipelagos and Australia in the east, and finally Antarctica in the south. Its "shores" were explored and settled by different but connected human communities in four main steps.

The first step corresponds to the emergence of the *Homo* genus in East Africa and its initial expansion to Eurasia between 2.5 and 1.85 Ma ago. This early settlement phase stretched from East Africa, via South Asia (Indian subcontinent) to Southeast Asia (Java and Eastern Asia).

The second step took place in the context of the expansion of modern humans, *Homo sapiens sapiens*, also called "Out of Africa 2." Sahul, the ancient continent made of Australia, New Guinea, and Tasmania, was reached around 65,000 years ago. At that stage, all the Indian Ocean shores were inhabited, with however, very sparse and widely scattered populations.

The third step happened in the Early Holocene with the early domestication of plants in the New Guinea Highlands followed by their expansion into Melanesia and Asia. And finally, the fourth stage is the expansion of speakers of Austronesian languages, spread from Hawaii and Easter Island in the Pacific Ocean in the East to the Comoros Archipelago and Madagascar on the western shore of the Indian Ocean.

This chapter focuses predominantly on steps 3, 4, and after. Starting with two series of independent but overlapping processes that took place during the Holocene—the last 10,000 years—and set the stage for the formation of distinct but interconnected Indian Ocean interaction spheres. The nature and distribution of human settlements in Southeast Asia strongly conditioned the developments taking place from step 3 to the present.

Sunda and Sahul Late Pleistocene/ Early Holocene Hunter-Gatherers

Climate change with its consequences had significant impacts on patterns and amplitude of human mobility. Continental landmasses' boundaries and topography changed considerably during the peak of the Late Pleistocene Glacial period, the Early and Late Holocene Global warming (Bird et al. 2011, Pelejero et al. 1999, Soares et al. 2016). The submergence of Sundaland and Sahul took place in three episodes. The first one, the Meltwater Pulse Ia (MWP) happened in 15,000–13,500 BP, triggering fast retreat of coastlines and initial flooding (Pelejero et al. 1999). The second episode, the MWP 1b, occurred in 11,500–10,000 BP and delineated the main configuration of the present-day landmasses and established the modern hydrographic conditions.

And finally, the third episode took place in 8,000–7,000 BP, with marginal effects on major landmasses' contours. As a result of these environmental processes, the South China Sea was connected to the tropical Indo-Pacific waters through a channel. The ancient Sunda continent was fragmented into Islands Southeast Asia (ISEA) with myriad archipelagos and Mainland Southeast Asia (MSEA). The ancient Sahul continent was dislocated into Australia, New Guinea, and Tasmania.

Sundaland and Sahul were settled by modern human—*Homo sapiens*—hunter-gatherer communities from at least 70,000–65,000 years ago (Habgood and Franklin 2008, Higham 2013). Madjedbebe, a rock shelter in Northern Australia, has its earliest levels dated to 65,000 BP featuring a broad-spectrum diet (Florin et al. 2020). In Eastern New Guinea, Ivane Valley sites dated to 49,000–43,000 BP present evidence of exploitation of taro and pandanus. Population expanded from these early settlements, and around 40,000 BP, medium and long-distance exchange networks developed all over Sahul, along with burial practices. Mining and quarrying emerged later, around 24,000 BP (Habgood and Franklin 2008). Farther north, in Sundaland, there are archaeological sites dated from c. 63,000 BP in Thailand, the Philippines, Laos, Indonesia, and Malaysia, with 45,000- to 35,000-year-old visual representation sites featuring hand stencils, mammals, and hunting scenes documented in Borneo and Sulawesi, particularly at Lubang Jeriji Saleh Cave.

Beside the two new hominin species discovered in ISEA in the last few years, *Homo floresiensis* on Flores Island in Indonesia and *Homo luzonensis* in Luzon in the Philippines, the legacy of ancient hunter-gatherer populations is traceable through archaeology and ethnology (Higham 2013). Late Pleistocene hunter-gatherers' sites are scattered all over the ancient Sundaland. Most of the MSEA sites are more or less directly connected to the Hoabinhian tradition. These sites located in upland regions are predominantly in caves and rock shelters. It is the case for Tam Pa Ling in Laos where a Homo sapiens skull dated between 63,000 and 43,000 BP was found, Lang Rongvien Cave, dated to c. 38,000–27,000 BP in Peninsular Thailand; Callao Cave, c. 60,000 PB in Luzon, Philippines; Tabon Cave, c. 30.000 BP also in the Philippines; the large cave of Niah in Borneo, c. 45,000 BP, where evidence for the exploitation of sago, taro, and yam was found; Dieu, c. 30,000 BP, Nguom, c. >23,000 BP, and Son Vi, c. 23,000–13,000 BP in Vietnam.

Open-air shallow prehistoric sites do not preserve well in the archaeological record, providing a distorted view of past settlement systems. As suggested by ethnographic observations: "rock-shelters are but one component of their occupation strategy. During the dry season, the Mani prefer to live in their temporary encampments in the cool rainforest, retreating to cave shelters only during the period of rains" (Higham 2013: 24). With the rise of sea level and changes in the hydrographic networks, a number of sites were located in broad riverine floodplains and later, around 5000 BP, on raised beaches in the context of what Charles Higham (2013) called "maritime adaptation."

Contemporary hunter-gatherer communities of small-statured individuals (Negritos) survive in a few pockets in Southeast Asia. It is the case for the Andamanese (Andaman Islands), the Semang and Mani (Peninsular Thailand), and the Aeta (Philippines). In fact, the spread of millet and rice farmers profoundly impacted hunter-gatherer systems and lifeways. Some communities were entirely absorbed in farming societies and adopted their languages. Others withdrew to rainforest refugia, where they became small-bodied dark-skinned humans through biological adaptation. "Andamanese and Semang haplogroups not only have a deep indigenous ancestry but also link with an original movement of anatomically modern humans (AMHs) from Africa. This stems from the finding that the lineage L3 is the parent African base for the expansion of AMHs out of Africa" (Higham 2013: 22).

aDNA and Genomics Perspectives

Recent high-resolution phylogeny research shows shared paternal ancestry of Han, Tai-Kadai, and Austronesian speakers. Even if focused exclusively on China, the study points to the existence between 9,000 and 5,000 years ago of different subbranches of the paternal haplogroup O1a-M119 in the Yangtze River delta, labelled as "Southeast China Neolithic Communities," ancestral to Austronesian Han, and Tai-Kadai speaking populations (Sun et al. 2021: 11, Wang et al. 2021).

Genomic research conducted on the peopling of Southeast Asia by McColl et al. (2018) provides a complex population dynamics model involving at least four ancient populations. Following the expansion of modern humans, the older layer is made of Mainland Hoabinhians (Gr. 1) "who share ancestry with present day Andamanese Onge, Malaysian Jehal and Ancient Japanese Ikawazu Jomon" (McColl et al. 2018). A change of ancestry occurred around 4000 BP coinciding with population expansion from East Asia into Southeast Asia during the transition to farming. These incoming waves of East Asian migrations were associated with speakers of Austroasiatic, Kradai, and Austronesian languages.

New Guinea Neolithization and Its Aftermath

C. O. Sauer's (1952) prediction on the early origins of agricultural practices in the tropics was finally verified with the findings from Kuk Swamp in Highlands New Guinea. The swamp, formed in a previous Pleistocene lake basin, is located in the Upper Wahgi Valley at 1,560 meters above sea level in interior New Guinea. Long-term environmental and archaeological research that started in the late 1970s revealed agroforestry and plant management practices stretching from the Late Pleistocene to the mid-Holocene in three main phases (Denham 2009, Denham et al. 2003, Denham, Haberle and Lentfer 2004, Denham and Haberle 2008, Denham and Mooney 2008, Denham and Barton 2014).

Phase 1 evidence dated to 10,220–9910 years BP, found in better-drained paleochannel levees at slightly higher elevation, consists of runnels, pits, postholes, and stake-holes. The Pleistocene forest was cleared with the assistance of fire and openings were used to grow taro (*Colocasia esculenta*), yams (*Dioscorea alata*), bananas (*Musa*, var accuminata), and sago (*Metroxylon sagu*).

Phase 2 remains consist of a well-preserved paleo-surface with evenly spaced circular to subcircular mounds very likely used to grow yams and taro. There are in addition other less patterned features with the whole phase 2 dated to 6950 to 6440 years BP.

And finally, phase 3 remains are comprised of ditch networks connected to major drainage channels dated from 4350 to 2800 years BP. They were built in two distinct chronological sequences: from 4350 to 3950 BP for the early series and 3260 to 2800 BP for the later one.

Musaceae [bananas] phytoliths [plants silica micro-skeleton] are present in high percentage in Phase 1 sediments suggesting deliberate planting in wooded environment. Phase 2 landscape consists of a degraded forest shifting to human induced grassland. The frequency of *Musa* sp. phytoliths

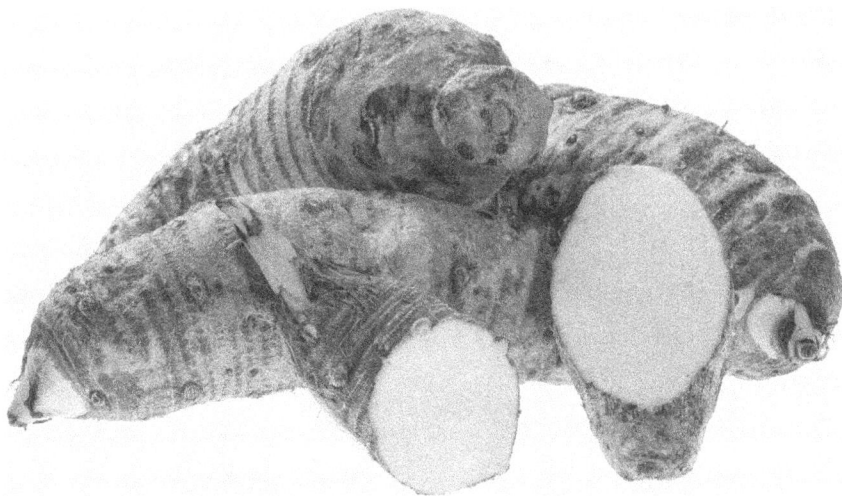

Figure 2.1. Taro (*Colocasia esculenta*). *Gonzalo Calle Asprilla / iStock / Getty Images Plus / Getty Images*

Figure 2.2. Purple Yams (*Dioscorea alata*). *PixHound / iStock / Getty Images Plus / Getty Images*

Figure 2.3. Bananas (*Musa accuminata*). *Joydeep / Wikimedia Commons / CC BY-SA 3.0*

Figure 2.4. Sago (*Metroxylon sagu*). ilbusca / DigitalVision Vectors / Getty Images

is sustained and relatively high, pointing to routine cultivation of domesticated bananas along the wetland margins (Denham et al. 2003: 191–92). From phase 2 on, Highlands New Guinea grew a number of crops, including bananas, taro, yams, sugarcane (*Saccharum officinarum*), and breadfruit (*Artocarpus altilis*) that will initially expand west to Southeast and South Asia, and later East to the Pacific and West to the Indian Ocean.

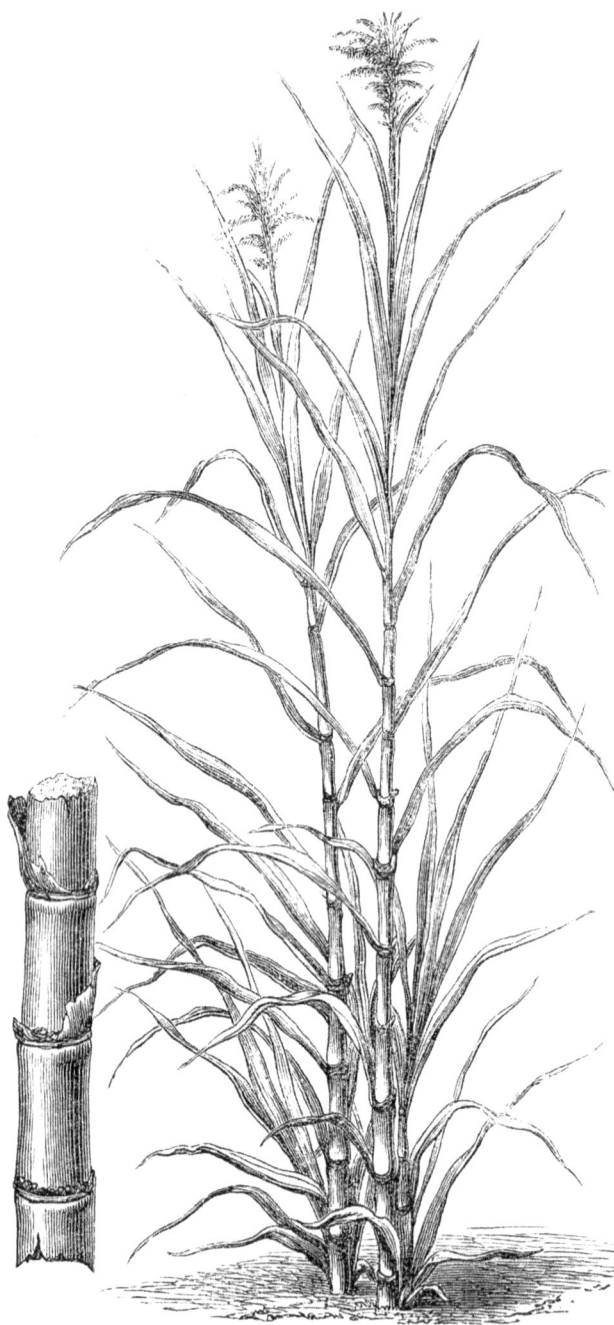

Figure 2.5. Sugarcane (*Saccharum officinarum*). *Nastasic / DigitalVision Vectors / Getty Images*

Figure 2.6. Breadfruit (*Artocarpus altilis*). *BergmannD / iStock / Getty Images Plus / Getty Images*

Wild varieties and progenitors of bananas, taro, and yams are found in most of the tropical South, Southeast Asia and New Guinea, from Pakistan and Northern India, China, Malaysia, Borneo, to Papua New Guinea. "The greatest diversity of wild *Colocasia* species appears to extend from NE India to southern China within the Himalaya region of mainland Southeast Asia. . . . Based on genetic analyses, it could have been domesticated several times in different locations over a vast area ranging from India to South China, Melanesia and northern Australia" (Chair et al. 2016: 2). Taro domestication appears to have taken place independently in southeast Asia and New Guinea, with a possible additional domestication center in Yunnan and southern China (Beaujard 2017: 55–56). Different parameters point to New Guinea as the area of origins and domestication of *Dioscorea alata*, with a secondary expansion area in Sulawesi (Beaujard 2017: 45). The domestication of *Musa acuminata* took place in New Guinea around 7000 BP. "The genomes of practically all bananas eaten today derived from one or the other sub-species *bankssi* [originating from New Guinea] and *errans* [originating from the Philippines], and sometime both" (Beaujard 2017: 153), with *errans* a later addition to *bankssi*. Consequently, the geographic distribution of genotypes involved in bananas' domestication required human's translocation of plants, most likely under vegetative forms of cultivation, across vast regions (Perrier et al. 2011: 1).

Domesticated bananas are seedless. Most of the New Guinea early domesticates reproduce vegetatively. Cuttings or whole plants must have been carried by seafarers with the intention of "transporting their landscapes." "It was small scale, village or lineage groups of farmers and seafarers who played the key role in the peopling of the Pacific and the cultural transformation of Neolithic Island Southeast Asia." (Fuller et al. 2011: 544).

Domesticated bananas spread to Southeast Asia and India, where they hybridized with other varieties. Their phytoliths are recorded at Fahien Cave in Sri Lanka dated to 6000 BP, Kot Diji in Pakistan dated to 4500–3900 BP, Munsa in Uganda dated to 5492–5100 BP, Xincun site, coastal Guangdong in China dated to 5050–4060 BP, and Nkang in southern Cameroon, Central Africa dated to 2700–2500 BP.

However, the earliest domesticated varieties spread from New Guinea from 7,000 to 6,000 years ago and hybridized with other local varieties along their expansion trajectories. In their analysis of data from Xincun site in coastal Guangdong province in China, Yang et al. (2013) concluded that:

> roots and tubers were the staple plants foods in this region before rice agriculture was widely practiced. . . . During 3350–2470 BC, humans exploited sago palms, bananas, freshwater roots, acorns, job tears as well as wild rice. A dominance of starches and phytoliths from palms suggest that the sago type palms were an important plant food prior to the rice in south subtropical China. (Yang et al. 2013: 1)

The expansion of New Guinea cultivars through seafaring expeditions and land transfers through Southeast Asia archipelagos, Southern China, Sri Lanka, and India created the first interaction sphere along the eastern flank of the Indian Ocean in the late-Early to Mid-Holocene period (Beaujard 2005, 2017, 2019).

THE EXPANSION OF SPEAKERS OF AUSTRONESIAN LANGUAGES

The Austronesian language family consists of more than 1,200 languages spread on about half of the globe, from Easter Island and Hawai in the east and Northeast to Madagascar in the west (Padilla-Iglesias et al. 2020). It is comprised of two main branches: Western Austronesian with such languages as Malay, Indonesian, Javanese, Malagasy, and Tagalog; and Eastern Austronesian mostly from the southern Pacific with Samoan, Tongan,

Tahitian, Maori, Hawai'ian, etc. (Blust 1984–85, 2019). With the significant exception of the Comoros and Madagascar located at the extreme western edge of the geographic distribution of speakers of Austronesian languages, the Austronesian core, which includes Taiwan and the Philippines, is situated along the eastern edge of the Indian Ocean. Groups of Austronesian speakers expanded from that core to Indonesia, Melanesia, Micronesia, and the western Indian Ocean (Comoros, Madagascar), and finally to Polynesia, reaching Hawaii, Eastern Island, and New Zealand.

The nature, processes, and chronology of the expansion of speakers of Austronesian languages are still debated by researchers. Taiwan presents the greatest linguistic diversity of the Austronesian speakers' world. For Blust (2019), "since the area of greatest diversity is favored as the primary center of dispersals both in linguistics and botany," Taiwan is the area of dispersal of speakers of Austronesian languages. For Soares et al. (2016: 311) however, referring to the Pan-Asian SNP Consortium research, "the diversity of Taiwanese aboriginals is likely a subset of the ISEA—Islands Southeast Asia—diversity, implying that the dispersals between Taiwan and the ISEA took place in the reverse direction."

Historical Linguistics Outline

The Austronesian languages classification and its cultural and chronological implications are addressed if differently by Blust (1984–1985, 2019) and Blench (2010) with the former providing a chronological outline he cautiously termed as "informed speculation" (Blust 1984–1985: 54). Speakers of the Proto-Austronesian language spread from Mainland China to Taiwan around 4500 BCE bringing with them cereal agriculture and domestic animals. A split occurred approximately 1,000 years later with the expansion out of Taiwan resulting in the formation of Formosan (F) and Malayo-Polynesian (MP) languages. MP languages spread west and east around 3000 BCE, leading to the formation of Western (WMP) and Central Eastern (CEMP) Malayo-Polynesian branches. In a fourth step that occurred around 2500–2000 BCE, Central (CMP) and Eastern (EMP) Malayo-Polynesian diverged, with large-scale expansion in the Pacific Ocean resulting in the formation of South Halmahera–West New Guinea and Oceanic languages.

> The one conclusion that the linguistic evidence forces upon us again and again is that the dramatic migrations of the Polynesians were but the end point of a millennia-long journey that began far to the west and north. (Blust 1984–1985: 59)

Geographic and relative social isolation drove the formation and evolution of Austronesian languages (Padilla-Iglesias et al. 2020). In the process, the expanding seafarers communities carried with them animals and plants from different origins, domestic animals and commensals such as pigs, chicken, dogs and plants like rice, millet, breadfruit, paper mulberry, bananas, yam, taro, etc. (Chang et al. 2015).

Archaeological Perspectives

The "Out of Taiwan" hypothesis championed by historical linguistics research involves partial or total demic diffusion from China mainland, the introduction of domesticated plants and animals, and the diffusion of this "Neolithic package" first in the Philippines, then ISEA, Melanesia, Polynesia, reaching Hawaii, the Easter Islands, and finally New Zealand. Without going into details at this point, archaeological research supports historical linguists' conclusions. From 5000 BCE, hunter-gatherers settled along the south and southeast China coastline, with most specializing in the exploitation of marine resources (Hung 2019, Hung and Zhang 2019). Their sites, predominantly made of shell middens, are located along the coast and on the offshore islands of Fujian, Guangdong, Guangxi, Hainan, and Taiwan, at such places as Kequitou, Fuguodon, Jinguishan, Chinpinglong, Dawei I, and Dawei II. They formed different regional cultures: the Kequitou culture of the Fujian coastline, the early phase of the Dabenkeng culture of Taiwan, and possibly the Da But culture of Northern Vietnam (Bellwood 1995, Zhang and Hisao-chun 2008). Yang et al. (2018) published results that map the southward expansion of rice farming from the Middle Yangtse Valley "through the mountainous region of Wuyi and Nanling . . . areas of Western Fujian and North Guangdong by 5000 CalBP. . . . Continued expansion into coastal areas of East China Sea and South China Sea . . . crossing the Taiwan Strait around 4500–4000 CalBP" (Yang et al. 2018: 1496). Rivers' systems were preferential pathways for such expansion, particularly the Min, East, and North Rivers, as indicated by archaeobotanical remains from NLi (NW Fujian) and Laoyuan (North Guangdong). The former located on the bank of the Min River in NW Fujian contained rice macro remains dated to 5000–4100 CalBP and the latter in North Guangdong, located along a tributary of the East River has rice and millet remains dated to 5000–4500 CalBP.

Coastal Neolithic settlements, based on pottery presence in the archaeological record, have been documented at Xiantouling, Shiweishan, Chenqiaocun, Kequitou, Tanshishan, and Dabenkeng in Guangdong, Fujian, and Taiwan. "Until now, no evidence of rice or millet farming before 3000 BCE has been found in coastal southern China." (Hsiao-Chun and Zhang 2019: 63). In Taiwan, Early (3500–2800 BCE) and Late (2800–2200 BCE) Dabenkeng assemblages have been recorded at more than forty sites: Dabenkeng in Taipei, Fengbitou in Kaoshiung, Nanguanli, Nanguanlidong and Dachangqiab in Tainan, Changguang in Taidong, and Guoye on Magong island in Penghu (Hsiao-Chun and Zhang 2019: 61). Ancient rice remains dated from 4500–4000 CalBP have been recorded at a little more than ten sites in Taiwan and the Strait. It is the case for Zhishanyan, YuLi and Dalongdong in the North; Yingpu and Anhelu on the central west coast; Youxianfang and Fengbitou in the southwest; Chaolaiqiao in the southeast; and finally, Kending at the south end (Deng et al. 2017, Galipaud et al. 2014).

The "Neolithic package" derived from the Middle Yangtse valley appears around 3000 BCE along China's southern coastline and islands. It is marked by the introduction of rice and millet, red-slipped pottery, bark cloth technology, loom weaving, and dogs, pigs, and very likely water buffalo in Mid-Holocene Taiwan (Ardika and Bellwood 1991, Bellwood 1995, 2013, Deng et al. 2017, Hung 2019, Hung and Zhang 2019, Jiao 2017, Kelly 2017, O'Connor 2015, Rolett et al. 2007, Tsang 1992, Yang et al. 2018). Neolithic sites are recorded along the Fujian, Guangdong, and Guangxi coastline, and watercraft skills were necessary to cross the strait to Taiwan. Foragers groups were already present in most of the former Sunda and Sahul continents. Many of their open-air sites submerged by the rise in sea levels are now inaccessible, providing a distorted view of ISEA late Pleistocene hunter-gatherer settlement densities.

Farming practices introduced to Taiwan around 3000 BCE, spread in its different biotopes, and resulted in the consolidation of rice farming cultures for almost 1,000 years. Taiwan Neolithic crops and related material culture, with plain and red-slipped pottery, spread to coastal and hinterlands favorable localities in the Philippines, Borneo and Sulawesi from c. 2500 to 1500 BCE.

The geographic distribution of elements of the "Neolithic package" was mapped by different researchers (Kelly 2017, Krigbaum 2003, O'Connor 2015). Domesticated rice is recorded in the archeological record of Andarayan in the Cagayan Valley of Northern Luzon in the Philippines at 3400±125 BP, Gua Sireh Cave in Sarawak at 3850±260 BP, and Ulu Leang in South Sulawesi at 4000 BP. Red-slipped pottery is recorded at Chaolaiqiao and Donghebei in southern Taiwan at 4200 BP. It is present in the Batanes Island between Taiwan and Luzon, Nagsabaran and Magapit sites in Northern Luzon, and Minanga Sipakko and Kamassi sites in Sulawezi, ranging from 4000 to 3500 BP. In addition, "schist and slate adzes with morphology similar to Neolithic specimens from Taiwan and the Philippines as well as their manufacturing debris were also recovered" (O'Connor 2015: 13). Domestic pig (*Sus scrofa*) and domestic dog (*Canis familiaris*), dated respectively to 3200 Cal BP and 2400 Cal BP have been recorded at the Savidug Dune site in the Batanes Islands; Nagsabaran in the Philippines with possibly water buffalo, dated to 4400 Cal and 2500 Cal BP; in Sulawesi, at Karama River sites of Minaga Sipakko, 3500 Cal BP for pig and 1000 Cal BP for dog; 4000 Cal BP for pig at Liand Bua in Flores island, Indonesia; a 2867±26 BP dog burial at Matju Kuru in Timor-Leste; 3260±70 BP and 2330±70 BP for pig and dog at Uattambi, on Kayoa island; and finally 3100 Cal BP for pig along with red-slipped pottery at Banda Island (O'Connor 2015).

In Kalimatan for example, the earliest Neolithic levels are dated to 2000–1700 CalBCE at Niah cave, 2800–2200 CalBCE at Gua Sireh, and 750–450 CalBCE at Lubang Angin (Kelly 2017).

Expanding Austronesian worldviews are conveyed through visual representations found on coastal limestone cliffs and subsumed under the category of Austronesian Painting Tradition. "Aside from small anthropomorphs, boats dominate the figurative rock art repertoire and vary from simple schematized boats to more representational examples showing details such as high raked prows, and/or decorated prows, central sails and steering oar" (O'Connor 2015: 45).

The importance of rice declined in the equatorial latitudes, with subsistence systems shifting to greater reliance on tropical plants, tuber crops, and fruits that were already adopted by local foragers. The expansion in Melanesia—the Lapita expansion—took place from 1600 to 1000 BCE.

In all the cases, "Neolithic groups were faced with new challenges which may well have involved adaptation toward secondary foraging and/or systematic food production and collection. These trends in diet likely reflect patterns that mirror larger more fundamental aspects of subsistence, settlement, and mobility" (Krigbaum 2003: 302). Diet reconstructions, based on enamel stable carbon isotopes from specimen collected at Niah Cave, Gua Sireh, and Lubang Angin in Borneo, show that broad-spectrum subsistence, combining gathering, hunting, fishing, consumption of wild and cultivated root crops and grain, nuts, vegetables, invertebrates, and small trapped vertebrates was very likely the rule (Krigbaum 2003), with no evidence for the reliance on a single crop. As demonstrated above, adaptive flexibility is the sine qua non requirement for successful mobility.

The Genomic Dimensions

Genomic research addresses the expansion of humans, animals, and plants. Chang et al. (2015), Matisoo-Smith (2015) comments, and Penailillo et al. (2016) examine the phylogeography of the Pacific paper mulberry (*Broussonetia papyrifera*), its use, cultural importance, and origins. It is traced back to its undisputable Taiwan origins and has profound implications for the understanding of Austronesian languages speakers' expansion. Ko et al. (2014), Soares et al. (2016), Skoglund et al. (2016), and Spriggs and Reich

(2020) address directly or indirectly the human genomic aspects of the "Out of Taiwan" hypothesis.

Ko et al. (2014) have designed a two-pronged methodology to identify the Early Austronesians in and out of Taiwan. They rely, on the one hand, on the complete mitochondrial (mt) DNA genome sequence of an -8000 years robust thirty-year-old 1.6-meter-tall male skeleton from Liang Island in the Taiwan strait. On the other hand, they collected 550 mtDNA genome sequences from eight aboriginal (Highland) Formosan and four other Taiwanese groups.

Liang Island is located at 24 kilometers from Fujian coastline and 180 kilometers northwest of Taiwan. The skeleton buried in a supine tightly flexed position at the base of a shell midden is dated to 8320–8060 Cal BP. As suggested by Hsiao-Chun and Zhang (2019: 72), this individual can be assigned to the Australo-Papuan flexed burial tradition of maritime-adapted hunter-gatherers.

Ko et al. (2014: 430) found evidence of population expansion around 8,000–10,000 years ago, when early Austronesians diverged from Han ancestors and expanded into Taiwan Haplogroup E. They entered in North Taiwan and spread south. Their conclusion is straightforward: "Thus Lingdao man is the oldest genetic relative of Aboriginal Formosans. Furthermore, his lineage traces back to ancestral M9 lineages along coastal China. . . . We estimate the initial divergence between Formosans and Han to be around 8–10,000 years" (Ko et al. 2014: 431).

Soares et al. (2016) designed a different approach and methodology. They combined genome-wide mtDNA data and Y chromosome to investigate the ancestry of Austronesian- speaking populations. Relying on what they called "the most comprehensive analysis of the region to date," they reached three main conclusions: 1) That there is a pre-Neolithic common ancestry for Taiwan and ISEA populations; 2) There were two small-scale migrations via Taiwan in the Later Holocene; and finally, 3) There were language shift and small-scale migrations rather than large-scale population expansions of speakers of Austronesian languages. In other words, they assert the "the spread of the red-slipped pottery Neolithic and Austronesian languages in ISEA were indeed accompanied by dispersals of seafarers from Taiwan, but beyond the Philippines the primary mechanism for the spread of both was acculturation" (Soares et al. 2016: 311). That assertion is highly debatable, as will be shown later. It is clearly not relevant for the colonization of the Comoros Archipelago and Madagascar by speakers of Austronesian languages in the Western confines of the Indian Ocean (Beaujard 2017, 2019).

The analysis of Xu et al. (2012), focused on the estimation of the time and amount of admixture involving Asian and Papuan ancestry across East Indonesia, was carried out through two studies. One with about 50,000 Single Nucleotide Polymorphism (SNP) analyzed in a sample of 288 individuals from thirteen Austronesian- and two Papuan-speaking populations in Indonesia and Papua New Guinea. And the other made of around 680,000 SNP analyzed from thirty-six individuals sampled from seven populations in Indonesia and twenty-five others from Papua New Guinea. The results of their research "refute suggestions that the Asian ancestry observed in Indonesia largely predates the Austronesian expansion or that the Austronesian expansion was not accompanied by large-scale population movement" (Xu et al. 2012: 4579). Their analyses of genome-wide data point to "a strong and significant genetic impact associated with the Austronesian expansion in Indonesia, just as similar analyses have pointed to a genetic impact associated with the Austronesian expansion through Near and Remote Oceania" (Ibid.).

P. Skoglund et al. (2016) present the results and significant implications of genome-wide ancient DNA (aDNA) analysis of four burials: three dated to 3100–2700 BP from Vanuatu and one dated to 2700–2300 BP from Tonga, compared with 778 samples of present-day East Asians and Oceanians. It shows that the first settlers of these lands, with very little or no Papuan ancestry, originated from Southeast Asia. The aDNA data "show irrefutable evidence of 3 independent prehistoric population movements in Vanuatu" (Spriggs and Reich 2020: 11): 1) An initial peopling by First Remote Oceanian population of East Asian ancestry; 2) the spread of Papuan ancestry in Late and/or post Lapita period and admixture with local population; and finally, 3) gene flow from Polynesia affecting different parts of Vanuatu in different ways.

All three works mentioned above (Ko et al. 2014, Soares et al. 2016, Xu et al. 2012) comfort the "Out of Taiwan" hypothesis. The first focuses exclusively on Taiwan populations' ancestry. The second addresses the wider expansion of speakers of Austronesian languages and de-emphasize the impact of demic diffusion. And finally, the third, exploring time and amount of admixture, emphasizes widespread population movements. The probable causes of the observed population expansions, tangentially alluded to from time to time, are not addressed in any of these papers.

Linguistic, archaeological, and genomic research converge in support of the "Out of Taiwan" hypothesis as the most parsimonious explanation of the origins of speakers of Austronesian languages (Bellwood 1995, 2013, Blench 2010, Blust 1984–1985, 2019, Chang et al. 2015, Matisoo-Smith 2015, Ko et al. 2014, Penalillo et al. 2016, Skoglund et al. 2016, Spriggs 2011, Spriggs and Reich 2020, Soarez et al. 2015). However, there are still some disagreements on the meaning of some factual observations (the spread of pottery, domestic animals, and cultivated plants) as well as the nature, causes and amplitude of population movements. As is generally the case in research problems requiring multidisciplinary approaches, disciplinary lenses and jargon can create difficulties. To avoid such situations of confusion, Spriggs and Reich (2020: 10) understandably "advocate the use of specifically genetic terms for genetic entities (First Remote Oceanians, Papuan), cultural terms for cultural entities (Lapita), and linguistic terms for linguistic entities (Austronesian/Non Austronesian)." It is a minimalist approach to transdisciplinary research that is supposed to address complex intricate issues. Human demography is biological and social. Both aspects can be separated theoretically but when it comes to the explanation of population dynamics common concepts such as age, sex, life expectancy, fertility and mortality rates, etc. at the intersection of biological and social dynamics are what is required, not a single disciplinary lexicon.

MODELING THE AUSTRONESIAN EXPANSION

With varying emphasis and differences, most researchers accept the historical fact of the expansion of speakers of Austronesian languages. The phenomenon is investigated through different lenses, from paleoclimatology to paleo-genomics, with interesting and compelling results. But why did ancestral Austronesian take it to the sea after approximately 1,000 years of stasis in Taiwan? What processes triggered populations movements? How did these movements unfold? And what were the broader social and economic consequences for the people involved? (Spriggs and Reich 2020: 12).

Some basic facts have to be clarified at this juncture. Shared material culture traits are not necessarily an indication of single coherent biological population. Different biological populations can share the same material culture and different material culture traits can be adopted by different segments of the same biological population. Languages can be learnt and whole groups can experience language shifts. Differential preservation limits researchers' access to the kind of high-resolution data they may need to fine-tune and address the problems they are interested in. But a simple qualitative modeling can help bring to the fore the dynamics operating in the "black box" of expanding populations.

Why Did They Move?

P. Bellwood (1995: 108–10) suggested a number of reasons that may have triggered and fueled Ancestral Austronesian seafaring: 1) population growth caused by reliable food supply; 2) the transportability and reproductibility of agricultural economy; 3) technological innovations and the development of seafaring traditions; 4) the existence of cultural rewards for courage and daring explorations feats; and finally, 5) the drive to access prestigious exotic materials and goods.

Most of the ISEA archaeological record is obtained predominantly from rock shelters and cave sites. Open-air settlements with relatively large excavation exposures of settlement features are not available, making all attempts at the reconstruction of past social organization off limits (Higham 2017). Beside technological innovation in seafaring (the invention of outrigger canoe), four intersecting dimensions can be relied upon to model the probable causes of the initial ancestral Austronesian expansion: 1) climate and environmental change; 2) population growth; 3) social organization (with its inherent value systems) and patterns of residence; and finally, 4) the dynamics of subsistence systems.

In the climate and environmental change dimension (Hu et al. 2008, Lim et al. 2019, Liu and Feng 2012, Park et al. 2019, Wu et al. 2014), abrupt climate change as well as periodic short-term changes in climate variables such as the total amount, periodicity, and annual distribution of rainfall without major climate crises, can have significant effect on people's lives and food supply. Low precipitations and patchy rainfall distribution can trigger famines within a single year. Too much rain in too short a time can cause devastating floods and soil erosion, detrimental to crops. In both scenarios, people may adjust by shifting back to strong reliance on hunting and gathering, splitting into smaller scattered groups, or migrating to better places. Even if they cannot be confidently inserted in the model, exceptional natural disasters, like volcanic eruptions, earthquakes, and tidal waves can trigger settlement relocation.

It is generally assumed that the advent of food production triggered population growth, resulting in what J. P. Bocquet-Appel (2008) termed the neolithic demographic transition (NDT). Sedentism had a significant impact on women's fertility. It resulted in a decrease of birth interval following a reduced breastfeeding time; decreased the maternal stress for carrying babies in multiple forager moves; and finally, initiated better metabolism for maternal nutrition. Food-producers with higher fertility than foragers and reliable food supply in sedentary contexts resulted in a sharp increase in birth rate. However, "with the appearance of village life and the corresponding increase in local population density, higher mortality soon followed the increase in fertility" (Bocquet-Appel 2008: 52). Sustained positive birth/mortality ratio over a favorable time segment thus axiomatically resulted in population growth; situations that could have generated social stress and tensions depending on the characteristics of the social organization under consideration.

Most of ISEA was already populated by mobile forager groups before the kickoff of the earliest seafaring speakers of Austronesian languages. Archaeological evidence suggests contacts between the expanding rice and millet farmers and local hunter-gatherers. Such situations feature different social organizations, different languages, differential and unbalanced matrimonial circulation, and differential reproductive success (Thomas et al.

2006). Farmers tend to have higher fertility and birth rates than foragers. In an almost standard case of hypergamy, farmer males tend to take foragers females as spouses; the opposite move, with female farmers espousing forager males is exceptional. These interactions if articulated on demographic disparities between the two populations involved could have resulted in language replacement, with foragers adopting farmers language, significant culture change manifest in new material culture elements and traits, and finally, profound genetic transformations:

> Significant genetic transformation of a population could . . . occur if there were disparities in fertility between two populations. This could be influenced by lifestyle or social organization. Relatively small-scale migrations of people could result in disproportionate transformations of local genetics if migrants and their descendants tended to be positioned at the top of stratified societies. (Booth 2019: 11)

Social organization

Social organization with its inherent value systems and patterns of residence are the crucial matrix difficult to access for the remote past. Ethnographic and historical data can however be relied upon to suggest some plausible scenarios. Claude Lévi-Strauss (1987) crafted the concept of "house societies" to refer to a form of social organization common in Indonesia, Melanesia, and Polynesia that has puzzled anthropologists because of the fluidity of kinship formations. A "house" is a corporate body with an estate combining material and immaterial goods (Kahn 2014, Santos and Donzelli 2007–2008, Ting 2005). A house society is accordingly a social structure in which kinship and political relations are organized around membership in corporately managed dwelling not around descent groups or lineages. "A common characteristic of Austronesian house-societies is that features of dwellings served symbolic rather than purely functional purposes" (Kahn 2014: 22).

Austronesian longhouses generally shelter a whole village, up to sixty families under the same roof. They present three main attributes: they are raised aboveground and built on piles. They generally tend to have large saddleback roofs and decorative finials. The ground level is used for storage and livestock. On the platform raised on piles, there is a long gallery connecting all the living quarters of the individual families. The house is the effective institution for access to farming land and the transmission of names, goods, and privileges. Some members of a longhouse can migrate and build a new longhouse after population growth triggers fragmentation. Tension and rivalry can also lead to fission. This happens when a competitor to the incumbent headman cannot find enough support to displace him. The challenger and his supporters might then decide to leave that longhouse and begin their own (Ting 2005).

Life under the same roof has strong implications for the wider system of material and social reproduction (Santos and Donzelli 2007–2008). The "longhouse" was probably the core organizational module of the expanding speakers of Austronesian languages. It was very likely the unit in charge of outrigger-canoe construction operations, logistic planning of high-sea fishing and expeditions, as well as subsistence activities and agricultural production (in this case, rice cultivation).

Contrasting the Melanesian big-man versus Polynesian chief as the Non-Austronesian and Austronesian divide, Lin and Scaglion (2019: 268) suggest that "there were social tendencies stressing stricter genealogical rules regarding symbolic and natural resources in early AN-[Austronesian] speaking communities that enabled and promoted, but did not always lead to, the development of hereditary leadership." It is highly probable that the early Austronesians' genealogical principle that bars junior branches from accessing land and inheritance was a significant push factor to rapid maritime expansion and seafaring (Bellwood 1996, Fox 1995).

The house society model draws attention to the architectonic manifestation of social organization (Kahn 2014: 18) and is, as such, amenable to archaeological investigation. Unfortunately, "as a consequence of the dearth of archaeological research in Southeast Asia dedicated to the investigation of settlement patterning, construction techniques and function, assessments of social organization and change rely heavily on mortuary data" (Higham 2017). Most of the sites excavated in ISEA are either shell middens, rock shelters, or caves (Bellwood 1995, 2013, Higham 2013, Krigbaum 2003, Kelly 2017, Ko et al. 2014, O'Connor 2015, Rollet et al. 2007, Tianlong 2007).

The corporate nature of the social organization of speakers of Austronesian languages can be adjusted to different kinds of sites—open-air villages, caves, and rock-shelters—even if archaeological research is still lagging behind in revealing wide-scale site structures. Excavation size varies considerably from case to case, ranging from small test pits to larger exposures. The Chaolaiqioa site in southeastern Taiwan, for example, was probed with a 2 x 1.5-meter test pit revealing a 1-meter-thick deposit with occupation evidence in Layer III dated to 4200–4000 BP (Deng et al. 2017). Kequitou, a shell midden in coastal Fujian dated to 6500–5500 BP, was sampled on 700 square meters, revealing one burial, twenty-one shell pits, and one hundred small post molds arranged in two clusters, probably piles from raised house platforms (Hsiao-Chun and Zhang 2019: 57). The Laoyuan site in the East River drainage of Northern Guangdong, dated to 5000–4500 CalBP, is estimated to extend over 5,000 square meters, with 433 square meters excavated, revealing eight burials, forty-five pits, and 135 postholes, direct indication of houses built on pikes. Unfortunately, the site map is still unpublished. And finally, the Chaling site, northeast of Guangzhou City in the Pearl River delta, revealeda number of house foundations and postholes in addition to eighty-three pits and 112 burials (Yang et al. 2018: 1496).

As indicated by the archaeological record at hand, the exploitation of wild resources, from hunting, fishing, and gathering was a constant in all the excavated sites. Rice—where it could be grown—and pork were very likely staple foods, but it is difficult to assess the proportion of their contribution to the overall diet of the expanding populations of speakers of Austronesian languages. Cultural anthropology research on rice-growing populations emphasizes rice's central role as material substance and symbol. "Rice is both a key staple food and a central socio-cultural metaphor, being at the same time a powerful operator of distinction and an essential mediator of human recognition" (Santos and Donzelli 2007–2008: 35).

Rice Farming

Rice cultivation is labor-intensive and features the highest preindustrial human densities (Boserup 1965). It is comprised of two main forms: wet and dry. Wet rice cultivation requires significant investment in hydraulic infrastructure construction to provide an adequate and controlled quantity of water at any time during the crop growth. There are different rice varieties with different maturation times between sowing and harvesting. It is 130–135 days for long-maturation, 113–125 days for medium-maturation, and 110 days for fast-maturation varieties. With constant maintenance, adequate water management, and the addition of new soil and manure, farmers can obtain two to three rice harvests a year per paddy field, with an average yield of 1,000 kilographs/acre, for a relatively long production period (Fong et al. 2015, Xin et al. 2018). The average yield per acre of rainfed or hill rice is 1.7 ton per hectare, significantly less than in paddy fields. In his analysis of the Iban longhouse, J. Ting (2005) shows that for these farmers practicing slash-and-burn agriculture, soil nutrients are depleted after three successive years of production, triggering the relocation of the longhouse and a fifteen-year-long fallow period for the cultivated plot.

Rice cultivation thus generates two distinct settlement strategies. Labor-intensive paddy cultivation tends to be relatively stable with a denser population. Rainfed or hill rice cultivation on the other hand, tends to be spatially extensive and more sensitive to annual variations in precipitation, with either periodic relocation of dwelling features, search for new agricultural lands, and/or out-migrations.

Initial Out of Taiwan: Why Did They Take It to the Sea?

The constant interaction between environmental parameters, human demography, social organization, settlement patterns, and agricultural practices sketched briefly above generates nonlinear dynamics. The Austronesian longhouse was very likely the core feature of the social organization of speakers of Austronesian languages. Its structural fluidity allowed for greater adaptive flexibility, either through the creation of new longhouses following population growth and/or fission to defuse internal tensions. Ancestral Austronesians took approximately 1,000 years to spread from the northeast to the southwest of Taiwan, settle in all agriculturally sustainable environments, and interact with the island forager populations. Pushes for out-migration were probably punctuated, separated by longer period of stasis. The invention of the outrigger canoe allowed for the initial expansion to the islands southwest of Taiwan and Luzon in the Philippines around 4150 BP. The dynamics of dry rice farming is critical for modeling the expansion of speakers of Austronesian languages in ISEA. Sustained population growth, differential reproductive success, absorption of forager groups, and short-term environmental perturbations impacting rice production may have triggered the initial seafaring expeditions southwestward, to the Philippines.

Holocene climate history is generally partitioned into three distinct segments: The Early Holocene, the Holocene Climatic Optimum (HCO), and the Late Holocene (Lim et al. 2019, Park et al. 2019, Wu et al. 2014) with however significant intra-segment climate variability. Hu et al. (2008) analysis based on calibrated ^{18}O isotopes and focused on Southwest China shows "that rainfall was 8% higher than today during the HCO (*ca* 6000 BP), but only 3% higher during the Early Holocene. Significant multi-centennial variability also occurred, with notable dry periods at 8.2 ka [ka = 1,000 years], 4.8–4.1 ka, 3.7–3.1 ka, 1.4–1 ka and during the Little Ice Age" (Hu et al. 2008: 221).

A major worldwide climatic event happened in the Late Holocene, at 4200–4000 BP. "This '4000 Cal yr BP Event' is reported to have played an important role in the collapse of three major civilizations" (Liu and Feng 2012: 1181), notably Ancient India, Ancient Egypt, and Mesopotamia. A deep-sea core (Core 255, 25° 12'N/123° 07' E) on the path of the Kuroshio current along the southeast flank of Taiwan "exhibits a marked cooling event that lasted from 4500 to 3300 Cal yr BP. . . . This drastic cooling was interpreted to reflect the Late Holocene intensification of the Asian winter monsoon" (Liu and Feng 2012: 1182).

Data from the Zhejiang province in East China show sustained expansion of prehistoric cultures in the context of agricultural and Maritime civilizations before 4000 Cal yr BP. After 4000 Cal yr BP however, the dry-cold climate as well as the deterioration of the coastal maritime environment led to the contraction and collapse of prehistoric cultures (Wu et al. 2014: 669).

A multi-proxy study of a thirty-meter-long sediment core from the estuarine floodplain of Seomjin River in South Korea, an area under the influence of the Kuroshio current, provides compelling evidence on climate change and past societal responses (Park et al. 2019). Accordingly, the pollen zone 2–4.4 ka to 1.6 ka BP—features "a noticeable decline in *Quercus* from zone 2, and increase in *Pinus*, *Artemisia* and *Poaceae*. This change indicates that the HCO ended and the climate deteriorated" (Park et al. 2019: 4). Late Holocene climate appears to have been modulated by a c. 500-year cycle, "leading to abrupt climate deterioration at 4.7 ka, 4.2 ka, 3.7 ka, 3.2 ka and 2.4 ka BP in the study area" (Park et al. 2019: 7). Settlement evidence points to a fast-expanding population of rice farmers from 3500 BP on, taking advantage of the improved climatic conditions. By c. 2800 BP however, the number of settlements dropped drastically. "The agrarian subsistence economy may have been heavily undermined by an abrupt drying and/or cooling event," and rice farmers finally abandoned their sedentary lifestyle around 2400 BP when faced with another abrupt drying and/or cooling event (Park et al. 2019: 11). Considering the strong linkages between the Yayoi culture in Japan and the Songuk-ri culture in South Korea, the authors finally argue for a plausible southward migrations of rice farmers to wetter areas suitable for growing rice, even crossing the sea to Japan and initiating the Yayoi culture around 2800 BP.

The timing of the initial expansion of the "Neolithic package" out of Taiwan coincides with the Late Holocene 4200–4100 Cal yr BP dry/cooling event. "The diagnostic red-slipped pottery, along with spindle whorls, Taiwan nephrite ornaments, and stone adzes first appeared in Eastern Taiwan in 4200 BP and then Batanes islands and the Cagayan valley of northern Luzon afterwards" (Deng et al. 2017). Neolithic rice farming communities expanded in different parts of Taiwan, in Xuntangpu in the northwest, Niumatou in the central west, Niuchouzi in the southwest, and Fushan in the southeast. Taiwan appeared to have witnessed sustained Neolithic population growth, with a total of some forty-three sites dated to 4500–3500 BP, all settlements much larger than in the previous period.

In c. 4200 BP, a combination of an abrupt shift to dry/cooling climate, larger farming populations, and tectonic uplifting resulted in limited amount of flat alluvial and coastal terrain suitable for growing wet rice. That convergence of independent factors triggered a profound crisis for Taiwan Neolithic farming communities. The only reasonable solution was out-migration in search for suitable coastal farmland to release the pressure on those staying behind. It is very likely that such cycles, with differential combinations of demographic, climatic and environmental, and social and cultural variables, occurred again and again, sustaining technological innovations and shaping coastal and maritime oriented Austronesian speakers' traditions.

Go West! Austronesians in East Africa

Malagasy is an Austronesian language spoken today in Madagascar. It belongs to the Southeast Barito (SEB) languages group of Kalimatan in Indonesia (Adelaar 2016, Beaujard 2011, 2017, Brucato et al. 2018, Crowther et al. 2016, Pierron et al. 2017, Regueiro et al. 2008).

Madagascar is located in Western flank of the Indian Ocean, at 450 kilometers east in the southeast periphery of the African landmass, and at 6,000 kilometers from Southeast Asia. The expansion of speakers of Austronesian languages to East Africa which is now securely dated to the seventh or eighth century CE is considered to have been "the single most astonishing fact of human geography for the entire world" (Crowther et al. 2016: 6635). The processes involved in this achievement, investigated from a broad range of disciplines, are hotly debated by scientists. Number of issues are raised concerning the population and settlement histories of Madagascar, the Comoros, and the East African coast; the logistics involved in the transfer of groups of speakers of Austronesian languages from Borneo to the southwestern shore of the Indian Ocean, and the demographic, cultural, and subsistence processes involved.

Sustained archaeological research provides scattered but consistent evidence of human presence in Madagascar from the Early Holocene to its successful colonization by ancestral Malagasy. Cut marks on animal bones have been recorded in different parts of the island. A bone from an elephant bird— *Aepyomis maximus*, an ostrichlike creature that stood more than three meters high and weighed more than three hundred kilograms—found near Ilakaka in the south central part of the island is dated to 10,500 BP (Lawler 2018: 1059). A radius from a now-extinct large sloth lemur (*Palaeopropithecus ingens*) found at Taolambiby in the southwest is dated to 402–204 CalBCE. And, finally, a hippopotamus (*Hippopotamus lemerlei*) bone from Anjohibe cave in the northwest is dated to 2288–2035 CalBCE (Dewar et al. 2013: 12583). Moreover, Dewar et al. (2013) present evidence "that stone tool-using foragers occupied Madagascar before the iron-using agriculturalists who were the earliest previously known settlers; and that these foragers were active in northern Madagascar at least as early as 2000 BCE." The recorded early human presence may have been discontinuous, but the source area was undeniably East Africa.

In logistical terms, direct seafaring expeditions from Borneo to Madagascar are unlikely. The formation of the Srivijaya Empire in the seventh century CE provided sea links between Indonesia, India, Arabia, and East Africa, through

Malay-controlled shipping companies. For Adelaar (2016: 89), migrants from Borneo were transported on Malay ships. Beaujard (2011: 170) in contrast thinks that, "it is hardly likely that Malay ship masters would have chosen crews of men with no seafaring experience (and accompanied by women)," even if he acknowledges the possibility of the presence of other crew members on the ship. In fact, both researchers consider different populations on board the ships. While Adelaar is clearly referring to Malay ships' passengers, Beaujard focuses narrowly on the ships' crews members only. Passengers are supposed to disembark at destination and ships' crew members are expected to stay aboard to service the ship. Whatever the case, successive groups of migrants originating from Kalimatan Southeast Barito in Indonesia landed in the Comoros and settled in the Archipelago in 800–900 CE. It is from the Comoros Archipelago population bottleneck, where admixture with Bantu speakers took place, that speakers of Austronesian languages colonized the larger island of Madagascar.

The genetic structure of the Malagasy population is unanimously characterized as southeast Asian and East African with however significant differences in data interpretations (Adelaar 2016, Brucato et al. 2018, Pierron et al. 2017, Regueiro et al. 2008). On the average, the genetic makeup of the Malagasy population is 66.3 percent African and 33.7 percent Southeast Asian (Regueiro et al. 2008) with important regional variations. "The distribution of ancestral components based on genome-wide data indicates that people in the highlands in the center of the island have mostly Asian ancestry (>65 percent), whereas people from the coastal regions have higher African ancestry (>65 percent) (Pierron et al. 2017: 3). While Pierron et al. (2017: 5) write that "both GLOBEtrotter and ALDER analyses date the single admixture event between 500 and 900 BP," they went on to assert that they "identified a recent split of proto-malagasy population from southern African Bantus around 1500 BP and an older split from South Borneo between 3000 and 2000 BP." Their conclusion "that Indonesian populations may have arrived on Madagascar before African populations" (Pierron et al. 2017: 5) is surprising and unsupported.

Linguists have shown that the coherence and unity of Bantu loanwords and grammatical features found across all Malagasy dialects can have but one explanation: an initial Austronesian settlement on the African mainland and/or the Comoros. It is generally accepted that there is a bottleneck pattern in the settlement of Madagascar. The proto-Malagasy, or the migrants were already a mixed Asian-African population before setting foot on the great island (Adelaar 2016: 83). Brucato et al.'s (2018) results back linguistic and archaeological evidence featuring the Comoros Archipelago as the earliest contact locale between Austronesians and Africans in the West Indian Ocean, resulting from "the dispersal of a group genetically close to the present Banjar population from Southeast Borneo around the end of the first millennium" (Brucato et al. 2018: 65). The Comoros Archipelago is consequently the primary gateway for Austronesian gene flow into the Swahili corridor at the beginning of the second millennium.

"The earliest detected admixture event in Madagascar occurred during the late 11th century in groups located on the easternmost coast of the island. This postdates the earliest date of admixture in the Comoros, which is estimated to be in the 8th century for the communities of Anjouan, the eastern island of the archipelago" (Brucato et al. 2018: 65).

Archaeological and archaeobotanical evidence provide additional support to the Comoros as the primary gateway. "Dusum ware," popular in Southeast Asia during the Srivijaya Empire, was found at the Dembeni site on Mayotte in the Comoros Archipelago. Archaeobotanical data showing that Asian crops are earlier in the Comoros than at sites in Madagascar support the scenario of indirect colonization of the latter from the former, or elsewhere in Eastern Africa (Crowther et al. 2016). There are significant regional variations in the genetic makeup of the Malagasy population detected by Pierron et al. (2017). They can however be explained by social practices such as preferential matrimonial networks, and/or limited or avoided intermarriage between distinct ethnic groups (Thomas et al. 2006). Based on genomic, archaeological, archaeobotanical, and linguistic data, the most parsimonious explanation for a relatively rapid colonization of Madagascar by an African-Asian population is that of a secondary colonization from the Comoros Archipelago gateway. "The Comoros were settled at an early date by a Southwest Asian population that was later genetically and linguistically swamped" (Crowther et al. 2016). Paleoclimatic research in the western part of the Indian Ocean (Kench et al. 2020, Kuhnert et al. 2014) points to cooling/dry events dated to 234–605 CE (Common Era) and 1481–1807 CE. In the former, corresponding to the "Late Antiquity Ice Age," the sea level dropped to –0.88 m and in the latter, coeval with the Little Ice Age, it dropped to –0.89 m. It is not known if the Late Antiquity cooling/dry event had any direct impact on out-migration from Borneo, but the relative synchronism with the rise of the Srivijaya Empire and the initial arrival of Austronesian to the Comoros Archipelago is worth singling out.

Madagascar and the Comoros

The earliest evidence of human presence on Madagascar consists of three femora of an extinct hippopotamus with cut marks made with iron tools. They were found at Lamboharana and Ambolisatra in Southwest Madagascar and dated to 80–380 CE (Dewar and Wright 1993: 428). Evidence for human settlement is however particularly shallow in the southwest and almost everywhere else on the island before the later part of the first millennium CE. In general, traces of these early sites, found along the eastern, south-western, and north coast, point to transient camps occupied by small visiting crews. Longer-term and very likely permanent settlement developed later in the first millennium CE from the eighth century onward. It is the case at Nosy Mangabe, a 520-hectare island in the northeast, and the Sandrakatsy phase site of the Mananara valley. The Comoros islands were settled during this time period, with Dembeni phase villages ranging in size from less than 0.5 hectare to 5 hectares. In Northern Madagascar, Nosy Mangabe and Sandrakatsy yielded evidence for iron metallurgy, chlorite schist wares, as well as silver, gold, glass, and carnelian beads. Dembeni phase groups were organized into small iron-using farming and fishing communities, cultivating rice, millet, coconuts, beans, and possibly citrus fruit (Wright 1993: 660).

The first two or three centuries of the second millennium CE were characterized by relatively unchanged and stable subsistence and craft traditions without a noticeable trend toward intensification. Major transformations took place nonetheless, within the context of social ideologies and organizational patterns of human communities (Wright 1993, Dewar and Wright 1993). Larger and more populous centers emerged.

In the Comorian archipelago, Dembeni grew to reach fourteen hectares in size and appears to have been surrounded by a rampart. Villages measuring one to three hectares as well as numerous smaller hamlets dotted the landscape of the archipelago. Comparable change occurred in Madagascar but on a larger scale. Most of the recorded sites are found in the north and southeast. The rest of the island appears to have been very loosely inhabited with isolated village sites found at Fiekena in the central highlands and Rezoky in the southwest. Mahikala in the bay of Ampasindava on the northwest coast had a walled area measuring more than sixty hectares. It was a harbor and point of entry of the Indian Ocean trade goods. The town was very likely part of a larger settlement system that included a number of smaller contemporary sites, all measuring less than one hectare. The cave site of Andavakoera, as well as villages and hamlets from Irodo, Lanivato, Bemanevika, and Sandrakatsy, are all located along the northeast coast. In the remaining part of the island, there is evidence of settlements including small villages or larger sites like Andranosoa that include multiple embankments over an area of some thirty hectares with concentrations of mud-house remains (Wright 1993: 668). There was a significant intensification of the Indian Ocean exchange systems along with the widespread adoption of Islam in coastal areas.

From the fourteenth to the sixteenth century, when a Portuguese fleet reached the northwest coast of Madagascar, the island appears to have gone through comparable transformations if looked at from a settlement pattern perspective. Sites clusters articulated around one larger center of approximately five hectares in size were comprised of five to ten smaller settlements. Such patterns have been recorded in the Bay of Antongil in the northeast, northern Androy in the south, Imerina in the central highlands, and southern Anosy in the southeast (Dewar and Wright 1993). Islamic port towns emerged at Kingany, Nosy Manja, and Vohemar along the northwest and northeast coasts. The centers of settlement clusters were the residences of paramount leaders. From then on, complex chiefdoms appear to have developed everywhere on the island and fueled the fierce rivalry and competition that took place later in the eighteenth century (Wright 2007).

HUBS, NETWORKS, AND FLOWS:
THE INDIAN OCEAN WORLD SYSTEM

Starting with the initial expansion of *Homo erectus* in Southeast Asia some 2–1.8 million years ago, followed by modern human—*Homo sapiens sapiens*—settlement in Sundaland and Sahul, biological and cultural connections have crisscrossed all the territories reached in constant multidirectional flows. Plants and cultivars domesticated in Highlands New Guinea spread to Asia and Africa. African plants, such as finger millet (*Pennisetum glaucum*) and sorghum (*Sorghum bicolor*), spread to Asia, specifically in the Arabic peninsula and India. The landing of the first waves of speakers of Austronesian languages in the Comoros Archipelago in the second half of the first millennium CE connected the east and west shores of the Indian Ocean. That "cycle of events" put in place human and cultural links that channeled ideas, peoples, plants, and material culture in all directions and generated the Indian Ocean world system.

Maritime Exchange Networks

Distinct exchange networks inserted in different geo-cultural areas stretching from China in the East to the East African coast in the West were linked through sea traffic. At its peak, the Indian Ocean world system was articulated on five relatively large regional hubs or cores. From west to East, they were: 1) the East African coast through its Swahili city-states stretched from Somali in the north to Mozambique in the south; 2) The Arabic peninsula and the Persian world in the north-northwest; 3) the Indian subcontinent in the center-north; 4) the mainland and islands, Southeast Asia in the southeast; and finally, 5) China in Eastern Asia. Each of these political and economic hubs/cores influenced and was influenced by all the others, operating with maritime technologies and "know-how" with however distinct merchant ship designs.

The dominant regional powers involved in the Indian Ocean maritime networks changed over time (Beaujard 2017, 2019, Li 2020, Szczepanski 2019). In the initial phase that started in the second half of the first millennium BCE, the Persian Achaemenid empire (550–350 BCE), the Mauryan Empire in India (324–185 BCE), the China Han Dynasty (202 BCE–220 CE); and finally, the Roman Empire in Egypt and the Near East (33 BCE–475 CE) were the main powers involved. Along with trade in goods, silk, porcelain, glazed wares, etc., Indian merchants spread Buddhism, Hinduism, and Jainism to Southeast Asia and China. In addition, well before the emergence of Islam, Christianity and Judaism were the expanding religions in the Indian Ocean (Sekand 2013).

The second phase, from c. 400 to 1500 CE, lasted for a little more than 1,000 years. It witnessed the emergence of Swahili city-states along the East African coast, the rise and expansion of Islam, and the settlement of speakers of Austronesian languages in the Comoros Archipelago and Madagascar. The main participants powers included the Umayyad (661–750 CE) and Abbasid (750–1258 CE) empires in the Arabic peninsula and Persian Gulf, the Chola Empire (200 BCE–1279 CE) in southern India, the Srivijaya Empire in Southeast Asia, the Angkor Civilization (800–1327 CE) in MSEA, and finally, the Tang (618–907 CE), Song (960–1279 CE), and Ming Dynasty (1368–1644) in China.

If all major empires and states benefited from the economic and trade activities through customs duties and taxes, all were however not directly involved in the daily maritime trade transactions. Trade operated through specialized institutions, articulated on trading diasporas, circulation societies, and overlapping social networks based on geography, ethnicity, and religion (Sekand 2013).

East Africa–Persian Gulf

As indicated in the *"Periplus of the Erythraean Sea,"* East African trade was predominantly connected to the Arabic Peninsula/Persian Gulf core, extended from Egypt to Persia, including the Red Sea, the Gulf of Aden, the Hadramout coast, the Persian Gulf, and the Arabian Sea up to the West India coast (Sekand 2013). Persian loanwords, principally nautical terms, are found in Ki-Swahili, the language of East African coast and some local East African traditions credit the foundation of some East African ports to Shiraz (Horton et al. 2011). Persian ceramic dated to the third through fifth centuries CE is found at Ras Hafun in Somalia in the north, Chibuene in Mozambique in the south, and Ngazidja Island in the Comoros Archipelago. Ceramic assemblages collected from Manda (Chittick 1984) and Shanga (Horton et al. 1996) contain vessels from Siraf, unglazed storage jars, and white glazed wares, as well as Chinese stoneware. Al-Masudi (896–956 CE) reported that there were regular voyages from Oman and Siraf to the Bilad al Zanj—the land of Zanj—in particular to the port of Qanbalu (Pemba Island) at the beginning of the tenth century CE; adding that ivory was the main export, along with ambergris and timber, in this case mangrove poles (Horton et al. 2011). Enslaved Africans were one of the main commodities, as shown indirectly by the Zanj uprising from 869 to 883 CE around Basra in the Tigris-Euphrates delta that is considered to have contributed to the late-ninth-century crisis of the Abbasid caliphate (Popovic 1999).

From the third century to the fifteenth century CE, there were constant adjustments in the Arabic Peninsula/Persian Gulf trade networks. In the fifth to eleventh centuries, Kis and Hormoz at the head of the Persian Gulf were the main ports trading East African products to India, Egypt, and the Far East. In partially overlapping developments, the main centers of East African trade shifted to the south of the Arabian coast, at Aden or Western India from the seventh century to the thirteenth century (Horton et al. 2011).

The India Subcontinent

The India subcontinent comprised of India and Sri Lanka, with its myriad of states and thousands of kilometers of coastline has very long maritime and commercial traditions going as far back as the Indus Valley civilizations in the early third millennium BCE (Beaujard 2019, Mambra 2019). Despite shifts in wealth and political fortunes, naval constructions were well established in a number of ports, effective international trade entrepôts. Lothal and Bharuch in Gujarat were among the oldest ports of India. The former, probably the oldest port of the subcontinent dated as far back as 4,500 years ago, traded with West Asia and Africa, exporting jewelry, textiles, and mineral ores. The latter, located at the estuary of the river Narmada, also an important naval construction locality, traded with Arabs, Greeks, Romans, Africans, Egyptians, and Chinese. Muziris in Kerala, Poompuhar in Tamil Nadu, Arikamedu in Pondichery, Calicut on the Arabian Sea coast, and Tuticorin were crucial nodes of the Indian Ocean maritime trade (Mambra 2019). Muziris, active from the first century BCE to 1341 CE when it was destroyed by a tsunami, exported black pepper, pearls, diamonds, ivory, and semiprecious stones. It imported textiles, wine, wheat, and gold coins. Its trade network connected it to the Roman Empire, Egyptians, Greeks, Assyrians, Phoenicians, and Persians. Poompuhar specialized in the spices trade from c. 200 BCE to c. 500 CE. It imported horses from the Persian Gulf, as well as goods from Sri Lanka and Indonesia. Arikamedu, a Chola port and bead-making center active from the second century BCE, specialized in trade with the Roman Empire. It exported beads, textiles, terra-cotta artifacts, jewelry, and spices. Calicut, active in the first half of the second millennium CE, exported pepper, cloves, cinnamon, and textiles, and imported Chinese ceramics and European pots after Portuguese arrival. Tuticorin, at five hundred kilometers southwest of Chennai, specialized in fishery and pearls. As shown by the Godavaya ship-wreck in Sri Lanka (Di Mucci 2015), semifinished products like iron bars from India were parts of the traded goods, as were also enslaved Africans represented today by the Siddies living in Karnataka, Gujarat, and Hyderabad in India and Makran and Karachi in Pakistan (Jasdanwalla 2011).

Mainland and Islands Southeast Asia

Southeast Asia between the Indian and Chinese worlds witnessed the for-mation of Javanese kingdoms and the emergence of the Khmer state and the Srivijaya Empire. The latter was not a centralized state but relied on a system of alliances. It rapidly became a powerful "thalassocracy" controlling regional and interregional maritime routes. "The Sea Peoples provided crews for the ships and received part of the revenue, and the 'center' redistributed the goods in the course of Patron-Client relationships" (Beaujard 2019: 89). Srivijaya ships sailed in South China Sea, India, the Persian Gulf, the Comoros, Madagascar, and East Africa, carrying and distributing a broad range of merchandises, including sandalwood from Timor, camphor from Sumatra, spices from the Moluccas, mirobolan, malachite and textiles from Syria, ivory, rhinoceros horns from East Africa, textiles and ceramics from China, and enslaved Africans to a certain extent, etc. "The thalassocracy was primarily a hub connecting the system's cores to its various peripheries" (Beaujard 2019: 91), such as the Thai-Malay Peninsula, Mainland Southeast Asia Khmer state and Champa, as well as Javanese kingdoms. Srivijaya had moderate craft production but was the main gateway of the Indian Ocean trade to the South China Sea.

East Asian Connections

Ongoing research unearths more and more evidence of contact between East Asia and Africa (Li 2015, 2020, Holl 2020, Kusimba et al. 2020). It is not yet known precisely when Chinese goods reached Africa for the first time in the past. Archaeological research provides some clues. An Austrian expedition excavating in Thebes, at Deir el Madina in the burial ground of the kings' workmen, found the remains of silk in the hair of a thirty- to fifty-year-old female mummy dated to 1075–945 BCE, the Hyksos Twenty-first Dynasty (Li 2005, Lubec et al. 1993, *Renmin Ribao*–April 2, 1993). The silk industry certainly originated from China, where archaeologists "have found textiles in a mysterious tomb dating back nearly 2,500 years in eastern Jiangxi Province, the oldest to be discovered in China's history" (*People's Daily* online, August 26, 2007). The silk industry, trade, and consequently the Silk Road are thus much older than thought and probably reached Egypt through Persia. The silk found in the Thebes burial could have been introduced by the Hyksos. Trade and cultural exchanges between China and Egypt were well established during the Han Dynasty [206 BCE–220 CE] (Sun Tang 1979 in Li 2005).

Evidence of Chinese material culture has been recorded in East Africa, from Egypt to South Africa, along the coast as well as in the hinterland. Chinese porcelain represented by "Longquan wares, Jingdezhen Qingbai wares, Fujian celadon and Qingbai wares, and blue and white, copper red wares from Jingdezhen were all found in the coast of Kenya. . . . Changsha wares were found in Shanga, celadon shards produced in Guangdong found in Shanga, and Fanchang ware made in the tenth century were discovered in Manda" (Li 2015: 49).

Numerous coins from different historical periods were also found in different parts of East Africa:

> Coins of the Song Dynasty were . . . found by the British in Zanzibar, the Song coins made in 11th–12th centuries were found in Mogadishu in 1898. In 1916, Chinese coins were discovered at Mafia Island in Tanzania, including one of Song Emperor Shenzong (1068–1085). Qinyuan *Tongbao* of Song Emperor Ningzong (1168–1224) and Shaoding *Tongbao* of Song Emperor Lizong (1205–1264) were discovered in Gedi of Kenya. In Kilwa, six coins were found, includingone Chunhua *Tongbao*, four Xining *Tongbao*, and one Zhenghe *Tongbao*. The most significant discovery is in Kazengwa of Zanzibar in 1945, where 176 coins were found. Among them, 108 are of the Northern Song Dynasty, fifty-six of the Southern-Song Dynasty, four of the Tang Dynasty, and eight not identified. In 1991, the currency of the Song was discovered in Aihdab in the Sudan by a Japanese archaeologist, this was the first time for this type of discovery in the region. (Li 2015: 49)

According to Li (2005: 60), Du Huan, a Chinese from the Tang Dynasty (618–907 CE) and war captive at Baghdad where he spent several years, visited Africa in the eighth century, sometime around 762. The book he wrote when he returned to Guangzhou, Jingxingji (经行记,"Record of My Travels"), was lost and is now known only through quotes in other books. It is therefore not known which part of Africa he may have visited, even if Egypt and Northeast Africa appear to have been the most reachable.

In the first half of the fifteenth century, the Ming Dynasty decided to project Chinese naval power all over the Indian Ocean. Emperor The Yongle (1403–1424) appointed Zheng He was the chief admiral of a large fleet—the "Treasure Fleet." The latter organized a number of expeditions, seven in total, from 1405 to 1433, generally termed "Zheng He travels" (Deng 2005,

Dreyer 2006, Ferrand 1919, 1922, Filesi 1970, Levathes 1997, Viviano 2005). The "Treasure Fleet" sailed to the East Africa coast in the fourth (1413–1415), fifth (1416–1419), and sixth (1421–1422) voyages, docking at Mogadishu, today in Somalia, Malindi, and Mombasa in today's Kenya. They exchanged Chinese goods for African ones, including live animals like zebras and giraffes. (Prinsloo et al. 2005, Beaujard 2007). In addition, some of the descendants of Chinese sailors from Admiral Zheng He fleet living in the small island of Pate were interviewed by Kristof (1999) for the *New York Times* and visited by Li Xinfeng (2017).

In summary, there are scattered but significant evidence for the presence of Chinese goods and people in African past. These interactions started in the early first millennium BCE, became more frequent with time through the Han (206 BCE–220 CE), Tang (618–907 CE), Song (906–1279), Yuan (1271–1368), and Ming (1368–1644) dynasties, peaked in the fifteenth century and were cut short by an imperial ban on foreign trade and naval expeditions.

Beyond the presence of surprising animals like zebra and giraffe (Chou Ju-Kua 1911, Ferrand 1919, 1922, Filesi 1970, Wheatley 1961, Talib and Samir 1988), a number of Africans, through different indirect channels ended up living in China as early as the first quarter of the eighth century. According to the Chronicle of the T'ang Dynasty, the king of Srivijaya from Palembang in Sumatra offered a Zanj (Black) girl, among other things, as tribute to the Emperor in 724 (Talib and Samir 1988: 732, Ferrand 1922). This practice was repeated several times during the next centuries, in 813, 818, and 976. In 813 and 818, the rulers from Kalinga, an Indonesian kingdom, offered several Zanj boys and girls in three successive missions to the T'ang emperor Hsien Tsung. In 976, under the Sung dynasty, the Imperial court received " a black K'un Lun slave with deep set eyes and black body" (Chou Ju-Kua 1911) from an Arab trader (Talib and Samir 1988: 732).

Although, indirectly and through Arab and Indonesian middlemen, the trade in enslaved Africans reached China, principally through the entry port and distribution hub of Guangzhou. The enslaved Africans were "employed on shipboard to caulk leaky seams below the water-line from the outside as they were expert swimmers who do not close their eyes under water" (Chou Ju-Kua 1911: 31–32, Talib and Samir 1988: 732, Wheatley 1961: 55). Others were gate guards and household servants for the wealthy families in metropolitan areas. According to Chou Ju-Kua (1911: 32), "many families buy black people to make gatekeepers of; they are called *kui-nu*, or 'devil-slaves' or *hei siau ssi* (black slaves or servants)." There is clearly much more research to be done in this direction, if oral histories and archives of ancient Cantonese elite families and landowners can be collected and studied systematically.

The great Moroccan world traveler and explorer Abu Abdullah Muhammad ibn Abdullah Al Lawat Al Tanji Ibn Battuta—Ibn Battuta for short—visited

China in the middle of the fourteenth century. He was born on February 24, 1304, at Tangiers and died at Marrakech in 1377. He traveled all over the ancient world, covered some 120,000 kilometers in twenty-nine years. Ibn Battuta arrived at Guangzhou in China in 1345 (Ibn Battuta 1982). He was particularly interested in local crafts, boat construction, and porcelain making and visited a number of places and towns. He traveled north to Hangzhou, which he presented as the largest of the cities he had ever seen. He could not reach Beijing and returned to Guangzhou in 1346 to sail to Sumatra.

It is also claimed that Admiral Zheng He "Treasure Fleet" took some foreign dignitaries back to China to visit and pay homage to the Ming emperors. It is not clear if some Africans from the Swahili city-states of Mogadishu, Malindi, or Mombasa were involved in these visits. In summary, from as early as the eighth century, Africans were present in Chinese imperial courts and in some wealthy families from southern China.

CONCLUSION

The genesis of the Indian Ocean world system can be traced back a few thousand years. Dispersals of humans, cultivated plants, domesticated animals, and technologies were aspects of the cultural and economic connections and exchange systems (Dalton 1968, Polanyi et al. 1957, Renfrew 1975, Rotstein 1970, Sabloff and Lamberg-Karlovsky 1975) that operated from the initial expansion of modern humans to Sahul to the Austronesian settlement in Madagascar. Trade and exchange, "the mutual appropriative movements of goods between hands" (Polanyi 1957: 266), were core mechanisms of the Indian Ocean world system. Relying on exchange systems spatial manifestations, C. Renfrew (1975: 41) identified ten trade modes ranging from direct access to port of trade, all of these modalities implemented in varying degrees in the Indian Ocean world system. Whatever the case however, trade requires personnel, commodities, organization, transportation, and value. There are different organizational forms of economic life and different patterns of evolution. To frame the analysis of trade in "an evolutionary context is to suggest a departure from a notion of unilineal development that would tend to see earlier economies as miniature replicas or potential versions of our own market economy" (Rotstein 1970: 117). In other words, ancient trade systems are not impoverished forms of present-day market economy. They have their own logic, organization, and value systems. K. Polanyi (1957) identified nonmarket trade organizational forms in ancient societies, articulated on reciprocity and redistribution.

Trade can be partitioned into three main classes that are partially or totally applicable to different historical periods (Polanyi 1957, Rotstein 1970): 1) gift trade; 2) administered trade; and 3) market trade. In the gift trade, exchange consists of high- value gifts among elite members of the involved societies. Sociological criteria are determining factors of the value of the exchange goods. There is no required strict equivalence between the exchange items. A precious jewel can be offered in exchange for a giraffe. There are many known cases of gift exchanges between Chinese and Africans of different ranks and social positions, from emperors to special envoys.

Administered trade operates within more or less explicit agreement between trading partners. The value of exchanged goods is stable and set by political arrangements. The transactions conducted by Zheng He mariners for example, probably combined gift and administered trade. China wares, porcelain, and celadon from different workshops were ordered and loaded in ships, sold to Arab, Persian, or Indian middlemen. These commodities were shipped to the west flank of the Indian Ocean and exchanged for African goods. Even if it is not explicitly mentioned in ports imported and exported merchandises, and as far as Arab, Persian, Indian, and Malay traders are concerned, human cargo was certainly part of the "goods" shipped from the East African coast. Slave labor was used in the Arabic Peninsula, the Persian Gulf, India, ISEA, and China, particularly in the thriving metropolis of Guangzhou.

And finally, market trade, applies predominantly to later economic systems, with laws of supply and demand as price-fixing mechanisms and more impersonal transactions. Gift and administered trade still operate within the contemporary predominantly market trade, depending on social and political circumstances.

The dense transaction networks that crisscrossed the Indian Ocean and surrounding lands—the continental and the maritime Silk Roads—from at least the first millennium BCE clearly set the stage for the first globalization. Its attraction was plain and evident in the European push—Portuguese and Spaniards—to reach India. The Spaniards with Christopher Columbus sailed west and landed at Bariay in Cuba on October 28, 1492, in the Caribbean, convinced they had reached China. The Portuguese sailed south, with Vasco da Gama reaching Calicut in India on May 20, 1498. On their way, they flexed their military might by firing cannons at Mombasa and stopped at Malindi to hire a skilled local mariner who guided them to Calicut in India. The circumnavigation of Africa hooked the Indian Ocean world system to the opening Atlantic World. That linkage struck a deadly blow to East African coastal Swahili city-states and paved the way for the Atlantic enslaved trade and centuries of European domination.

Chapter 3

Origin and Expansion of Speakers of Chadic Languages

The Chad Basin and the Origin of Speakers of Chadic Languages

INTRODUCTION

Virtually all speakers of Chadic languages have their home in the southern half of the Chad Basin with however a western extension in North Central Nigeria. The basin sits at the gravity center of Africa. It is a sedimentary formation stretched from the Sudanian Savanna in the south to the desert landscape of the Tenere in the north, and an endorheic watershed fed by rainfall and watercourses from the south and west: the Logone, Chari, El Beid, Yedseram, and Yobe rivers (fig. 3.1). The study area, located in the southern part of the basin, extends from the latitude of the Maiduguri-Bama-Limani-Bongor ridge, the Early Holocene Mega-Chad 320 meters above sea level (asl) shoreline to 282 meters asl level present-day lake level.

Paleoclimatology and Environment

Geological, palynological, and paleoecological research (Durand et al. 1983, Maley 1981, Schneider 1994, Servant 1983, Servant-Vildary 1978, Servant and Servant-Vildary 1980) show that the extent and depth of Lake Chad changed several times in the past. For the last ten thousand years, the major transgressive episode dates from the Early Holocene, when the Mega-Chad had the NW-SE oriented Maiduguri-Bama-Limani-Bongor ridge at 320 meters asl as its southern shoreline. From the Mid-Holocene on, with

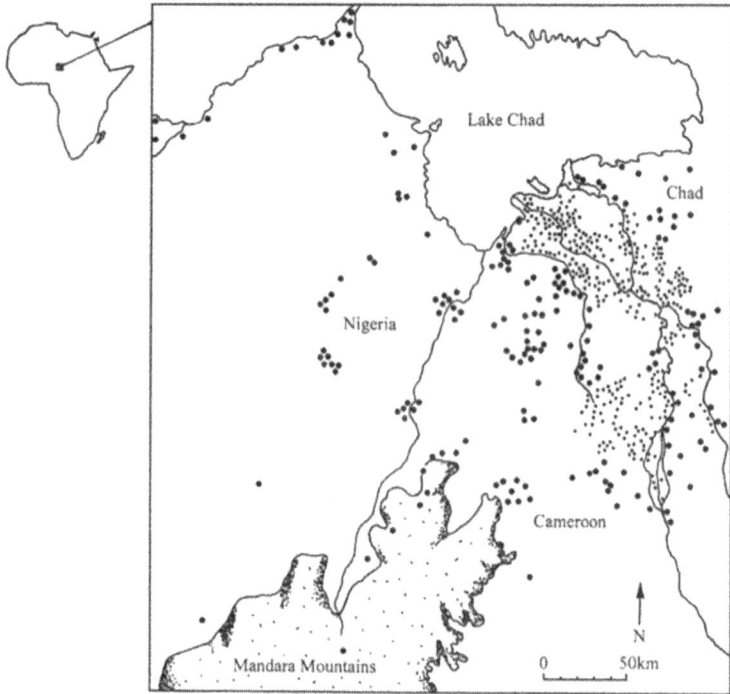

Figure 3.1. Distribution of archaeological sites in the Chadian Plain. *Created by the author*

significant fluctuations, climatic conditions changed and generated a long-term trend toward the reduction of both the size and depth of the Early Holocene Mega-Lake Chad.

The Chadian plain, essentially along the southern half of the basin, is dotted with thousands of archaeological sites of varying size and shape (Lebeuf 1981: 14). Mound density is relatively lower in the western portion of the plain from the Cameroon border westward to the Hawsaland in Nigeria and Niger (fig. 3.2). It is however important to note that the number of excavated sites is extremely low compared to the total number of recorded and mapped settlements (Lebeuf 1969, 1981, Lebeuf et al. 1980, Connah 1981, 1984, Holl 1987, 1988, 1993a, b, c, 2002, Holl et al. 1991, Breunig n.d. a. b, Breunig 1994, 1995, Breunig et al. 1992, Breunig et al. 1993, David and Sterner 1987, 1989, MacEachern 2012, Magnavita et al. 2006, Rapp 1984, Gronenborn 1998, 2013, 2016, Neumann 1995).

Figure 3.2. View of a Chadian plain mound shape and stratigraphic profile. *Created by the author*

Brief History Synopsis

Two renaissance geographers, Fra Mauro (1400–1464) and Giovanni Lorenzo d'Anania (1545–1609) provide some insight into the southern Chad Basin political landscape in the fifteenth and sixteenth centuries. Fra Mauro mentioned Mandera—for Mandara—and Mergi—-for Margi—in his 1459 world map. In his Cartographica del Mundo (Map of the World) published in Genoa in the sixteenth century, Giovanni Lorenzo d'Anania referred to some kingdoms from the Lake Chad area. He explicitly mentioned Makary, Gulfey, Afade, Kusseri, Logon, and Alph (Houlouf), and offered a glimpse of their political systems and mortuary customs at the death of their kings. Within the same period, also in the sixteenth century, Ahmad Ibn Furtu, a Bornu scholar, imam of the capital city (Birni Ghazzargamu) Friday mosque, and panegyrist of King Idriss Alauma, completed the writing of a book, *Kitab al ghazzargawat al Barnu*, on his king's deeds. He narrates the wars of expansion of the Bornu state from its core in the Yobe River Valley to the north, east, and south. The conquered or exterminated populations were generally called "Sao," referring to the "Others," non-Kanuri speakers, who were clearly the first settlers of the land. These early settlers were all speakers of one or another Chadic language, derived from the evolution of the Central Chadic language subfamily. These Chadic speakers were organized into ranked and centralized societies. They dwelt in small towns surrounded by moats and earthen ramparts. Depending on circumstances, these Chadic polities were called chiefdoms, or kingdoms, and their rulers, called *miarre*—or sultans (in the later Arabized form). The Chadic polities nearest to the Bornu heartland, Makary, Afade, Ndufu, etc., were conquered and integrated in the expanded Bornu kingdom. Those located on the outer periphery, like Kusseri, were coerced into a tributary status with a Kanuri plenipotentiary appointed in residence to oversee the local government. Others, as was the case for Lagwan, resisted Bornu pressures and went on an expansionist policy of their own. Bornu imperial policy waxed and waned; the "Kanurification" of the elite went a long way, leveling cultural differences but amplifying the hunt for captives. Islam spread.

European explorers of the nineteenth century (Denham 1820, Barth 1850, and Nachtigal 1870) witnessed the political situation of the area. The Bornu Empire was tilting toward its end. The Langwan kingdom, sandwiched between two regional superpowers—the Bornu empire in the north-northwest and the Barma kingdom in the south-southeast—succeeded in preserving its independence through shrewd diplomatic maneuvering. The situation was further complicated by the sudden irruption of Rabbeh, a slave trader and adventurer from the Bahr el Ghazzal in Sudan, and the onset of European colonization.

The organization of some of these Chadic polities was investigated by French ethnographers, starting with Marcel Griaule, Jean-Paul Lebeuf, and A. M. D. Lebeuf, Vincent (1991) and Forkl (1983, 1985). A. M. D. Lebeuf (1969) wrote a remarkable book that includes ethnohistory and detailed descriptions of the political and territorial organization of the polities she had investigated. The famous "Sao Culture" owes a great deal to the M. Griaule–inspired book *Les Sao Legendaires.* Even if investigated much less intensively, comparable developments and evolutionary trajectories resulting in the emergence and formation of Hawsa city-states and kingdoms took place in the western flank of the "Chadic Land" (Gronenborn 2011, Gronenborn et al. 2012, Sule and Haour 2014). The Southwest-Central Chadic area witnessed the emergence of the Wandala kingdom along the northern margins of the Mandara mountains at the end of the fifteenth/beginning of the sixteenth century. Initially a Bornu vassal, it converted to Islam in the eighteenth century and devastated the whole area with slave-raiding expeditions, triggering the influx of settlers into the Mandara highlands.

In summary, by the middle of the second millennium CE, centralized political formations were constitutive of the southern Chad Basin human landscape, in Central and Western Chadic speakers' areas. How did these Chadic polities emerge? How were they organized? How did they grow and adjust to changing sociopolitical circumstances?

Archaeology of the Chadian Plain

The archaeology of the Chadian plain—the southern shore of Lake Chad—entered the world of archaeological scholarship at the very beginning of the twentieth century. F. Wulsin (1932) from Harvard University sunk a number of trial trenches at Gulfey on the left bank of the Shari River. The archaeological deposits he probed were exposed by the meandering river. His results were above all descriptive and did not spark any interest in researching the archaeology of the area.

A more sustained research effort started with the involvement of Marcel Griaule and Jean-Paul Lebeuf, both ethnographers without formal training in archaeology. M. Griaule was the leader of the French 1931–1933 Dakar-Djibouti expedition, championing the study of African beliefs systems. He was fascinated by the folk traditions of the Chadian plain inhabitants, collected and translated an impressive number of local oral traditions, and published his inspired book *Les Sao Legendaires*. The purpose of their archaeological research project was simple and straightforward: to document, trace, and reconstruct the origins of the "mysterious Sao." They coined and popularized the concept of "Sao Civilization." The term "civilization" was a common currency in those days partly based on the concept of "Kultur Kreis" elaborated by German ethnologists (Forkl 1983, 1985). Despite its vagueness, it conveyed the idea of cultural templates that manifest themselves more eloquently in artworks. The Sao produced an intriguing statuary in clay. They made large well-fired clay vessels (So pots). They manufactured fine items of personal adornment in clay, copper, alloyed copper, iron, and brass. They built cities protected by moats and earthen ramparts.

Griaule and Lebeuf organized no fewer than four archaeological expeditions. They tested tens of sites in search for artworks and published several extensive reports in the *Journal de la Societe des Africanistes*. The material they collected was generally described after a substantial introduction based on ethnohistorical sources. The archaeological record was thus used to support ethnohistorical scenarios that already staged the Sao's cultural achievements. On the other hand, ethnohistorical sources were used to justify and interpret the archaeological record. And the recorded archaeological finds were used to back the ethnohistorical narrative of Sao cultural developments. The circularity of the approach was plain and obvious; migrations were the engine of cultural change. The understanding of the origins and evolution of the "Sao Civilization" became more and more elusive (Lebeuf 1969, 1971).

In the 1960s, Jean-Paul Lebeuf and A. M. Detourbet shifted their field methodology with the Mdaga excavation (Lebeuf et al. 1980). They adopted a more scientific approach with tighter stratigraphic control, radiocarbon dating, and a more elaborate sampling strategy. The concept of "Sao

Civilization" was dropped even if the term remained in use. The results of the project were startling. Mdaga was inhabited for more than two millennia, from c. 450 BCE to 1800 CE. Subsuming such a long occupation under the heading of "Sao Civilization" became clearly untenable. The excavation of Sou Blame Radjil supported the findings from Mdaga, putting the concept of "Sao Civilization" to a final rest.

In parallel to research by J. P. Lebeuf and A. M. D. Lebeuf in Cameroon and the Republic of Chad, G. Connah (1983), then from the university of Ibadan, Nigeria, launched an archaeological project in Bornu. He selected a number of sites along a north-south transect, from the Mandara Mountains in the south to the Yobe River Valley in the north. His project was framed in environmental and adaptive terms, with an explicit interest in the patterns of human adaptation to the Chadian wetland context. The 60 x 5 meter and 11.5-meter-deep trench of Daima was spectacular and productive. The evolutionary sequence reconstructed from the series of tested sites stretched from the Late Stone Age (c. 2000 BCE) to the sixteenth century CE, including the advent of iron technology traced to the later part of the first millennium BCE. Connah (1983) also found charred sorghum remains dated to 800 CE, as well as evidence of round mud houses. He probed the central part of Birni Ghazzargamo (the capital city of the Bornu kingdom), sunk a number of probes in the royal palace compound, and described its architectural layout. He surprisingly refrained from any discussion of the emergence of the Kanuri state (Holl 2000) and simply alluded to the urbanization process that may have driven the political apparatus of the Kanuri Imperium.

In the early 1990s, the University of Frankfurt launched a joint project with Nigeria's University of Maiduguri, led by P. Breunig. The project, rooted in "cultural history," included an important environmental component. The aim was clearly to understand the impact of the Holocene climatic change on human settlement location and subsistence systems. With some variations, they too adopted a transect strategy and sampled the major landforms, from the Bama-Limani-Bongor ridge in the south, to the Yobe River Valley in the north. Kursakata, a mound site previously excavated by G. Connah, was re-excavated by D. Gronenborn. An intensive archaeobotanical program was carried out by K. Neumann. P. Breunig directed the excavation of Late Stone Age sites at Konduga, Gajiganna, and Dufuna (including the famous 8500 BP dugout). Gronenborn (1998, Gornenborn et al. 2012) conducted excavations at a burial site in Hawsaland and focused on more recent sites, including Dikoa, the nineteenth-century headquarters of Rabbeh. Holl (1988, 1994, 1996, 2002) carried out a long-term regional archaeological project focused on Houlouf. And finally, the Mandara Archaeological project directed by N. David (2012) investigated cultural development along the northern periphery of the Mandara mountain range, land of Southern Central Chadic speakers (MacEachern 1993, 2012, 2015). Cattle and sheep/goat husbandry appeared to have been practiced in the area for at least four thousand years. Agriculture on the other hand, was a latecomer. Bulrush millet was cultivated around 1000 CE.

Out of a total of more than 1,500 recorded mounds, less than fifty have been surveyed, excavated or tested in the Chadian plain (Wulsin 1932, Griaule and Lebeuf 1948, 1950, 1951, Lebeuf et al. 1980, Connah 1981, 1984, Rapp 1984, Holl 1988a, 2002). In general however, a chronological framework pertaining to phases and settlement sequences have been achieved despite differences in the terminology used by individual authors; Sao I, Sao II, and Sao III for Lebeuf (1969, 1981); Daïma I, Daïma II, and Daïma III for Connah (1981); Pré-Sao, Early-Sao, and Late Sao for Rapp (1984); and Late Stone Age or Late Neolithic, Early Iron Age, Late Iron Age, and Islamic (Holl 1988b). Sustained research shows this chronological framework to be an extremely simplified view of a much more complex evolutionary process (David and Sterner 1989, Breunig 1992 et al., 1993, Holl 1994, 2000, 2002, 2004).

Two Late Stone Age localities have been discovered in Nigeria and Cameroon in the southernmost part of the Chadian plain, along the 320 meter asl. Maïduguri-Bama-Limani-Bongor Early Holocene Mega-Chad shoreline. Due to the dynamics of lacustrine environments during that period of high lake level, it is highly probable that most of the sites were either destroyed or buried under thick layers of sediments, as shown by the Dufuna dugout found under five meters of sediment. Another series of Late Stone Age settlements, dating from c. 4000 BP to 2500 BP, have been recorded. With the exception of Bornu 38 or "Bama Road site A" situated on the ridge, most —Bornu 70 or Shilma, Kursakata, Daïma, and Gajiganna in Nigeria, Sou Blamé-Radjil, Deguesse, and Krenak in Cameroon—are located farther north in the ecological and sedimentary context of the Chad Lagoonal Complex. This Chad Lagoonal Complex is a presumable evidence of the Late Holocene Lake Chad shoreline that may have fluctuated between 287 and 285 meters asl.

Chadic Speakers in the Chad Basin

Historical linguistic data cannot be used as straightforward support for archaeological and historical reconstructions of past cultural evolution. These sets of scientific evidence have to be initially considered relatively independently. Historical linguistic material provides students of the past with exciting and challenging models of a peculiar kind of historical processes that cannot be neglected. Details of linguistic evidence and methodological and theoretical diversity of historical linguistics are not discussed here (Vansina 1994). Linguists as well as archaeologists, historians, and anthropologists agree and disagree on different issues of their respective research fields. Suffice it to say that languages are dynamic systems constituted of a multiplicity of subsets, such as idiolects (i.e., individual speech), sociolects (i.e., idioms of specific social group), and dialects (i.e., localized variants). "A language is therefore a dialect continuum" (Vansina 1974: 174). In such a dynamic system and depending on circumstances, forces of differentiation are countered and balanced by those of homogenization.

Chadic languages are distributed into three major branches; the Western, exclusively in Nigeria today, the Central, in Nigeria and Cameroon, and the Eastern Chadic almost exclusively in the Republic of Chad. Each of these branches is divided into two subbranches; northwestern and southwestern in the first, southwestern and northeastern in the second and third. The glottochronological work carried out by Barreteau and Jungraithmayr is based on a comparative list of one hundred words from fifty-two Chadic languages: fourteen from the western branch, twenty-eight from the central branch, and ten from the eastern branch (Barreteau 1987b, Barreteau and Jungraithmayr 1987, 1993: 106). The rationale behind the glottochronological method formulated by Swadesh is based on the evaluation of the retention rate of words from the basic vocabulary from an earlier linguistic background. Simply stated, it can be said that the retention rate decreases with time (Swadesh 1955, Embleton 1986); it is, however, not constant.

According to Barreteau and Jungraithmayr (1993), the earliest split between the Eastern and Western/Central Chadic branches, which feature 26 percent common words roots, occurred around 4500 BP. It was followed around 4200 BP by a second split between the Western and Central branches. Between 4100 and 4000 BP, the three branches were divided into two subbranches each, mostly into eastern and western language groups. If the focus is narrowed on the Central Chadic branch, Kanuri, a Saharan language, expanded during the last millennium and probably accelerated the divergence between southwestern and northeastern Central Chadic subbranches. According to glottochronological data, this split occurred around 3900 BP. From that time, from c 2650 BP to 1450 BP, linguistic drift generated the development of nine languages within the Cameroonian part of the Chadian plain. It is worth emphasizing the fact that it is not the absolute dating per se of periods of split between languages that is really relevant, but essentially the time-ordering or relative chronology of the sequence. Considered from that perspective, the glottochronological research on Chadic languages provides an exciting and useful tool and a much needed and welcome challenge for archaeologists, historians, and anthropologists.

There are amazing parallels between the historical linguistic reconstruction of the expansion of Chadic languages and what can be learned from the scanty available archaeological evidence, as will be shown later. It can be suggested that speakers of Proto-Chadic dialects settled along the Maiduguri-Bama-Limani-Bongor ridge during Middle/Late Holocene around 4000 BP. Their territories may have extended from the western part of the ridge to the Early and Mid-Holocene Chari delta in the East, between the lake shoreline in the north and the Mandara Mountains in the South. The long-term reduction of the size and depth of the lake have generated diverse strategies to cope with the ever-changing ecosystems including the colonization of new land made accessible by the shrinking Lake Chad.

Chadic Genomics

Genomic research is picking up in Africa, opening an unprecedented access to the dynamics of past African populations in general and Chad Basin speakers of Chadic languages in particular (Cerny et al. 2009, Cerezo et al. 2011, Cruciani et al. 2002, Fan et al. 2019, Haber et al. 2016, MacEachern 2012, Shiner and Rotimi 2018, Tucci and Akey 2019). Different methodologies are tested to achieve different objectives. Haber et al. (2016) revealing multiple Holocene Eurasian migrations looks at the Chad Basin genetic diversity via a comparative analysis of 480 samples collected from Chad, Yemen, Lebanon, and Greece and the whole genome sequencing of nineteen individuals. Fan et al. (2019) and Lorente-Galdos et al. (2019) show that patterns of African population structure are predominantly shaped by linguistic affiliation and geographic distance. Shriner and Rotimi (2018) and Cerny et al. (2009) provide data directly relevant to the origins of Chadic speakers.

   Cerny et al. (2009) look at the phylogeography of the mitochondrial L3f haplogroup to trace the migration of Chadic-speaking pastoralists. They assert that "the result of our study supports an East Africa origin of mitochondrial L3f3 clade that is present almost exclusively within Chadic speaking people living in Chad basin." There was accordingly a Chadic-Cushitic split in the Early Holocene followed by a westward migration of speakers of proto-Chadic languages. They suggest the Wadi Howar—the Sudan segment of the Bahr el Ghazzal connecting Lake Chad to the Nile—to have been the migration route of proto-Chadic pastoralists. The Shari River drainage with its multiple tributaries appears to have been the optimal migration route in view of available archaeological evidence. The southward expansion of speakers of Nilo-Saharan languages has probably amplified the westward push of speakers of proto-Chadic languages.

   Shriner and Rotimi (2018) investigate the genetic history of the population of the Republic of Chad through an integrated analysis of genotype data from 751 individuals from Burkina Faso, Chad, Mali, South Sudan, and Sudan. As far as the speakers of Chadic languages are concerned, they found Eastern African ancestry in the Hausa (Nigeria) and Mada (Cameroon);

"detected two waves of gene flow. The first occurred 133 generations ago between Eastern Africa and West Central African references. The second wave introduced Arabian ancestry 10 generations ago" (Shriner and Rotimi 2018: 6). Accordingly, genetic evidence shows that speakers of proto-Chadic languages were originally from the Nile Valley and arrived in the Chad Basin "approximately 3700 years ago" (Shriner and Rotimi 2018: 9).

CONCLUSION

A combination of linguistic, genetic, and archaeological data point to the southern shore of the Holocene Mega-Chad, particularly the Maiduguri-Bama-Limani-Bongor shoreline and the successive Shari deltas, as the most likely homeland of speakers of proto-Chadic languages.

CLIMATE CHANGE, CULTURAL LANDSCAPES, AND CHADIC EXPANSION

Introduction

Climate change is the ideal illustration of punctuated equilibria with different periodicities (Holl 2020c). Higher-resolution paleoenvironmental research with focus on the Holocene has now allowed the detection of many abrupt climate change events (Armitage et al. 2015, Phelps et al. 2019). During the Early Holocene (c. 9000–7000 BP), the Mega-Chad was at its maximum height, with its shoreline fluctuating between 325 and 320 meters above sea level (asl). Its extent is estimated at 330,000 km² and its maximum depth fluctuated between 150 and 175 m (Schneider 1994: 43). According to Servant and Servant (1980), and based on geological, palynological studies and diatoms analyses, the climate was cold in general, with minor seasonal variation in rainfall (Servant 1983, Servant-Vildary 1978). Important fluctuations have however been recorded. Around c. 8500 BP the lake's water level was high. It was followed by a sharp decrease between c. 7600 and 7300 BP. The lake was probably divided into smaller lakes or lagoons, with large extents of land accessible to human settlements. Another high lake level recorded around 6900 BP lasted for 1500 years with a minor regression around 6500 BP (Servant 1983, Maley 1981, Durand et al. 1983). The lake's size was reduced compared to the previous period; its shoreline fluctuated between 300 and 295m asl. The climate was tropical—sub-desertic to Sudano-Sahelian, characterized by sharply contrasted seasons, with drastic seasonal variation of lake water levels.

The Mid-Holocene Environment

A Mid-Holocene abrupt climate event is documented worldwide. In the Chad Basin, shells from Goz Kerki regressing 325–330 meter shoreline in the north dated to 5310–4980, 5440–4970, and 4520–4190 BP indicate a Mid-Holocene high-stand around 5000 BP, after which "the lake level fell dramatically, and dunes of the Erg du Djourab within the northern Bodele catchment became active" (Armitage et al. 2015: 8545). Data from the Mega-Chad lake partly summarized in Armitage et al. (2015) point to an abrupt end of the African humid period (AHP) equally documented in East and North Africa, indicating a rapid, centennial-scale drying all over the large paleolake Mega-Chad Basin after c. 5000 BP. Phelps et al. (2019) show that "the most obvious increase in the domestic animal climatic niche (c. 4500 BP) occurred during the end of the AHP when both a strong reduction in the tropical trees and Sahelian grassland cover and spatially extensive dust mobilization occurred" (Phelps et al. 2019: 9). It is during that period that proto-Chadic pastoralist groups are hypothesized to have reached the southeastern flank of the Chad Basin through the Mid-Holocene Chari River drainage.

The present-day lake, with water level at 282 meters on the average, extended over 20,000 to 25,000 square kilometers, was formed in the middle of the second millennium CE. There is a higher-resolution chronology for the lake's levels fluctuations during the last millennium, c. 1000–2000 CE. The lake's open water had disappeared several times in the past and during the last thirty years, as was the case in 1984 and 1990. The paleoecological changes of the Holocene Lake Chad outlined above (Hohn et al. 2020) offered opportunities as well as constraints to Late Stone Age populations' expansion and colonization of new territories.

Late Stone Age Hunter-Gatherer Settlements

During the early settlement phase, shifting lake levels may have been detrimental to the preservation of the Early Holocene archaeological record. A handful of sites were recorded in the Nigerian part of the plain, one at Konduga in the 320-meter shoreline and the other at Dufuna in the Yobe drainage.

The Bama ridge consists of a near parallel series of sandbars. The inter-bar valleys are filled with sand deposits several meters deep located in former river channels. Surveys carried out between Bama and Maiduguri in Nigeria have shown that cultural remains are often found in such clayey fills. According to Breunig et al. (1992: 14), "the most probable origin of this redeposited material might have been the top of the ridges. The large number of sites suggests an intense prehistoric settlement in the area under consideration." Unfortunately, none of these recorded sites was tested, beside the relatively shallow evidence from Konduga.

The surface extent of Konduga is unknown. The ridge is twelve meters high in the north flank of the site, and the landscape five meters lower in the south. Two excavation units were tested, exposing a 1.2-meter thick cultural deposit made of three layers: the top layer (0–0.5 meter) consists of a grayish-brown sand; layer 2 (0.5–0.8 meter) is composed of a light yellowish-brown sand, and finally layer 3 (0.8 meter–1.2 meters) constituted of pale brown fine gravel. The collected archaeological finds amounted to 450 pieces, mostly potsherds found around and within a sandpit at the ridge top below one meter of consolidated sand (Breunig et al. 1992: 14). The recorded potsherds are decorated with rocker-stamping (or comb) technique. Pieces of rounded charcoal that seem to have been mobilized by lake waves are dated to 6340±250 BP (KN-4300). The earliest Late Stone Age settlement phase is unfortunately still very poorly documented. If there were any other Stone Age foragers sites in this sandy and clayey plain as suggested by the discovery of the Dufuna dugout, they still have to be found.

Even if it cannot be considered as a settlement *stricto sensu*, the Dufuna dugout, found in the upper Yobe River Valley along the Gana River and dated to c. 8000 BP, is the earliest evidence of human presence in the Chadian plain and the oldest watercraft in Africa. This dugout, 8.5 meters long, fully preserved, was found buried under five meters of lacustrine sediment. It was made from *Detarium senegalensis* wood, a tree usually found in the closed forest and fringing forest of the moister savanna regions (Breunig 1995: 16). The spectacular find of the Dufuna dugout attests to a mastery of watercraft by early Late Stone Age inhabitants of the Chadian plain. No early and contemporaneous habitation site has yet been found

Mobile Pastoralists Settlements

There are very few sites with clear indications of pastoralism. Five have been recorded so far, two in Nigeria at Gajiganna and Shilma, and three in Cameroon, at Blabli, Deguesse, and Krenak. The last two sites will be discussed later in the context of the Houlouf regional archaeological project.

Blabli is a flat site, presumably a small camping locality measuring one hectare in surface extent at one kilometer north of the Bama ridge (David and Sterner 1987: 2–8). The site consists of a single cultural horizon twenty centimeters thick, encompassed within fluviolacustrine deposits. Radiocarbon dates run on an ovicaprine bone fragment suggests that the locality was settled between c. 7000 BP and c. 4500 BP (David and Sterner 1989: 7). The evidence at hand suggests that a single cultural horizon site does not necessarily mean that a settlement was inhabited for a short episode, the formation of a cultural horizon depending on the nature of the building material used and the frequency and length of occupation. Different and distinct small herders' groups may have settled on the one-hectare site of Blabli at different seasons, times, and periods of the Early and Middle Holocene.

The recorded material culture includes pottery and stone artifacts. They show a finely made and well-fired pottery, mainly decorated with comb impression. One terra-cotta figurine of *Bos sp.* as well as ground and polished stone axes were recorded. Bones of domesticated cattle were identified among the faunal remains along with those of domestic sheep/goats (David and Sterner 1987: 5). No evidence of plant remains was recorded. Minimally at least, the inhabitants of Blabli can be considered as mobile stock breeders, who settled on Lake Chad's shores and beaches during episodes of low water levels (dry season camping), a site location strategy practiced by present-day pastoral-nomadic groups in the Chad Basin (Holl 2003).

Gajiganna (12° 15' N–13° 12' E) is a twin mound complex situated at the edge of a clay depression in the western part of the Bama Deltaic Formation, sixty kilometers northwest of Maiduguri in Nigeria (Breunig 1992el alet al., 1993; Breunig 1994). The site complex extends over two hectares, with the larger Mound B measuring 150 meters in diameter. The cultural sequence of Gajiganna A is two meters thick and comprises two cultural horizons, the lower dated to 2930±60 BP. The Gajiganna B cultural deposit is three meters, with three cultural horizons. The earlier one is dated to 3140±110 BP, the middle one dated from 3040±120 BP to 3150±70 BP, and the later and upper cultural layer dated to 2740±50 BP.

The stratigraphic sequences of both mounds suggest a complex settlement history of the site, starting from the western part of the complex, with an initial installation on eroded dunes sloping from east to west. The occupation sequences, continuous in Mound B and discontinuous in Mound A, may have resulted from the expansion and contraction of the inhabited space as well as shifting location of dwelling facilities. If radiocarbon dates are taken into consideration, there seem to have been at least four—if not five—occupation phases at Gajiganna instead of two: That is, from the earliest to the latest: (1) the Basal Cultural Layer (Mound B); (2) the Lower Cultural Layer (Mound B); (3) the Lower Cultural Layer (Mound A); and (4) the Upper Cultural Layer (Mound A and B).

Subsistence patterns consist of a combination of livestock herding, hunting, fishing, plant gathering, and collecting of mollusks. As far as livestock is concerned, numerous cattle figurines and cattle and sheep/goat bones were recovered. "The economy of the prehistoric settlements was dominated by domestic animals: goat, sheep, and cattle. Domestic dogs were probably raised as well. Sheep were rare in comparison to goats and cattle played the most important role among livestock. More than 60% of the bones of all mammals represented in the archaeological record belong to cattle. Small clay figurines indicate a southern breed" (Breunig et al. 1993: 31).

The recorded material culture consists essentially of pottery, lithics, and bones. Pottery includes jugs, open bowls, and globular vessels, without parallel in other Chadian plain sites. The lithic material consists of bifacially retouched arrow-points with concave bases made of chalcedony or quartz, and grinding equipment made from Damboa-area sandstone (130 kilometers in the southwest), granite and microdiocrite from the Mandara Mountains, and basalt used for the manufacture of celts and adzes obtained from the Bui area (Garba 1993). The bone industry is attested by chisels, harpoons, points, and ornaments.

Four burials were found in the upper cultural layer of mound A; three of adults and one of a child. Two adults and the child were buried next to each other, and one of the adult skeletons has one arm and the skull missing (Breunig et al. 1993). The dead were buried within dwelling features; lying on their sides, arms flexed, and hands before the face.

The predominance of cattle among animal bone remains does not automatically mean that the former inhabitants of Gajiganna were nomadic pastoralists. The large amount of pottery—even if highly debatable—can be used as an indication of sedentary life. There is however no evidence of agriculture in the early stages of Gajiganna occupation. The site, located on the edge of a clay depression in a totally flat landscape, was probably under permanent flood threat during rainy seasons. Gajiganna was a regularly visited place, probably a "permanent dry season camp. A large pit more than 2.5 m wide and about 2 m deep, situated downslope in the exposed section of Mound 3, can be interpreted as evidence of a shallow well dug in an area with a high-water table. This practice is common among Shuwa-Arab pastoralists during their dry season camping in the seasonally flooded *yaere* clay depression of the Houlouf region" (Holl 2003).

Sedentary Mixed-Farming Villages

A sample of sites featuring sedentary farming villages is presented in this section to showcase the diversity of temporal and locational situations that presided over the formation of these ancient communities. The cases are selected from Nigeria (Bama Road Site, Kursakata, Shilma, and Daima), Cameroon (Sou Blame Radjil), and Chad (Mdaga).

Bama Road Site (11° 32' N–13° 40' E) is an elongated mound, 300 meters long, 250 meters wide, and 3 meters high, located at some 2.5 kilometers northwest of Bama. Two trial trenches 3 x 2 meters each (Cutting I and II), were tested on the site. The archaeological deposit, which measures 3.40 m in maximum thickness, is sitting above a dark gray sand and gravel sedimentary unit. The site seems to have been settled from the beginning of the second millennium BCE. The earliest settlement phase is dated to 3830±250 BP (N 793). The material items collected from the basal Late Stone Age levels consist of thirty-four potsherds, some decorated with comb-stamping technique and two bone tools. The bulk of Late Stone Age occupation occurred during the first millennium BCE, as suggested by material evidence collected from Spits 1 to 13 in both probes. Series of superimposed living surfaces containing burnt soil, ash lenses, and charcoal suggest that the site may have been settled permanently during the accumulation of spits 6 to 10, between one meter and two meters in the stratigraphic section.

In general, the repertoire of material culture consists of pottery, bone tools, stone axes, grinding equipment, and very few pieces of flaked stone. The pottery, mostly plain and highly fragmented, includes globular and sub-hemispherical pots, some with fully everted rims. Small bowls were predominant. When present, decoration consists of mat impressions, grooving, ridging, and comb-stamping (Connah 1981: 87). Few fish and mammal bones were collected but unfortunately not identified. Freshwater mussel (*Aspartharia* spp.) shells were also collected, suggesting their use as a food resource (Connah 1981). Four burials, two infants and two adults, were found within both trial trenches. According to Connah (1981: 85), the Bama Road Site can be considered as consisting "of a series of at least semi-permanent villages" at the end of the second millennium BCE. The buildup of a 3.4-meter-thick cultural deposit suggests that the settlement may have been visited from time to time during the early occupation phase, frequently occupied, for longer periods or even a quasi-sedentary village

Sou Blame Radjil (12° 12' N 14° 41' E) is a twin-mound complex located on the shore of an intermittent stream, measuring fourteen hectares in surface extent. A twenty-five-square-meter excavation unit was set on the highest point of the western and largest mound (Rapp 1984), revealing a 4.4-meter-thick cultural deposit made of eleven occupation levels. The initial Late Stone Age occupation found in levels V (2.2–2.7 meters) to XI (4.05–4.4 meters) is bracketed between 2280±170 BP and 3280±360 BP. The early occupation material culture consists of thirty-six sherds decorated with roulette impressions and comb-stamping. Most of the deposit of levels VII (3–3.25 meters) to XI (4.05–4.4 meters), 1.4 meters of the deposit, consists predominantly of hard clay with a minor component of silt, varying from brown to gray, interspersed with burnt occupation surfaces. As suggested by evidence from Daima, to be considered later, Late Stone Age habitations prior to the advent of iron metallurgy consisted of wood and grass. However, the available radiocarbon dates suggest that the buildup of levels VII to XI lasted from c. 3200 to c. 2500 BP, close to the one-meter-per-millennium accumulation rate suggested by Maley (1981) for Lake Chad sediments. The deposit thus seems to have been accumulated by natural processes of aggradation generated by successive flooding events. The repertoire of material culture consists predominantly of pottery, bone tools (9 points and harpoons from the excavation, and 116 others, 90 complete and broken harpoons, 20 points and 6 chisels from the surface), and stone artifacts. The stone raw material, syenite and sandstone, was obtained from the Mora Hills and Mandara Mountains 150 kilometers to the south. The bulk of Sou Blame Radjil Late Stone Age occupation occurred during the second half of the second millennium BCE, between c. 2500 and 2200 BP, when the pattern of occupation of the locality may have shifted from an intermittently settled sand island to a more permanent sedentary village.

Kursakata mound (12° 19' N–14° 14' E), 450 meters long, 275 meters wide, and 5 meters high, is situated on a presumable beach ridge along the Lake Chad shoreline dated to c. 4000–3000 BP. The settlement was probably located in a lacustrine environmental setting, likely on the immediate lakeshore. A small test excavation was carried out from the central and highest point of the mound, revealing a 5.87-meter-thick archaeological sequence. The recorded cultural deposits sit on natural *Firki* clay, "but the immediate surroundings suggest that the mound formed on the edge of a slightly elevated sandy area adjacent to a *Firki* plain. Such sandy areas in the *Firki* most commonly consist of the sand islands rising through the clay" (Connah 1981: 91).

The site stratigraphy consists of finely banded clay layers, some of them iron-hard. With the exception of a shallow hearth discovered at 5.44–5.5 m, at the bottom of the cultural deposit, no other dwelling feature has been recorded. A charcoal sample from the hearth is dated to 2880±140 BP (N 480). Additional research carried out by Gronenborn (1998) shows the earliest site occupation to date to c. 3000 BP. The mound buildup seems to have resulted from successive semipermanent settlements from the beginning of the first millennium BCE to sometime in the first millennium CE. Late Stone Age occupation levels at the bottom of the site sequence contain a relatively low quantity of cultural remains. The quantity of potsherds varies from twenty-six to thirty-eight, with however the majority of clay figurines and all the stone artifacts recorded in these early deposits. "Bone tools and ground axes are absent; even grindstones and grinders/pounders are rare, but clay figurines of animals, figurines of strange upright type, and fired fragments of the distinctive figurine clay are relatively common" (Connah 1981: 97). The decoration of Kursakata Late Stone Age potsherds shows strong similarities with that from the Bama Road Site and Sou Blame Radjil. Five main decoration techniques have been recorded: comb-stamping, grooving and ridging, wiping and smoothing, rouletting, and mat impressions.

As far as subsistence patterns are concerned, mixed farming, hunting, and fishing appear to have been regular food-procurement strategies. The collected faunal remains were unfortunately too fragmented and virtually unidentifiable. Cattle and sheep/goat bones have however been identified, and fish bones were retrieved all along the stratigraphic sequence. 70 percent of the identified fish remains belong to two species, Nile perch (*Lates niloticus*) and catfish (*Clarias* sp.) (Connah 1981: 98, Gronenborn 1995). Evidence of cultivated millet, *Pennisetum glaucum*, dated to 1000 BCE has been recorded (Neumann 1995). Wild plants such as wild rice (*Oriza* sp.) and wild fruits (*Celtis integrifolia, Ziziphus* sp., and *Viles* sp.) were also extensively collected.

The sample of ten excavated tombs provides entry into burial customs. All these tombs were found virtually at the same depth, suggesting the presence of a cemetery. "Four or five of the deceased were infants but five were adults or at least adolescents" (Connah 1981: 95). The dead were laid on their sides, in flexed position without predominant orientation, with no grave goods with the exception of eight clay beads found in one of the skeletons. "The burials appear to have been placed in shallow graves then filled with lumps of *Firki* clay and appeared to have been put in 'blind,' without much idea of the position of previous burials" (Connah 1981: 95); such characteristics suggests an intermittent settlement.

Kursakata Late Stone Age occupations appear to have been highly intermittent. This pattern of occupation may have depended on the amplitude of Lake Chad c. 4000–3000 BP seepage, seasonal fluctuations, and changing levels. According to paleoclimatic research (Maley 1981, Schneider 1994), the actual Lake Chad level and shoreline fluctuated between 296 and 290 meters asl. Consequently, depending on the combination of climatic parameters, rainfall and evaporation, the site may have been either accessible or flooded.

Shilma or Bomu 70 (11° 55' N–14° 21' E) is a flat site located in the middle of an extensive clay formation within the Chad Lagoonal Complex. Judging from surface inspection, the site is 800 meters long and 400 meters wide. Two test excavations carried out on the highest points revealed a one-meter-thick archaeological deposit (Connah 1981: 142). The recorded cultural deposit, sitting on a thick *Firki* clay, is capped by a compact to loose sand and clay sediment with vertical cracks. It consists of finely bedded horizontal "absolutely iron hard" clay bands containing some ash, probably representing remains of dwelling floors. The initial site occupation happened at the end of the first half of the first millennium BCE, from 2720±120 BP (N 792) to 2680±180 (N 791). The settlement appears to have been inhabited for only a few centuries, abandoned at an unknown time, likely during the second half of the first millennium BCE. For Connah (1981: 45), "The conclusion seems inescapable that we are dealing with a mixed assemblage resulting from periodic occupation spread over a considerable time. Even now a tiny settlement still exists at Shilma, actually on the site, and over the years I have seen it both abandoned (1967, 1969) and occupied (1978)." Add to the probable intermittent occupation that this site has experienced the fact that the *firki* clay (of which it is mostly composed) is subject to deep, regular cracking and gradually inverts its profile . . . and it can be guessed why the assemblage is mixed. The evidence from Shilma does not fit in the model of steady emergence of sedentary settlement with a unidirectional shift from mobile hunting-gathering to sedentary food-producing societies which is assumed to explain the development of human colonization of the Chadian plain as epitomized by the "success" of Daima, a model which is at variance with more recent observations on local and contemporary settlement dynamics (Connah 1981, Holl et al. 1991, Holl 1993, 2002, Holl and Levy 1993). It easily appears that Shilma was settled on a seasonal basis, frequently visited during a few centuries and then abandoned. It points to an alternative site use, part of a broader spectrum of settlement location strategies encompassing short duration seasonal camps and permanent sedentary villages.

The material culture repertoire consists mostly of potsherds, a few bone tools—harpoons, points, and miscellaneous worked objects—and grinding equipment. Pottery is decorated with five dominant techniques: grooving and ridging, twisted cord roulette, miscellaneous rouletting, wiping and smoothing, and mat impression. In this regard, the ceramic material shows strong similarities with data from Bama Road Site, Sou Blame Radjil, and Kursakata, pertaining to closely linked decoration traditions. No faunal remains are reported. Shilma seems to have been settled during a relatively dry period.

Daima (12° 12' N 14° 30' E) is a subcircular mound measuring 250 meters long and 170 meters wide. It is not far from the shore of El Beid River, an intermittent stream. Eight trenches were excavated, the most impressive being Cutting VIII (50 x 6 meters). The recorded cultural deposit measures 11.5 meters in maximum thickness. The excavation has demonstrated that the base of the mound actually rests on the *Firki*, but the immediate surroundings of Daima consist of a moderately extensive sandy area, which, like Kursakata, seems not to be a typical sand island rising through the clay. However. as the excavation showed, the *Firki* clay beneath the Daima mound is relatively thin with sand beneath. "The initial Daima settlement have accordingly grown on a small sand island and then extended onto the edge of the *Firki* as time went on" (Connah 1981: 100). Daima 1 at the base of the mound sequence is dated from 2550 BP±50 (2520±110 BP (I-2945) to 2400±95 (I-2372). It contained a refuse dump with animal bones, potsherds, a bone harpoon, and a clay animal figurine (Connah 1976, 1981: 113). Few postholes were found but were not organized into meaningful dwelling plans.

The cultural remains repertoire is diversified and consists of potsherds, anthropomorphic and zoomorphic clay figurines, bone tools, stone arti-facts, and grinding equipment. Six main techniques were used for pottery decoration during the Late Stone Age Daima I occupation: comb-stamping, comb-drawing, grooving and ridging, wiping and smoothing, plaited cord rouletting, and mat impressions. Small pots and bowls, the former with thick-ened rim and everted curved neck, and pot-lids were the most frequent vessel shapes. Most of the grinding equipment and axes were manufactured on stone raw material from the Mandara Mountains (Connah 1981, Connah and Freeth 1989). Bone tools comprise numerous harpoons, spatula tools, a few points, and miscellaneous pieces

As shown by the burial from Spit 51 in which the deceased was hit with a harpoon, this class of artifact was a dual weapon not only as tool for fishing (Connah 1981: 117). Twenty burials were exposed in Daima 1 deposits, pos-sibly, however, only seven of them are from the Late Stone Age. The recorded burials, all without grave goods, "ranged from some with merely flexed legs to others so tightly contracted that the knees almost touch the chest" (Connah 1981: 115).

Faunal remains suggest the subsistence of Daima I Late Stone Age people to consist of livestock husbandry with predominantly cattle and sheep/goat, fishing, hunting of waterfowl and few wild mammals, and wild plant gath-ering. However, it was probably part of a broader mixed economy likely complemented by sorghum cultivation, even if plant macro-remains were not found in the earlier deposits but only later in Daima III occupation levels. In contrast to Shilma, the settlement at Daima was successful, but it is far from certain that Daima 1 inhabitants were sedentary farmers right from the begin-ning. The site may have been frequently settled on a seasonal basis for a few centuries and turned into a permanent village-based community, tentatively during Daima II in the first half of the first millennium CE.

Mdaga (12° 12' N–15° 03' E) is an elliptical mound, 300 meters long, 185 meters in average width, and 8 meters high, located in the northwestern por-tion of the Chari Deltaic Formation. It is sited on the shore of the Linia, a seasonal tributary of the Chari River and surrounded by an impressive earthen wall, 6 meters in average width at its base with four gates. Stratigraphic cor-relations and radiocarbon dates suggest the earthen wall to have been built between 1000 and 1200 CE (Lebeuf et al. 1980, Holl 1987, 1988, 1993c). The site excavation was implemented through fifteen trenches. The exposed archaeological deposits are 5–5.5 meters thick, made of ten or eleven occupa-tion levels depending on trenches.

Late Stone Age people settled on a sand island around 2375±150 BP (Gif 742)–2150±135 BP (Dak 10). The sample of their cultural remains is rather poor, made up of four burials, the base of a four-legged pot, one grooved stone, and fish bones of Nile perch (*Lates niloticus*) and catfish (*Gymnarchus niloticus*).

If judged from the quantity of cultural remains collected from 284-square-meter and 5.50-meter-thick sampled units, Mdaga appears have been inhabited discontinuously. At the time of its pioneer occupation, the settlement was probably situated on a lake island or immediately on its shore. Clay sediment characteristic of most of the Late Stone Age deposits may thus have been accumulated by seasonal floods and/or during shorter periods of higher lake levels.

Emergent Complexity

The presentation of the main sites excavated in the southern Chad Basin plain provides the necessary chronological outline of Chadic settlement development. They are however too scattered over very extensive territory to allow for the full grasp of the processes involved in the long-term forma-tion of Chadic polities. The work carried out in the context of the Houlouf regional archaeological project (1981–1991) was designed to address that problem. That investigation of the emergence of Chadic polities focused on site-location strategies, settlement hierarchy, evidence of social inequality, differential consumption of scarce exotic goods, and the differential treatment of the deceased. The quantity, quality, and resolution of data obtained through archaeological investigations vary considerably in time and space.

In African archaeology, the emergence of complex societies tended to be addressed almost exclusively in historical terms during the colonial period up to the 1970s. Research was focused on major trade entrepôts (Awdaghost, Great Zimbabwe, Kumbi-Saleh, Mapungubwe, Niani, Gao, etc.) and capital cities of the late first/early second millennium kingdoms. The archaeology of social complexity is fraught with theoretical and empirical difficulties. There is persistent disagreement on the very definition of complexity when used in the study of the evolution of social systems. (Earle 1991, Holl 1985, 1986, 1993. 1994, 2002, McIntosh 1995, McIntosh 1998, Feinman and Marcus 1998, Insoll 1996, Wright 1998, Yoffee 1993). How do researchers choose between alternative evolutionary pathways? What is the scientific status of inferences derived from the archaeological record?

There is disagreement among scholars on the genesis and the evolu-tion of complex societies in Africa (Connah 1987, Holl 2004, Insoll 1996, MacDonald 1998, S. K. McIntosh 1995, R. J. McIntosh 1998, McIntosh and McIntosh 1980). Current interpretations focus on political centralization, craft specialization, settlement hierarchy, and social ranking as comple-mentary facets of the process leading to the emergence and reproduction of complex social systems. Archaeologists' theoretical guesses have however to be tested through their relevance and capacity to further an understanding of the material record of past societies. They have the onerous task of deciphering their material record and reconstructing the range of evolutionary trajectories followed in different parts of the continent.

Houlouf: A Chadic Polity in the Making

The Houlouf Archaeological Project was framed to trace the emergence of Central Chadic polities and investigate their evolution through time. As such, it required a significant tightening of the study area boundaries to allow for a rigorous grasp of the material record at hand. The Houlouf region is located along the Savanna-Sahel margins of the Chadian plain in the northernmost part of the Cameroons. The area, settled at the very beginning of the second millennium BCE, is still inhabited by speakers of Chadic, Semitic (Arabic), and Saharan languages. The delineated study area measures 400 square kilometers, a 20 x 20-kilometer square set in what is considered by the local population to be the heart of the "Land of Houlouf" (Holl 2002). It is divided into three ecological zones: 1) the Logone-Shari River valley with its sand islands and shores colonized by *Borassus aethiopicum* palms; 2) the arbustive savanna with a vegetation made predominantly of *Acacia* sp. and thorny shrubs, and finally, 3) the hinterland depression, called *yaere* in local Arabic, flooded during the rainy season, and turning into prime grassland after the annual flood during the first half of the dry season. The nature and regional distribution of soils appear to have played important roles on site-location strategies and decisions.

Fourteen mounds distributed into ten settlements were mapped and tested, providing a four-thousand-year-long occupation sequence ranging from c. 1900 BCE to the present. The surveyed and excavated mounds vary considerably in size and shape, with one consisting of a multi-mound complex. With the exception of the main excavation at Houlouf which measures 120 square meters, most of the sites were investigated with 3 x 4-meter-deep probes revealing the mounds' stratigraphy (fig. 3.3).

The settlement sequence of the study area is divided into five phases of varying length, subdivided into subphases A and B. The phasing is based on significant change in regional settlement patterns and site distribution, resulting either from the foundation of new settlement or abandonment of previously settled localities.

With the exception of the pioneer settlement phase (Deguesse Phase) which is rather long and still poorly investigated, the subphases range from 200 to 250 years. At the end of the third and very beginning of the second

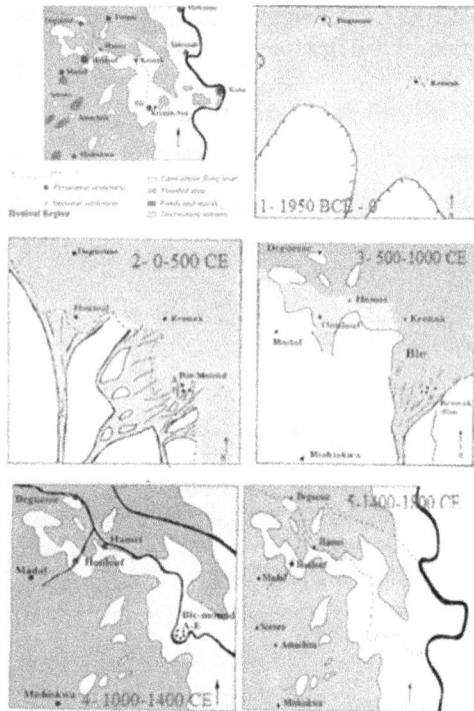

Figure 3.3. Chronology and settlement phases of the Houlouf polity. *Created by the author*

millennium BCE, Lake Chad was much larger and deeper. The study area was then part of the lake bottom (Holl 1988, 1994, 1996, 2000, 2002).

Deguesse Phase (BCE 1900–0): Pioneer Herders

Deguesse phase settlements dated from c. 1900 BCE to 0 CE were recorded at the bottom of two sites' trenches, at Deguesse and Krenak (fig. 3.3). Settlement evidence is shallow. It consists mostly of livestock dung deposits with very few cultural remains. The region was then inhabited by mobile herders, relying on abundant wild grain or practicing a kind of not yet fully documented management of annual plants that still escapes archaeologists' grasp. Both sites are located at nine kilometers from each. Based on the exposed sedimentary sequence, they were very likely sand islands settled during low-water regimes, that is, during the dry seasons.

Krenak Phase (0–500 CE):
Autonomous Farming-Fishing Communities

The Krenak phase (0–500 CE) witnessed a significant increase in the number of settled localities. During Krenak phase A (0–250 CE) there were three settled localities (Deguesse, Krenak, and Houlouf), all confined to the northwest of the study area (fig. 3.3). There is a clear shift toward a more sedentary lifestyle with bulkier dwelling facilities. A single grinder in syenite suggests the existence of imported material from the Waza-Mora-Mandara mountain range 200–250 kilometers to the southwest. During Krenak phase B (250–500 CE), settlement was extended to the southeast with the foundation of the Ble-Mound complex, consisting of three distinct small tells. Craft specialization is represented by a blacksmith workshop. There is a broader range of imported high-value items such as carnelian beads, alloyed copper, and coarse stone artifacts (fourteen in syenite, two in rhyolite, one in quartzite). The recorded villages are surprisingly equidistant, located at five kilometers from one to its nearest neighbor, along marshlands in a deltaic context. Few horse bones (one first phalanx, one distal end of left tibia, and proximal femur) were found at Houlouf in level II, suggesting the import of prestigious riding animals.

Mishiskwa Phase (500–1000 CE): Bipolarization Process

The Mishiskwa phase (500–1000 CE) corresponds to the extension of human settlement in the clayey hinterland depression. During Mishiskwa phase A (500–750 CE), the number of settled localities increased to ten, and then eleven during Mishiskwa phase B. The settlement system appears to have consisted of two distinct patterns. The pattern found in the northwest consisted of five almost equidistant villages with Houlouf in a central position. The southeastern pattern (the Ble-Mound Complex and Krenak-Sao) is comprised of five tightly clustered sites, with one isolated case (Mishiskwa) in the south. Craft specialization is represented by iron-smelting furnaces, blacksmiths' workshops, weaving artifacts, and textile dyeing installations. There is a significant increase in the diversity and amount of imported high-value goods, in the context of competing central villages.

Ble Phase (1000–1400 CE): Competition and Rivalry

During the Ble phase (1000–1400 CE), Krenak in the Houlouf orbit and Krenak-Sao in the Ble-Mound Complex area are abandoned. A new site is founded at Ble-Mound C, set on a silted channel of the ancient Logone River delta. There is a significant trend toward economic intensification with massive evidence for fish-smoking in the Ble-Mound Complex, iron-smelting furnaces, and forge installations. The manufacture of clay headrests and intensive salt production are new additions to the craft repertoire. Imported goods include carnelian and glass beads, a broad range of artifacts in alloyed copper, and cowrie shells.

The settlement system is clearly bipolar with Houlouf and the Ble-Mound Complex as competing centers, with significant import of exotic prestige items and presumably warfare. The whole area was witnessing the emergence of centralized political systems with peer-polity interactions ranging from elective alliance to outright war. An adult male buried with a pair of spurs suggests the emergence of a class (or social category) of warrior-horsemen (fig. 3.4). The same level revealed a rich female burial with a range of imported prestigious materials. Houlouf Level VI provides indisputable evidence of purposeful destruction of salt-production installations, probably resulting from raiding or more extensive warfare. Comparable evidence has also been recorded at the Ble-Mound Complex with systematic decapitation of terra-cotta figurines as well as several hundreds of almost calibrated spherical to subspherical coarse stone used as missiles. The Houlouf earthen rampart was built during the Ble phase in this context of competition and rivalry.

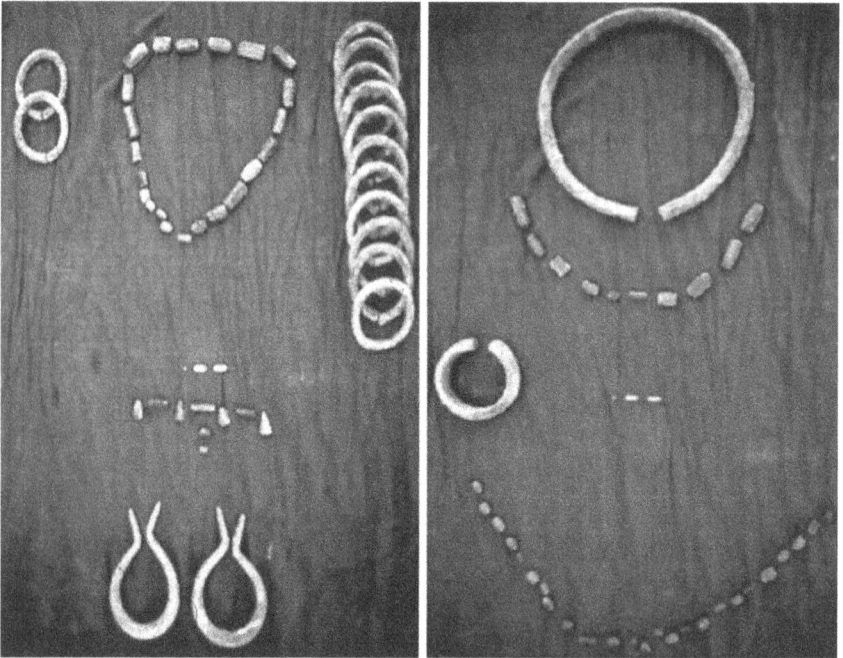

Figure 3.4. Personal adornment of the warrior-horseman and high-ranked woman. *Created by the author*

Houlouf Phase A (1400–1600 CE):
The Rise of Houlouf Chiefdom

During Houlouf phase A (CE 1400–1600), the number of settled localities dropped dramatically from nine to three, with only Houlouf, Deguesse, and Amachita left as inhabited settlements (fig. 3.3). The beginning of Houlouf phase coincided with the onset of a particularly dry and arid period—The Little Ice Age—that lasted for 100 to 150 years.

Houlouf is the central settlement of a polity that will include seven settlements during Houlouf phase B (1600–1800 CE). An elite cemetery reveals specific rules of etiquette, orientation and position of the deceased, for a tiny group of individuals. The structure and spatial layout of this cemetery suggests the existence of four factions or descent groups (Holl 1988, 1994, 2002), all jockeying for power and prestige in the shadow of the ruler probably represented by the "effigy jar" found at the center of the graveyard, and probably symbolizing the paramount chief or the king. The most prestigious among them seems to have belonged to the class of warrior-horsemen. Burials are marked by superimposed large clay vessels—also known as So pots. The deceased are buried in a sitting position, their feet resting in a pot, all facing southwest, the direction indicated by the central effigy jar. Most of the individuals buried in the Houlouf cemetery belonged to a select group of elite members. Many were warrior-horsemen, some officeholders, and a few, ritual specialists (Holl 1994, 2002). Rulers as well as successful officeholders display their status with items of horsemanship, specific dress code, and elements of personal adornment. The copper figurine of the horse rider, may recapitulate the essence of Chadic warrior-horsemanship.

The remains of the rulers' residence, still called the "Sultan Palace," is located on a higher small mound—forbidden to archaeologists. This relatively impressive complex was probably built during the Ble phase. The chronological uncertainty could however not be settled because of a legitimate excavation prohibition. At the peak of its power, the chiefdom was centered at the earthen-walled 15.5-hectare city of Houlouf.

CENTRALIZATION, SOCIAL DIFFERENTIATION, AND CHADIC SOCIAL FORMATIONS

Introduction

The period bracketed between 500 and 1200 CE witnessed the development of ranked and centralized societies in the Chadian plain, the Hawsaland, and the Mandara Mountains (David 2008, Holl 2002, Lebeuf 1969, MacEachern

2012a, Sutton 1979). The formation of Chadic polities involved differential concentration of population over the landscape, the connection with long-distance trade networks, the amplification of craft specialization, and the development of social ranking (Connah 1976, 1981, Holl 1988, 2000, 2002, 2003). They are materialized through settlement rank-size locational patterns, "prestige-goods" distribution, and specific burial protocols.

Central settlements, presumably important sociopolitical centers, are characterized by the presence of an impressive earthen rampart. Some of these walled cities such as Makari (Macari), Gulfey (Calfe), Afade (Afadena), Wulki (Ulchi), Kusseri (Uncusciuri), Sao (Sauo), Houlouf (Alph), and Logone (Lagone), located in the Central Chadic speakers' land, were mentioned as chiefdom centers at the end of the sixteenth century (d'Anania 1582: 350). Similar and contemporaneous evolutionary processes took place in Hawsaland, among speakers of Western Chadic languages, with the formation of *Hausa bakwai,* the traditionally claimed "seven initial Hawsa city-states" (Biram, Daura, Gobir, Kano, Katsina, Rano, and Zaria). Ethnohistory, either the Bayajida or the Sao legends, is made up of political charters serving actual local sociopolitical purposes (Cartwright 2019, Sutton 1979). The Hawsa homeland was very likely located along the southwest shore of Lake Chad. With Lake Chad shrinking, ancestral speakers of Western Chadic—Proto-Western Chadic—languages moved westward, and from the Hadejia-Daura-Kano region expanded west up to Sokoto and beyond. Through a "hawsazation" process, other small and scattered linguistic groups were absorbed and adopted the Hawsa language. "The 15th century is seen as a watershed. It is then . . . that the emergence of city-states in east Hawsaland—Kano, Katsina, Zazzau—first becomes obvious and that Hawsaland clearly connects itself with the cultural and commercial network of the Sudan, the Sahara, and its islamizing features" (Sutton 1979: 185). Despite the relative paucity of archaeological evidence (Gronenborn 2011, Liesegang 2009, Sule and Haour 2014, Sutton 1979, 2010), there are convincing data in support of emerging elites and social ranking in the Hawsaland core, as will be shown below (Gronenborn et al. 2012).

The North-Central Chadic Area

In the North-Central Chadic area, graveyards and burials in large jars are found almost exclusively in strict association with earthen-walled settlements (table 3.1). Survey data without archaeological testing show this to be the case at Kabe, Kala-Kafra, Maltam, Kala-Maloue, Logone-Birni in Cameroon, and Ngala in Nigeria. Some isolated burials in jars were excavated at Gulfey, Kusseri, and Logone-Birni, and more substantial cemeteries were studied at Sao and Houlouf in Cameroon and Midigue and Mdaga in the Republic of

Chad. The surface extent of the studied sites varies from seven (Mdaga) to 20.3 hectares (Sao), and they are located on the shores of intermittent river courses. In this flat landscape, the regional distribution of earthen-walled settlements can be analyzed with locational models. Thiessen polygons suggest that each of the mapped sites was the political center of a territorial unit. Smaller territorial units are situated in the middle of the study area and larger at both ends. Three of the centers—Makari in the north, Kusseri in the center, and Logone-Birni in the south—are paramount centers, located at fifty to sixty kilometers from one to the next. The settlement rank-size hierarchy is thus constituted of at least three levels: 1) open mounds of different but generally small size villages; 2) earthen-walled sites as former villages chiefdoms and later district centers, and finally, 3) paramount central settlements. The construction of an earthen rampart, the development of cemeteries, and competition for territories were different facets of the same sociopolitical process (Holl 1994). Archaeological data from cemeteries can be used to evaluate the accuracy of the above-mentioned hypothesis.

With the exception of one extended burial from Mdaga cemetery, all the recorded tombs are jar-burials. These jars were not always used for the same purpose everywhere. At Houlouf, jars were used as "tombstones," without direct contact with the body of the deceased and always situated .3 to.5 meter above the heads of the buried individuals. In this cemetery, the dead were buried in a sitting position, all facing southwest, their feet in a pot. At Sao, Mdaga, and Midigue, jars were used as coffins. In all the cases, the number of jars per tomb varies from one to three. The surface extent of observed graveyards vary from 38.50 (Houlouf) to 180 square meters (Midigue Intra-muros), with the number of burials in each ranging from eleven (Sao) to thirty (Midigue Intra-muros). Two of the studied cemeteries (Mdaga and Midigue Extra-muros) are located outside the city's earthen rampart. According to informants cited by Lebeuf et al. (1980: 96), graveyards located out of the cities' ramparts were those of blacksmiths and their relatives. It is therefore not surprising that almost all of the excavated burials from these cemeteries were devoid of grave goods. In terms of spatial patterning, the density of burials varies from 0.15/square meter (Sao) to 0.67/square meter (Houlouf) and the average space per tomb, from 1.48 square meters (Houlouf) to 6.27 square meters (Sao) (table 1). In cemeteries located in the cities, burials are distributed into different clusters. Such a pattern suggests the existence of different social factions among those who were buried in these specific formal disposal areas (Holl 1994, 2002).

The differences in the distribution of grave goods are not detailed here (table 3.1). They are however comprised of diverse items sets and raw materials that can be partitioned into two broad categories: local and exotic. Locally made items (clay beads, smoking pipes, pottery, zoomorphic, and

Table 3.1: Distribution of grave goods in the excavated North Central Chadic central settlements

Site	Sao	Mdaga	Midigue intra-muros	Midigue extra-muros	Houlouf
Settlement Size					
Length (m)	580	350	350	350	450
Width (m)	350	200	200	200	400
Surface (ha)	20.30	7.00	7.50	7.50	15.90
Shape	Ellipsoidal	Ellipsoidal	Ellipsoidal	Ellipsoidal	Subcircular
Mortuary Evidence					
Cemeteries					
surface (m²)	69	109	180	47.50	38.50
Number of tombs	11	22	30	13	26
Density	0.15	0.20	0.16	0.27	0.67
Average space per tomb (m²)	6.27	4.90	6.00	3.65	1.48
Burial facilities					
Jars	17	28	57	13	32
Grave goods					
Nb of tombs with grave goods	10	26	30	–	23
Nature of grave goods					
Carnelian beads	449	11	255	–	914
Glass beads	162	10	22	–	1
Alloyed copper	130	7	43	–	71
Pottery	6	11	9	–	22
Others	6	1613	17	–	25

anthropomorphic terra-cotta figurines) are recurrent but in very small quantities. Exotic goods, carnelian, and glass beads (long cylindrical and opaque bleu), and artifacts in alloyed copper—connected to warfare and horsemanship—are relatively abundant, but their distribution between settlements and burials is highly skewed.

At Houlouf, for example, the frequency of carnelian beads per tomb varies from 1 to 174, and that of alloyed copper artifacts from 1 to 12 (Holl 1994, 2002). Exotic items were obtained through interconnection with long-distance trade and used as symbols of prestige and power. In the Chadian basin, in 1100–1600 CE, such trade networks linked enslaved procurement areas to redistribution centers and markets places of North Africa and the Nile Valley, via the Sahara, Bornu kingdom and Hawsa polities in the north and west, and Bagirmi kingdom and Darfur in the east.

Developments in the Western Chadic Area

In the western confine of the Western Chadic languages area there is a rich and intriguing ethnohistory backed by written sources that have been analyzed and discussed by generations of historians (Sutton 1979, 2010). Published archaeological surveys and excavation are relatively scarce compared to the Central Chadic area. The excavation of Durbi Takusheyi cemetery provides an extraordinary archaeological entry into the formation of early Hawsa city-states. The site is located at the epicenter of the *Hawsa bakwai*—the traditionally claimed seven initial Hawsa city-states—between Katsina and Daura. In the recorded oral traditions, Daura is suggested to be the most ancient town of Hawsaland, a locality from which all the other Hawsa city-states gain their legitimacy.

The cemetery is comprised of eight burial mounds organized into two subsets along the shores of a seasonal stream. Tumulus T6 and T7 are located along the north shore, at approximately 500 meters from the southern subset. T1 and T2 are located in the northeast of the southern group, T8 at its south-west end. And finally, T3, T4, and T5 are set in a triangular arrangement at the center. T1 and T3 were tested in 1907 by the British resident administrator H. R. Palmer with the assistance of the Emir of Katsina. T2, T4, T5, and T7 were excavated in 1992 by the Bayreuth University team led by D. Lange and G. Liesegang (2009). And finally, a new project, focused essentially on the restoration and public display of the previous campaigns archaeological finds, was carried out by the Romisch-Germanisches Zentralmuseum (Mainz) led by D. Gronenborn (2012).

The material collected from the excavation of T3 was lost. T1, at the northeast end of the southern subset, was excavated in 1907. It contained a single central tomb of an individual buried in a sitting position, with a rich and diverse array of grave goods. They include: a rusty iron sword blade; an iron spearhead; an alloyed-copper arm-ring; metal plates; pottery; a grinding stone; and sheep bones (Gronenborn et al. 2012: 260).

T4, at the southwest of the central triangular arrangement, also contained the remains of an individual buried in a sitting position in the central chamber (Gronenborn et al. 2012: 260). The accompanying grave goods consist of a metal rod; spiked anklets—in fact, horseman leg-guards (Holl 1994, 2002); ivory arm-rings at the right arm; and a cap stitched with cowrie shells. Two charcoal samples date T4 to 1260–1295 calCE (KI 3627) and 11225–1285 calCE (HD 15569/15537).

T5, at the northeast of the central triangular arrangement, has a single central burial of an individual in a sitting position (Gronenborn et al. 2012: 263). The recorded grave goods are made of: metal bars, a metal plate containing cowrie shells and glass beads; an iron spoon; a metal bangle; ivory rings; cowrie-shell belt; massive metal anklets—in fact symbolic leg-guards for high-ranked warrior-horsemen; and a massive bangle around the right forearm (Holl 1994, 2002).

Finally, T7 in the northern cluster is not only the richest monument of the whole cemetery, it is also remarkably a female burial. The position of the deceased is unfortunately not known. There is no indication of her burial posture in the available report. It would have been particularly interesting to know if she was also buried in a sitting position as all the other documented individuals, or if there was a specific treatment of a deceased high-ranked female. Her grave goods consisted of: one metal bowl; two metal buckets; two gold rings and bracelet in a bowl; two gold earrings, gold finger ring and gold pendent; and carnelian beads (Gronenborn et al. 2012: 265).

Data from Durbi Takusheyi graves are similar and parallel to the material exposed at the Houlouf cemetery. The deceased are buried in a sitting position with a diverse assortment of local and exotic goods. Warrior identity is well emphasized via alloyed-copper horsemen leg-guards and archers alloyed-copper wrist-bands (Holl 1994, 2002). There are imports from Egypt or the Near East, but most of the raw material represented had a West African origin. Gronenborn et al. (2012: 263) asserts in reference to alloyed copper anklets and bangles that "it appears, however, there are no published exact parallels," but this is inaccurate. Such evidence was published as early as 1988 (Holl 1988, 1994, 2002). The additional suggestion that "the carnelian beads may come from Fezzan but also from Gujarat in India" (Gronenborn et al. 2012: 265) ignores the fact that there was an important carnelian production area in the Tilemsi Valley, stretching from the Adrar-n-Ifogha to the Niger Bend in present day Mali (Gaussen and Gaussen 1988), less than one thousand kilometers west of the Hausaland. This information was already reported in the eleventh century CE by Al Bakri as follows:

> Another road from Tadmekka to Ghadamis: you go from Tadmekka for six days over the country inhabited by the Saghmara and then through the waterless waste for four days before attaining water, and then through another waterless region also four days. In this second waste is a mine of stone called *tasi-n-nasamt*, which resembles agate (*aqiq*). Occasionally you may find in one stone various colors such as red, yellow, or white. Sometimes, though very rarely, a large, fine stone is found. When such a stone is brought to the people of Ghana, they value it extravagantly and pay a high price for it. They consider it to be more splendid than any other precious object. This stone is polished and pierced by means of another stone called *ti-n-tuwas* in the same way as rubies are polished and pierced with emery. Iron would make no impression on it at all without the *ti-n-tuwas*. (Al Bakri in Levtzion and Hopkins 1981: 86)

Beside carnelian beads, copper and alloyed copper, gold, and iron obtained in different parts of West Africa were sold and distributed through the long-distance trade networks that crisscrossed the whole continent.

The development in Central and Western Chadic speaking areas present striking parallels. The cemetery of Houlouf replicates the formation of a sociopolitical elite that emerged in the western Chadic area in the fourteenth and fifteenth centuries CE. The development of cemeteries occurred during the thirteenth through sixteenth centuries, a period that witnessed an extensive resettlement that took place after the abandonment of the area in c. 1350–1450 CE because of adverse climatic conditions (Maley 1981). Occupation gaps were recorded in all the tested mounds stratigraphic sequences. At the end of the fourteenth century (1380 CE), groups of Arabs pastoralists started to move into the Chad Basin and were present in the plain in 1500–1550 CE (Holl 2003). In the same sixteenth century, King Idriss Alawma, ruler of the Kanuri kingdom of Bornu, initiated a policy of systematic expansion and conquest of the Chadic polities located along the western and southern shores of Lake Chad (Zeltner 1980, Holl 1993, 1994, 2000, 2003, Holl and Levy 1993).

In the Shadow of Empires

Beyond patterns of settlement hierarchy and the regional distribution of sites, the control of the *means of legitimation* is the critical step in the emergence and routinization of elite groups among speakers of Chadic languages. Archaeological evidence from Central and Western Chadic speaking areas point to the development of centralized political systems between 1000 and 1400 CE, coalescing into competing polities. The intensification in long-distance exchange and craft specialization went along with accelerated occupational differentiation (warrior, horsemen, officeholders, ritual specialists), and a narrower definition of the legitimate use of symbols of prestige and achievement. As shown by Baines and Yoffee (1998: 234) in their comparative study of Mesopotamia and Egypt, the emergence and maintenance of elites, and then of elites within elites, lie at the heart of civilization: unfortunately in this case, inequality is fundamental. "Elites control symbolic resources in such a way as to make them meaningful only when it is they who exploit them. This appropriation of meaning is complementary to, and at least as important as, other legitimation available to controlling individuals or groups" (Baines and Yoffee 1998: 234).

During Houlouf phase B, from 1650 CE onward, the Houlouf chiefdom, sandwiched between the expanding Imperial Bornu state and the rising competitor of the Lagwan paramount chiefdom, lost its autonomy and became a peripheral center of the Lagwan Kingdom. The Latter conquered Houlouf, Kabe, Kala-Kafra, Tilde, and Jilbe polities along its northern and northwestern boundary as buffer to the expansionist ambitions of the rising powerful Bornu Empire. The latter defeated and conquered all Chadic polities—chiefdoms, Sao-Gafata, Sao-Tatala, etc. along the southwest shore of lake Chad and most of the north-central Chadic area, imposed tributary relationships to the Wandala kingdom in the south, and the Hausa city-states in the west. The other north-central Chadic polities consolidated their respective territories as three paramount chiefdoms emerged from the long-term peer-polities interaction that operated in the Chadian plain during the major part of the second millennium CE. The Makari chiefdom in the northwest was conquered and annexed as a province of the expanding Bornu Empire in the sixteenthcentury. The Mser chiefdom, in the central and eastern part of the Chadian plain, with its center at Kusseri was conquered in the sixteenth century by Bornu troops, turned into a dependent province (protectorate), with Bornu officials appointed to supervise the local government and ruler. And finally, the Lagwan kingdom, in the southeast, with its capital city at Logone-Birni, preserved part of its political autonomy but was tributary to both the Bornu and Bagirmi kingdoms. Both "superpowers" were archrivals, constantly competing for regional primacy during almost two centuries, from the late seventeenth to the end of the nineteenth century, very frequently using the Lagwan kingdom territory for troops maneuvers and battle ground.

In the Western Chadic area, the Hawsaland was conquered in 1510 by a Songhai expeditionary force led by Askia Mohammed. Katsina, Kano, and Gobir became for a short time, tributary states, with a relative of the Songhai ruler appointed as vice-regent (Cartwright 2019, Gronenborn et al. 2012). At the same time, Hawsa city-states launched predatory raids to the south as far as the Benue Valley against Bauchi, Gongola, Jukun, and Yawuri (Cartwright 2019). After the demise of Songhai, the Bornu kingdom became politically dominant over Hawsaland and exacted tribute (Sutton 1979).

A coalescence of mountain dwellers and plains dwellers formed the Wandala kingdom, with its capital city shifting successively from Keroua to Doulo and finally Mora (Barkindo 1989, Chetima 2018, Hallaire 1965, MacEachern 1993, 2012, Mohammadou 1982, Vincent 1991). Archaeological surveys and excavations conducted by the Mandara Archaeological Project (David 2012, MacEachern 1996) mapped some 123 sites in northern Mandara ranging from the Late Stone Age to the twentieth century. The collected data show no evidence of human occupation of the Mandara highlands before the first millennium BCE. Tested sites like Doulo Igzawa (middle of the first millennium BCE), Manaouatchi-Grea (390 BCE–560 CE), and Ghwa Kiva (1250–350 to 800–200 BCE), are located along the massif periphery. "Known sites from the period after 750 BCE are located close to inselbergs and along the Mandara foothills. There continues to be no indisputable evidence for occupation of the highlands" (MacEachern 2012: 42).

Settlement was relatively dense in the plain. Chadic-speaking communities of mound-dwellers cultivating sorghum and rearing livestock adopted iron metallurgy during the first millennium BCE, displaying in the material culture rubric cultural continuity from earlier times. Mound settlements expanded considerably in the plain between 400 and 1400 CE. Occupation started trickling into the Mandara Highlands in the latter part of the first millennium CE as indicated by such sites as Ngoye Kirawa (780–1020 CE). The first half of the second millennium CE witnessed divergent evolutionary pathways in the plain and the mountains.

The construction of massive stone walls, called DGB (*diy-geb-bay* = ruins of chiefly residence in local Mafa language) developed in a limited portion of the northern Mandara (David 2008, MacEachern 2012a, 2012b). These constructions concentrated in a small territory were built between the thirteenth and the seventeenth centuries. DGB-1 and DGB-2 are only 100 m apart; and the most remote, DGB-8, built in the fifteenth century, is located 3.2 km southeast of DGB-1/2. and the former, the largest one, measuring 3,600 square meters (60 x 60 m). Parts of some of these monumental constructions were used for habitation and domestic activities, very likely in combination with yet to be determined ritual performances. Rainmaking rituals have been suggested (David 2008). But the multiphase arrangements, the architectonic modifications, and the heavy labor investment make such a simple and straightforward explanation unlikely. The "chiefly residence" denomination given to these sites raised interesting questions. Why are they concentrated in the same small area? Are they sequential or contemporaneous? There are logical answers to these two questions, but it is not certain that they are historically accurate. Concentration can be explained by the strong symbolic charge of certain part of communities' cultural landscapes. In such a case, emerging prestigious lineages will invest in monumental constructions there to build a clientele. Such process can operate either sequentially, with only one settlement in operation at a time, in a succession of aspiring lineages leaders' construction events, or simultaneously, with aspiring lineages leaders scrambling to make their presence visible in the core of their global cultural landscapes.

Parallel to the DGB phenomenon, the formation of the proto-Wandala state was kicked off at Keroua, an already inhabited locality at the end of the first millennium CE. Connections and exchanges with the Mandara Mountains provided iron to the emerging polity. As is the case for Bornu with Sayf ben Di Yazan, founder of the Sayfawa dynasty, and *Hausa-bakwai* with Bayajida, the founder of the Hausa ruling families, the "culture heroes who founded the ruling dynasty of the Wandala through their marriage with locals are said to have come from the North and East, from Yemen for example" (MacEachern 1993: 255).

During the first half of the second millennium CE, highlanders (montagnards) and lowlanders (in this case Wandalans) were linked by complementary economic exchanges. The Wandala kingdom emerged during the sixteenth century, immediately under the Bornu shadow (Barkindo 1989, Chetima 2018, Hallaire 1965, MacEachern 2015, Mohammadou 1982). Its rulers and elite converted to Islam at the beginning of the eighteenth century through the influence of Bornu clerics. Its predatory expansion through slave-raiding for the count of the Bornu kingdom resulted in the sharp depopulation of the plain and an influx of settlers in the Mandara highlands. The high population density and the practice of intensive agriculture in the Mandara Highlands from the second half of the first millennium CE to the present were a consequence of Wandala's constant predatory pressures. Hallaire captures the tragedy of the Wandala kingdom in the following terms: "a small militaristic state, famous for its cavalry, in perpetual war against the highlanders—montagnards—, against its powerful neighbor and ex-overlord of Bornu, then, in the nineteenth century against the Fulani" (Hallaire 1965: 58).

The area inhabited by speakers of southern central Chadic languages witnessed divergent evolutionary trajectories: the formation of a centralized ranked predatory social formation with the Wandala kingdom, its capital shifting from Keroua, Doulo, and finally Mora in the nineteenth century; chiefly formations, initially with the DGB phenomenon, adopted later by some populations of the plain and inselbergs along the Mandara periphery; and finally, autonomous but interlinked families and lineages homesteads distributed all over the Highlands landscape.

CONCLUSION

This chapter has addressed the long-term evolutionary trajectories of speakers of Chadic languages communities predominantly located in the southern part of the Chad Basin, and distributed today in three African states, the Republic of Chad in the east, Cameroon in the center, and Nigeria in the west. There is convincing genomic and linguistic evidence pointing to the East-African origins of initial groups of speakers of Proto-Chadic languages. These initial groups, adjusting to long-term Holocene climate fluctuations and practicing livestock husbandry drifted westward along the multiple tributaries of the Shari River to settle in the Mid-Holocene Shari Delta and the southern shore of the Mid-Holocene Lake Chad. From this Proto-Chadic homeland and following the steady shrinkage of Lake Chad, they expanded west, north, and east, generating in the process distinct communities of speakers of proto-western, proto-central, and proto-eastern Chadic languages. The archaeology of speakers of eastern Chadic area is nonexistent, and historical research is very limited. Territories of speakers of Central and western Chadic languages have witnessed more intensive archaeological and historical research, providing most of the data mobilized in the discussion.

The presence of Late Stone Age foragers dated to 8000–6000 BP is documented at Konduga along the Maiduguri-Bama-Limani-Bongor ridge—the Early Holocene Mega-Chad shoreline—in the south, and the Dufuna dugout in the Yobe River Valley in the north.

The recorded early pastoralist sites can be relied upon to suggest the drift and expansion of speakers of proto-Chadic languages. The Mblabli and Bama-Road site (7000–4000 BP) along the Early Holocene Mega-Chad shoreline may have been part of the initial settlement of speakers of proto-Chadic languages in the Chad Basin. Shilma and Gajiganna (4000–3000 BP) in the north and west point to the northwest expansion of speakers of proto-western Chadic languages. And finally, Deguesse and Krenak (3900–2000 BP) evidence the northward expansion of speakers of proto-central Chadic languages.

With significant chronological overlap and starting from 4000 BP, sedentary mixed-farming villages adopted iron metallurgy. They practiced agriculture and livestock husbandry, as well as hunting, fishing, and wild plants gathering, and spread all over the Chadian plain. These communities were all connected by long-distance exchange networks (Holl 2002). Stone raw material from the Mandara mountains and surrounding areas is found in all mound sites in the stoneless Chadian plain. Intensive fishing, fish-smoking, and salt production installations from the Houlouf region contributed to the interregional circulation of foodstuff (Holl 2002). Copper and alloyed copper objects, carnelian, and glass beads were imported from the surrounding lands, the Azelik-Teggida-n-Tesemt, the Tilemsi Valley, the Nupe territory, as well as North Africa and the Near East. They displayed sophisticated levels of craftmanship with incipient craft specialization. Pottery production reaching its peak with manufacture of polysemic terra-cotta figurines and copper/alloyed jewelry and status objects (Lebeuf and Lebeuf 1977, Holl 1988, 2002). The combination of all these processes triggered incipient urbanization leading to the emergence of central earthen-walled settlements in the first half of the second millennium CE.

Peer-polity interaction involving rivalry but also alliance sustained the emergence of ranked centralized power structures. Such developments are well documented in the northern, southern central, and western Chadic languages areas. It is the case for the emergence of Kotoko princedoms, chiefdoms, and kingdoms in the north-central Chadic languages area, the *Hausa-bakwai* and other city-states in the western Chadic languages area, and finally, the DGB sites of the Mandara Highlands and the Wandala kingdom in the south-central Chadic languages area. Less centralized political organizations based on relatively autonomous lineage homesteads also took shape during that period.

The intensification of interregional exchanges and long-distance connections accelerated urbanization, and the sustained expansion of Islam by traders and traveling scholars triggered quite comparable processes in Africa's Sudano-Sahelian belt. The convergence of all these dynamic processes resulted in a succession of emergence and collapse of multinational states, also called empires.

The Mali Empire (1200–1450) inaugurated that unstable imperial process based on predatory expansion and "wars without end" (Reyna 1990). The collapse of Mali in mid-fifteenth century provides room for the formation and rise to regional primacy of the Songhai Empire. Despite claims of "1000 years old Sayfawa dynasty" based on the misinterpretation of the transcribed "Epic of the Sayfawa rulers" (Holl 2000), Bornu was one among many interacting social formations along the southern shore of Lake Chad in the late fifteenth and early sixteenth centuries. Lake Chad completely dried up during the "Little Ice Age" (ca 1400–1600 CE), triggering important regional population redistribution. Shuwa-Arabs originating from the Nile Valley arrived in the Chadian plain around 1350 CE (Holl 2003). Kanem population shifted from the east to the southwest shore of the lake, bringing speakers of proto-Kanuri language in conflict-ridden contact with the northernmost speakers of central Chadic languages, the Sao-Ngafata, and Sao-Tatala. In the aftermath of the foundation of the Kanuri kingdom with its capital at Birni-Ngazzagamo, Bornu rulers launched a program of conquest and systematic expansion that was opposed and countered by Bagirmi kingdom with its capital at Massenya on the east bank of the Logone river. In an endless succession of military campaigns, *Mai* [King in Kanuri language] Idriss Alawma who ruled from 1564 to 1596, conquered and annexed rival Chadic polities in the Yobe River Valley and southwest shore of Lake Chad, imposed tributary relations to Hawsa city-states in the west and the Wandala kingdom in the south, extended the Bornu empire as far north as Bilma oasis and Fezzan. He was injured and died after direct confrontation with Bagirmi troops in 1596. Enslavement to feed the high demand of indentured labor of the Arabo-Muslim world fueled all political formations' predatory expansion. It is in that context that the Wandala kingdom, initially a Bornu vassal state, became its handmaiden for the provision of enslaved individuals, triggering by the same token the depopulation of the plain and the extensive colonization of the Mandara Highlands. The Lagwan kingdom, through the payment of two sides tribute to Bornu and Bagirmi, managed to keep a certain autonomy. Power shifted from the Sayfawa to the Kanemiyin dynasty at the beginning of the nineteenth century in the aftermath of the Sokoto Jihad, with a new capital built at Kukawa, almost on the Chad lakeshore.

The weakened and divided kingdom was easy prey for Rabbeh, an adventurer and enslaved trader from Sudan, who was at his turn defeated by French colonial troops in 1901 at Kusseri. Despite changing rulers, Chadic polities were particularly resilient and able to survive the succession of political regimes. The vestiges of this resilience are still visible in the "political architecture" of Kotoko princedoms in Cameroon, "Montagards" princedoms in the Mandara mountains, and Hausa city-states in North-Central Nigeria.

Chapter 4

Origins and Expansion of Speakers of Bantu Languages

The Formulation of the "Bantu Question"

INTRODUCTION

The Bantu Expansion is the "most important demographic, linguistic, and technological event in Sub-Saharan Africa" (Quintana-Murci et al. 2008: 1601). What has come to be known today as the "Bantu Question" was shaped in distinct and successive stages. In the nineteenth century, research focused initially on the census and classification of African languages. Then, its scope expanded to incorporate historical questioning in addition to and beyond the linguistic dimension. Researchers began to ask questions about the reasons for the strong similarities between certain languages and suggested scenarios to account for the present-day distribution of certain languages. Historians joined the questioning, and archaeological investigation was grafted onto the historians' questioning, bringing a new diachronic depth to the initial topics. Over the last few decades, bioanthropological and paleoenvironmental studies have joined the mix. With a little hindsight, one could in summary say that the Bantu question is the result of successive punctuated balances between population dynamics and environmental dynamics. This is a phenomenon of long-term demic expansion, stochastic but directional.

Language Distribution in Africa

Africa presents the highest linguistic diversity of all continents. There are 1,800 to 2,000 African languages depending on the differentiation criteria one relies on (Blench 2006). They are divided into four large families, the geographical distribution of which is in the form of large West/Northeast–East/Southeast diagonal bands (fig. 4.1).

The Afro-Asiatic family that spans the north of the continent, from the Horn of Africa to North Africa via the Sahara, includes around 200 languages. The Nilo-Saharan family with its 140 languages is found in the north-central and eastern part of the continent. The Niger-Congo family with over one thousand languages covers a third of the continent and includes two branches, the Niger-Congo A branch in West Africa and the Niger-Congo B branch (Bantu languages) in Central, East, and southern Africa. The Khoisan family comprises some thirty languages, most of which can be found in the western part of southern Africa with small pockets in East Africa. And finally, the Austronesian family, represented by Malagasy, is found only on the large

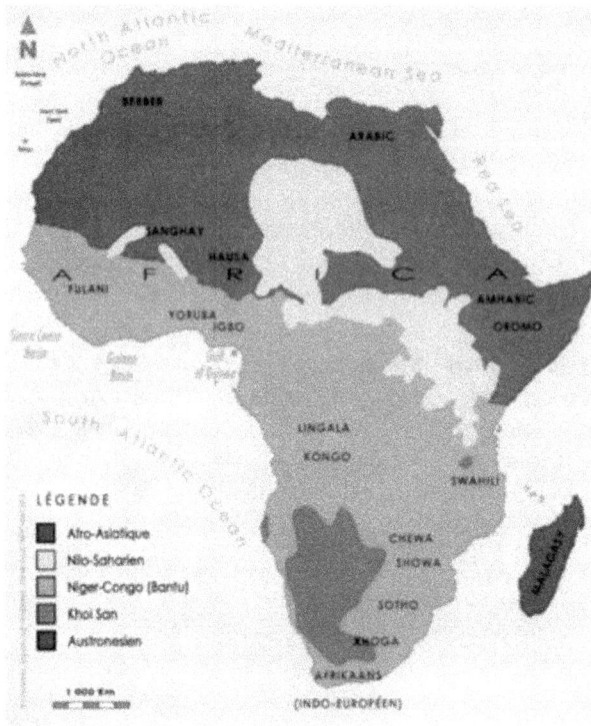

Figure 4.1. Distribution of major linguistic families in Africa. *Created on the author's behalf*

island of Madagascar on the southeastern flank of the continent. The distributional patterns of these large linguistic families alluded to above is clearly the result of historical processes, some of which, such as the Berber and Arab expansion, or the colonization of Madagascar (see part 2), are fairly well documented. Others are much less so. On a strictly cartographic level (fig. 4.1), the encapsulation of Khoisan by the Bantu languages is evocative of the process that generated this distribution. It is all the processes that led to the present-day distribution of speakers of Bantu languages that are examined in this chapter.

The "Bantu Question"

Three researchers were instrumental in shaping the Bantu question as it is known today. They are: Wilhelm Bleek (1827–1875), Henry Harry Hamilton Johnston (1858–1927), and Carl Friedrich Michael Meinhof (1857–1944). The first, Wilhelm Bleek, a German linguist and pioneer of comparative linguistics in Africa, undertook comparative research on different languages in the middle of the nineteenth century. He studied the relationship between Bantu and Xhosa languages, wrote a Zulu grammar, grouped West African languages together, and identified a Bantu language family spanning from central to southern Africa. The second, H. H. H. Johnston, explorer, scientist, and British colonial administrator, hypothesized the existence of an ancient population originating from West Africa and speaking an ancestral Bantu language (Johnston 1886, 1919), which would have spread by diversifying into East Africa. And the third, C. F. M. Meinhof (1906), German linguist and professor at the School of Oriental Studies in Berlin, developed research into the comparative grammar of Bantu languages and reconstructed a hypothetical ancestral Bantu language (*Ursprache*). He crafted the first general classification of African languages, a book that was authoritative in Africanist linguistic circles until 1955.

Languages, Populations, and Environment

The low degree of differentiation between the hundreds of Bantu languages recorded from the Nigeria/Cameroon border areas to the tip of South Africa suggests this diversification to be relatively recent, a few millennia ago at most. H. H. H. Johnston and C. F. M. Meinhof envisioned the existence of an Ancestral Bantu language that would have spread by diversifying into the rest of the subcontinent. However, the processes leading to the observed results remained completely obscure and many questions were raised. What was the area of origin of the initial speakers of Bantu languages? Could the observed dispersion of the Bantu languages be the result of a movement of populations? Could these be the cumulative results of linguistic borrowings flowing in all directions and leading to strong similarities in vocabulary, grammar, and syntax over a vast region? These questions, refined over time, have mobilized several generations of researchers from different disciplinary fields.

J. H. Greenberg (1955) and M. Guthrie (1967–1971) spearheaded the development of systematic research in Bantu linguistics. The former located the area of origin of speakers of Bantu languages along the Benue Valley in the Nigeria/Cameroon border area. The latter situated it in the southeast of the Congo Basin. The work of classifying African languages in general and Bantu languages in particular continued unabated from then on, and the debate generated by the differences between the Greenberg and Guthrie approaches were addressed during an international multidisciplinary conference "The Bantu Expansion" organized by the CNRS (Centre National de la Recherche Scientifique) in Villiers in France in 1977 (Bouquiaux 1980). Jan Vansina's opening remarks in his review of the three-volume *L'Expansion Bantoue* edited by L. Bouquiaux et al., according to which: "by now, I suspect, many historians are tired of the Bantu Expansion. It confuses many and they must wish that the question would just fade away, to reappear again once a consensus has been reached first among linguists and then between them and archaeologists" (Vansina 1983: 127), reflects the general feelings of "Bantuists" yearning for a consensus in the early 1980s. He nonetheless emphasized in the rest of the review that such a posture is misleading. In the final part of the review, picking one of the final contributions to volume 3—Meeussen's views on Bantu expansion—he singles out that contributor's conclusion, writing "it could be that we will not be able ever to really be precise as to how the Bantu expansion took place," asking readers to keep that in mind (Vansina 1983: 129–130). As is normal in complex research questions, there were conflicting views on how to proceed. But final statements on a final solution to a history research problem are epistemologically unsound. Despite the diversity of theoretical stances and conflicting views, the "Bantu Question" clearly became since then a problematic on the expansion of speakers and the formation of the series of languages very close to each other (Vansina 1983, 1984, 1990, Eggert 2006) spread from Nigeria/Cameroon to Southern Africa.

Linguistic Phylogenetics

Historical linguistic research on Bantu languages is proceeding, raising new issues, formulating news hypotheses, and testing more precise languages classifications (Bastin et al. 1999, Bostoen et al. 2015, Curie et al. 2013, Whiteley et al. 2018). For Bostoen et al. (2015: 359) for example, "most internal classifications of Bantu languages are based on lexicostatistics, a method for generating language trees through the calculation of lexical distance between pairs in terms of percentages shared basic vocabulary." Comparative analyses of basic lexica are therefore not dealing directly with written words but rely on numerical symbols that feature non-replicable authority opinion. "Bantu language classification and historico-geographical spread remain unresolved, with multiple competing hypotheses. The main reasons for the lack of consensus lie in the muddled methods of historical linguistics and resulting bowblerizing of empirical data" (Whiteley et al. 2018: 3). It is difficult to disprove a reconstruction with empirical evidence. Joseph Greenberg bluntly formulated this issue as follows:

> There exists in linguistics no coherent theory regarding the general classification of languages. . . . Any notion that historical linguistics has an utterly rigorous method, however slow, which reconstructs linguistic history step by step with complete precision is sheer myth. (Greenberg 2005: 153)

Whiteley et al. (2018: 1) build on these observations to suggest a new approach to Bantu language classification based on methods derived from DNA sequence optimization algorythms, considering basic vocabulary as sequences of sounds. Words, not numerical symbols, are the object of analysis, and the basic vocabulary comparison is central to the research. In lexical analysis, the higher the word frequency in form and meaning shared between two languages, the closer their historical relationship. Using the Swadesh 100 words list, Whiteley et al. (2018) applied standard approaches to lexical data to identify sound shifts from presence-absence patterns among paired languages.

The results of their work support the late split hypothesis (to be explained later) and shows that there is a large clade of languages south and east of the rain forest with inferred common descent from an ancestor in the northwest, without identifiable West, Southwest, and East Bantu. Looked at from the standpoint of physical geography, "the results depict an ancestral spread south and southeast from the lower to the middle Congo-River, following rivers and river valleys, with migrations into East Africa plateau via the land bridge between Lake Tanganyika and Malawi" (Whiteley et al. 2018: 11).

Historians and the Bantu Question

R. Oliver (1966) attempted to reconcile the results of the work of M. Guthrie and J. Greenberg. He did this by identifying four successive phases of expansion of the Bantu languages (fig. 4.2) by adding some socioeconomic characteristics and the little archaeological data available at that time.

Figure 4.2. (A) Current model of the spread of Bantu languages; (B) R. Oliver adaptation of M. Guthrie expansion of Bantu speakers; (C) the initial model of Bantu expansion with the Eastern and Western streams. *Created on the author's behalf*

The model of expanding populations of speakers of Bantu languages practicing agriculture and iron metallurgy has gradually established itself. Researchers began to be interested in the possible routes of these populations' movements. A lexicostatistical study, using the Swadesh list (one hundred basic vocabulary words), carried out on 137 Bantu languages by Heine et al. (1977) established once and for all Greenberg's hypothesis as the most parsimonious. From the "Benué valley: Nigeria—Cameroon border zone" nuclear zone, and because of the presence of humid equatorial forest, we were then considering a first strategy to bypass the northern edge of the forest (fig. 4.2A).

This first series of early movements would have resulted in the formation of Eastern Bantu languages. A second axis of expansion is taking place along the western fringe of the equatorial forest, giving rise to the western Bantu languages (fig. 4.2C). The populations of speakers of the languages of these two branches would then have converged in the savanna area south of the equatorial forest. Expansion into the rest of the southern part of the continent was initiated from these latitudes, both along the coasts and inland, to reach Natal in South Africa in the early centuries CE. Archaeologists (Phillipson 1977, 1994) using linguistic reconstructions have developed scenarios for the settlement of the subcontinent (fig. 4.2C). Phillipson (1977, 1994) for example, brings together all the archaeological entities of the Great Lakes region and East Africa under the designation of the "Chifumbaze Complex." Farther south, T. Huffman (2007) makes a strong correlation between Eastern and Western ceramic and Bantu traditions.

The Debate: Objections and Refutation

Looked at from the perspective of research history, critics of the dominant model of the Bantu Expansion can be grouped into three categories, all of which contest the validity of the proposed migrations scenario. For Lwanga-Luniigo (1976), the concept of one-way migration, which has played a very important role in speculation about the history of Africa appears to be a real obsession. In his opinion, the "migrationist mania" has caused profound difficulties in the reconstruction of Bantu history. He considers the work of J. Greenberg and M. Guthrie to be only unconfirmed hypotheses. For him, the supposed migrations from West Africa to Central, East, and then South Africa never took place. In his opinion, in this immense space stretching from West Africa to South Africa, it is "almost impossible to determine the precise point of origin, archaeological data being scarce and uncertain, insufficient and unconvincing linguistics." He therefore suggests that populations have moved little but that widespread linguistic borrowings have resulted in the current distribution of Bantu languages (Lwanga-Luniigo 1976).

J. Vansina (1984, 1990, 1995) presented a series of objections quite similar to that of Lwanga-Luniigo but relying on more recent and much richer lexicostatistical data (Bastin et al. 1999, Eggert 2006: 313). These data collected from corpus of vocabularies from 440 out of 600 languages made it possible to construct seven tree models (Stammbaum model) according to the theoretical assumptions and statistical techniques used. The tree model has a certain rigidity and only allows the formation of new languages from mother languages without any hybridization. From this perspective, new languages are formed by successive stages of dialect formation, supported by geographic distancing—remoteness. In developing his method of "words and things," J. Vansina (1990, 1995) draws on the intertwining of observed word distributions to write a cultural history of the settlement in the humid equatorial forest. The waves propagation model (Wellen model), according to which "words and things" are propagated over vast areas, step by step, and from one dialect community to another, appears to him to be the best suited to make sense of the history of the Bantu languages and the present-day geographic distribution patterns. This model accommodates possibilities of hybridization as well as a multiple origin of new languages. Vansina (1995) therefore rejects the hypothesis of Bantu expansion and considers that the Bantu languages in fact constitute only a gigantic continuum of dialects. In other words, languages can spread while people remain stable, in the geographic sense of the term. From that perspective, there was no Bantu expansion in the classical sense of the concept, but multiple interlocked dynamics through which some languages are being formed while others are driven to extinction.

A testable reconstruction of the history of languages can only be done within the framework of a multidisciplinary approach. The fundamental question has always been how to craft appropriate research questions and put this multidisciplinary approach into practice. M. Eggert (1992, 2008) highlights what he rightly termed a vicious circle, relying on the case of David Phillipson's research. He outlines the successive adjustments of Phillipson's archaeological reconstructions to the different historical linguistics scenarios. For him, some linguists rely on the conclusions of certain archaeological syntheses to support the validity of their conclusions. And some archaeologists start from the reconstructions of some linguists to link past material culture with linguistic entities (Eggert 2008: 307–312). He acknowledges that there have been significant advances in research over the past three decades, but insists that archaeological research is still in its infancy in most of Central Africa and the humid equatorial forest zone. The available data on pottery, metallurgy, settlements, and lifestyles are not only very fragmentary but also widely scattered. The history of the occupation of the humid African equatorial forest is barely sketched:

> Empirical data rather than armchair reasoning are clearly required in order to reconstruct the settlement processes associated with the dispersal of Bantu languages. If dispersal was brought about by migratory movements—as the majority of Bantuists, archaeologists, cultural anthropologists, and historians argued—then we ought to search for whatever tangible evidence of these

migrations might have survived. With regard to the equatorial rainforest. . . . [in] Vansina's synthesis of where, when, and how Bantu languages came to be spoken, there was far too little non-linguistic evidence to be convincing. (Eggert 2008: 312)

This fully justified observation leads the author to formulate two suggestions. He believes that each of the disciplines involved in research on Bantu languages should comply first with the obligation to clarify its methodological expectations and resolve its empirical difficulties before allying itself with the others. "The obligation to first clear up one's own methodological and empirical difficulties before joining forces" (Eggert 2008: 321). Superficially, this suggestion, which appeals to common sense—also called "abstract empiricism"—appears reasonable at first glance. However, the process of scientific research does not operate that way. Expecting each discipline to solve its research questions before sharing results with others is a conceptual and methodological fallacy. Scientific research is an endless process in which principles, theories, and methods are in constant development. The solution of old puzzles begets new questions.

Eggert draws on the example of the state of archaeological research in Africa humid equatorial forest to support his suggestion. In his opinion, the absence of connections between the ancient and stylistically varied pottery traditions of the interior of the Congo Basin and the pottery of other regions both inside and outside of the equatorial rain forest is a fundamental problem that should be solved first. This surprising proposition is based on the postulate of unambiguous relations between population, language, culture, and pottery. In other words, the establishment of genealogical links between the various prehistoric "ceramic traditions" of Central Africa is a sine qua non condition for any attempt at a multidisciplinary approach to the Bantu question: "until archeology can solve this specific problem, archaeologists should not actively participate in any debate on 'Western Bantu expansion'" (Eggert 2008: 321).

It is difficult to understand how the resolution of a question of chronology of all ancient ceramic traditions of the humid equatorial Africa rain forest constitutes a sine qua non condition for the participation of Central Africa archaeologists in the multidisciplinary investigation of the expansion of speakers of Bantu languages. Pottery is only a minute subset of empirical archaeological data. Many other data categories can be mobilized in this investigation. Suggesting a moratorium on multidisciplinary research while waiting for the resolution of the relationships between and chronology of pan-equatorial Africa rain forest ceramic traditions is clearly misleading. Disciplinary isolationism is a dead end. On the contrary, the multidisciplinary approach should be amplified by integrating bioanthropological, paleoenvironmental, archaeological, and cultural anthropology and historical research. In addition to comparative and historical linguistics, these disciplinary fields make decisive contributions to the understanding of different facets of the expansion of speakers of Bantu languages (Holl 2015, 2017).

DECIPHERING BANTU SPEAKERS'
POPULATION DYNAMICS

Linguistics and history have played a foundational role in framing the "Bantu question." Both disciplines have generated elaborate research protocols to understand and explain that issue. Archaeology was grafted to the topic but operated up to a certain point in a circular logic emphasized by M. Eggert. Linguistic findings were used to make sense of archaeological data, and archaeological data were relied upon to validate linguistic reconstructions. All fields of scholarship have witnessed significant improvements in both theoretical and empirical methods and techniques. It is however, the entry of new ways of tracking evidence on the history of speakers of Bantu languages, in a kind of multidisciplinary new synthesis, that has now provided sounder explanations of the expansion of speakers of Bantu languages. Such new and complementary ways of addressing the Bantu Problem revolve around the rapidly growing field of genomics and ancient DNA (aDNA) research, the more sophisticated and higher resolution input of paleoclimatology and paleoenvironmental sciences, the renewed and more regionally focused archaeological research protocols, and finally, more integrated and systematic understanding of the dynamics of subsistence systems and social formations.

Genomics and aDNA perspectives

Despite significant progress in the last decade, Africa is still trailing behind as far as genomics and paleo-genomic research are concerned. The continent "remains under-studied with only 85 ancient genomes published . . . relative to 3500 from Eurasia" (Wang et al. 2020: 1). Despite that undisputable fact, however, thanks to the rapid progress in genomics and aDNA research, the different facets of bioanthropology are playing an increasingly decisive role in the reconstruction of human populations history in Africa and anywhere else. Genomic reconstructions of populations' relatedness make it possible to explore various aspects of human relationships and trace the genealogies of groups near and far. aDNA research provides critical specific time-place evidence backing genomic-derived reconstructed population scenarios:

Studying aDNA offers a unique opportunity to access genetic variation of past populations and enables us to put past populations in context of present day genetic variation. Human groups from all regions of the world, have unique histories of migrations, admixture, and adaptation, which has shaped their past. (Vicente and Schlebusch 2020: 8)

The accelerating pace of research on present and past African populations offers entries into African populations' interconnectedness (Berniell-Lee et al. 2009, Choudhury et al. 2020, Curie et al. 2013, Li et al. 2014, Gelabert et al. 2019, Lipson et al. 2020, Lombard et al. 2018, Prendergast et al. 2019, Quintana-Murci et al. 2008, Vicente and Schlebusch 2020, Wang et al. 2020, Schlebusch and Jakobson 2018, Schlebusch et al. 2017, Sengupta et al. 2020, Skoglund et al. 2017, Wang et al. 2020).

Learning from aDNA Research

As far as the deep history of African populations is concerned, the still modest but sustainably increasing aDNA research provides anchor data that can be contrasted with and compared to genomic data from modern-day Africans.

Lipson et al. (2020) reconstructed the genome-wide ancestry profiles of four children from Shumlaka, a foragers' site from Western Cameroon, located in the putative cradle of speakers of Bantu languages. The studied samples belong to two distinct chronological segments with two individuals each. The oldest sample is dated to eight thousand years ago and the younger one to three thousand years. The revealed genome-wide ancestry of these four individuals links them to contemporary West Central Africa foragers from Cameroon, Gabon, and the Central African Republic, with no relationship to speakers of Bantu languages. Lipson et al. (2020) inferred Africa-wide phylogeny reveals widespread admixture and three prominent radiations: 1) An early modern human split; 2) East African divergences; and 3) the expansion of ancestry associated with Bantu speakers.

The genome-wide aDNA analysis of sixteen prehistoric Africans by Skoglund et al. (2017) offers a comprehensive reconstruction of prehistoric Africa population structure. The processed data were collected from three Western Cape South Africa individuals (2300–1300 BP), four from coastal Kenya and Tanzania (1400–400 BP), one from interior Tanzania (3100 BP) and seven from Malawi (8100–2500 BP). The study reveals: 1) "an unknown cline of geographically structured hunter-gatherer population stretching from Ethiopia to South Africa; 2) a deep structure in West Africa predating the divergence of the ancestors of Southern Africa hunter-gatherers from other population lineages; and finally, 3) the profound impact of food producing populations. The last and third aspect emphasizes the difficulty of relying only on the genomics of present-day populations to reconstruct past African population dynamics (Skoglund et al. 2017: 67).

Schlebusch et al. (2017) analyzed genome-wide sequences of seven individual archaeological samples from Kwazulu-Natal: three two-thousand-year-old Stone Age foragers from Ballita Bay A, B, and Doonside and four 300–500-year-old samples from Iron Age individuals from Newcastle, Eland Cave, and Nfongosi. The foragers' genomes is similar to today's Southern San and place the divergence of modern humans at 350,000–260,000 years ago. Iron Age samples, on the other hand, are related to West Africans, and cluster "with groups from Angola, supporting the Late-Split linguistic hypothesis " (Schlebusch et al. 2017: 652).

Prendergast et al. (2019) analyze generated genome-wide aDNA from forty-one individuals from East Africa archaeological contexts. Three are dated to the Later Stone Age, thirty-one belong to the Early Pastoral and Pastoral Neolithic, one to the Iron Age, and six to the Pastoral Iron Age. The study features a four-stage model of Eastern Africa populations from the recent past. 1) Later Stone Age individuals are part of a forager genetic cline that stretched from Ethiopia to South Africa. 2) Early Pastoral and Pastoral Neolithic individuals are more closely related to present-day speakers of Afro-Asiatic languages. 3) Pastoral Iron Age individuals are related to present speakers of Nilotic languages. And finally, 4) the Iron Age child from Deloraine Farm in Kenya shares ancestry with West Africans, specifically, speakers of Bantu languages. In summary, "genome-wide data from 41 ancient eastern Africans show that archaeological complexity during the spreads of herding and farming is also reflected in genetic patterns, which indicate multiple movements and gene flow among ancestrally distinct groups of people (Prendergast et al. 2019: 9).

Wang et al. (2020), with its eloquent title "Ancient genomes reveal complex patterns of population movement, interaction and replacement in Sub-Saharan Africa," provides an accurate state of the "art" on Sub-Saharan Africa aDNA research. The study relying on food production strategies as a sampling tool presents the analysis of genome-wide data from twenty ancient Sub-Saharan Africans from Botswana (four individuals dated to 1000–1300 BP), Kenya (ten individuals dated to 3900–300 BP: three East African foragers, five Pastoral Neolithic herders, and two Iron Age farmers), Uganda (one individual dated to 400–600 BP), and the Democratic Republic of Congo (five individuals dated to 200–795 BP). The selected food production strategies are arranged along a temporal cline, with 1) Eastern and Southern Foragers groups; 2) Eastern African Pastoral Neolithic groups; 3) Iron Age groups; and finally, 4) Bantu Iron Age. The analysis highlights the contraction of diverse once continuous hunter-gatherers' populations and early admixture between pastoralists and foragers that predate Bantu ancestry in East Africa and southern Africa. "The data also reveal that this interaction between herders and foragers was very unbalanced, with hunter-gatherer ancestry entering pastoralist populations, but little flow in the other direction" (Wang et al. 2020: 6).

The aDNA research available so far features extensive hunter-gatherer populations all over the continent that ended up divided into Western, Central, and Eastern Africa subsets. The advent and expansion of food production triggered multilayered and differential admixtures, between farmers and foragers, herders and foragers, farmers and herders. Farmer-forager admixtures initially took place in West and East Central Africa via the expansion of speakers of Bantu languages and cascaded to reach Eastern and Southern Africa later. Herder-forager admixtures initially took place in Eastern Africa from Ethiopia-Somalia-North Kenya southward, reaching Botswana, Namibia, and South Africa later but before the arrival of Bantu farmers. And finally, farmers-herder admixtures essentially took place in Eastern and Southern Africa.

Forays into Genomics

With diverse methodologies, sampling strategies, and regional coverages, most of the selected genomic case studies support the reconstructions derived from Sub-Saharan Africa aDNA research (Alves et al. 2011, Breniell Lee et al. 2009, Castrì et al. 2009, Coelho et al. 2009, Gelabert et al. 2019, Li et al. 2014, Quintana-Murci et al. 2008, Plaza et al. 2004, Sengupta et al. 2020).

Li et al. (2014) investigate the signal of Bantu expansion across a large panel of sub-Saharan African populations in an attempt to outline its timing and dispersals routes. They sampled six populations distributed into the three main Bantu groups: forty-eight individuals (Bulu and Lemande) from Cameroon for the Western Bantu; forty individuals from Pare (Tanzania) and Luhya (Kenya) for Eastern Bantu; and finally, forty-one individuals from Xhosa and Venda (South Africa) for Southern Bantu. Their study reanalyzes microsatellite DNA markers known to capture signatures of recent population history because of their fast mutation rates. The results support the observation of a primarily demic diffusion of Bantu-speaking people from West Africa and clearly visualizes the spread of West African genetic component throughout sub-Saharan Africa" (Li et al. 2014: 2019).

Quintana-Murci et al. (2008) investigate the origins of Central Africa foragers and farmers and their interaction. They looked at mitochondrial (mt)DNA variation in 1,404 individuals from twenty farming and nine foraging communities of Central Africa: 983 Bantu farmers and 421 forest foragers.

The mtDNA data presented . . . suggest that the ancestral population in Central Africa that eventually gave rise to the modern-day AGR [farmers] and PHG [Forest foragers] populations, consisted principally of L1c clades that have survived to give diverse forms observed among AGR, and essentially a single lineage among western PHG. (Quintana-Murci et al. 2008: 1601)

Sengupta et al. (2020) focus on the genetic structure and complex demographic history of South African Bantu speakers through the analysis of genome-wide data of over 5,056 individuals from eight major South Eastern Bantu groups. The study provides strong evidence for fine-scale population structure, aligned with geographic distribution and congruent with linguistic phylogeny. From a background of extensive southern Africa forager populations, there are: 1) small-scale migration of pastoralists from East Africa some two thousand years ago leading to the formation of the populations of Khoekhoe herders; 2) then the formation of Bantu-speaking agropastoralist communities; and finally, 3) the arrival of European colonists. The admixture of the Southeastern Bantu and the Khoi-San took place some forty-five generations ago (1300 years), with Tsonga and Venda showing the oldest admixture date. Iron Age genomes are aligned along a north-south cline, with increasing levels of Khoi-San ancestry. And finally, "the comparison of mtDNA and Y-chromosome haplogroups distributions shows evidence for relatively higher maternal gene flow from Khoi-San into all Southeastern Bantu groups, with significant variations between groups " (Sengupta et al. 2020, preprint).

Castrì et al. (2009) examine the variability of mitochondrial DNA within the Shona and Hutu groups. The data obtained are compared with that of other peoples who speak various Niger-Congo languages. The results show that the Shona and the Hutu are genetically very similar to all other populations of speakers of Bantu languages. The characteristics of the observed genetic variability, in particular a great genetic homogeneity and the high levels of gene flow, support the model of gradual expansion of the populations of speakers of Bantu languages as well as strong interactions between the different descendant groups.

Coelho et al. (2009) fill a gap in genetic research on populations on the western flank of the Bantu expansion with samples collected in Angola and Namibia. They analyze patterns of the Y chromosome (paternal line), mitochondrial DNA (maternal line), and genetic variation in lactase tolerance, and examine levels of interaction with Kung-San groups and other populations in Sub-Saharan Africa. Componential analysis of different aspects of these markers shows: 1) that the gene pool of southwestern Angola derives from the western flank of central Africa; 2) that the genetic pool of Herero and Kuvale pastoralists results from strong interactions with the Kung-San lineages and presents a mutation favorable to the digestion of milk, probably originating in the non-Bantu zone of East Africa; 3) that demographic growth for both men and women had been sustained after the separation of the eastern and western branches which would have taken place four thousand years ago; and finally 4) that male populations were generally smaller with relatively low migration rates, suggesting patrilocality, female hypergamy, and exogamy.

Berniell Lee et al. (2009) look at the genetic and demographic implications of the Bantu expansion via paternal lineages. They carried out an analysis of a large collection of Y-chromosome markers—forty-one single nucleotide polymorphism (SNP) and eighteen short tandem repeat (STR)—in 883 individuals sampled from twenty-five populations of Cameroon and Gabon, twenty-two Bantu-speaking communities and three rain forest hunter-gatherers. The sample is made of unrelated males from twenty-one Gabonese populations, twenty Bantu foragers and one forest forager and four Cameroonian ones, two Bantu-Fang and Ngumba—and two foragers—Baka and Bakola. The analysis reveals "a recent origin for most patrilineal lineages in West Central African populations most likely resulting from the expansion of Bantu-speaking farmers that erased the more ancient Y-chromosome diversity found in this area . . . some traces of ancient paternal lineages are observed in these populations, mainly among hunter-gatherers" (Berniell-Lee et al. 2009: 1581). The data also reveal predominant maternal gene flow from foragers to Bantu farmers, "suggesting that the demic movements associated with the Bantu expansion involved more males than females " (Berniell-Lee et al. 2009: 1587).

The work of Montano's team (2011) also focuses on the Y chromosome of populations found in Nigeria, Cameroon, Congo, and Gabon. The sample includes 505 donors from seventeen populations. The results show an absence of correlation between genetic variation and linguistic diversity. They also contradict the dominant conception, which makes speakers of Bantu languages a group of homogeneous populations whose gene pool would have been formed during a relatively recent phase of expansion. The genetic heterogeneity observed in the Cameroonian portion could however be due to the presence of non-Bantu populations. Finally, the study highlights important differences in local demographic histories that would support the hypothesis of a much earlier triggering of the expansion of speakers of Bantu languages.

Alves et al. (2011) aim to show that the expansion of the Bantu populations is a relatively recent and rapid phenomenon. Nineteen Bantu populations from Mozambique to Angola were sampled. New analytical methods allow better measurement of genetic variations between populations on a transcontinental scale. The obtained results show very high genetic homogeneity of the main populations in the sampled geographic area. There are, however, a few more strongly differentiated populations: the Chopi of Mozambique, the Kuvale of Angola, and the Yao and Mwani in northern and the Nyungwe and the Sena in southern Mozambique. The great genetic proximity demonstrated indicates strong interactions between all these southern savanna populations. It is, however, difficult to reconcile these findings with the old models of separation between the eastern and western branches.

Plaza et al. (2004) analyze variations in mtDNA in Angola. This country, where contact was made with the Khoisan populations, is considered the head of the southernmost expansion of the Western branch. The results show that more than half of the mtDNA pool in the sampled region comes from West Africa, about a quarter from Central Africa, and 16 percent from East Africa. The study also detected the signal of large gene flows coming from Southeast Africa, showing that the so-called western and eastern branches were not separate entities south of the present forest. Other works present more nuanced results, particularly in the northwestern margins of the equatorial rain forest, the area of origin of the "Ancestral Bantu" (Berniell-Lee et al. 2009, Gelabert et al. 2019, Montano et al. 2011).

Genomic and aDNA research support the demic expansion model (De Filippo et al. 2012; Pakendorf 2011). The situations are much clearer on the southern and eastern flanks of the area of expansion of speakers of Bantu languages. They are much less so on the northwestern flank, the Niger Congo A and B contact zone, and the area of origin of speakers of Bantu languages. However, the short genetic distances observed for populations distributed globally south of the equator rather indicate a relatively recent expansion and, all things considered, relatively rapid. What would have been the triggering mechanisms of the expansion of the Bantu-speaking peoples?

Climate Change and Paleoenvironmental Dynamics

In their remarkable synthesis of the state of paleoenvironmental research in Atlantic Equatorial Africa during the last four thousand years BP, Vincens et al. (1999) outlined the congruence between pollen records and hydrological and hydrobiological data demonstrating "that an arid event has been the primary driving factor of this change, responsible of the main feature of the modern landscapes" in the covered study area. They show that all the investigated sites featured forested landscapes of two kinds between 4000 and 3500 years BP: mainland forests with a semi-deciduous facies on the one hand, and dense swamp forests on hydromorphic soils on the other hand. An abrupt vegetation change occurred from 3000 to 2500 years BP, resulting in fragmented forest with isolated enclosed savannas. That episode is followed by forest expansion from the existing refugia during the last millennium (Vincens et al. 1999: 881–82).

The significant intensification of paleoenvironmental research in Equatorial Africa over the past three decades (Bostoen et al. 2015, Brncic et al., 2009;

Desjardins et al. 2020, Giresse et al. 2020, Maley, Brennac 1998; Maley 2001; Maley et al. 2017, Lezine et al. 2013; Vincens et al. 2010) has confirmed and supported the pioneer synthesis of Vincens et al. (1999) and provided an expanded database of higher-resolution environmental information.

Numerous lacustrine and marshlands sequences—from lakes Barombi Mbo and Ossah in Cameroon, Lake Sinnda in western Congo, and Mopo Bai swamp in the Democratic Republic of Congo—were sampled (fig. 4.3). The data obtained allow researchers to reconstruct the broad lines of environmental changes during the second half of the Holocene. During the Holocene period, the humid equatorial forest of Central Africa experienced its maximum extension around 6000 BP. It then spanned the entire Adamawa Plateau. Since then, climatic crises have resulted in major setbacks. A broad array of paleoenvironmental data, essentially sedimentological and palynological obtained from deep coring in lake beds and swamps, are available from sites

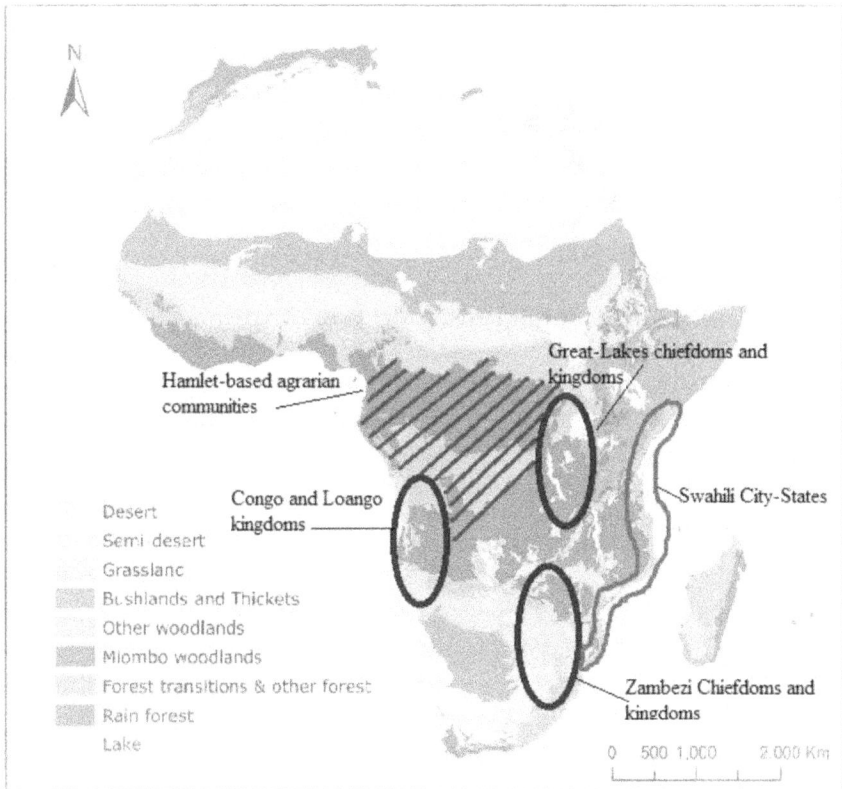

Figure 4.3. Distribution map of Bantu speakers' social formations in 1000–1500 CE. *Created by the author*

across Central Africa, in southern Cameroon, Democratic Republic of Congo, Western Congo and Gabon.

The first climatic crisis, called the "first fragmentation," is dated 4000 BP, and the second took place around 2500 BP. The first crisis, due to a sharp drop in rainfall (Neumann et al., 2012) resulted in a major contraction of the Equatorial Central African forest domain, marked by the expansion of savanna along its northern and southern peripheries, south of the Adamawa plateau in the north, along coastal Gabon in the west, and in the Niari in Western Congo (Giresse et al. 2020, Maley et al., 2012, 2017).

The second fragmentation, from 2500 to 2100 BP, is due to the installation of strong seasonality in the annual distribution of precipitation. This climatic regime with a strong dry season resulted from a southward shift of the inter-tropical convergence front (Bayon et al., 2012; Lézine et al., 2013; Maley et al., 2012; Neumann et al., 2012). The result of this major perturbation is forest fragmentation, a brief extension of savannas and rapid expansion of pioneer heliophilic species such as the oil palm, as well as a marked erosional phase. The landscape then consisted of "dry open forests with wooded savanna and dense rainforests 'micro-refugia' in favorable edaphic areas along rivers" (Maley et al. 2017: 3).

The Sangha River Interval (SRI) was formed during the second climatic crisis around 2500 cal yr BP (Giresse et al. 2020, Maley et al. 2017). "The opening of the SRI following the 2500 cal yr BP crisis constituted an important corridor for the rapid and large scale spread of Bantu speaking communities, who benefited from the major pioneering nature of the oil palm, that provided important food source. From the SRI, the Bantu were subsequently able to reach the inner Congo basin" (Maley et al. 2017: 7) as indicated by the site of Imbonga located at the center of the fluvial forest refuge and dated to 2350–2050 cal. yr BP (fig. 4.3).

It was during this period that pearl millet (*Pennisetum glaucum*), the remains of which were recently unearthed in southern Cameroon and central Congo (Kahlheber et al., 2009), spread to central and eastern Africa. The abrupt climate change that led to the fragmentation of the forest is also marked by strong erosion with deposits of coarse sedimentary materials, forming "stone-lines" in the sedimentary profiles. The reconstruction of the sequence of events that led to the fragmentation of the humid equatorial forest and the strong erosions observed give rise to interesting debates. For Bayon et al. (2012a; 2012b, 2019), the erosion intensification in the whole of the Congo Basin from 2500 BP is the consequence of massive forest clearing initiated by Bantu speaking farmers. For Maley (2012), Maley et al. (2017) and Neumann (2012), it was rather due to a set of natural causes resulting from radical climate changes dated to the second half of the third millennium BP. The issue debated by these researchers, "the relationship between the Late

Holocene Rainforest Crisis (LHRC) around 2500 cal yr BP in tropical West Central Africa and the main phases of Bantu expansion" (Giresse et al. 2020: 1), is either climate change impacted the equatorial rain forest and allowed easier migrations through a more open vegetation (Giresse et al. 2018, 2020, Maley et al. 2017) or the rain forest fragmentation was the consequence of human intervention (Bayon et al. 2019, Garcin et al. 2018).

Relying on data recorded from a ten-thousand-year-long sediment core from Lake Barombi in Southwestern Cameroon, Garcin et al. (2018) argue that the rain forest crisis was not associated with any significant hydrological change. Marshaling additional data from some 450 archaeological sites distributed in the northwestern half of the present-day equatorial Central African rain forest, they concluded that humans altered the rain forest ecosystem and left detectable traces in the sediments accumulated in the lake's deposit. Reviewing sedimentary data obtained from more than twenty locations in West and Central Africa: deep lakes in humid and montane forests, lakes and swamps marginal to the tropical forest, and shallow lakes and swamps, Giresse et al. (2018) show that the very low population density conveyed by the frequency and distribution of archaeological sites in the western portion of the equatorial rain forest was unlikely to cause the simultaneous environmental changes observed in Central and West Africa. Pioneer Bantu-speaking farming and iron-using communities took advantage of the fragmentation of the rain forest to spread initially through the SRI to the inner Congo basin, and progressively from there to the Great Lakes region, East and Southern Africa.

Human-Land Relationships along the Northwestern Margins of the Equatorial Forest in the Late-Holocene

The northwestern margins of the central Africa equatorial rain forest witnessed the initial steps of the expansion of speakers of Bantu languages. It is accordingly a crucial area to probe the characteristics and timing of human impacts on the vegetation and landscape during the Late Holocene. Recent high-resolution paleoenvironmental research has been carried out in southern Cameroon, northern Congo, and south-central Central African Republic (Biwole et al. 2015, Desjardins et al. 2020, Lupo et al. 2018, Lezine et al. 2013, Morin-Rivet et al. 2016, Morin-Rivat, Biwole et al. 2016, Vleminckx et al. 2014, Wotzka 2006). These projects provide better-grounded understanding of the processes that have impacted the environment, affected the present-day vegetation, and track human expansion and presence in the sampled areas.

Desjardins et al. (2020) address the "Natural versus Anthropogenic origins" debate on the cause of the large-scale environmental crisis that struck Equatorial Africa and presided over the genesis of the present-day wooded-grassland/forest mosaic. The investigation is carried through the analysis of isotopic signatures of soils organic matter in south-central Cameroon, in a study area that includes the large wooded grasslands and wooded grassland/forest mosaic zone of central Cameroon and the Grassfield plateaus between 4°25'–6°10'N; 10°05'–12°25'E and 600–1,800 meters above sea level (Desjardins et al. 2020: 2). They sampled twenty-nine sites including some from the Grassfield plateau. Relied upon as a vegetation marker, C^{13}, a heavy isotope, is less assimilated from the atmosphere by plants to build and maintain their tissues. Consequently, its residual proportion in soil organic matter is negative, with $\partial^{13}C$ [delta 13C] values ranging from -14 to -17%o in savanna soils to -24 to -27 in forest soils. The conducted analyses show that: 1) forest sites feature no significant alteration of the tree cover all along the Holocene, with however traces of contraction and/or expansion along the forest margins; 2) wooded grassland and grassland areas had more tree-covered landscapes than true forest in the Lower and Middle Holocene; and finally, 3) the forest mosaic/wooded-grassland experienced a lower-amplitude environmental crisis. The obtained results thus seem to "fit a climatic rather than anthropogenic origin of the vegetation opening in this region" (Desjardins et al. 2020: 1) of initial expansion of speakers of proto-Bantu languages.

Vleminckx et al. (2014), Biwole et al. (2015), and Morin-Rivat et al. (2016) examine the anthropogenic impact on current forest composition in southwest Cameroon in a study area located in the Ma'an National Park at 2° 10'–2°39' N, 10° 11'–10° 53' E East of the small city of Campo. They address three specific questions: 1) Does the forest composition reflect past disturbances? 2) If yes, are the recorded disturbances linked to human impact? And finally, 3) What is the spatial extent and the timing of these disturbances? Environmental data, specifically wood charcoal and oil palm endocarps, collected from twenty-five test pits distributed in three three-kilometer-long transects reveal the practice of slash and burn shifting cultivation as well as the presence of settlements of unknown size on hill slopes. Human activities are concentrated on two distinct periods: the earlier one lasting for one thousand years from 2300 to 1300 BP, and the latter one ranging from 580 BP to the present.

A field methodology similar to the one described above was used by Vleminckx et al. (2014) and Morin-Rivat et al. (2016) to collect the same category of environmental data in southeastern Cameroon, at 2° 30'–2° 39' N, 10° 42'–10° 76' E northeast of the Dja Reserve. Sixteen to nineteen test pits, also from three three-kilometer-long transects, set at 250 meters from one to next, revealed an occupation sequence starting from 2800 BP to the present with varying settlement intensity. Oil palm endocarps are ubiquitous in almost all test pits. The practice of slash-and-burn cultivation is confirmed along with possibly natural fires, as well as human settlement in the form of small hamlets on hill slopes. The regional settlement history is partitioned into four successive episodes: the first one with very low settlement intensity from 2800 to 2500 BP; the second with high settlement intensity for almost one thousand years, from 2300 to 1400 BP; the third with extremely low settlement intensity between 950 and 750 BP; and finally, the fourth and last episode with relatively moderate settlement intensity from 500 BP to the present.

Morin-Rivat et al. (2016) investigated patterns of environmental changes in the Sangha River Interval (SRI), a four-hundred-kilometer-wide region between northern Congo, south Central African Republic, and southeastern Cameroon. As a savanna corridor 2,500 years ago it may have facilitated the southward expansion of speakers of Bantu languages. Its vegetation consists predominantly of old growth semi-deciduous Celtis forest. The research project divided in two parts, examines the population and age structure of *Pericopsis elata, Terminalia superba, Erythrophleum suaveolens*, and *Triplochiton scleroxylon*, four "deciduous, emergent, pioneer light-demanding" (Morin-Rivat et al. 2016: 3) timber species monospecific in the SRI on the one hand. On the other hand, they look at the synchronism between the obtained timber information and paleoenvironmental, archaeological, and historical data. The population and age structure of the sampled timber species show the canopy trees to range in date from 142 to 164 years ago. Sedimentary and pollen analyses show the climate to have been "dry until 1200 CE, between 1250 and 1450 CE, and since 1850, with intermediate wet periods, in particular a long one between ca 1450–1850 CE." (Morin-Rivat et al. 2016: 4). $\partial^{13}C$ values from soil organic matter reveal two periods. The first one, a forest vegetation made of C3 plants until 1200 CE, and the second one from 1600 CE to the present, with grass cover, made predominantly of C4 plants. Human impact is indicated by an increase in fire use, both from the practice of slash-and-burn cultivation and natural fires, in 1300–1400 CE, and more substantially between 1550 and 1850 CE. Human presence indicated by pottery and iron production as well as salt exploitation is subdivided into three periods: the earliest one from 800 to 1100 CE, the second from 1300 to 1600 CE, and the third from 1700 to 1800 CE. Due to the impact of slave raiding and forced settlement along roads during the colonial period, human population density dropped considerably, allowing the recolonization of the savanna by forest trees.

The K. Lupo research team conducted a field project in the flank of the Ngotto Forest Reserve in the south-central Central African Republic along the northern margins of the Congo basin, in a 3,250-square-kilometer triangular study area (Lupo et al. 2018). Surveys and test excavations allowed the recording of ninety-eight artifact concentrations with pottery scatters, iron mining and smelting, and nineteen sites containing wood charcoal and charred oil palm endocarps. The collected data "provide a suite of chronometric age estimates that reflects persistent human use of the north-central Congo basin over the past 2500 years" (Lupo et al. 2018: 211). The study area human settlement history consists of three successive phases: 1) an early settlement phase by pottery-bearing groups by 2500 BP; 2) an intermediate low-density settlement phase between 1400 and 800 BP; and finally, 3) a later phase of intensive iron mining and smelting ranging from 1750 to 1840 BP particularly along the Lobaye River.

The sampled study areas arranged in a West-East mega-transect along the northern margins of the equatorial forest include: 1) the Ma'an National Park East of Campo, 2) the wooded grasslands and wooded grassland/forest mosaic zone of central Cameroon and the Grassfield plateaus; 3) the Mbang Site, northeast of the Dja Reserve in Southeast Cameroon; 4) the SRI in southeast Cameroon, northern Congo, South central Central African Republic; and finally, 5) the Ngotto Forest Reserve in the south-central Central African Republic. With minor variations, all these areas revealed the practice of slash-and-burn cultivation by pottery-bearing communities with knowledge of iron metallurgy, from c. 2800 BP to the present. Some researchers single out hiatuses in human histories in their study areas, pointing at population collapse as the explanation for the absence of radiocarbon dates in parts of the settlement sequence. The data from the Ngotto Forest Reserve and additional material from the northern Congo Basin does not support that conclusion. The current archaeological excavation methods used in Central Africa and the sampling strategies implemented in all the projects reported above do not allow to access individual site size. What the studies emphasizing occupation gaps "failed to consider . . . is that the summed distributions of calibrated radiocarbon dates, either as histogram or as probability-densities, reflect the probability that one of the sampled dates has a given range and not the population of humans or archaeological sites" (Lupo et al. 2018: 221).

Archaeological Perspectives

To avoid the circularity rightly pointed out by M. Eggert discussed earlier in the text, archaeological data have to be assessed first on their own merits for the identification and clarification of the settlement processes that resulted in the present-day distribution of Bantu-speaking farming communities. The detailed and comprehensive analysis of the initial settlement dynamics that took place in the northwestern half of the Central African rain forest is crucial, as what happened later in Eastern and southern Africa was literally the continuation of what started earlier in the northwest. It is generally accepted that Bantu expansion resulted in the spread of agriculture, iron metallurgy, sedentary lifeways, and pottery making to a certain extent, to mention but a few of these core dimensions (Holl 2015, 2017, Huffman 2007, Phillipson 2010).

The Spread of Agriculture

The cumulated Holocene settlements arranged into successive time-segments of different durations clearly feature a North/West—East/South clinal sites distribution. Very few sites, most located in Cameroon Southwest and coastal area—the eastern two sites belong to the Central Africa megalithic tradition—are dated to first half of the Holocene period. Settlements spread considerably East and South between 4500 and 2500 cal yr BP; a process that was amplified during the next two time-segments 2500–1500 and 1500–0 cal yr BP.

Agroforestry based on the exploitation of tubers, probably aerial and subterranean yams, was complemented by reliance on oil-plants trees such as *Canarium schweinfurtii* and pioneer plants like the oil-palm—*Elaeis guineensis*—recorded as plant macro remains in a large number of sites in the north and western half of the equatorial rain forest. The concentration of oil palm remains is particularly high in the SRI—Sangha River Interval. Cultivated pearl millet remains—*Pennisetum glaucum*—are found at Obobogo (3000–2100 cal yr BP), Biwambe-Sommet (2350 cal yr BP), Abang Minko (2200 cal yr BP) in southern Cameroon, as well as Boso Njafo (2270–2200 cal yr BP) in the central part of the Congo Basin in the Democratic Republic of Congo (Bostoen et al. 2015, Giresse et al. 2020). And finally, banana phytoliths—*Musa* sp.—are documented at Nkang (2500 cal yr BP), also in southern Cameroon. However, "because of this climate particularity, the initial farming system of pearl millet was no more than an episode of about 200–400 years in the settlement history of the Central African rain forest (Giresse et al. 2020: 11). The Northwest—South/southeast clinal distribution of pearl millet macro remains is obvious.

The Spread of Iron Metallurgy

New data collected during the last three decades point to unexpectedly early manifestations of metallurgical skills in different part of the continent (Bocoum 2004, de Foresta et al. 1990, Dupre and Pincon 1997, Essomba 1992, Eze-Uzomaka nd, 2009, Holl 2009, 2020, Pringle 2009, Zangato and Holl 2010). Early blacksmiths' workshops were excavated at Gbatoro in Djohong area in the Cameroons, and Oboui, in Ndio area in the Central African Republic (Zangato and Holl 2010). Both localities are situated in the northeastern part of the Adamawa plateau. Iron production activities are

156 Chapter 4

Table 4.1: Radiocarbon dates of the early ironworking sites in Northwestern Central Africa

Context	Sample	Lab No	Age BP (two sigma)	Calibrated BCE
Oboui blacksmith workshop				
Feature 6d	Charcoal	Pa 2223	3645+/-35	2135–1921
Feature 6c	Charcoal	Pa 2130	3635+/-35	2132–1900
Feature 6b	Charcoal	Pa 2095	3665+/-30	2136–1955
Feature 6a	Charcoal	Pa 2084	3675+/-30	2140–1958
Feature 6h	Charcoal	Pa 2203	3690+/-40	2198–1959
Feature 6j	Charcoal	Pa 2202	3995+/-40	2200–1965
Gbatoro blacksmith workshop				
Layer 2	Charcoal	Loean 132	3707+/-29	2153–2044
Layer 2	Charcoal	Pa 3835	3835+/-30	2368–2200
Gbabiri smelting site				
Layer 3 h2	Charcoal	OBDY 1515	2630+/-40	895–675
Layer 3 h1	Charcoal	Pa 1446	2670+/-40	902–794
Layer 4	Charcoal	Pa 1451	2680+/-40	906–797
Gbabiri blacksmith workshop				
Forge	Charcoal	Pa 1538	2640+/-40	895–773
Balimbe habitation site				
Layer 4	Charcoal	OBDY 1508	2980+/-40	1298–1026
Layer 5	Charcoal	OBDY 1111	3530+/-40	2135–1612
Bounboun habitation site				
Layer 4	Charcoal	Loean 135	3598+/-30	2025–1891
Betume habitation site				
Layer 5	Charcoal	OBDY 1112	4350+/-30	3490–2930
Nsukka Region, Nigeria				
Lejja	Charcoal	Ua 34416	1715+/-35	370–266
	Charcoal	Ua 34416	2370+/-40	520–410
	Charcoal	Ua 34415	4005+/-40	2571–2491

(Calibration IntCal04, (Reimer et al. 2004))

documented to have taken place as early as 3000–2500 BCE, in different contexts (table 4.1). It is the case in habitation sites like Balimbé, Bétumé, and Bounboun, smelting sites like Gbabiri, and forge sites like Ôboui and Gbatoro. The last two sites provide high-resolution data on the spatial patterning of blacksmiths' workshops dating from 2500 to 2000 BCE. As is the case for Gbatoro, the blacksmith workshop discovered at Oboui is particularly coherent in chronological and functional terms (table 4.1). The recorded installations include a forge furnace, a stone anvil for hammering the bloom, a clay vessel for quenching purposes, two charcoal storage pits, three refuse pits, and finally, one fire-place. All the steps of the forging *"chaine operatoire"* are represented in the excavated workshop. All the dated samples point to the same time segment, between 2300 and 1950 BCE.

Early iron smelting sites have also been recorded at Opi, Aku, Obimo, Obukpa, Owerre, Elu, and Lejja in the Nsukka region in southeastern Nigeria (Eze-Uzomaka 2009, nd.). The uncovered slag blocks weight 34 to 57 kilograms, with the oldest case dated to 2571–2491 CalBCE (Ua 34415: 4005+/-40 BP) (table 4.1). The massive evidence of early iron smelting activities in the Nsukka region are deeply embedded in local contemporary culture. "In the past, the chief or king of Lejja (Eze Lejja) is supposed to be descendant of a lineage of past smelters" (Eze-Uzomaka nd: 5). Strong links between political power and ironworking have been documented in Central Africa, among the Tiv, Margi, Sukur in Northwest, the Congo River Basin in the center, and the Great Lakes regions in the East (Dupre and Pincon 1997, Schmidt 2006, Vansina 1990). Early iron metallurgy evidence from Lejja in the Nsukka area (Nigeria), Gbatoro in Djohong area (Cameroon), and Oboui in Ndio region (Central African Republic), all dating to the late third/early second millennium BCE, point to the northern margins of the equatorial rain forest to have been a potential area of iron metallurgy invention in Africa (Holl 2009, 2020, Pringle 2009, Zangato and Holl 2010). These data reveal a dynamic picture of technological innovations with an indisputable north-south clinal distribution. Iron metallurgy evidence from Olinga in southern Cameroon is dated to 1096–910 Cal BCE and 700–370 CalBCE (Essomba 1992, Holl 2009: 419). These readings, initially contested as too early and unreliable, fit in the emerging evolutionary picture of a north-south gradient of iron metallurgy expansion. Iron metallurgy is present in Gabon from around 2600–2500 BP as indicated by the archaeological record of the Oyem, Moanda, and Otoumbi sites (Clist 1989), Congo (de Foresta (1990), and the Great Lakes region (Schmidt 2006).

Settlement Dynamics

It is now indisputable that Shum Laka, the oldest securely dated site in northwest Central Africa, was inhabited by forest foragers who adopted pottery use some five thousand years ago. The low-density archaeological coverage of this vast territory does not allow the reconstruction of empirically sound settlement dynamics and sites dispersals. The available data combining pottery analyses and settlement locations can nonetheless be used to outline some dispersals scenario to be tested in future research (Clist 1989, Clist et al. 2019, Clist, Kaumba et al. 2019, Huffman 2007, Phillipson 2010).

The excavated archaeological sites appear to have been mostly constituted of small hamlets during what is called the Neolithic/Early Iron Age. The Obobogo tradition recorded in Yaounde area in southern Cameroon is dated to 1000–600 BCE. Its pottery consists of open and closed forms with identical design arrangements on pots and bowls. Partly contemporaneous but latter cultural groups did emerge in Gabon, Congo, South Central African Republic, the central Congo Basin, and the Great Lakes region.

In the Congo Basin, the Imbonga tradition, documented on the left bank of the Congo River around Mbandaka, emerged in the second half of the first millennium BCE. Its signature material culture consists of pots and bowls, mostly flat based, decorated with rocked incisions and impressions. The Maluba/Batalimo tradition developed further north, lasted from 2150 to 1570 BP, with a distinctive array of decoration motifs and syntax on its pottery. The Ngovo tradition formed between the Congo River and the Angola border between 2200 and 1900 BP (Clist et al. 2019) provides new evidence showing that "during the EIA [Early Iron Age], the Lower Congo region of Central Africa had more regional variation in ceramic production than previously known." The hope to rely on pottery classification to clarify the expansion of speakers of Bantu languages as formulated in M. Eggert program has completely evaporated. Any correlation can only be made at the most superficial level, relying on almost ubiquitous decoration technique such as roulette and/or carved roulette impressions.

Four "pottery" traditions have been recorded in the Lower Congo region: the Ngovo Ware (420 cal BCE–130 CE), Kay Ladio ware (30–475 cal CE), Kitara Ware (230–524 Cal CE), and Gombe type pottery (340–765 cal CE). These traditions are partly/totally contemporaneous with coastal Atlantic Herringbone ware (198 cal BCE–766 cal CE) and Carinated Broadly Grooved Ware (253–585 cal CE). Interestingly, Kay Ladio Ware (30–475 cal CE) found in the wooded savanna "mark[s] the presence of the oldest known iron-using communities south of the Central Africa equatorial forest" (Clist et al. 2019: 521).

Finally, the Urewe tradition with dimple-base pottery and iron metallurgy is present in the Great Lakes region of the East Africa hinterland from 2500 BP on, at Gasiza I in Rwanda, Mirama in Burundi, and Katuruka in Tanzania. From there, speakers of Bantu languages reached the East Africa coast and spread south and southwestward (Huffman 2007).

Expansion Dynamics and Moving Frontiers

Linguistic, archaeological, and genetic data unambiguously show the expansion of speakers of Bantu languages to have resulted from demic diffusion processes with varying extent of admixtures with ancestral central Africa rain forest and ancestral Khoi-San foragers (Holl 2015, 2017). The dynamic processes that have triggered and sustained the expansion of Bantu-speaking populations, have however not been investigated systematically beyond the simple notion of migration (Grollemund et al. 2015, Russel et al. 2014). The forces driving expansionary population dynamics sit clearly at the interface of demography and subsistence. These structural relations, manifest in social organization, and methods and techniques of food production (Boserup 1965, Chayanov 1986, Darity 1980, Hammel 2005, Pollini 2014), can be relied upon to model the dynamics of the "Bantu moving frontier."

It goes without saying that expansion is triggered by population growth, with highs and lows. The speakers of Bantu languages admixed with forest foragers in the initial stages of the south/southeast expansion (Breton et al. 2021). The size of the initial settlements in southern Cameroon, Gabon, and Congo is not known but they were very likely in the range of small to large hamlets, connected by river courses and/or footpaths. Present-day communities of speakers of Western Bantu languages located in southern Cameroon and Gabon, the Bamileke, Bakoko, Bassa, Beti, Duala, Malimba, Yabassi, etc., have a series of coherent prefixed-identity names and tend to be organized into exogamic clans.

Les préfixes *ndo, ndog* ou *ndok* qu'on a dit être l'équivalent de *ba, ya, log, lok* et *long, bona* ou *bone*, ont non seulement les significations relevées plus haut, mais également d'autres significations comme "patrimoine de," "héritage de." (Tsofact 2006: 104)

[*The prefixes ndo, ndog, or ndok, said to be equivalent to ba, ya, log, lok, and long, bona or bone, have not only the meanings singled out above, but also other meanings such as "heritage from," "legacy of"* (my translation).]

Matrimonial alliances generate extensive networks and, depending on actual patterns of postmarital residence, sustain a constant circulation of men and women across connected communities. Among southern Cameroon Bantu however, postmarital residence is overtly patri-virilocal, with women leaving their parents to go live in the hamlet of their husbands' fathers. Accordingly, in the population dynamics dimension, demography, matrimonial networks, and patterns of postmarital residence sustain a nonlinear but constant flux and reflux of people from connected communities along moving frontiers, generating linguistic drift and the formation of new dialects and languages in the process.

As already suggested above, the subsistence of expanding speakers of Bantu languages included reliance on the exploitation of wild resources through hunting-gathering and fishing, and farming of grain (finger millet) and possibly tubers (yams). Such subsistence practices can be subsumed under the labels of agroforestry—protection and dispersal of useful trees (oil plants, *Elaeis guineensis* and *Canarium schweinfurthii*), horticulture through the practice of vegeculture, and grain agriculture (Boserup 1965, Darity 1980, Pollini 2014) through the practice of slash-and-burn cultivation. In her influential analysis of agricultural intensification, Boserup (1965) differentiated five stages arranged along increasing population densities: 1) forest fallow; 2) bush fallow; 3) short fallow; 4) annual cropping; and 5) multicropping. She has shown that forest fallow, at the lowest scale of agricultural intensification based on slash-and-burn practices, was the optimal agricultural strategy in low-density areas with available land.

Evidence for the use of fire for land clearing and agriculture dating from 3000 BP onward and coeval with initial expansion of Bantu farmers is now fully documented in Southern Cameroon and parts of Congo (Biwole et al. 2015, Morin-Rivat et al. 2016). Slash-and-burn agriculture, also called "shifting agriculture" or "swidden cultivation," "refers to land-use where a cropping period is rotated with a fallow period" (Pollini 2014: 1). It is an extensive land use, characterized by expansion over uncultivated land following population growth. The practice is highly rational. Forestland is cleared by fire. The burnt biomass provides nutrients that are deposited on the soil as ashes. The cropping of the cleared field lasts one to three years, with the fallow period usually three to twenty-five years (Boserup 1965, Darity 1980, Pollini 2014).

The interface between demography and patterns of subsistence is the core process in the expansionary dynamics of Bantu-speaking farmers. "When population density is low, land is abundant while labor is usually a strong limiting factor" (Pollini 2014: 3). The critical variable is accordingly labor, not land, making the recruitment and retention of people a key parameter in communities' sustainability and survival strategies. Chayanov's (1986) study of the demographic dynamics of Russian peasant communities at the beginning of the twentieth century has shown how the demographic evolution of a family affects labor demand and agricultural productivity. The consumer/producer (C/P) ratio of a newly formed couple drops sharply with the birth of their children [from 2/2 to 3/2 . . . 4/2 . . . etc.], and bounces back [4/3, 4/4] with the entry of the growing children in the family labor force. As inspiring as it is, Chayanov's analysis is based on the assumption of an autarkic nuclear family, a very unlikely social situation for the expanding Bantu farmers. "The Chayanov model of peasant economy is based on autarkic nuclear family household. Expansion to more complex households and kin groups common in peasant societies show that the sharp changes Chayanov observed in the Consumer/Producer ratio over the domestic cycle are smoothed by the intergenerational structure of complex households and extended kin groups" (Hammel 2005: 7043).

Expanding Bantu core social units may have been extended multigenerational families, polygamous families, or a combination of both. Unfortunately, central Africa archaeological research, generally based on small excavation units, does not allow a realistic assessment of early western Bantu settlement size. From what is emerging however, they were mostly small hamlet to small village size sites.

Available paleoenvironmental data indicate an acute climatic crisis between 3000 and 2500 BP, a crisis that triggered the fragmentation of the humid equatorial forest and the installation of the vast grass savannas. The Bantu expansion follows the fragmentation of the forest. Farmers, cultivating millet, have settled in the savannas and forest mosaic. The genetic data indicate a higher female mobility, with exogamy and tendency to patrilocality. The cumulative dynamics of agricultural, social and environmental systems suggest a model for the expansion of the speakers of Bantu languages. The initial cereal agriculture was carried out by shifting cultivation based on slash-and-burn practices (Biwolé et al. 2015, Morin-Rivat et al. 2016). Fields cultivated for one to three years are left fallow for three to twenty-five years. This is an extensive exploitation of territories with very low population densities.

The habitat would have consisted of small hamlets. In a stable demographic situation, daughter communities would form around mother communities, settling in similar environments. As long as there are sparsely populated territories, the increase in population will flow along corridors with optimal potential, preferably along hydrographic axes. Assuming a site-catchment of 5 kilometers in diameter per hamlet, a sustained population growth, and the creation of new hamlets located 5 kilometers from the previous one in each generation, one would have a periodic but sustained territorial expansion along a moving frontier. Such punctuated changes, derived from feedback loops between two dynamic systems, demography one the one hand, and subsistence on the other hand, do not require population pressure as such to take place. The combined dynamics of shifting slash-and-burn agriculture (Biwolé et al. 2015), population growth, the system of matrimonial alliances based on clan exogamy, and patri-virilocal postmarital residence maintain a constant flow of populations in space and time.

The settlement processes implemented by the expanding Bantu speaking communities were fundamentally stochastic and nonlinear, Brownian and directional movements with back-loops as will be shown below. The grass areas of the savanna along river courses, as was the case for the Sangha River Interval for example (Giresse et al. 2018, 2020), were preferentially occupied initially, and the interstitial spaces colonized later. The pioneer Bantu moving frontier reached the Great Lakes regions, the savanna south of the equatorial rain forest, East Africa coast, and southern Africa between 500 BCE and 500 CE. The regionalization processes triggered then resulted in different evolutionary trajectories in different parts of the sub-continent. Following the initial expansion, with interregional variations, some areas witnessing the clustering of higher population with the formation of larger settlements, ranging from large villages to cities in the next millennium from 500 to 1500 CE.

Seidensticker et al. (2021) provide interesting data on what they termed "population collapse" in 400–600 CE in the Congo Basin, a pattern already well documented (Lezine et al. 2013, Garcin et al. 2018) but interpreted differently. Relying on the summed probability distributions (SPD) of 1,149 radiocarbon dates, from 726 sites comprising 115 pottery styles, they outline two peaks in settlement intensity in the Congo Basin corresponding to the local Early Iron Age on the one hand, and Late Iron Age on the other hand, separated by low settlement intensity for about two hundred years equated with "population collapse." It is however the suggestion that these findings require an urgent reassessment of the Bantu expansion, formulated as "until now, the dispersal of Bantu-speaking communities in the Congo rainforest has tended to be seen as a single, and long-term, continuous, macroevent" (Seidensticker et al. 2021: 6) that is puzzling. Such views were pioneered half a century ago, in the mid-twentieth century (Wrigley 1960, 1961, Vansina 1980) and have since been laid to rest (Vansina 1990). On methodological grounds, radiocarbon dates summed probability distributions provide an acceptable proxy to demographic trends, but absolute sites frequencies have to be correlated with settlement size to make accurate demographic sense. A ten-hectare archaeological site is the equivalent of ten one-thousand-square-meter family hamlets. In addition, well-documented admixtures with forest foragers that may have had adaptive implications are not alluded to in the demographic scenario under consideration. In summary, the conclusions of Seidensticker et al. (2021) are misleading.

An evolutionary approach based on the SArFe model provides a robust and parsimonious explanation of the Congo rain forest situation documented by Seidensticker et al. (2021). Pioneer Bantu-speaking communities from the Congo Basin, probably organized into small widely scattered family-hamlets, experienced population bottlenecks, and maladaptation for these grain farmers faced with rain forest regrowth and expansion. Founder effect articulated on population redistribution along with a shift to different horticultural practices—oily plants, bananas, yams—triggered a new growth cycle in the Congo Basin rain forest, while the Great Lakes region and East and South Africa followed different evolutionary pathways.

BANTU SOCIAL FORMATIONS FROM 1000 TO 1500 CE

From 1000 to 1500 CE, speakers of Bantu languages reached the Eastern and Southern confines of the Africa southern hemisphere. Most of the Western Bantu area and the equatorial rain forest, from the Great Lakes to the Cameroon-Nigeria Bantu Homeland, was settled by small hamlet-size self-sustaining autonomous agrarian communities, connected by river courses and networks of footpaths. The development of chiefdoms and ranked societies in Southwestern Cameroons, for example, was triggered by the post-1500 collusion between the continental and Atlantic enslavement systems (Holl 2001, 2015).

The archaeology of the last three millennia of East and Southern Africa is the product of genetic and cultural recombination of distinct populations, forest and southern Africa foragers, Northeastern Africa pastoralists, Near Easterners, speakers of Austronesian languages, and Asians from the Indian Ocean. The Swahili civilization along the coast and the colonization and successful settlement of the Comoros Archipelago and Madagascar resulted from the trans-regional redistribution of population belonging to the Malayo-Indonesian world, Africa hinterland, and the southern portion of the Near East. The southern part of the continent witnessed a parallel developmental trajectory, with the emergence of chiefdoms and states in South Africa, Botswana, and the Zimbabwe plateau (fig. 4.3).

The Great Lakes Region and the Southwest

The Great Lakes region, the southwest, and the savanna-land south of the equatorial rain forest witnessed the development of complex chiefdoms and kingdoms during the second millennium. In the Great Lakes region, the development at Ntusi, Munsa, Bigo, Kibiro, Mubende, and other earthwork sites was remarkable. Large-scale cattle husbandry is documented at Ntusi. Kibiro witnessed an impressive intensification in the production of salt from the local brackish springs (Connah 1996). And an agricultural colonization took place in western Uganda (Reid 1997). However, tracing the precise evolutionary trajectory of any of the past Great Lakes polities is still hampered by the lack of sustained long-term archaeological research and terminological uncertainties (Robertshaw 1999, 2003). The savanna, from the Atlantic coast to the Great Lakes, witnessed the emergence of successive states that may have started at the end of the first or very beginning of the second millennium CE. It is the context for the development of Kongo, Loango, Tio, Mbundu, Kuba, Lozi, and Luba kingdoms. Archaeological excavations carried out at Kongo kingdoms' regional capitals like Mabata, Mpangu, Nsundi, Kindoki, and Ngongo Mbata point to scattered small farming communities as far back as 600 CE. Population concentrations and early urbanization kicked off around 1300 CE (Clist et al. 2015, de Maret 1997) and accelerated significantly with the connection to the Atlantic system and its trade of enslaved Africans.

East Africa Coast

The Swahili civilization emerged from an immense interaction sphere stretched along three thousand kilometers north-south and 20–250 kilometers east-west in coastal East Africa, from Mogadiscio in Somalia to Cape Delgado in Mozambique. Pastoralists from Cushitic ancestry expanded southward from c. 4500 BP. Groups of Bantu speakers practicing agriculture, gathering, hunting, and fishing, trickled into the Great Lakes regions and later along the East African coast from the first millennium BCE onward. Despite differences in the interpretation of the archaeological, historical and ethno-historical records, the African and Bantu roots of the Swahili civilization are now firmly established (Beaujard 2007, Kusimba 1999).

The development of Swahili city-states is spelled out in three major phases, with a fourth one (1500–1950), corresponding to foreign domination and colonization. During Period I (100 BCE–300 CE), settlements were small, founded and inhabited by iron-using farming communities, and characterized by a pottery tradition that can be traced back to 400 BCE in the Great Lakes region. This Kwale ware is found at Misasa in Tanzania, Kwale in Kenya, and Ras Hafun in Somalia.

Period II (300–1000 CE) is comprised of two phases: the Azanian (300–600 CE) and the Zanjian (600–1000 CE). It witnessed the kickoff of the urbanization process and the onset of international long-distance trade. The maritime trade became particularly active during the Zanjian phase, as indicated by the presence of carnelian beads, Partho-Sassanian tin, glazed Chinese porcelain, and Indian purple ware, as well as Egyptian glass. The outgoing component of the international exchange was very likely made of human cargo, as indicated indirectly by the "Zanj Revolt" that took place in southern Iraq, and lasted for some fifteen years, from 869 to 883. It threatened the very existence of the Abbasid Dynasty when whole detachments of Black soldiers of the Caliph army deserted and joined forces with the rebels (Popovic 1999). Among many others, settlements sprung up at places such as Chibuene, Masuguru, Kaole, Kilwa, Manda, Pate, and Shanga, etc.

The Swahili city-states strictly speaking emerged during Period III (1000–1500 CE). Each major city controlled a more or less extensive hinterland and coastal fringe, with docking areas for seafaring vessels. The coast was dotted with a string of towns, villages, and fishing stations. Particularly important urban centers emerged at Kilwa, Manda, Mogadiscio, Ras Hafun, and Ntwapa. Islam, which started to expand during the Zanjian phase, became a dominant well-established religion. The intensification of long-distance trade, the emergence of a class of wealthy merchants residing in mansion-like houses built of coral-stone, and local copper coinage, as well as the development of social ranking, all contributed to the thriving economies of the

East African Coast. Slavery was an "institution" geared to satisfy foreign and local demands. Congregation mosques, massive elite stone mansions, but also wattle and daub houses became distinct but complementary facets of East African urban landscapes. From 1500 onward, the irruption of the Portuguese (Subrahmanyam 2001), the Omani Arab conquest, and finally the European takeover sealed the demise of the Swahili civilization (Beaujard 2007, Kusimba 1999).

Southern Africa Developments

Food-producing communities practicing grain agriculture and livestock husbandry spread all over the southern part of the continent during the latter part of the first millennium BCE (Huffman 2007, 2020). Depending on areas, the newcomers interacted with Khoi-San foragers resulting in complex pattern of mutual influences. Livestock husbandry expanded in most of Namibia. Agriculture and livestock spread in Mozambique, Zimbabwe, and North/Northeast South Africa, while Khoi-San foragers moved away in parts of the Kalahari Desert. The developments to be discussed below focus on the emergence of the Zambezian chiefdoms and states (Huffman 1996, Pikirayi 2001, Sinclair et al. 1993).

Mapungubwe State

The Toutswe chiefdom in the Kalahari fringe of eastern Botswana and the Mapungubwe state in the Shashe-Limpopo valley are the earliest ranked societies to have emerged in Southern Africa at the very end of the first millennium CE (Pikirayi 2001). The latter developed into a full-fledged state for approximately two hundred years, from 1100 to 1280 CE. Excavation at Bambandyanalo, Mapungubwe, and Schroda revealed a connection to the international trade network of the Indian Ocean. In exchange, they provided products from the gold mines, animal skins and hides, as well as elephant tusks. Cattle husbandry was a central element in the Mapungubwe state political economy. It served as repository of wealth with success measured by the size of the herds any potential leader could marshal. Settlements were made of enclosures organized around cattle sheds. The central site that may have been the capital of the new emerging polity shifted from Schroda, to Bambandyanalo (K2), and then Mapungubwe.

Bambandyanalo, a mound site with huge rubbish middens, was an important village, part of a larger settlement system comprised of Pont Drift, Mmamgwa, Schroda, and Mapungubwe. Its inhabitants were predominantly cattle herders and elephant hunters, living in sun-dried clay houses with beaten earthen floors. It was abandoned during the second half of the eleventh century CE, for a new central site at Mapungubwe Hill. This new settlement complex, including a hill site for the rulers and elite members overlooking a lower one of sun-dried clay-and wattle houses for the commoners, emerged at the end of the eleventh century CE. Mapungubwe state (ca. 1100–1280) participated actively in the international long-distance trade and controlled a relatively extensive territory along the Shashe-Limpopo valleys. The settlement hierarchy with Mapungubwe as the largest and central site was divided into five distinct levels: 1) the dominant political center; 2) hilltop towns inhabited by elite members; 3) large villages; 4) hamlets; and 5) farmsteads (Huffman 1996, 2007, Pikirayi 2001). The state economy was predominantly anchored on cattle husbandry, long-distance exchange with the Indian Ocean coastal towns, and the flow of tribute extracted from dependent polities. The causes of the decline of Mapungubwe state are still poorly investigated (Pikirayi 2001: 116). Its population started to decline in the second half of the twelfth century CE. A combination of factors including droughts, soil depletion, shifts in international trade routes and, very likely, overtaxation, put an end to the existence of the first Zambezi state at the end of the thirteenth century CE. Regional primacy shifted hundreds of kilometers north-northeast to the Zimbabwe plateau, first in the Mateke hills where small villages and homesteads were already settled at the very beginning of the second millennium CE, between 1000 and 1200.

Great Zimbabwe State

The Great Zimbabwe state emerged at the very end of the thirteenth century CE on the plateau of the same name with settlement distributed between 500 and 1,300 meters above sea level. Its territory stretched along some three hundred kilometers, from the Runde River in the south to the Save River in the east and northeast. The economic basis of the Great Zimbabwe state was not qualitatively different from that of Mapungubwe. It combined intensive cattle husbandry with grain agriculture. The connection to the international Indian Ocean trade was however much stronger, with an intensified export sector involving copper, gold, ivory, gems, leather, and animal skins. The town of Great Zimbabwe, at the center of the southern half of the plateau, was the main center and capital of the state.

Almost all settlement included prominent stone buildings. They nonetheless differed in size. Homesteads clustered around small villages. The small villages generally attached to large villages. Large villages were part of a regional district dominated by small towns with the state capital at the top of the settlement hierarchy. Characteristically, all the regional centers and the Great Zimbabwe site are located along a southwest-northeast diagonal axis between the 800- and 1,000-meter contour lines. Nenga and Pamuuyu are located in the southwest; Great Zimbabwe and Majiri in the center-south, Musimbira and Chibvumani in the center-northeast, and finally, Matendere and Muchuchu in the north.

The spectacular architecture of the Conical Tower, Great Enclosure, and Hill Complex at Great Zimbabwe is a testimony to the prestige and power harnessed and displayed by the state rulers and elite. The "walling" styles of the mazimbabwes (stone towns) (Chipunza 1994, Chirikure 2021, Huffman and Woodborne 2020, Pikirayi 2001, 2017) have been arranged into successive variants, with P (poor) walls as the earliest, followed by PQ (poor and high quality) walls, and finally, Q (high quality) walls, with the status of the floating R walling style ambiguous. This walls systematics based exclusively on the quality of the construction is problematic if taken as a chronological yardstick. Despite this limitation and using these walling styles as chronological proxies, it is possible to map the phases of construction of the Great Zimbabwe Hill Complex. The latter appears to have been in a constant process of extension and remodeling. It expanded from west to east, from the Western Enclosure built with P(E) walling style in c. 1000 CE. During this early stage, the enclosed complex measured approximately 1,700 square meters (Holl 1996: 85). During the second extension phase, that may have lasted up to c. 1150 CE and characterized by P(L) walling style, the complex almost doubled in size and included a number of new units such as the Cleft Rock and the Southern Enclosures—a series of short walls connecting large boulders in the northeast. The Western Enclosure was extensively remodeled. A monumental wall, forty-two meters long, 2.9 meters wide, and 3.4 to 3.76 meters high, with a doorway and topped by a series of four micro-conical towers, was built along the west flank of the complex. An additional monumental wall was built along the south side. The enclosed space measured 2,700 square meters at the end of the second extension phase. The construction of the Hill complex was completed with the third (PQ) and fourth (Q) walling styles, from c. 1150 to 1450 CE. The Eastern and Recess Enclosures were added at the southeastern end of the complex, and extensive remodeling took place along the south side. A series of new walls measuring 25 meters in length, 1.7 to 3 meters in height, and 1.1 to 1.4 meters in width, was built parallel to the previous south wall providing a narrow passageway to the eastern half of the complex. A similar architectural device was used during the construction of the Great Enclosure in the Valley Complex. At the peak of Great Zimbabwe State power, from 1300 to 1450 CE, the Hill complex measured some 4,950 square meters in surface extent. It was then divided into five main components: the Western, Cleft rock, Southern, Recess, and Eastern enclosures. The Eastern Enclosure was devoted to state ceremonies and rituals as suggested by the discovery of a series of six carved soapstone birds, soapstone bowls, and geometric pattern decoration on stone monoliths and bowls. The heavy investment in the construction and monumentality of the whole southern side of the Hill Complex that overlooks the lower City of the Valley Complex was very likely designed as an unmistakable display of the prestige and power of the Great Zimbabwe ruling elite.

The demise of Great Zimbabwe state was gradual but accelerated in the middle of the fifteenth century CE. when emerging competing states of Torwa, Mutapa, and others captured the bulk of the international long-distance trade. The post-fifteenth-century period saw the arrival of a new player on the international scene, the Portuguese. They negotiated trade agreements with many African polities along the Indian Ocean coast and the Southern Africa hinterland. However, most of the time, competition was fierce, involving successions of attacks, counterattacks, and retaliation. The Portuguese won and imposed a series of trade regulations and monopoles that ruined the previously thriving economies of the Swahili city-states (Kusimba 1999).

CONCLUSION

The expansion of speakers of Bantu languages is the result of the long-term interaction of several dynamic systems. Climate change, and more precisely the modification of the circulation of air masses that generated a climate with a strongly marked dry season, triggered the fragmentation of the great humid equatorial forest. In this context, the opening up of grassy savanna spaces favored the southern extension of cereal agriculture based on pearl millet cultivation (Eggert et al. 2006). There was no need to bypass the forest as initially thought. Genetic data show that there are no noticeable cleavages between a western and an eastern branch that would have merged later on the southern flank of the equatorial rain forest. Matrimonial alliance systems show a significant absorption of women from hunter-gatherer communities, both the ancestors of the Equatorial rain forest foragers and those of the southern Khoi-San. The expansion along certain privileged corridors, the extension over vast territories, and the linguistic drift led to the formation of various dialects and then languages derived from a common origin. Genetic research has now firmly shown that the expansion of speakers of the Bantu languages was essentially a relatively rapid phenomenon of demic diffusion that took place over approximately two millennia.

Chapter 5

Genesis and Expansion of Cattle Pastoralism in Africa

Livestock and Pathogens

INTRODUCTION

In Africa, the development of food-producing economies was spread over almost the total time range of the Holocene period, with different parts of the continent experimenting with specific combinations of technical and socio-cultural practices involving humans, plants, and/or animals. This chapter focuses on one aspect of the emergence and routinization of food production, namely cattle husbandry. It explores different facets of the spread of cattle pastoralism across the continent as can be reconstructed from the archaeo-logical record. It focuses on some of the implications of these developments in connection with the spread of zoonoses, and especially bovine tuberculosis (bTB) (Brass 2007, 2017, Clark and Brandt 1984, Clutton-Brock 1993, 1997, Gauthier 1987, Gifford-Gonzales 2017, Holl 1998a, b, 2004, 2006, Jousse 2004, Lander and Russell 2018, Prendergast et al. 2019, Robertshaw 2021, Smith 1992, Stock and Gifford-Gonzales 2013, Wendorf and Schild 1998).

The developmental and/or social evolutionary processes that resulted in the adoption of new subsistence strategies focused on livestock husbandry are considered from their broadest perspective. Such broad perspective involves discussion on ecosystem dynamics and paleoclimatic changes, variation in settlement/subsistence systems as materialized by period-specific regional site distribution and recorded food remains, and the diversity and variation in material culture remains. Once the archaeological space/time framework of the origins and spread of livestock in Africa is in place, the focus shifts to the etiology and history of tuberculosis—predominantly bTB—and the examination of their implications for past and current human and livestock health in the continent.

Tuberculosis (TB), a very contagious infectious disease caused by the *Mycobacterium tuberculosis* (MT) pathogen, has affected humanity as early as three million years ago. MT modern strains that appear to have emerged around 20,000–15,000 years ago were transmitted to livestock, especially cattle, during the domestication process in the Near East and probably India. Bovine TB (bTB) has since been a constant health threat to humans, livestock, and wildlife. In Africa, the early history of TB infection, either via human-to-human or livestock-to-human transmission, is virtually unknown with very few exceptions. Zooarchaeological research, rightly still focused on species identifications, has not yet implemented a systematic search for TB pathologies in archaeological faunal assemblages. Accordingly, this chapter will rely on evidence of cattle sacrifice in the Sahara during the Neolithic period to formulate a provocative hypothesis according to which the ritual practices involving cattle sacrifices and burial may have been cultural strategies to handle livestock acute zoonoses, including among others bovine tuberculosis (bTB).

The undisputable evidence of cattle/livestock sacrifices recorded in the Eastern, Central Sahara, and West African Sahel are generally interpreted in terms of performative rituals geared to alleviate environmental stress and handle detrimental consequences of climate change. Instead of a direct correlation between climate fluctuations and ritual performance, and despite the predominant loose chronological resolution, it is hypothesized that the sacrifice and burial of untouched complete animals' carcasses makes more sense as "culturally sanctioned" prophylactic measure against looming livestock and human health threat. The proposition is falsifiable and may convince zoo-archaeologists to go back to the drawing board to look for evidence of infectious diseases in archaeological faunal remains.

POST-PLEISTOCENE ADJUSTMENTS AND INNOVATIONS

Africa is a massive continent literally straddling the equator. That situation has significant climatic and biogeographic implications. Most of the continent experiences monsoons with summer rainfall regimes. The Mediterranean fringes north of the Tropic of Cancer and south of the Tropic of Capricorn are sustained by winter rainfall regimes.

The hunter-gatherer populations inhabiting the continent during the Later Pleistocene had to deal with profound climate instabilities. In the northern hemisphere, vast swathes of the continent were emptied of their populations during the Last Glacial Maximum, circa 20–18000 to 12–10000 BP. Humans were mostly concentrated in refuge areas, along the Nile Valley (Jebel Sahaba, Waddi Kubbaniya), the Mediterranean coast (Iberomaurusian), the Atlantic coast (Site of the Bingerville Highway, Cote d'Ivoire) and southwestern Cameroon Grassfield (Fiye-Nkwi, Mbi Crater, Shum Laka). A recolonization movement began with the return of the humidity and the Early Holocene Wet Phase. This new dynamic led to important innovations in subsistence, technologies, and culture. Mobile foragers invented the bow and arrow and practiced selective hunting of a limited number of animal species, Barbary sheep (*Ammotragus lervia*) in North Africa and the Sahara and the giant eland (*Taurotragus derbianus*) in southern Africa. The "Capsians" adopted the intensive exploitation of aquatic resources in the chotts of the northern Saharan fringe of the Maghreb. It was in this general atmosphere of transformation that significant innovations occurred in different parts of the continent. These innovations materialized as the invention of pottery, wild sorghum cultivation, the rearing of " captive" Barbary sheep, and the domestication and/or adoption of cattle.

Making and Using Pottery

The production and use of pottery became widespread between 8000 and 6000 BCE in the continent's northern hemisphere. Such pottery was found in the eastern Sahara (Nabta Playa), the Bandiagara Escarpment in southeastern Mali (Ounjougou), the Tibesti region of northern Chad, the Tadrart Acacus in southwestern Libya, the Tassili-n-Ajjer and Hoggar mountains in the Algerian southeast, and the Air Mountains in Niger. The vessels recorded in the eastern Sahara sites, at Nabta Playa and Bir Kiseiba, were small bowls probably used for food and drink consumption. Those of the Central Sahara, from Tagalagal, Amekni, Site Launay, etc., presented a greater diversity of shapes and sizes. They included large hemispherical pots with rounded bases, globular pots with everted lips, and smaller-sized hemispherical bowls. Large containers were used for storage of liquids and foodstuffs, such as the wild grain that was gathered regularly. Medium-sized pots would have been used for cooking while bowls were for the consumption of food and other substances.

The Cultivation of Wild Sorghum

The exploitation of wild grain and other plant resources was marked by a certain intensification during the first millennia of the Early Holocene as indicated by data from Nabta Playa in the eastern Sahara (Biehl et al. 1999, Wasylikowa and Dahlberg 1999) and Uan Afuda and Ti-n-Torha in the central Sahara (Barich 1992, 1998). Panicoid grasses (*Panicum* sp.*, Pennisetum* sp.,

Setaria sp.) were common in the central Sahara sites. Plant macro remain samples taken from site E-75–6 (Nabta Playa) indicate the presence of 127 taxa including a significant component of "useful" plants (Wasylikowa and Dahlberg 1999: 29–31). Among these plants, there is a large group of wild grasses including *Brachiaria* sp., *Digitaria* sp., *Echinochloa colona, Panicum turgidum*, Paniceae A type, Paniceae B type, Paniceae indet., *Sorghum bicolor* ssp., *Arundinaceum* and *Urochloa* sp. Sorghum remains from 187 samples were found in the excavations of all dwellings and silo pits. "Sorghum grains occur in all the huts, indicating that it was always available in the area. It was collected in similar quantities as other food plants, except in three huts, where much larger quantities were found. These huts also had a lower diversity of food plant species" (Wasylokowa and Dahlberg 1999: 22–23).

These remains were morphologically wild and frequently collected in the Nabta Playa basin. Some of this sorghum may also have been grown using the technique of flood-recession farming—*decrue* technique. The wet sediments exposed by the receding waters were sown with seeds and the young shoots were transplanted later. Overall, the data from Site E-75–6 of Nabta Playa indicates a focus on sorghum, remains of which were found in all dwellings. The duration of this "experiment" is uncertain, but the sorghum grown in Nabta Playa was still morphologically wild.

Management of Wild Animals

Consolidated dung layers of Barbary sheep were uncovered in Uan Afuda Cave, on the Eastern slope of the Tadrart Acacus in southwestern Libya. The data, collected in layers 1 and 2 of excavation I, at the entrance and in the upper part of the stratigraphy of the excavation inside the cave, dates from c. 8300–8500 and 8000 BP (Di Lernia 2001). The massive accumulation and compaction of the deposits attest to the non-accidental nature of the uncovered evidence. Additional micromorphological and palynological data and analyses of macro remains were used to reconstruct some of the events that took place at Uan Afuda Cave between 8500 and 8000 BP. The hunter-gatherers group who settled in Uan Afuda Cave at the end of the Pleistocene/beginning of the Early Holocene mainly hunted Barbary sheep and gathered wild grain and fruits. The Early Holcene Uan Afudians were able to catch young Barbary sheep that could not escape and take them back to their dwellings. The data collected indicates the provision of food and protection for the animals. It is highly unlikely that the captured animals were kept in the cave for their entire existence. It is easy to imagine the use of ropes and tethering stones that would have allow them to graze in the cave vicinity during the day, with the cave used as a shelter at nighttime for both humans

and animals. Although the Barbary sheep were raised in captivity, it is difficult to know whether they were tamed and/or able to breed in captivity. They
were clearly not domesticated. The number of captive animals present at any
given time in the cave is unknown. As modern contemporary analogues show
in almost every part of the world, tamed wild animals tends to be pets, not
food. A few individuals would not be enough to compensate for the lack of
meat. However, if the selection of captive individuals focused on females,
these could in time have supplied milk and guaranteed sustainable diets to
Late Pleistocene/Early Holocene hunter-gatherers during lean periods.

Overall, the end of the Pleistocene and the beginning of the Early Holocene
was characterized by three converging trends. First, a trend toward territorial-
ization marked by the repetitive occupation of the same sites; second, a trend
toward intensive exploitation of certain animal species and plant resources
as indicated by Barbary sheep hunting and taming in the Tadrart Acacus and
the collection and/or cultivation of wild sorghum in the Nabta Playa basin.
And finally, third, a trend toward the diversification of material culture with
the invention/adoption of pottery. These trends, regulated by climate changes,
increased during the Holocene with however significant regional variations.
Interesting contrasts appear regarding the cultivation of wild grasses; the
intensive exploitation and cultivation of wild sorghum seems to have been
confined to the eastern Sahara, in Waddi Kubbaniya and Nabta Playa basins
respectively. Wild millets and other panicoids were predominant in the
Central Sahara sites, particularly at Ti-n-Torha, Uan Tabu, and Uan Afuda in
the Tadrart Acacus in southwestern Libya.

The Shift to Food Production

The emergence of food-producing economies is a key moment in the economic and social development of humankind. The consequences of these
changes were certainly not revolutionary when they initially took place. It is
unlikely that in their early stages these historic changes occurred in the form
of a "Great Leap Forward." In fact, some data show that the first communities living partly on agricultural produce in the Fertile Crescent experienced
severe health consequences (Cohen and Armelagos 1984). The average stature
fell considerably compared to that of the Upper Palaeolithic and Mesolithic
populations. "Owing to poor diet throughout childhood, the dimensions of the
skull, pelvic inlet, and long bone shafts, as well as general dental health, were
depressed below any reasonable health norm" (Angel 1984: 62). Situations
varied considerably, but the health status of all the early Neolithic populations was initially negative and improved much later (Angel 1984, Goodman
et al. 1984). Accordingly, in its initial steps, the shift to food production
was not that "great leap forward" guaranteeing a sustainable food supply to

"endangered" Late Pleistocene/Early Holocene hunter-gatherers. What were the factors that compelled humans to follow these routes? Answers vary but are generally articulated on three variables: climate changes, demographic pressure, and/or exchange dynamics. Depending on periods and places, these key variables combined to produce the particular situations that will be examined in this part of the book.

The end of the Pleistocene and the Early Holocene were marked by significant global climate change. The impact varied depending on local circumstances but overall, the continent experienced a sharp increase in precipitation, recharging groundwater levels and reactivating river systems. The Early Holocene was the golden age of small and large Saharan lakes. Surplus water from Lake Mega-Chad ran into the Bahr el Ghazzal and the Wadi Howar and flowed into the Nile. Terminal Paleolithic and Mesolithic hunter-gatherers spread to all areas of the continent. The old model asserts that African food-producing economies as well as all technological and cultural innovations were derived from the Near East (Clark and Brandt 1984).

CATTLE DOMESTICATION: A BRIEF REVIEW

There are two widely accepted areas of cattle domestication in the world, Southwest Asia for *Bos taurus* and South Asia for *Bos indicus* or Zebu, with however a third possible one, the Eastern Sahara, still hotly debated (Arbukle and Kassebaum 2021, Bradley et al. 1996, Decker et al. 2014, Gebrehiwot et al. 2020, Kim et al. 2017, Mwai et al. 2015, Perez-Pardal et al. 2018). The cattle domestication process was kicked off among Early Holocene foragers hunting large wild bovids, *Bos primigenius*—auroch—in Southwest Asia, Europe, and North Africa, and *Bos nomadicus* in the Indian subcontinent.

As far as the presence of domesticated cattle in Africa is concerned, the predominant narrative places its center of domestication in Southwest Asia during the Early PPNB (Pre-Pottery Neolithic B, ninth millennium BCE) in the context of the early farming communities of the Fertile Crescent. In fact, "the narrative of the appearance of domestic cattle in the 9th millennium BCE is largely a mirage. Domestic phenotypes in fact appear in the 8th millennium" (Arbuckle and Kassebaum 2021:10), preceded by millennia-old scattered traditions of management of wild animals. The study by Verdugo et al. of sixty-seven ancient bovines reveals three distinct Neolithic lineages in Southwest Asia. "A" is reflected in the Early Neolithic Balkans (with origin in SW Asia); "B" is identified in Neolithic Anatolia and Iran; and "C" is found in Southern Levant" (Arbuckle and Kassebaum 2021: 14). The Southwest Asia cattle domestication is accordingly non-centric.

The possibility of cattle domestication from the North Africa *Bos primigenius* stock is worth discussing. Bradley et al. (1996) conducted the analysis of a large data set comprising mtDNA displacement loop (D loop) sequences from ninety contemporary cattle sampled on three continents. Their results pointed to a pre-domestic separation for the ancestors of African and European bovines. The analysis by Decker et al. (2014) of worldwide patterns of ancestry, divergence, and admixture in domestic cattle reveals regardless of analytical method or sampled subset, three major cattle groups: Asian indicine, Eurasian taurine, and African taurine. They observed that African taurine diverges significantly from Eurasian taurine, displaying a large portion of wild African auroch ancestry. "If African and Asian taurines were both exported from the Fertile Crescent, in similar numbers at about the same time, we would expect them to be approximately equally diverged from European taurine" (Decker et al. 2014: 3). It is however not what is observed from the data at hand. "African taurines were consistently revealed to be more diverged from European and Asian taurines" (Decker et al. 2014, Geberhiwot et al. 2020, Mwai et al. 2015). Because of this divergence, a third domestication of cattle in Africa is still an open question. For Decker et al. (2014: 5) the divergence resulted from high level of wild African auroch introgression (20 percent ancestry from wild African auroch) through admixture with an ancestral population in Africa.

Hanotte et al. (2002) have addressed the origins and migrations of cattle in Africa through the genetic imprint of a continent-wide sample of fifty-two populations of indigenous African cattle from twenty-three countries, thirty-one *Bos taurus* and nineteen *B. indicus*. They found: 1) that the major process of *B. indicus* influence centered on East Africa, via seaborne transfer, instead of land connection between Egypt and the Arabic Peninsula, and this despite humped cattle paintings in the XIIth Dynasty second millennium BCE tomb; 2) that their " PC3 [Principal Component] results support local domestication rather than Near-East introduction as plausible origin of African cattle" (Hanotte et al. 2002: 338).

The initial cattle population of Africa was exclusively taurine. All contemporary African cattle do carry a taurine mtDNA. All tropical humped cattle (*Bos indicus*) derived from domestication processes that took place in South Asia some eight thousand years ago. "Humped zebu-like cattle were introduced to Egypt from the Levant (3400–3000 BP), but present African Zebu cattle are the result of multiple introduction" (Perez-Pardal et al. 2018: 2). The latter's phylogenetic analysis shows that all zebu Y-chromosome haplotypes are partitioned into three lineages: $Y3_A$, the most predominant and cosmopolitan lineage; $Y3_B$, observed only in West Africa; and finally, $Y3_C$, predominant in North and South India. "The cryptic presence of $Y3_B$ haplotypes in West Africa, found nowhere else, suggests that these haplotypes might represent the oldest zebu lineages introduced to Africa c. 3000 BP and subsequently replaced in most of the world" (Perez-Pardal 2018: 2).

With the genuine possibility of local cattle domestication in Eastern Sahara, African cattle pastoralism has multiple sources, from Northeast Africa and Southwest Asia for taurine and South Asia for indicine, through multiple introductions and admixture. "The rinderpest panzootics of 1889–1896 are estimated to have annihilated up to 80% of herds in many regions or over 5.2 million African taurine cattle and resulted in zebu being massively reintroduced along the eastern coastline of Africa, largely replacing African taurine bulls" (Perez-Pardal et al. 2018: 2). Today, Africa has 180 cattle breeds, 150 of which are indigenous including *Bos taurus*, *B. indicus*, Sanga (indigenous taurine + zebu), and Zenga (zebu + Sanga).

EXPANSION OF LIVESTOCK HERDING IN AFRICA

The end of the Last Glacial Maximum was characterized by a general warming of the climate resulting in an important wet phase in most regions in the continent's northern hemisphere. The Late Pleistocene populations concentrated in the refuge areas of the Nile Valley, the Mediterranean coasts, the Highlands of southwestern Cameroon, Cote d'Ivoire Atlantic Coast, and Central Saharan Mountain Ranges spread out once again to the newly available hospitable lands. The Early Holocene nonetheless experienced significant climate fluctuations with brief but severe arid phases as was the case in 9800–9600 BP and 9200–9100 BP (Wendorf and Schild 1998) documented in the Nabta Playa Basin in the eastern Sahara. The pioneering phase of the adoption/domestication of cattle took place in an area stretching from the Tadrart Acacus plateau in southwestern Libya in the west to the Eastern Sahara and Nile Valley in the east (Marshall and Hildebrand 2002, Holl 1998a, 2004, Wendorf and Schild 1998). This phase is dated from 10000 to 8000 BP. Large bovid bones identified as *Bos taurus* were collected in Nabta Playa, Bir Kiseiba, and Ti-n-Torha. During the El Adam phase of the Early Neolithic (10,800–9800 cal. BP), the sites contained a few bones and teeth of *Bos*, many gazelle and hare remains, plus several bones from turtle, jackal, birds, and small rodents, indicating a rather poor environment, comparable to the northern fringe of the Sahel. El Adam phase hunter-herders probably came from the Nile Valley and ventured into the desert to take advantage of the pastures fed by summer rains. "They used their cattle as a renewable resource" (Wendorf and Schild 1998: 101), relying on milk and its by-products instead of meat. Site E-75–6 of the El Nabta phase dating from 9100 to 8900 BP marked an important change in the Early Holocene occupation of the Playa. It contained the remains of at least fifteen circular dwellings, each flanked by a bell-shaped silo, and all arranged in two or three parallel lines with three 2.5 m-deep wells. E-75–6 was occupied during the dry season, a period during which the intensive gathering of wild sorghum was added to the rearing of a few head of cattle and the hunting of gazelles and hares. This scenario, debated since the publication of these results by F. Wendorf and R. Schild team (1998), Stock and Gifford-Gonzales (2013) is challenged in a recent work: "The results from modern DNA analyses, coupled with (a) this re-examination of the ecological underpinnings of the early African cattle domestication model and (b) the dates of the appearances of caprine and cattle domesticates in a minimum of two diffusionist waves via different land and sea routes from a current bracketed date of c. 6300 BCE onwards, show that the time has come to abandon the long-standing hypothesis of an early Holocene independent centre of cattle domestication in Northeast Africa" (Brass 2017).

The new study asserts that Early Holocene large bovid bones from Nabta Playa were those of wild aurochs. However, it does not take into consideration the presence of domesticated cattle before 6500 BCE in the archaeological sites of the Central Sahara in the Acacus (Holl 2004) and in Nubia (Sudan) in the Wadi al Arab site dating from 8500–6500 BCE (Stock & Gifford-Gonzales 2013). From the northeast of the continent initial cattle husbandry with latter admixture with Near Eastern taurines expanded to the rest of the continent, westward and southward (Brass 2007, Finucane et al. 2008, Gifford-Gonzales 2017, Jousse 2004, Lander and Russell 2018, Prendergast et al. 2019, Robertshaw 2021).

Northeast Africa

Northeastern Africa is certainly the key area for the investigation of at least part of the origins of livestock husbandry in Africa (Wendorf and Schild 1998). Cattle mtDNA suggesting an early split (ca. 25,000 BP) between African, Eurasian, and Indian wild populations of *Bos* lends support to the idea of possible cattle domestication in Eastern Sahara (Bradley et al. 1996). During the Late Neolithic period (ca. 7500–7400 cal. BP) livestock and mostly cattle are involved in complex rituals comprising burials in megalithic features. According to Wendorf and Schild (1998), this clear focus on cattle is probably a precursor to the worship of Hathor in Pharaonic Egypt.

Even if still debated (Brass 2017), the Nabta Playa archaeological record has changed our views on the nature of cultural development not only in northeastern Africa but also in Africa as a whole. Dakhleh Oasis, at approximately five hundred kilometers north of Nabta Playa, presents an important and intriguing time lag in the appearance of livestock in the archaeological record between both areas. The Dakhleh Oasis sequence consists of three major cultural phases. The oasis was inhabited by almost sedentary hunter-gatherers with no indication of food production during the Masara cultural unit (ca. 8800–7000 BP). Livestock herding of cattle and sheep/goats is attested during the Bashendi A and B cultural unit (ca. 7000–5500 BP). At the end of the studied settlement sequence, which lasted up to Old Kingdom times, Sheikh Muftah groups were more sedentary with their sites preferentially located in the oasis lowlands. Cattle husbandry was initially a local development that may have also concerned part of the Central Sahara. Each playa basin or oasis presents some peculiarities that are still poorly understood; the time lag of three thousand years in the appearance of cattle bones in the archaeological record of Nabta Playa and Dakhleh Oasis is particularly intriguing. It is however likely that Dakhleh oasis cattle resulted from a latter Near East stock as suggested by the synchronic occurrence of sheep/goat, a Middle Eastern domesticate.

The archaeological record does not allow for an accurate investigation of the transition from foraging to livestock husbandry in the Nile Valley south of Khartoum for several reasons outlined by W. Wetterstrom (1993: 202–203): 1) the paucity of relevant sites and a huge discontinuity in the archaeological record; 2) the nature of the bioarchaeological record that "is by no means a lucid blueprint of [past] subsistence practices." In general, mixed-farming settlements dating from ca. 5000 to 4000 BCE have been recorded from the upper to the lower Nile (Hassan 1985, Krzyzaniak 1978, 1991, Wetterstrom 1993) at such sites as Kadero, Badari, El-Omari, Merinde, and the Fayum area.

Central Sahara

Archaeological evidence from the Central Sahara concerning the issue of livestock husbandry can be split into two categories; the first one includes rock paintings and engravings particularly numerous in the Tassili-n-Ajjer, Messak, and Ahaggar (Holl 2006, Muzzolini 1995; Le Quellec 1993). The second is comprised of archaeo-zoological evidence, the samples of animal bones collected from controlled excavations. Almost all the sites with published archaeo-zoological data are located in the Tadrart Acacus along the Algero–Libya boundary. It is the case for Ti-n-Hanakaten (Aumassip 1978), Ti-n-Torha cave complex (Barich 1974, 1987, Gauthier 1982, 1987, Gauthier and Van Neer 1982), Uan Muhuggiag (Mori 1965, Barich 1987), Fozzigiaren, Uan Afuda, and Uan Tabu (Di Lernia and Cremaschi 1996, Cremaschi et al. 1996).

Evidence for Late Pleistocene paleoclimatic change and settlement distribution in the Libyan Tadrart Acacus are provided by Di Lernia and Cremaschi (1996), as well as interesting data on early management of wild Barbary sheep (Cremaschi et al. 1996). Regularly visited settlements with stratified deposits situated in rock shelters are concentrated in the Middle Acacus. Shallower sites are found along the former lakeshore, a few kilometers east of the Acacus Plateau. Cremaschi et al. (1996) have recorded more than 150 sites.

Evidence from Uan Afuda Cave clarifies and complexifies the picture of the evolutionary trends at work in the Tadrart Acacus during the Early Holocene period. A layer of consolidated Barbary sheep dung was recorded in stratigraphic Unit 1 with radiometric dates ranging from 8000 to 8900 BP (Di Lernia and Cremaschi 1996). The finding provides evidence for an unsuspected know-how in wild animal management already mastered by Early Holocene Central Saharans. Cattle bones are recorded from contexts dated to 7000 BP onward at Uan Muhuggiag, Fozzigiaren, Ti-n-Torha cave complex, and probably Ti-n-Hanakaten, which is the southernmost among the tested Tadrart Acacus sites. This area played the role of a gateway in the transfer of livestock from the Eastern Sahara to the Western part of Africa. The faunal remains from two key sites, Ti-n-Torha East and Uan Muhaggiag, are considered in more detail below.

Ti-n-Torha East is a shallow rock shelter located on the east of the Ti-n-Torha circus at seven hundred meters above sea level in the northern part of the Tadrart Acacus. The site is extended over approximately two hundred square meters, of which eighty-three square meters were excavated (Barich 1974). A series of five huts' stone foundations set along the cave wall have been exposed as well as a 1.8-meter-thick stratigraphic sequence, divided into five occupation levels dated from c. 9000 to 7500 BP. The faunal remains sample made of 1,004 bones was analyzed by Cassoli and Durante (1974), Gautier (1982), and Gautier and van Neer (1982). The discussion conducted below intends to outline the importance of the diet-breadth model in attempts to understand subsistence changes, and in this case, the adoption of cattle pastoralism. The analysis examines changes in Ti-n-Torha East archaeological sequence faunal spectra and this in connection with K. Flannery (1969) concept of "broad spectrum revolution." (BSR) (Stiner 2001, Zeder 2012). BSR, equivalent to "Niche Construction Theory" (NCT), refers to hunter-gatherers broadening their resource bases through the exploitation of increasing numbers of animal and plant species prior to the shift to food-producing economies.

As far as Ti-n-Torha East is concerned, no animal bone was collected from the earliest occupation layer R. base. Fifty-three bones belonging to twelve animal species were collected from layer R. Inf. Level R. Sup yielded 145 bones distributed into nineteen species. In level CII the number of recorded animal bones jumps to 649 pieces belonging to forty species. And finally, the bone frequency falls back to 157 pieces from twenty-four species in the uppermost level CI.

In all the recorded cases, Barbary sheep is the preferential animal game; but as far as the faunal spectra are concerned, there is a sustained increase in the number of species from level R. Inf to CII, varying from twelve to forty, followed by a sharp drop to twenty-four in level CI. It is worth noting at this juncture that two large metapodials (from level CII and CI) have been assigned to a large bovid (Gauthier and van Neer 1982: 97). The appearance of a large bovid species in a context of "constantly" broadening faunal spectrum may be significant. It may signal a solution to an enduring subsistence crisis, a fact that may explain why the faunal spectrum is significantly narrowed during the occupation of level CI, and this shortly before the onset of genuine pastoral nomadic lifeways as shown by the evidence from Uan Muhuggiag further south.

The site of Uan Muhuggiag in the Tadrart Acacus plateau, on the bank of wadi Teshuinat at nine hundred meters above sea level, was settled from c. 7500 to 3700 BP (Barich 1987, Belluomini and Manfra 1987). It is characterized by the presence of paintings on the cave's walls (Mori 1965) and a stratigraphic sequence made of seven distinct occupation levels. The amount of recorded stone tools varies from a minimum of seventy-seven pieces in the earliest occupation level (level 2d) to a maximum of 406 found in level 2a. Two animal bone collections, here termed the Pasa and Barich collections, are available for analysis. The Pasa collection is made of faunal remains from ten distinct archaeological layers (I to X), and the Barich collection from seven (Layers 1, 1a, 2, 2a–2d). As judged from the frequency distribution of animal bones, hunting seems to have played a minor role in Uan Muhuggiag subsistence systems, clearly based on livestock husbandry of sheep/goats and cattle. In both collections, Barbary sheep (*Ammotragus lervia*) is the preferentially hunted species, with bone frequency ranging from one to twenty-seven. Uan Muhuggiag cave is clearly a pastoral nomadic seasonal station; both collections nonetheless suggest different evolutionary patterns. In the Barich collection, sheep/goats are predominant all along the seven recorded levels following a pattern of sustained increase, with proportion relative to cattle varying from 3/2 in the earliest level 2d, 2/2 in level 2c, 28/11 in level 2b, 22/15 in level 2a, 26/3 in level 2, 24/6 in level 1a, and finally, 98/3 in level 1. The pattern observed in the Pasa collection has much more contrast. Sheep/goats are slightly predominant in the two earliest levels with proportion relative to cattle varying from 1/1 in level X to 5/0 in level IX. Cattle is then predominant in the following five levels, with proportion of 5/8 in level VIII, 1/6 in level VII, 1/2 in level VI, 5/6 in level V, and 16/20 in level IV. The pattern shifts again toward the predominance of sheep/goats, with 18/15 in level III and 11/10 in level II, and finally ends with the predominance of cattle, with a relative proportion of 5/9 in the uppermost level I.

Thanks to the relative richness of the archaeo-zoological data from Uan Muhuggiag, no simple evolutionary scenario can yet be offered to explain the differences between both collections of animal bones. Cave paintings are difficult to interpret, not only because of difficulties in assigning narrow precise time ranges but also because of the ambiguity and polysemy of the meanings of visual representations. They are widespread in Africa and are divided into two main overlapping categories: engravings, which are the most widespread, and paintings, which seem to be restricted to higher elevations in the Tadrart Acacus, Tibesti, Jebel Uweinat, Ahaggar, and especially the Tassili-n-Ajjer (Muzzolini 1995). A broad range of motifs is represented in rock artworks; it is nonetheless uncontroversial that pastoral scenes are largely represented in the Tassili-n-Ajjer. The case of the Tassili-n-Ajjer suggests the existence of mature and well-developed pastoral–nomadic societies in at least some parts of the Central Sahara from the later part of the Early Holocene onward.

Test excavations indicate the presence of mobile hunter-herder groups in the area around 6500–6000 BP (Holl 1995: 76–77). It is worth noting that the Tassili-n-Ajjer is a difficult terrain with steep valleys, cliffs, and inselbergs; painting stations are preferentially concentrated in the landscape portion situated above 1,200 meters asl. It is highly probable that part of the landscape dotted with hundreds of painting stations was not an ordinary mundane component of the Tassilian pastoralists behavioral space. The concentration of Saharan visual representations "masterpieces" in the Tassili-n-Ajjer suggests a peculiar status of that "Highland" (Holl 1995, 2006). It may have had some connection with initiation and rites of passage and/or prowess and skills necessary to achieve genuine adulthood. The Mathendous and other Libyan and Moroccan Atlas Rock images sites consist mostly of engravings (Le Quellec 1993, Muzzolini 1995) comprising representations of cattle, wild fauna, and humans, both males and females, some of them with strong symbolic implications.

North Africa

In the east, mixed farming was already well represented in the Nile Delta and the Fayum Depression by c. 5000 BCE. Barley, emmer, and flax were the main cultivated plants, while sheep, goats, cattle, pigs, and dogs were kept. "The donkey, an indigenous African species, was first domesticated in the Nile valley at about this time" (Phillipson 1993a: 136). In the western coastal part of North Africa, the "Neolithic" culture traits, basically pottery, ground stone implements, and arrowheads, were recorded in a relatively restricted area along the southern shore of the Gibraltar Straits in northern Morocco

(Martinez-Sanchez et al. 2018a, b, Salazar-Garcia and Garcia-Puchol 2017). According to Camps (1982), cattle and sheep/goat bones were found in some of these sites, associated with Cardial pottery, as is the case at El Khril near Tangiers. "Throughout this area it seems likely that the introduction of domestic small stock was broadly contemporary with the beginning of pottery manufacture: bones of such animals were recorded from the lowest levels of El Khril and may represent the first type of farming to be practiced in this part of north Africa" (Phillipson 1993a: 142). Two cave sites, Haua Fteah in Cyrenaica in the Machrek and Cappeleti cave in Algeria in the Aures Mountains, with their archaeozoological material studied by E. S. Higgs (1967, 1979), provide important clues. Haua Fteah is the Arabic name of an impressively large natural cave on the northern coast of Cyrenaica in Libya. It is located approximately half a mile from the coast at about sixty-five meters above sea level; its opening is some twenty meters high and sixty meters wide (Mc Burney 1967: 1–3). An impressive archaeological sequence, with almost continuous settlement evidence spanning the past 100–80,000 years was recorded. The sequence is divided into settlement phases of varying length. It is Phase F recorded in layers VIII–VII, dated to 5000–2700 BCE, and termed "Neolithic of Libyco-Capsian Tradition" (Mc Burney 1967: 327), that is of interest in this discussion. According to Mc Burney (1967), the cultural transformations attested in Phase F do not suggest any substantial ethnic change. Such transformations include the first appearance of domestic sheep/goat, the introduction of pottery, and pressure-working in flint tool manufacture. These changes occurred while the predominant lithic tradition preserved the major characteristics of the preceding Phase E Libyco-Capsian (c. 8000–5000 BCE), with minor alteration of some details. Haua-Fteah domesticates consist exclusively of sheep/goat. A comparison of the mean dimensions of measurable Caprini bones from the site sequence shows without exception that "there is a sharp and consistent fall in mean bone size from Libyco-Capsian layers to the Early Neolithic" (Higgs in Mc Burney 1967: 315). There is no indication that the decrease in bone size was gradual as may be expected from a long-term local process of domestication. The change was abrupt. In addition, the number of young animals butchered shifted from 2–11 percent in Phases A to E to 25–32 percent in Phase F Neolithic levels (Higgs in Mc Burney 1967: 313), suggesting the development of herd management strategies. Some peculiar "cultural practices" have also been reported: "in spit 1955/7 there are 23 scapulae, 20 humeri, 16 metatarsals and many broken fragments of sheep or goat less than 1 year old. The small carcasses were probably buried intact for most of the fragile bones were recovered" (Higgs in Mc Burney 1967: 318). It is clear that the young animals were not eaten; the cave was large enough to shelter humans and their flocks, as protection against predators as well as sheepfold during parturition. Finally, for E. S.

Higgs (1967: 317), the abrupt establishment of domestic sheep/goat at Haua Fteah "suggests that they were domesticated at an earlier date elsewhere. This would be in accordance with the prior appearance of few sheep or goat bones in the preceding Libyco-Capsian."

Cappeleti Cave is situated in the Aures Mountains range in the Constantine province in Algeria. The cave, located on the northwestern slope at 1540 m above sea level at sixty to sixty-five meters above wadi Berbaga, measures approximately eighty square meters in surface extent divided into two "rooms" (Roubet 1979). The stratigraphic sequence is almost continuous without noticeable break probably due to the slow rate of sediment accumulation in the cave context. The recorded archaeological sequence spanning over a little more than two thousand years is divided into four occupation periods. The earliest series of occupation episodes termed Period I and recorded at the base of the stratigraphic section (deposit 11) is dated from 6530–6250 to 5900–6150 B.P. The cave was then settled for the first time by groups of ovicaprid herders, bringing with them a "Capsian-like" pottery with conical-base vessels, bone and stone tools, grinding equipment, and, finally, elements of personal adornment (beads, pendants). The second occupation series, Period II, is dated from c. 5900 to 5740–6140 BP; the third from ca. 5740 to 5400–6140 BP; and finally, the fourth from 4670–6130 to 4360–6130 BP. The material culture from the whole archaeological sequence clearly belongs to the Capsian Tradition (Balout 1955; Camps 1974, 1982; Roubet 1979) and was thus termed "Neolithic of Capsian tradition." The repertoire of stone tools consists of rare ground axes, grinding equipment, varying proportion of geometric, notched, and denticulated pieces, as well as arrowheads. The subsistence system was clearly a broad spectrum one with livestock husbandry predominant; freshwater and terrestrial mollusks as well as wild fruits and berries were collected; wild boars, antelopes, gazelles, and migratory birds were hunted. The cave was generally settled on a seasonal basis, in spring, summer, and part of fall, as suggested by plant macro remains and juvenile sheep/goat bones (Roubet 1979: 392, 515). As far as livestock is concerned, sheep and goat bones are by far the predominant species with 10,407 bones out of a domesticates total of 12,050. Their proportion relative to cattle varies from 299/43 in Period I, 3777/751 in Period II, 5370/663 in Period III, and, finally, 790/357 in Period IV (Roubet 1979: 384–91). Unfortunately, kill-off patterns were not examined at the level of each occupation series. The data available nonetheless suggest the existence of a mature pastoral system based on transhumance between the lowlands settled in winter and the highlands visited for the rest of the year. The aging of butchered animals using different bones shows a converging pattern: 1) 98 percent of radii proximal and humeri distal ends belong to animals less than ten months old; 2) 55 percent of tibias and metapodials distal ends belong to animals less than two years old; 3)

70 percent of radii distal, femurs proximal, as well as calcaneum belong to adult individuals, but aged less than three and half years; 4) 82 percent of tibias proximal and femurs distal ends belong to adult individuals, but less than three and half years old; and finally, 5), teeth eruption shows that 73 percent of the studied sample belong to young animals, less than two years old (Roubet 1979: 392). The size of the site points to a relatively small group, a special-purpose group of young herders for example, or a single family or household.

West Africa

There is a clear chronological cline in the distribution of livestock remains in West Africa archaeological sites, with a relatively sharp southern limit that may have coincided with an ecological/cultural boundary (Finucane et al. 2008, Holl 1998, 2004, Jousse 2004). The limit may have been ecological because of the presence of tsetse fly or cultural because different foodways were developed in wetter southern areas. In the present state of research, there is no single evidence for livestock in northwestern Sahara, in the extensive area situated between the Atlas and the Aures Mountains in Morocco and Algeria in the north, to the Ahaggar in the east, and the Tanezrouft in the south, along the Mali–Algeria boundary (Balout 1955, Aumassip 1986). This area seems to have been settled, according to the vagaries of Holocene climatic change, by mobile forager groups, some of them with pottery linked to the "Capsian" world as is the case at Wadi Zegag (Camps 1974, 1982, Holl 2004, Lihoreau 1993). It can safely be considered that the northwestern portion of the Saharan Desert did not act as a corridor for the transfer of livestock from North to West Africa (Holl 1998a, 1998b, 2004).

As far as West Africa is concerned, the earliest sites with livestock remains dated to 6000–5000 BP are Adrar Bous and Arlit, located along the western edge of the Tenere and the Air Mountain range in modern Niger (Smith 1992). Presumably, domesticated cattle then spread south and southwestward, with a fluorescence of food-producing communities between ca. 4500 to 3500 BP, at Tintan and Chami along the Atlantic Coast of Western Sahara; Taoudenni basin at Erg-in Sakane, Adrar-n-Ifogha, and Tilemsi valley in modern Mali (Finucane et al. 2008); Dhar Tichitt in Mauretania; Eghazzer basin and Azawagh valley in modern Niger (Holl 2013); Kintampo culture area in Ghana, Gajiganna in Bornu State in Nigeria, as well as mounds sites of northeastern Nigeria, northern Cameroon, and western Chad (Connah 198, Holl 2002). Two cases are singled out here; the first concerns the presence of livestock in early context of Kintampo culture sites in Ghana (Stahl 1985, 1993, Anquandah 1993), and the second deals with Gajiganna in northeastern Nigeria (Breunig et al. 1993, 1996).

In general, judged from what is known on mid-Holocene climatic change, Kintampo culture settlements found at Bosumpra, Mumute, Kintampo rock shelters, Bonoase, Boyasi hill, Daboya and Ntereso, etc., were located in the forest/savanna ecotone, with characteristically shifting vegetation boundaries. "In many respects, the Kintampo complex represents a major departure from the 'typical' Late Stone Age [complexes]," with "aspects of continuity with the preceding Punpun phase which underlie the 'new' elements" (Stahl 1993: 265). The new elements alluded to include the evidence for exploitation of sheep/goat, oil palm, presumably yam cultivation, and, finally, a move toward increased sedentism. The degree of reliance on exotic animal species is still unclear, and the debate on the status of the recorded animal bones is still going on as summarized by Anquandah (1993: 258). Although there seems to be general agreement that faunal remains of ovicaprids recovered from Kintampo K6 contexts and Ntereso are those of domesticates, there is no consensus about the character of eight bovid bones found at K6, since the remains appear to belong to creatures smaller than the grassland buffalo and modern *Bos* spp. Similarly, there is uncertainty as to whether the faunal remains of guinea fowl (*Numida meleagris*) found in K6 rock shelter level 3 belong to domesticated, tamed, captive, or wild species. Faunal remains of what have been claimed as *Bos* sp. excavated from Mumute have not been scientifically identified. From this short overview, it appears that the livestock side of the "Kintampoan" foodways is still poorly understood and deserves more systematic investigation in the future. It is probably in ecological and cultural contexts, like the Kintampo culture one, that few goat variants went through a selection process, leading to nanny goats, widespread today in humid equatorial Africa.

Gajiganna is a site complex made of two low mounds located in the northern part of the Bama Deltaic Complex in northeastern Nigeria (Breunig et al. 1996). This sedimentary formation combining longitudinal dunes and material deposited by the rivers Ngadda and Yedseram comprises slightly raised sandy areas, clay plains, and depressions, generating a gentle undulating topography. The site occupation sequence recorded in two distinct excavation probes (Gajiganna A and B) has been partitioned into two major units: an upper cultural layer dated to 1200–900 BCE, and a lower cultural layer dated to 1500–1200 BCE in calibrated C^{14} dates. Gajiganna thus seems to have been settled for an approximate duration of 600 years (Breunig et al. 1996: 125). The subsistence base of past "Gajigannans" appears to have been particularly broad, with mollusk exploitation (*Aspartharia* sp., *Pila* sp., and *Limicolaria* sp.), fishing (*Gymnarchus* sp., *Clarias* sp., etc.), hunting of birds and a broad range of wild mammals, and, finally, livestock husbandry. Evidence for wild fruit gathering was also recorded but it is not known if there was any initial reliance on cultivated crops (Breunig et al. 1993, 1996).

It is clear from the frequency distribution of animal bones that: the economy of the prehistoric settlement was dominated by domestic animals: goat, sheep, and cattle. Domestic dogs were probably raised as well. Sheep were rare in comparison to goats. Cattle played the most important role in livestock herding. More than 60 percent of the bones of all the mammals represented in the archaeological record belong to cattle. Small clay figurines indicate a southern breed (Breunig et al. 1993: 31). Archaeo-zoological data on domestic animals from Gajiganna are puzzling; further research is planned to clarify some of the issues linked to seasonality; "the cattle and goat remains comprise several juvenile and neonate specimens which should allow us to determine approximately the season during which they died" (Breunig et al. 1996: 130). However, it is not known if there is any significant change in kill-off patterns or herd management strategies between the lower and the upper cultural layers, the species frequency having been tabulated from all the collected faunal remains lumped in a single six-hundred-year sample and published as a global set for each excavation unit without stratigraphic levels differentiation. More specifically, one would like to know if the proportion of cattle relative to sheep/goats is constant throughout the site occupation, which was about six hundred years long. In fact, judged from the section of Gajiganna B Mound (Breunig et al. 1996: 124), the site sequence is made of five archaeological levels, from bottom to top: 1–3: basal cultural layers 7, 6, and 5; 4: lower cultural layer 4; and finally, 5: upper cultural layer 3. From an integrated regional perspective, the Gajiganna sequence needs to be linked to that of neighboring contemporary settlements to be tested in the future. From the present-day evidence alone, there are important indications for a some-what consistent reliance on livestock in the western part of the Chad Basin by the middle of the second millennium BCE (cf. part 3). The Chad Basin ecosystem as well as present-day climatic pattern can be used to suggest that Gajiganna was part of a broader, more comprehensive settlement-subsistence system in which pastoral activities may have been particularly concentrated and intensive during some seasons in specific parts of the landscape. The status of the "Gajigannan" settlement subsistence system is not yet clear: 1) Were they specialized pastoralist groups living on the edge of and interacting with agriculturalist settlements? 2) Were they components of mixed farming communities (predominantly young male herders) that happened to deal with livestock herding during the lean seasons? As is usually the case in archaeology, Gajiganna raises a number of interesting issues that can help orient the discussion on pastoralist territoriality in West Africa. A few hundred kilometers east, in the Cameroonian part of the Chad Basin, with major climatic, sedimentary, and vegetation patterns similar to those of the Gajiganna area, thick deposits of livestock dung have been recorded at the base of Deguesse mound and dated to 3350+/-270 BP(Ly-4177), calibrated to 1890–1430 BCE

(Holl 2002). In his previous research in the archaeology of Bornu, Connah (1981) has recorded the presence of domestic animals, cattle and sheep/goats dating from 1000 BCE onward, along a south–north transect stretching from Bama Road Site on the Bama ridge in the south to the Yobe River valley settlements in the north (Yau, Birni-Ghazzargamo), on the western shore of Lake Chad.

East Africa

Unfortunately, very little is known about the archaeology of southern Sudan, eastern Central African Republic, northeastern Congo, and northern Uganda. It is highly probable that these poorly investigated areas may have witnessed the south and southeastward transfer of domesticated animals. As far as the development of food production is concerned, the situation is not particularly better documented in Ethiopia. "It is surprising and disappointing that very little archaeological endeavor has so far been devoted to elucidating the early history of Ethiopian food-production. Indeed, only one localized field project has so far been devised specifically to illuminate this matter- . . . and, . . . the post-Pleistocene prehistory of Ethiopia has been investigated only cursorily" (Phillipson 1993b: 346). Domesticates—cattle, sheep, goats, horses, donkeys, and camels—are reported mostly from rock art stations, as clay figurines representing humped and humpless cattle, or from inscriptions referring "to cattle and small stock in large numbers, generally as tribute, booty, or army provisions" (Phillipson 1993b: 355). Finally, what can be referred to as firm archaeozoological evidence for domesticates comes from the earlier level of Lalibela Cave, dated to ca. 500 BCE, and consists of bones identified as those of cattle and sheep/goat.

In general, more intensive fieldwork was carried out in different parts of Eastern Africa on the development of food-producing economies, in Kenya mostly but also in parts of Tanzania (Robertshaw 2021). D. Gifford-Gonzales (1998, 2017) addressed one of the most intriguing issues in the understanding of the geographic distribution of "pastoral-Neolithic" sites in eastern Africa. An important time gap is observed in the spread of domesticated animals from Northern to southern Kenya. "Pastoralists entered northern Kenya during the third millennium BCE, but their arrival in southern Kenya and northern Tanzania is on present evidence dated only to the end of the second millennium" (Robertshaw 1993: 358). Robertshaw (1993) states that "similarities between ceramics from northern Kenya and undated sites in the south suggest that future research will bridge the chronological gap" and, as such, considers the situation to be an artifact of insufficient research. D. Gifford-Gonzales (1998) addressed that intriguing chronological and distributional case. Her explanation is grounded in community ecology, using epizootiology as a variable in the explanation of the differential distribution of cattle in the land-scape. It is thus suggested that the recorded differential distribution may have resulted from the existence of pathogens—viruses propagated by wildebeest in their natural home range, generating virulent and lethal sickness for cattle. Early pastoralist groups developed patterned avoidance behaviors of infested areas and were accordingly confined to territories with very low densities or even no population of wildebeest, expanding into new areas according to variation in the distribution of wild fauna. The model is a robust one, sus-ceptible to further testing and refutation with archaeo-faunas. This approach is complemented by an integration of a social interaction perspective. She suggests the existence of well entrenched differences in worldviews between expanding pastoralist groups and aboriginal hunter–gatherers, a fact that may explain selective borrowing, or the adoption of some cultural features or material items. Such a cultural tapestry make sense of some puzzling patterns in the distribution of material culture remains and the intricate culture–history framework of the whole area under consideration.

Prendergast et al. (2019) relied on genome-wide aDNA data from the skeletal material of forty-one burials distributed in Kenya and Tanzania, three from the Late Stone Age, thirty-one from Early pastoral and Pastoral Neolithic, one from Farming Iron Age, and six from Pastoral Iron Age, to decipher patterns of expansion of livestock in East Africa. They document a multistep process in a four-stage model as follows, with Late Stone Age individuals belonging to the Forager genetic cline:

1. Admixture in NE Africa, with equal Sudanese Nilotic speakers' ances-try on the one hand, and Northern Africa/Levantine groups (Afroasiatic speakers).
2. Admixture of these NE Africans with East African Foragers.
3. An additional component of Sudan related ancestry [Nilotic] contribut-ing to Iron Age pastoralist groups.
4. And finally, Western Africa ancestry (Bantu) appearing with the spread of farming.

The earliest East African pastoralist groups were formed some five thou-sand years ago around Lake Turkana and from there evolved through admix-ture into Elmenteitan and Savanna Pastoral Neolithic.

South Africa

The spread of Early Iron Age (EIA) communities in the southern half of Africa (Lander and Russell 2018) was rapid with settlements already estab-lished in Transvaal by the third century CE and the early fourth century CE in Natal (Plug and Voigt 1985). For T. Maggs (1994–1995: 173). The EIA arrived as a package that included metallurgy, crop cultivation, settled village life, livestock husbandry and distinctive ceramics (cf. part 4). Domestic animals were introduced in southern Africa between 2,400 and 1,800 years ago, with the earliest occurrence of cattle dated to c. 380 BCE documented at Salumano in Zambia (Plug 1996: 516).

In general, however, early cattle remains dated between c. 250 and 550 CE were recorded at Nkope in Malawi, Broederstroom, Happy Rest, and Kwagandaganda in South Africa (Plug 1996, Plug and Voigt 1985). In Mozambique there is no evidence for animal husbandry in Kwale and Matola Tradition contexts, with the only exception from later occupation at Zitundo. Sheep/goat and cattle bones were found in the south and south-central part of the country, at Chibuene and Massangir, where they are dated from the mid to late first millennium CE (Sinclair et al. 1993). By the middle of the first millennium CE, from c. 500 CE onward, domesticates including cattle, sheep, goats, dogs, and chicken, all components of mixed-farming economies involving the cultivation of millet (*Pennisetum typhoides*), sorghum (*Sorghum bicolor*), and a legume (*Vigna unguiculata*), are widespread in southern Africa. Consistent occurrence and on average larger samples of domestic animal bones dating from the second half of the first millennium CE have been reported from Namaga, Bulila, Salumano, and Isamu Pati Mound in Kalomo district in Zambia; Matope court and Namichimba in Malawi; Magogo, Msuluzi, and Ndondodwane in Natal; Lydenburg Head Site, Le6, Ficus A, and Ficus B in Transvaal; Zhizo and Toutswe. Tradition sites such as Taukome, Shroda, and Pont Drift and Commando Cop in Botswana; as well as at several localities in Zimbabwe (Pwiti 1994–1995, 1996, Plug and Voigt 1985, Plug 1996, 1997, Clutton-Brock 1994–1995, Kiyaga Mulindwa 1993, Huffman 1982, 1986).

It is probably during this formative period that the major characteristics of the Bantu Cattle Culture System were developed and laid down (Huffman, 1982, 1986, 1996). The Bantu Cattle Culture System as analyzed by Huffman comprises two distinctive components: the Central Cattle Pattern and the Zimbabwe Culture pattern. The Central Cattle Pattern found among most Bantu speakers of southern Africa reflects "their attitudes to economy, society, and religion [and] result[s] in a specific arrangement whereby an outer arc of houses, arranged according to some alternating system of status, surround a central zone that contains cattle byres, grain storage facilities, elite burials, and the men's court" (Huffman 1986: 296). The central cattle area characteristic of this pattern was thus "a focus of male economic, ritual and political activity" (Huffman 1986: 299). Huffman considers the Central Cattle Pattern to have emerged in the eighth and ninth centuries CE among Zhizo Tradition Bantu agriculturalists from the Shashi-Limpopo basin, and from

there expanded through large scale migration, in parallel with the development of long-distance Indian Ocean trade.

The Zimbabwe Culture Pattern first developed at Mupungubwe Hill by
the early beginning of the second millennium CE. It is characterized by an
upslope shift of the royal court, with monumental architectural remains,
totally dis-embedded from commoners' habitations. It corresponded to the
development of a bureaucratic class in a system in which "royalty controlled
access to wealth and political power" (Huffman 1986: 304). Relying on
Venda ethnography, Huffman (1986) quotes evidence according to which
"royalty was said to have owned all the cattle, so that bride-price of commoners consisted of small stock, hoes and so on and no commoner could afford
a royal wife." Settlement hierarchy, regional distribution of sites, and kill-off
patterns support the idea of a tight control of the elite and members of royal
households on the livestock (Barker 1988, Denbow 1983). "It has been clear
for some time that cattle dominate most Zimbabwe faunal samples from the
central plateau (Great Zimbabwe, Harleigh Farm enclosure, Khami). All the
samples were cattle dominated, all had low proportions of small stock and
game, and all except that of the Acropolis midden and Khami had similar age
composition, with about 30% of cattle killed under 30 months and the rest
mature" (Barker 1988: 228). Of the cattle bones from the Great Zimbabwe
Acropolis midden, 75 percent belong to animals under thirty months of age;
this midden certainly contains refuse from the king, his kin, and close advis-
ers. The refuse from the royal quarter at Khami is also characterized by an
unusually high number of young animals. "It seems clear that the slaughter of
calves was a particular feature of the royal life style if not of the Zimbabwe
economy as a whole" (Barker 1988: 228). The pattern of meat production and
consumption recorded at royal sites was probably based on surplus young
male cattle collected as tribute from surrounding communities.

With the development of the Zimbabwe Culture Pattern, "cattle keeping played a critical role in the territorial organization of the main series of
Zimbabwe enclosures on the Central Plateau" (Barker 1988: 229). The fact
that Huffman extends the Central Cattle Pattern back in time into the first millennium CE is still a matter of an ongoing debate, even if acknowledged as an
important contribution to the studied topic, supported as it is by some empirical evidence from sites like Broederstroom and Kwagandaganda. According
to Maggs (1994–1995: 176–77), there are numerous cultural attributes within
the Early Iron Age that are not explained by the Central Cattle Pattern or the
southern Bantu ethnography. Three of them are mentioned: 1) the very importance of cattle and the centrality of their pens is not entirely established, as it
has been generally suggested that sheep and goats were more important than
cattle to the Early Iron Age communities; 2) the issue of central grain storage
pits and elite burials is complex and still unresolved; and finally, 3) Natal

evidence shows that iron smelting, and not only forging, was practiced in central parts of settlements, suggesting that the idea of exclusion of smelting from ordinary living space is not accurate in all the known cases.

The western part of southern Africa, from Angola to the Cape Province in South Africa, witnessed a different path for the adoption of livestock husbandry. Early occurrences of sheep bones found in the Cape Province and dated from 2100 to 1900 BP (Inskeep 1997, Smith 1997) are still poorly understood and support the view formulated by Plug (1996: 516) according to which "sheep are also associated with Khoi pastoralists from a somewhat earlier period. At present it is not clear how these pastoralists obtained their livestock." Very little is known about the archaeology of eastern and southern Angola; the expansion of nomadic pastoralism in Namibia has been subject of sustained investigation by John Kinahan (1993, 1994–1995), while Smith (1992, 1997) has been involved since many years in renewed archaeological research on pastoralism in the Cape Province. He describes the paradox involved in the relationship between pastoralists and hunter-gatherers from a broad range of ethnographic case studies. He shows that herders generally rely on hunter-gatherers for their success in their expansion in new ecological and climatic zones; but at the same time, they drive the hunter-gatherers on the peripheries of the most productive lands and tend to despise them. In his archaeological case study based on evidence from Kasteelberg and Witklip in the Cape Province (Smith 1998), he shows how different parallel cultural universes have coexisted for centuries, without radical alteration of their respective material culture, economy, and traditions. He thus suggests that "such continued separation indicates a formative class structure in the pastoral environment, with hunters at the bottom of the social hierarchy"(Smith 1997: 211). In Namibia, archaeological evidence from the Hungorob ravine, eighty kilometers inland in the desert interior and the!Khuiseb Delta coastal dune-fields, shows that pottery arrived half a millennium before livestock, in this case mostly sheep. At Falls rock and Snake rock shelters in the Hungorob ravine, pottery occurred between 2100 and 1800 BP. It arrived south in the!Khuised Delta between 1500 and 1200 BP. (Kinahan 1993, 1994–1995). In the Hungorob ravine, "the paintings clearly suggest a shift in religious practice towards the end of the rock-shelter sequence. Taken together, with the introduction of pottery and the abandonment of the rock-shelter sites once livestock was established in the area, the evidence on the whole favors a local transition to pastoralism rather than the displacement of hunters by immigrant pastoral groups" (Kinahan 1993: 377). After 1000 CE, a settlement system with, on the one hand, small homesteads with stock enclosures in the upper reaches of the ravine, near main waterholes and rock art sites, and large encampments at the ravine entrance, on the other hand, was well established as a transhumance axis. It was later connected to an extensive network of aggregation and dispersal sites widely distributed across the Namib.

Data from southern Africa thus offer a number of scenarios ranging from the adoption of livestock husbandry by groups of hunter-gatherers, the process of which is still poorly investigated, to the migration of whole culture groups with more or less highly integrated food-ways. Livestock husbandry spread in the southern portion of the continent before farming, and relatively rapidly from today's Namibia southward and eastward. Lander and Russell (2018) synthesized this complex expansion history to Southern Africa in a series of chronological maps. In Sequence I Map 1, ranging from 551 to 351 BCE, sheep and pottery reached the Western half of Southern Africa as seen at Leopard's Cave in Namibia. Slightly later, evidence of decorated pottery is found in southern Mozambique. In sequence II Map 2 (350–150 BCE), the earliest sheep bones from South Africa are found at Spoegriver cave, a LSA forager site. Pottery is widespread and documented in multiple contexts. And finally in sequence III Map 3 (149 BCE–51 CE), the earliest cattle bones associated with sheep remains are found in a LSA site in Botswana while pottery and sheep are documented in many more sites in Namibia.

In summary, the expansion of livestock and adoption of pastoralism kicked off from Northeast Africa, following multi-episode introductions and admixtures took several millennia to reach both the western and southern edges of the continent. The process was always in state of flux, with pushes and pulls according to environmental conditions. The area out of reach in ancient time, and this for obvious environmental reasons, was the equatorial rainforest. During the past millennium however, and more precisely the past few decades, Fulani pastoralists expanded southward, along the northern edge of the equatorial forest, in the Central African Republic as well as Cameroon. Livestock, and especially cattle has always been involved in the fabric of herders' social systems. It was—and still is—integrated in loose expanding and dissipative nomadic and/or ranked societies in northeastern, western, and eastern Africa, in loosely differentiated sedentary societies practicing mixed agropastoral village-based economies in west Africa and the Nile valley, as well as in strongly differentiated and ranked societies in Southern Africa. In some cases, certainly in eastern and southern Africa, livestock expanded along with migrating groups. In others, as is the case for Namibia and probably the largest part of the Cape Province hinterland, the presence of domestic animals initiated far-reaching transformations of previous prehistoric hunter-gatherer societies, generating the formation of new cultural identities. "The history of African pastoralism explains the contemporary genetic composition of African cattle. . . . Domesticated within the continent but genetically influenced by centers of cattle domestication in the Near East and the Indus valley, modern African breeds represent a unique genetic resource at a juncture when there is an urgent need to improve livestock productivity for the benefit of the present and future human generations" (Hanotte et al. 2002: 3390).

HANDLING CATTLE: OPPORTUNITIES AND CHALLENGES

As is the case for all living organisms, cattle spread in most parts of Africa with their pathogens and variable adaptive plasticity to different environmental settings. Cattle pastoralism involves constant adjustment to environmental parameters, juggling with animal needs (health, water, and pasture), human needs (subsistence, social sustainability, and health), as well as the constitutive variability of climate parameters, essentially seasonality and climate cycling. Successful pastoralists' traditions have to strike a balance—usually instable—between all key parameters mentioned above through cultural creativity and flexibility. In this regard, increased aridity for example affects all components of the local biospheres. It impacts fodder and water, two key variables of sustainable livestock husbandry. Poor grazing and water shortage affect livestock and human health, increase susceptibility to diseases (contagious bovine pleuropneumonia, Rift Valley fever), death, and pastoralists' impoverishment. It also heightens intergroup conflicts triggered by raiding/counter-raiding as a livestock replenishing strategy.

Climate change and global warming impacts are more obvious today. Assembled data show that "climate change drives the emergence of diseases where arthropods vectors are sensitive to environmental changes" (Tomley and Shirley 2009: 2639, McDaniel et al. 2014). Zoonoses account for approximately 60 percent of new disease introduction. "Ungulates are the most important non-human host, both in terms of the number of zoonotic pathogens species supported as well as among emerging and re-emerging zoonotic species" (McDaniel et al. 2014). Pathogens susceptible to affect humans and cattle are bacterial (42 percent), parasitic (29 percent), viruses (22 percent), and prions (infectious proteins 2 percents). Consequently, " both the CDC [Centers for Disease Control] and the NIAID [National Institute of Allergy and Infectious Disease] have listed approximately half of all bovine zoonotic pathogens as both biological weapons (52%) and as potential emerging pathogens (50%)" (McDaniel et al. 2014: 14). Disrupted environments have dire consequences for pastoral communities in the present, and very likely in the past too (Di Lernia 2006, Di Lernia et al. 2013, Holl 2013, Pantuliano and Pavanello 2009, Western and Finch 1986).

Beside the usual seasonal mobility patterns, pastoralists, past and present, generally rely on two main strategies to handle environmental crises: migration in search for new more favorable lands on the one hand (Holl 1998, 2013,

Phelps et al. 2019); or local cultural adjustments (Di Lernia 2006, Di Lernia et al. 2013) via "Bad Times" innovative livestock management strategies. Western and Finch's (1986) observational and experimental research on cattle husbandry in drought contexts provides pertinent referents. "The reduction in food maintenance requirements when nutritive conditions deteriorate, and the rapid weight increase when they improve" (Western and Finch 1986: 87) are adaptive livestock responses to drought. Tight mating controls allow for cattle birth to take place in the rainy season to optimize availability of milk for calves and human consumption.

In the "cultural" context under consideration, cattle were likely the ultimate social currency. Livestock numbers—large herds—were thus geared to store surplus "meat on the hoof," with surplus from good seasons providing reserves for poor ones (Western and Finch 1986). In "bad years," meat from surplus cattle or sheep and goat is the only reliable food in the dry season. Pastoral-nomadic groups with large herds can accordingly "take greater risks, and prudently . . . slaughter and consume animals in anticipation of their death from starvation" (Western and Finch 1986: 89), and one may add, epizooties.

Zoonoses and Bovine Tuberculosis

There is a direct correlation between cattle herds' health and pastoralists' well-being. Cattle as well as humans can be hosts to unlimited number of pathogens, some transmissible in one or both directions, with differential health impacts. Zoonoses caused by pathogens triggering animal diseases—epizooties—are a constant threat to pastoralists' livelihood and social well-being. McDaniel et al. (2014) have listed forty-five bovine zoonotic pathogens in their review of the epistemology from a public health perspective. Bovine zoonoses are shown to be evenly dispersed around the world, with bacterial pathogens the largest taxonomic group representing 42 percent. They affect different organs and part of human's body. "Several bovine zoonoses of serious public health concern cause pulmonary infections in humans, the most important being zoonotic tuberculosis caused by *Mycobacterium bovis*. . . . or rarely *M. tuberculosis*" (McDaniel et al. 2014: 3).

Etiology of Tuberculosis and Genomics of the Mycobacterium Tuberculosis Complex

Tuberculosis (TB), a highly contagious infectious disease currently affects "nearly 2 billion people worldwide with around 10.4 million new cases of TB each year" (Barberis et al. 2017: 9). It is caused by *Mycobacterium tuberculosis* (MT) and affects the respiratory tract principally, but also bones, gastrointestinal, joint, nervous system, genitourinary tract, and lymph nodes, as well as skin with inflammatory infiltration, formation of tubercles and calcification, necrosis, and fibrosis (Barberis et al. 2017, Koch 1882). MT has very ancient origins. An early progenitor might have infected early hominins in East Africa some three million years ago, and the common ancestor of MT modern strains may have appeared 20,000–15,000 years ago. The *Mycobacterium tuberculosis* complex is comprised of seven species, including *M. bovis* and *M. tuberculosis*, "one of the most devastating bacterial pathogens of humans" (Berg et al. 2011: 670). Tuberculosis, caused either by *M. tuberculosis* or *M. bovis*, is transmitted through breathing droplets from infected human and/or animal subjects and consumption of unpasteurized milk and/or infected meat. Bovine tuberculosis (bTB) transmitted by cattle essentially is endemic among many African pastoralist populations today (Abdelaal et al. 2019, Abdou et al. 2011, Cason et al. 2014, Cleveland et al. 2007, de Garine-Wichatitsky et al. 2013, Dejene et al. 2016, Gumi et al. 2012, Ibrahim et al. 2012, Loiseau et al. 2020, Ndukum et al. 2010, Rasolofo-Razanamparany et al. 1999, Sichewo et al. 2020). Current field observations in different parts of the continent, in North, West, Central, East and southern Africa, point to the increasing threat paused by bTB to cattle production, pastoralists livelihood, and public health, as well the spillover of *M. bovis* to wildlife. The role of livestock as source of human infection is well documented, proceeding through housing—sharing confine living space with cattle, mixing cattle with sheep/goats, contact with animal fluids, and consumption of unpasteurized milk and infected meat.

One of the most effective way of protecting cattle herds is "selective cropping of old, debilitated animals . . . to remove . . . chronic shedders of the disease" (de Garine-Wichatitsky et al. 2013: 1351). How these carcasses are disposed of in African traditional pastoral contexts can be of interest for archaeological investigation of past practices. Such practices are not documented in African cultural anthropology literature but modern practices in handling severe livestock outbreaks as was the case at a pig farm in Namibia are instructive. "Upon confirmation of the diagnosis of African swine fever, the remaining 45 pigs were immediately culled, and the carcasses burned and buried on the farm under the supervision of a state veterinarian" (Samkange et al. 2019: 3).

Genomic research on the *Mycobacterium tuberculosis* complex allows us to map the evolutionary history and geographic trajectories of its multiple strains (Behr 2014, Brosch et al. 2002, Galagan 2014, Garnier et al. 2003, Inlamea et al. 2020, Loiseau et al. 2020, Muller et al. 2009, Orlova and Schurr 2017, Roberts 2015, Witas et al. 2015). The tale of *M. tuberculosis* is a story of how what was most likely a soil bacterium evolved to become one of the most successful human pathogens in history (Galagan 2014), through several transmissions and animal pathogenesis stretched on some 2.8 million years. *M. tuberculosis* spread with human migration out of Africa some

70,000–67,000 years ago reaching India and the Indian Ocean. A second dispersal took place 46,000 years ago reaching the Middle East, Europe, and Asia, expanding later to the Americas. According to Galagan (2014: 311), "during this period, a clone of *M. tuberculosis* that was originally adapted to cause human tuberculosis evolved to infect a non-human mammal, and thus began the transition into non-human ecotypes (*M. bovis*). Such infections then spread to other animals, including cattle, goat, oryx, seals, etc . . .

> It has long been thought that human tuberculosis had its origin as a zoonosis, with *M. bovis* jumping the species barrier and host adapting to humans to become *M. tuberculosis* at the time of cattle domestication 10,000–15,000 years ago" (Garnier et al. 2003: 7881). Brosch et al. (2002) document an evolutionary bottleneck for the *M. tuberculosis* complex 15,000–20,000 years ago. Their research shows that the 100 *M. tuberculosis* complex strains were composed of 46 *M. tuberculosis* strains isolated in 30 countries, 14 *M. africanum* strains, 28 *M. bovis* strains originating in 5 countries, 2 *M. bovis* bacillus Calmette-Guerin vaccine strains, 5 *M. microti* strains, and 5 *M. canetti* strains. The genome of *M. bovis* is smaller than that of *M. tuberculosis*, suggesting that the former is " the final member of a separate lineage represented by *M. africanum*, *M. microti*, and *M. bovis* that branched off from the progenitor of *M. tuberculosis* isolates. (Brosch et al. 2002: 3687)

It has a very large host spectrum infecting a wide range of mammalian species including humans and its early branching suggests that its emergence predates animal domestication, even if domestication may have accelerated its spread to livestock.

Not only did the initial domestication of cattle happen much latter, in the eighth millennium BCE, in Southwest and South Asia, and possibly NE Africa, but also new research using deletion analysis offers a scenario for the evolution of the *M. tuberculosis* complex. Accordingly, *M. tuberculosis* is situated closer to the common progenitor of the complex than *M. bovis*, with the latter evolving from a progenitor of the *M. tuberculosis* complex as a clone showing distinct host preference (Garnier et al. 2003).

Analyses of the evolutionary history of *M. bovis* set the stage for the understanding of the dynamics of ancient and present African cattle populations (Berg et al. 2011, Inlamea et al. 2020, Muller et al. 2009). The study based on 1,235 *M. bovis* genotypes from all over the continent with forty-five new samples from Mozambique shows a strong correlation with the archaeological record. 1) There is a broad North-South diversity gradient, with maximum diversity focused on the proximity to the Near East, where *M. bovis* likely emerged with cattle domestication. And 2), the genetic diversity of *M. bovis* is geographically clustered around the continent, with the Algeria–South

Africa instances resulting from recent European introductions (Inlamea et al. 2020: 1).

Two *M. bovis* clonal complexes have been identified in Africa. The first, named African 1 (Af1) by Muller et al. (2009) is dominant in *Bos taurus* in West and Central Africa. The second, named African 2 (Af2) by Berg et al. (2011) is dominant in *Bos indicus* in East Africa. *M. bovis* African 1 is widespread in Mali, Burkina Faso, Cameroon, Chad, and Nigeria. The origin of the progenitor of Af1 clonal complex is not yet known. If it is assumed that "West central African cattle were infected with a prior population of *M. bovis*, then the Af1 clone could have arisen with a selective advantage, and spread throughout the region, going to fixation in Nigeria, Cameroon, and Chad and replacing the previous population" (Muller et al. 2009: 1957).

It is clearly demonstrated that the consumption of unpasteurized animal milk facilitates zoonotic transfer and is the major mode of transmission of bTB to humans. This pattern points to a coevolution of humans, cattle, and pathogens that enhance the endurance of the disease.

The lactase persistence trait evolved independently in different African populations owing to distinct genetic events (Anguila-Ruiz et al. 2020, Ranciaro et al. 2014, Tiskoff et al. 2007), allowing adult to digest milk and consequently adopt livestock husbandry and pastoralists lifeways. Direct archaeological evidence of the processing of dairy products is documented in Sahara Neolithic visual representations (Holl 2006) and material culture (Dunne et al. 2018). Potsherd samples from Kadero (4600–3800 BCE, Sudan), Takarkori (6370–6100 BCE, Libya), and Gueldawan (5000–4900 BCE, Algeria) present evidence of animal fat congruent with milk. The assembled evidence summarized so far in this section point to the high probability of two-way transmission of bTB—from cattle to human, and human to cattle—during the formation and expansion of African pastoralisms.

Brief Archaeology of Tuberculosis

Despite the lack of direct archaeological evidence from all over the continent, it is axiomatic from data presented in the previous section that bTB had impacted ancient African pastoral societies. Osteoarticular and skeletal lesions of tuberculosis are generally found in the lumbar and thoracic vertebras, hip and knee joints as well as epiphysis and metaphysis of long bones (Harkins et al. 2014, Roberts 2015, Witas et al. 2015, Zink et al. 2003). When the skeleton is affected, it essentially points to evidence of chronic infection, meaning that the subject had tuberculosis for some time before dying.

The earliest confirmed paleopathological evidence of human TB is documented in pre-cattle domestication Southwest Asia. Two instances have been recorded in Syria, at Dja'de el Mughara dated to 8800–8300 BCE in the

North and Tell Aswad dated to 8200–7600 BCE in the South (Baker et al. 2015). Another set, almost contemporaneous to Syrian data and dated from 9250 to 8160 BP (calibrated) years ago, is reported from Atlit-Yam in coastal Israel (Hershkovitz et al. 2008). Later cases pointing to the presence of TB are documented in Germany (5400–4800 BCE), Hungary (fifth millennium), Poland, Portugal, and the Americas (Harkins et al. 2014).

Data from Egypt, a molecular study on three geographically distinct and time-delineated populations, so far, the best documented case study on the archaeology of tuberculosis in Africa (Zink et al. 2003) deserves a closer analysis. The studied sample consists of eighty-three individuals: seven from the Early Dynastic Necropolis of Abydos (c. 3500–2650 BCE), thirty-seven from the Middle Kingdom-Second Intermediate period (2100–1550 BCE), and finally, thirty-nine from the New Kingdom—Late Period, Thebes (1450–500 BCE). Eighteen cases showed evidence of aDNA of the *M. tuberculosis* complex. Of nine cases with morphological indications of tuberculosis spondylitis, 6 revealed evidence for mycobacterial aDNA. Five out of twenty-four cases without pathological alterations tested positive; and finally, seven out of fifty unaltered vertebral bones tested positive.

Comparatively, there was minor variation in the proportion of affected/ unaffected individuals between all three population samples, suggesting that: "tuberculosis was prevalent in Ancient Egypt since very early periods of this civilization" (Zink et al. 2003: 239). The findings pointed to *M. tuberculosis* or *M. africanum* specific signature, but no *M. bovis*–specific pattern was found.

ANCIENT PASTORALISTS COPING STRATEGIES: LIVESTOCK FOCUSED RITUALS

There is no doubt that ancient African pastoralist communities had to deal with epizooties and virulent outbreaks. Genomic research points to the constant presence of *M. bovis*, the pathogen cause of bTB affecting cattle and humans. The disease could have been rampant, peaking under particular circumstances, with devastating consequences for livestock and human health. In such extraordinary circumstances, one has to expect extraordinary measures such as the performance of propitiatory and curative rituals involving cattle and other livestock, as well as the reliance on medicinal plants to protect livestock and humans' health.

Archaeological evidence pertaining to special treatments of cattle/livestock remains, including complete carcasses, partially articulated parts, as well as disarticulated and piled bones disposed of in especially built features, are documented in different regions of Africa north hemisphere, from the

Nile Valley and Eastern Sahara (Egypt) to the Tilemsi Valley (Mali), via the Messak plateau (Libya), and the Tenere and Eghazzer basin (Niger) (Brass 2007, Di Lernia 2006, Di Lernia and Manzi 2002, Di Lernia et al. 2013, Holl 1998a, b, 2013, 2020). Such material signatures, polysemic by definition, can be arranged into two distinct but complementary "behavioral" categories. Category I, includes burial of "untouched" whole carcasses and/or portions of articulated animal parts. Category II is made of single/multiple species collections of livestock remains. Both categories refer to different but complementary ritual practices. Category I points predominantly to either "propitiatory" or "prophylactic" rituals geared to fend off misfortune, correct bad situations, and/or influence the course of future events. Category II pertains to celebratory and festive " thanksgiving" practices, such as "feasting" marking important social events, like weddings, funerals, group reconciliations, victories, etc.

The emergence and expansion of the cultural practices outlined above, generally subsumed under the term of "cattle burials," tend to be conceptualized in strictly religious-adaptive terms, as adjustments to erratic Mid-Holocene climate change (Di Lernia 2006, Di Lernia and Manzi 2002, Di Lernia et al. 2013). Adaptation to environmental change is a critical imperative for all life-sustaining systems. The concept is however too generic and requires some fine-tunning to allow the decipherment of the processes of interest in long-term past human socio-cultural evolution. As will be shown later, Category I ritual performances involving complete untouched cattle carcasses could have been—among many other goals—enacted as part of a culling strategy to remove sick animals from a herd and by so doing stop the spread of infectious diseases.

Animal burials exist during the Badarian, Nagada, and Maadi Buto periods in the Nile Valley. In the Eastern Sahara, nine tumuli excavated at the Northern end of Nabta Playa basin contain articulated/disarticulated cattle remains: a young cow's complete skeleton in Tumulus (T) E-94–1n dated to 5400 BCE; articulated/disarticulated cattle bones of three individuals in T-E-94–1s; four individuals (two subadult and two young adult) in T-E-96–4; two individuals (one juvenile, one young adult) in T-97–6 dated to 4500 BCE; and finally, one or two subadults in T-E-97–16 (Brass 2007, Di Lernia 2006: 53). Interestingly, all the represented specimens are young to very-young animals, not yet at reproductive age, and as such, susceptible to culling without endangering the communities' herds reproduction.

A few hundred kilometers West in Southern Libya, forty-two stone monuments were excavated along the Wadi Bedis meander in the Edeyen Murzuq Lake Basin, an area claimed to represent "locales of social importance and enduring value for Messak pastoral groups" (Di Lernia et al. 2013). Twenty-two of these monuments dated from 5149/4895–4120/3820 BCE contain livestock remains (cattle, sheep/goats and other ungulates). Eight monuments dated to 4668/4554–4225/4091 BCE contain cattle [large ungulates] remains only; six monuments dated to 5149/4895–4120/3820 BCE include cattle and sheep/goat [small ungulate] remains; four monuments dated to 4243/4093 BCE contains only sheep/goat [small ungulates] remains; one monument has equids and small ungulates [*ovis/capra*] remains; and finally, five monuments dated to 4358/4328 BCE–171/287 calCE revealed the presence of undetermined faunal remains.

Further West, in the Tenere portion of the Sahara in Northern Niger, cattle burials have been recorded in the Adrar Bous. A complete carcass was found in one case; a partially burnt right fore quarter in a tumulus at Site ABS1; a second tumulus dated to ca 5370–4830 BCE with charred cattle bones; a third tumulus with unspecified cattle remains dated to ca. 5500–4900 BCE; and finally, an additional cattle burial found at Agoras-in-Fast (Brass 2007: 6).

In southern Niger, Chin Tafidet, an extensive dry-season camping site dated from 4500 to 3400 BP and located in the western portion of the Eghazzer Basin, contains overlapping evidence of human settlement, humans and livestock burials. Eighteen complete cattle, three sheep/goats, and two shepherd dog burials have been recorded (Paris 1984, 1992) overlapping with human tombs. The presence of cut marks on cervical vertebrae of some specimens suggests that these animals, aged four to eight years, were sacrificed and buried in association with humans. Twelve out of the seventy-five recorded human burials were excavated. The deceased were buried without grave goods in clusters combining humans and cattle inhumations. Four such clusters were identified (Paris 1992). It is worth noting the fact that shepherd dogs and sheep/goat burials were not associated with human burials. An identical and contemporaneous feature of patterned association between human and cattle burials was recorded at Ikawaten in the north, but the reported find is not yet published in detail. From these mortuary data, it can be inferred that small groups of pastoral nomads used to bury their dead in one of their major dry-season camping areas (Holl 1998b, 2013) where important rituals involving livestock were performed from time to time.

Finally, at Karkarichinkat in the Tilemsi valley (Mali) at the western end of the distribution of archaeological manifestations of such practices, revealed a fully articulated cow buried in a grave pit surrounded by a set of postholes dug in the primary occupation level of the site in Trench 1-B/C dated to 4500 BP (Finucane et al. 2008: 84).

RITUALS: PROPITIATORY, PROPHYLACTIC, AND/OR CELEBRATORY?

Evidence for special treatments of livestock, especially cattle remains in early African pastoralists cultural contexts is plain and undisputable. The practice of slaughtering animals (sacrifice), sharing their meat, and burying their bones (complete carcasses or fragments) in especially built installations, is clearly documented in the cases under consideration. Identifying the goals of the performed rituals is however a more challenging issue. If human burials cannot be interpreted as evidence of "human cult," the behavioral patterns represented in the performed rituals involving complete or partial cattle carcasses can hardly qualify as "Cattle Cult" geared "to cope with drought and famine, using this precious resource as an offering to superhuman entities" (Di Lernia 2006: 60, Di Lernia and Manzi 2002). Human-livestock relationships are polysemic and versatile. There are multiple human-to-human reasons for performing rituals using cattle and livestock as media. The assumed connection to divinities is not only a commonsense assumption but also a cultural imposition (Schwartz 2017). Sacrifices and offerings to honor the ancestors do not require a divine interference. Those carried out to fend off the "evil eye" or "bad luck" do not require a divine intercession either. They deal exclusively with human affairs. The "religious connotations" alluded to in the literature generally used as *deus ex machina* are interesting assumptions but non-explanatory propositions. It is however the human/human/ natural forces rationale that is the anchor of the discussion carried out in the remaining part of this discussion.

Archaeologists' tools are particularly blunt and severely limited when it comes to addressing the palimpsestic nature of archaeological sites. By necessity, archaeological compressed timeframe distorts the perception of how events actually happened in the past. A ritual performance is a specific space-time event. It is scheduled to take place at specific time, in a specific place, for a specific reason, in the actual community cultural landscape. If the monument dated to 171/287 CE is removed from consideration, the series of ritual events represented in the Messak archaeological record took place from 5149/4895 to 4120–3820 BCE, a little more than one thousand years. Twenty-two ritual events over a period of 1029/1075 years, point on average to one ceremony every 46.77/48.86 years, or once every two generations. There were equally twenty-two ritual events—interesting coincidence with the Messak—recorded during the 4500–3400 BP intermittent seasonal occupation of Chin Tafidet in the Eghazzer basin, over 1,100 years. Accordingly, there was on the average one animal burial event every fifty years, almost two generations depending on actual life expectancy. If the three sheep/goat and the twin dog burials events are excluded, eighteen cattle specimens were culled, sacrificed, and buried during the 1,100-year-long settlement use, at a frequency of one ritual event every sixty-one years, more than two generations. Considering the implications of the data from the Mid-Holocene Messak (Libya) and the Eghazzer basin (Niger) presented above, mitigation of zoonoses appears to have higher explanatory potentials within the context of constant adjustment to actual environmental conditions.

The Messak plateau Mid-Holocene pastoral groups used the shores of the Edeyen Murzuq lake as a rainy season camping area and the higher ranges of the plateau for dry seasons, using streambeds as transhumance corridors. Some specific places—along the Wadi Bedis meander for example—were consecrated and used for important ritual events. Plants micro- and macro remains from the Messak provide additional clues on humans and livestock health issues then under consideration.

Pollen evidence points to a desert shrublands. Plants, flowers, and fruits were used as offerings. The recorded species—*Rumex cyprus* and *R. vesicarius*—flower in spring from March to April. The whole plant has important medicinal properties. It is rich of constituents (flavonoids, C-glycosides, oxalic acid, tannins, mucilage, mineral salts and vitamin C). ". . . The leaves and seeds are collected and prepared fresh or as a powder for internal use, to treat liver diseases and as a laxative. Traditional medicine uses the plant as an antiscorbutic, appetizer, astringent, carminative, stomachic and tonic, and for jaundice. The leaves are eaten fresh and much appreciated for their acid taste" (Di Lernia et al. 2013: 25).

Cattle, sheep/goats, and exceptionally an equid, were butchered, some buried entirely, others cut, shared, roasted and eaten, their bones collected for burial in especially built monuments. Butchered sheep/goats tend to be younger while cattle are represented by adult animals. Three specimens are >18 to 24 months old. But most of the butchered cattle specimens are four to ten years old, with four- to six-year-old animals sacrificed in six cases. Interestingly, when sex was determinable, the specimens happened to be bulls (Di Lernia et al. 2013: 15–16, table 4). Surplus animals appear to have been selected.

Selective butchering, likely at the beginning of the rainy season, with associated medicinal plants, point to a different kind of crisis management. Health issues concerning livestock, humans, or both, could have emerged infrequently during harsh dry seasons. The ritual performances could have been family and/or collective exorcism and enabler of new/renewed alliances between pastoral groups scattered all over the Messak plateau during the long dry seasons. Animal epizooties could have happened. Some cattle zoonoses, including bTB, could have affected humans. Calls to and support from successful ancestors could have been part of needed social healings.

The archaeology of that hard-to-perceive dark side of biological and cultural adaptations deserves to be investigated more thoroughly in the future.

CONCLUSION

Zoonoses and their related infectious diseases are part of biological inter-connectedness. Outbreaks are not rare. But the present one, triggered by the COVID-19 virus, is so far unique in human history due to its global reach and impact. Limited infectious disease outbreaks have certainly affected past African pastoral-nomadic communities in the Sahara and elsewhere (Holl 2020). Chin Tafidet, a dry-season site west of the Eghazzer basin (Niger) and the Messak plateau pastoral groups using the shores of Lake Edeyen Murzuq as a rainy season camping area and the higher ranges of the plateau during dry seasons were part of pastoral-nomadic groups' annual territories. Some specific areas—along the Wadi Bedis meander, for example—were consecrated and used for important ritual events. Cattle, sheep/goats, and occasionally an equid were butchered. Some were buried entirely, and others cut, roasted, and eaten, and their bones collected for burial in monuments especially built for that purpose. Slaughtered sheep/goats tend to be younger, while the cattle remains indicate adult animals. Three specimens are> eighteen to twenty-four months old. But most of the butchered cattle specimens are four to ten years old, with four- to six-year-old animals sacrificed in six cases. Interestingly, when sex was determinable, the specimens were bulls (see Di Lernia et al. 2013, 15–16, table 4). Only surplus animals appear to have been selected. Selective butchering, likely at the beginning of the rainy season, points to different kinds of crisis management. Health issues, concerning livestock, humans, or both, could have emerged infrequently during harsh dry seasons. The ritual performances, very likely exceptional and infrequent, were gatherings of family members or larger social groups enabling new/renewed alliances between pastoral groups scattered all over the Messak plateau or the Eghazzer basin during the long dry seasons. Such gatherings could have also been used to perform rituals to drive away the "evil eye." Animal epizooties could have happened. Some cattle zoonoses like bTB may have affected humans. Calls to and support from successful ancestors were part of the needed social healings. In some cases, sick animals could have been butchered, burnt to dispel the "evil eye," and buried entirely without anyone eating their meat. In others, healthy but weak animals were butchered, their meat shared to celebrate the renewal of alliances with other pastoralists groups, and the animals' bones collected and "memorialized" in a stone monument. In other cases, depending on the size of the attendance, cattle and sheep/goat and undetermined large/small bovids were culled, butchered, shared, and consumed in feasting episodes. And finally, to seal matrimonial alliances, healthy oxen could have been butchered, all or part of their bones buried in consecrated monuments to cement the alliance between two distinct pastoralist groups.

In fact, one has to expect these more than thousand-year-long ritual scripts to feature some diversity and polysemy. The butchering, sharing, and consumption of a "wedding ox," among many other options, has no connection with the adaptation to climate change. The archaeology of these hard-to-perceive sides of biological and cultural adaptations deserves to be investigated more vigorously in the future. Almost 75 percent of the recent major global disease outbreaks have a zoonotic origin (Asante et al. 2019). Human tuberculosis (TB), for example, can be contracted from infected cattle, and this is identifiable in the archaeological record (Galagan 2014; Kemunto et al. 2018; Muller et al. 2013). Bovine TB, prevalent in all major livestock-producing countries of the developing world and Africa, is strongly correlated to cattle density (Muller et al. 2013). TB, one of the most devastating human infectious diseases transmitted by *Mycobacterium bovis,* occurs through close contact with infected cattle or the consumption of contaminated animal products. About eight million new active cases that lead to nearly 1.5 million deaths are recorded annually (Galagan 2014: 307). The accelerated urbanization of Africa and the increasing demand for animal protein, estimated to increase by 50 percent by the year 2030 (Salman and Steneroden 2015: 3), drive a profound change in the landscape of infectious diseases that affect humans and animals (Asante et al. 2019).

Humans, particularly Africans, have to be prepared to face extraordinary health crises in the future. Unfortunately, there is a significant imbalance in the attention given to zoonotic diseases (Kemunto et al. 2018). Those posing global economic and health threats are, rightly so, focused on, and taken care of. Unfortunately, this happens at the expense of the endemic diseases that affect populations with little political clout, such as the present-day descendants of African Neolithic pastoral-nomadic communities.

As extensively demonstrated in this work, mobility in its multiple embedded dimensions is the core space-time process of human biological and cultural evolution. Effective research models are elegant, simple, and parsimonious. It is the case for the SArFe model formulated and tested in this book. SArFe is fractal-like in its time dimension with embedded iteration levels. It operates in the punctuated equilibrium rationale, is nonlinear, with the dissipative characteristics of human populations dynamics (Elredge and Gould 1972, Mandelbrot 1982, Prigogine and Stengers 1984).

This work is anchored on concepts derived from nonequilibrium thermodynamics as a key point to understand the behavior of living systems crafted by Prigogine (1977, Pulselli et al. 2004). "We see now that even for phenomena on our own level, the incorporation of thermodynamic elements lead to new theoretical structures. . . . Time appears with its full meaning associated with irreversibility or even with history, and not merely as a geometrical parameter associated with motion" (Prigogine 1977: 264). All living systems called "dissipative structures" are open, meshed in constant exchange of matter, energy, and information within and without, operating nonlinearly far from equilibrium. Nonlinearity expresses the non-direct proportional relationship between input and output in dynamic systems. Living systems as dissipative structures, are "open systems in steady state that maintain themselves in life by self-organizing due to material and energetic fluxes received from outside and from systems with different conditions" (Pulselli et al. 2004: 382).

The SArFe model is accordingly, the core of the global evolutionary archaeological perspective presented in this book. It is effective in fully addressing both biological and cultural aspects of most well documented cases of population expansion. In Africa, it can be applied to a multiplicity of cases, such as the Berber expansion (Tamazight, Taqbaylit, Tamashep, Tuareg, etc.) from coastal North Africa to the central and southern Sahara, the expansion of speakers of Saharan languages (Songhai, Kanuri, and Kanembu) in North-Central and West Africa, Afroasiatic expansion (Arabic, Chadic, Cushitic) in North, Central, and East Africa, Indo-European expansion (Greek, Roman) in North Africa, Egypt, and Nubia, as well as Niger-Congo expansion (Mande) in West Africa. The SArFe model provides a robust and integrated approach for the elaboration of a global evolutionary archaeology.

The expansion of human populations all over the globe, a global phenomenon encompassing biological and cultural dimensions that took a few million years to complete as "out of Africa 1 and 2," is the ideal SArFe test case. The Holocene case studies are embedded fractal-like iterations of SArFe 4, with the focus on the expansion of *Homo sapiens sapiens*. The selected cases addressing the origin and expansion of speakers of Austronesian, Chadic, and Bantu languages, as well as cattle domestication, the genesis of African cattle pastoralism, and the spread of bovine tuberculosis, framed in shorter time segments, predominantly feature cultural selection and language formation. They have less to do with speciation *stricto sensu*, but still present multiple phenotypic adaptations resulting from variable forms of adaptive radiation and founder effect. The future colonization of the Moon and possibly the planet Mars will very likely trigger SArFe 5 in a zero-gravity nonbiological universe of an entirely human-made environment.

All the core dimensions of the extended evolutionary synthesis are differentially but systematically addressed in the five case studies presented in this book. Directionality manifests itself as the time arrow, population flows, linguistic drift, and material culture evolution. Phenotypic plasticity, the ability of a specific genotype to generate variants under different environmental conditions, is obvious through the different facets of human expansion as well as cattle domestication and the emergence of distinct cattle breeds. The concept can also be relied upon, metaphorically, to address patterns of inventions and spread of material culture. Expanding populations colonization of new territories showcases reciprocal causality. The member of the expanding population "transport their landscape" materially—plants, animals, material culture—and ideally; adjust it fully or partially to their new habitat, and via cultural niche construction change it and are changed by it. Locational and subsistence decisions are generally articulated on a narrow range of targets in optimal circumstances, or in situations of relative stability. Such locational and subsistence patterns are passed from one generation to the next (inheritence), constantly adjusted to actual cultural and environmental circumstances. In all the case studies presented in this work, the tempo and mode of change have been shown to be punctuated, with in between relatively longer periods of stability (stasis), despite the relatively coarse resolution of archaeological time assessments.

Conclusion

As extensively demonstrated in this work, mobility in its multiple embedded dimensions is the core space-time process of human biological and cultural evolution. Effective research models are elegant, simple, and parsimonious. This is the case for the SArFe model formulated and tested in this book. SArFe is fractal-like in its time dimension with embedded iteration levels. It operates in the punctuated equilibrium rationale and is nonlinear, with the dissipative characteristics of human populations dynamics (Elredge and Gould 1972, Mandelbrot 1982, Prigogine and Stengers 1984).

This work is anchored on concepts derived from nonequilibrium thermodynamics as a key point to understand the behavior of living systems crafted by Prigogine (1977, Pulselli et al. 2004). "We see now that even for phenomena on our own level, the incorporation of thermodynamic elements lead to new theoretical structures. . . . Time appears with its full meaning associated with irreversibility or even with history, and not merely as a geometrical parameter associated with motion" (Prigogine 1977: 264). All living systems called "dissipative structures" are open, meshed in constant exchange of matter, energy and information within and without, operating nonlinearly far from equilibrium. Nonlinearity expresses the indirect proportional relationship between input and output in dynamic systems. Living systems, as dissipative structures, are "open systems in steady state that maintain themselves in life by self-organizing due to material and energetic fluxes received from outside and from systems with different conditions" (Pulselli et al. 2004: 382).

The SArFe model is, accordingly, the core of the global evolutionary archaeological perspective presented in this book. It is effective in fully addressing both biological and cultural aspects of most well-documented cases of population expansion. In Africa, it can be applied to a multiplicity of cases, such as the Berbers' expansion (Tamazight, Taqbaylit, Tamashep, Tuareg, etc.) from coastal North Africa to the central and Southern Sahara, the expansion of speakers of Saharan languages (Songhai, Kanuri, and Kanembu) in North-Central and West Africa, Afroasiatic expansion (Arabic, Chadic,

Cushitic) in North, Central, and East Africa, Indo-European expansion (Greek, Roman) in North Africa, Egypt, and Nubia, as well as Niger-Congo expansion (Mande) in West Africa. The SArFe model provides a robust and integrated approach for the elaboration of a global evolutionary archaeology.

The expansion of human populations all over the globe, a global phenomenon encompassing biological and cultural dimensions that took a few million years to complete as "out of Africa 1 and 2, is the ideal SArFe test case. The Holocene case studies are embedded fractal-like iterations of SArFe 4, with the focus on the expansion of *Homo sapiens sapiens*. The selected cases addressing the origin and expansion of speakers of Austronesian, Chadic, and Bantu languages, as well as cattle domestication, the genesis of African cattle pastoralism, and the spread of bovine tuberculosis, framed in shorter time segments, predominantly feature cultural selection and language formation. They have less to do with speciation *stricto sensu*, but still present multiple phenotypic adaptations resulting from variable forms of adaptive radiation and founder effect. The future colonization of the Moon and possibly the planet Mars will very likely trigger SArFe 5 in a zero-gravity nonbiological universe of an entirely human-made environment.

All the core dimensions of the extended evolutionary synthesis are differentially but systematically addressed in the five case studies presented in this book. Directionality manifests itself as the time-arrow, population flows, linguistic drift, and material culture evolution. Phenotypic plasticity, the ability of a specific genotype to generate variants under different environmental conditions, is obvious through the different facets of human expansion as well as cattle domestication and the emergence of distinct cattle breeds. The concept can also be relied upon, metaphorically, to address patterns of invention and the spread of material culture. Expanding populations' colonization of new territories showcases reciprocal causality. The members of the expanding population "transport their landscape" materially—plants, animals, material culture—and ideally; adjust it fully or partially to their new habitat, and via cultural niche construction change it and are changed by it. Locational and subsistence decisions are generally articulated on a narrow range of targets in optimal circumstances, or in situations of relative stability. Such locational and subsistence patterns are passed from one generation to the next—inheritance—constantly adjusted to actual cultural and environmental circumstances. In all the case studies presented in this work, the tempo and mode of change have been shown to be punctuated, with in between relatively longer periods of stability—stasis—despite the relative coarse resolution of archaeological time assessments.

References

Abdelaal, H. F. M., D. Spalink, A. Amer, H. Steinberg, E. A. Hashish, E. A. Nasr, & A. M. Talaat. 2019. Genomic polymorphism associated with the emergence of virulent isolates of Mycobacterium bovis in the Nile Delta. *Scientific Reports* 9: 11657.

Abdou, R., Boukary, E. Thys, E. Abatih, D. Gamatie, I. Ango, A. Yenikoye, & C. Saegerman. 2011. Bovine tuberculosis prevalence survey on cattle in the rural livestock system of Toradi (Niger). *PLOS One* 6(9): e24629.

Adelaar, K. A. 2016. Austronesian in Madagascar: A critical assessment of the works of Paul Ottino and Philippe Beaujard. In *Early Exchange between Africa and the Wider Indian Ocean World*. Edited by Gwyn Campbell. Pp. 77–112. New York: Palgrave.

Aguila-Ruiz, A., C. M. Aguilera, & A. Gil. 2020. Genetics of Lactose intolerance: An updated review and online interactive world maps of phenotype and genotype frequencies. *Nutrients* 12: 2689.

Aiello, L. C. and M. Collard. 2001. Our newest ancestor? *Nature* 410: 526.

Akhilesh, K., S. Pappu, H. M. Rajapara, Y. Gunnell, A. D. Shukla, & A. K. Singhvi. 2018. Early Middle Palaeolithic culture in India around 385–172 ka reframes Out of Africa models. *Nature* 554: 97–101.

Algaze, G. 1993. *The Uruk World System: The Dynamics of Expansion of Early Mesopotamian Civilization*. Chicago: Chicago University Press.

Alves I., M. Coelho, C. Gignoux, A. Damasceno, A. Prista, & J. Rocha. 2011. Genetic homogeneity across Bantu-speaking groups from Mozambique and Angola challenges early split scenarios between East and West Bantu populations. *Human Biology* 83(1): 13–83.

Anania d,' G. L. 1582. *L'universale Fabrica del Mundo*. Venice.

Anapol, F., R. Z. German, & N.G. Jablonski, editors. 2004. *Shaping Primate Evolution: Form, Function, and Behavior*. Cambridge: Cambridge University Press.

Angel, J. L. 1984. Health as a crucial factoring the change from hunting to developed farming in the Eastern Mediterranean. In M. N. Cohen and G. J. Armelagos (eds.) *Paleopathology at the Origins of Agriculture*. Pp. 51–74. Orlando: Academic Press.

Anton, S. C., R. Potts, & L. C. Aiello. 2014. Evolution of early homo: An integrated biological perspective. *Science* 345(6162): 1236828. DOI: 10.1126/science1236828.

Anquandah, J. 1993. The Kintampo complex: A case study in sedentism and food-production in sub-Sahelian west Africa. In *The Archaeology of Africa: Food, Metals and Towns*, edited by T. Shaw, P. Sinclair, B. Andah, and A. Okpoko, pp. 255–60. London/New York: Routledge.

Anton, S. C., & C. W. Kuzawa. 2017. Early Homo, plasticity and the extended evolutionary synthesis. *Interface Focus* 7: 20170004.

Arambourg, C. and Coppens, Y. 1968. Sur la decouverte dans le Pleistocene inferieur de la vallee de l'Omo (Ethiopie) d'une mandibule d'Australopithecien. *Comptes Rendus des Seances de l'Academie des Sciences* 265: 589–590.

Arbuckle, B. S. and T. M. Kassebaum. 2021. Management and domestication of cattle (Bos taurus) in Neolithic Southwest Asia. *Animal Frontier* 11(3): 10–20.

Ardika, I. W. and P. Bellwood. 1991. Sembiran: The Beginnings of Indian contact with Bali.

Antiquity 65: 221–232.

Ardrey, R. 1966. *Territorial Imperative*. New York: Dell.

———. 1976. *The Hunting Hypothesis: A Personal Conclusion Concerning the Evolutionary Nature of Man*. New York: Athenium.

Argue, D., C. P. Groves, M. S. Y. Lee, & W. L. Jungers. 2017. The affinities of Homo floresiensis based on phylogenetic analyses of cranial, dental, and postcranial characters. Journal of Human Evolution. DOI: 10.1016/j.jhevol.2017.02.006

Armitage, S. J., C. S. Bristow, & N. A. Drake. 2015. West African Monsoon dynamics inferred from Abrupt fluctuations of Lake Mega-Chad. *Proceedings of the National Academy of Science* 112(28): 8543–8548.

Arnold, B. 1998. Les pirogues neolithiques de Paris Bercy: Traces de travail et techniques de Façonnage. *Archeonautica* 14: 73–78.

Asante, J. et al. 2019. Systematic review of important bacterial zoonoses in Africa in the last decade in light of the "one Health" Concept. *Pathogens* 8(2): 50–79.

Asfaw, B., T. White, O. Lovejoy, B. Latimer, S. Simpson, & G. Suwas. 1999. *Australopithecus garhi*: a new species of early hominid from Ethiopia. *Science* 284: 629–635.

Ashley, C. Z., A. Antonites, &P. D. Fredriksen. 2016. Mobility and African archaeology: An introduction. *Azania: Archaeological Research in Africa* 51(4): 417–434.

Atkinson, Q. D. 2011. Phonemic diversity supports a serial founder effect model of language expansion. *Science* 332(346). DOI: 10.1126/science.119995.

Atkinson, Q. D., A. Meade, C. Venditti, S. J. Greenhill, & M. Pagel. 2008. Languages evolves in Punctuational Bursts. *Science* 319: 588.

Aubert, M., Setiawan, P., Oktaviana, A. A. et al. 2018. Paleolithic cave art in Borneo. *Nature* 564: 254–257.

Aubert, M., R. Lebe, A. A. Oktaviana, M. Tang, B. Burhan, Hamrullah, A. Jusdi, Abdullah, B. Hakim, J.-x. Zhao, I. M. Geria, P. H. Sulistyarto, R. Sardi, & A. Brumm. 2019. Earliest hunting scene in prehistoric art. *Nature* 576: 442–445.

Aumassip, G. 1978. In-Hanakaten: Bilder einer Ausgrabung. In *Sahara: 10.000 jahre zwischen Weide und Wuste*, edited by R. Kuper, pp. 208–213. Museen der Stadt, Koln.

———.1986. *Le Bas-Sahara dans la Prehistoire*. Paris: Editions du CNRS.

Baedke, J., A. Fabregas-Tejeda, & F. Vergara-Silva. 2020. Does the extended evolutionary synthesis entail extended explanatory power? *Biology and Philosophy* 35: 20.

Baines, J. and N. Yoffee. 1998. Order, legitimacy, and wealth and Ancient Egypt and Mesopotamia. In *Archaic States*, edited by G. Feinman and J. Marcus, pp. 199–260. Santa Fe: School of American Research Press.

Baker, J. L., C. N. Rotimi, & D. Shriner. 2017. Human ancestry correlates with language and reveals that race is not an objective genomic classifier. *Scientific Reports* 7: 1522. DOI: 10.1038/s41598-017-01837-7

Baker, O., O. Lee, H. Wu, G. S. Besra, D. E. Minnikin et al. 2015. Human tuberculosis predates domestication in ancient Syria. *Tuberculosis* 95: S4–S12. DOI: 10.1016/j.tube.2015.02.001.

Balout, L. 1955. *Prehistoire de l'Afrique du Nord*. Paris: Arts et Metiers Graphique.

Balter, M. 2001. Scientists spar over claims of earliest human ancestor. *Science* 291: 1460–1461.

Barberis, J., N. L. Bragazzi, L. Galluzaa, & M. Martini. 2017. The History of tuberculosis from the first historical record to the isolation of Koch bacillus. *Journal of Preventive Medicine and Hygiene* 58: E9–E12.

Barich, B. E. 1974. La serie stratigrafica dell uadi Ti-n-Torha (Acacus, Libia). *Origini* 8: 7–157.

———. 1987. *Archaeology and environment in the Libyan Sahara: The excavations in the Tadrart Acacus, 1978–1983*. Oxford: British Archaeological Reports.

———. 1998. *People, Water, and Grain: The Beginning of Domestication in the Sahara and the Nile Valley*. Roma: l'Erma di Bretschneider.

Barker, G. 1988. Cows and kings, Models for Zimbabwe. *Proceedings of the Prehistoric Society* 54: 223–239.

Barkindo, B. M. 1989. *The Sultanate of Mandara to1902: History of the Evolution, Development and Collapse of a Central Sudanese Kingdom*. Wiesbaden: Franz Steiner Verlag.

Barras, C. 2018. Tools from China are oldest hint of human lineage outside Africa. *Nature* Jul. 11, 2018. DOI: 10.1038/d41586-018-05696-8.

Barth, H. 1965. *Travels and Discoveries in North and Central Africa*. London: Frank Cass

Bartlett, J. 2017. Evolutionary teleonomy as a unifying principle for the extended evolutionary synthesis. *Bio-Complexity* 2: 1–7.

Bastin, Y., A. Coupez, & M. Mann. 1999. Continuity and divergence in the Bantu languages: perspectives from a lexicostatistic study. Tervuren: *Annales sciences Humaines* 162.

BattÛta, I. 1982. *Voyages III. Inde, Extrême-Orient, Espagne & Soudan*. Paris: Librairie François Maspero, Collection FM/La Découverte.

Bar-Yosef Mayer, D. E. 2020. Shell beads of the Middle and Upper Palaeolithic: A review of the earliest records. In *Beauty in the Eye of the Beholder: Personal Adornments across Millennia*, edited by M. Margarit and A. Boroneant. Pp. 11–25. Targoviste: Editura Cetatella de Scaun.

Bar-Yosef Mayer, D. E., Vandermeersch B, and Bar-Yosef O. 2009. Shells and ochre in Middle Paleolithic Qafzeh Cave, Israel: indications for modern behavior. Journal of Human Evolution 56(3): 307–314.

Bar-Yosef Mayer, D. E., Groman-Yaroslavski I, Bar-Yosef O, Hershkovitz I, Kampen-Hasday A, Vandermeersch B, et al. 2020. On holes and strings: Earliest displays of human adornment in the Middle Palaeolithic. *PLoS ONE* 15(7): e0234924. https://doi.org/10.1371/journal.pone.0234924

Bayon, G., Dennielou, B., Etoubleau, J., Ponzevera, E., Toucanne, S., Bermell, S. 2012a. Intensifying weathering and land use in iron age central Africa. *Science* 335. https://doi.org/10.1126/science.1215400.1219e1222.

———. 2012b. Response to Comments on "Intensifying Weathering and Land Use in Iron Age Central Africa" *Science* 337, 1040.

Bayon, G., Schefuß, E., Dupont, L., Borges, A.V., Dennielou, B., Lambert, T., Mollenhauer, G., Monin, L., Ponzevera, E., Skonieczny, C., André, L.. 2019. The roles of climate and human land-use in the late Holocene rainforest crisis of Central Africa. *Earth Planet. Sci. Lett.* 505, 30–41.

Beaujard, P. 2005. The Indian Ocean in Eurasian and African World-systems before the 16th Century. *Journal of World History* 16(4): 411–465.

———. 2007. East Africa, the Comoros Islands and Madagascar before the sixteenth century. *Azania: Archaeological Research in Africa* 42(1): 15–35.

———. 2011. The First Migrants to Madagascar and their introduction of plants: Linguistic and ethnological evidence. *Azania Archaeological Research in Africa* 46(2): 169–189.

———. 2017. *Histoire et Voyages des Plantes cultivees a Madagascar avant le 16e siècle*. Paris. Karthala.

———. 2019. The *World of the Indian Ocean: A Global History.* Volumes I and II. Cambridge: Cambridge University Press.

Bechly, G. 2018. Rewriting Human Origins, ongoing in East Asia. https://evolutionnews.org/2018/11/rewriting-of-human-origins-ongoing-in-east-asia/.

Belluomini, G., and L. Manfra. 1987. Radiocarbon dates from the Tadrart Acacus massif. In *Archaeology and Environment in the Libyan Sahara: The Excavations in the Tadrart Acacus, 1978–1983*, edited by B. E. Barich, pp. 327–330. Oxford: British Archaeological Reports.

Bellwood, P. 1995. Austronesian Prehistory in Southeast Asia: Homeland, Expansion, and Transformation. In Bellwood, Peter, J. J. Fox and D. T. Tryon, editors The Austronesians: Historical and Comparative Perspectives. Canberra: Australian National University.

———. 1996. Hierarchy, Founder Ideology and Austronesian expansion. In *Origins, Ancestry and Alliance: Explorations in Austronesian Ethnography.* Edited by J. J. Fox and C. Sather. 18–40. Canberra: Australian National University.

————. 2013. *First Migrants: Ancient Migration in Global Perspective*. London: Wiley-Blackwell.

Berg, S. M. Carmen Garcia-Pelayo, Borna Muller, Elena Hailu, et al. 2011. African 2, a Clonal Complex of *Mycobacterium bovis* Epidemiologically Important in East Africa. *Journal of Bacteriology* 193(3): 670–678. doi: 10.1128/JB.00750–10.

Berger, L. R., De Ruiter, D. J., Churchill, S. E., Schmid, P., Carlson, K. J., Dirk, P. H. G. M., Kibii, J. M.. 2010. *Australopithecus sediba*: A New Species of Homo-like Australopithecus from South Africa. *Science* 328: 195–204.

Berger, L. R. et al. 2015. *Homo naledi*, a new species of the genus *Homo* from the Dinaledi chamber, South Africa. *eLife* 2015: 4:e09560. DOI: 10.7554/eLife.09560.

Behr, M. A. 2014. Comparative genomics of Mycobacteria: some answers, yet more new questions. *Cold Spring Harbor Perspectives in Medicine* 5.a021204

Bergstrom, A., C. Stringer, M. Hajdinjak, E. M. L. Scerri, and P. Skoglund. 2021. Origins of Modern Human Ancestry. *Nature* 590: 229–237.

Berniell-Lee, G., F. Calafell, E. bosch, E. Heyer, L. Sica, P. Mouguiama-Daouda, L. Van der Veen, J.M. Hombert, L. Quintana-Murci & D. Cosmas. 2009. Genetic and demographic implications of the Bantu expansion: Insights from Human paternal lineages. *Molecular Biology and Evolution* 26(7): 1581–1589.

Binford L. R. 1973. "Interassemblage variability-the Mousterian and the 'functional' argument," in *The Explanation of Culture Change*. Edited by Colin Renfrew. London: Duckworth.

————. 1981. *Bones: Ancient Man and Modern Myth*. New York/London: Academic Press

Bird, M. I., W. E. N. Austin, C. M. Wurster, L. K. F. Field, M. Mojfahid & C. Sargent. 2011. Punctuated. Geology Eustatic Sea Level rise in the Early Mid-Holocene. *Geology* 38(9): 803–806.

Biwolé A. B., Morin-Rivat J, Fayolle A., D. Bitondo, L. Dedry, K. Dainou, O. J. Hardy & J. L. Doucet. 2015. New data on the recent history of the littoral forests of southern Cameroon: An insight into the role of historical human disturbances on the current forest composition. *Plant Ecology and Evolution* 148(1): 19–28.

Black, D. 1926. Tertiary Man in Asia—The Chou Kou Tien discovery. *Science* 64 (1668): 586–587.

Blanton, R. E. 1998. Beyond Centralization: Steps toward a Theory of Egalitarian Behavior in Archaic States. In *Archaic States*, edited by G. Feinman and J. Marcus, pp. 135–172. Santa Fe: School of American Research Press.

Blench, R. 2006. *Archaeology, Language, and the African Past*. Lanham: AltaMira Press.

————. 2010. Remapping the Austronesian Expansion. In Bethwin Evans, editor, *Festschrift for Malcolm Ross*. Pp. 1–25 Canberra: Pacific Linguistics.

Blust, R. 1984–85. The Austronesian Homeland: A Linguistic Perspective. *Asian Perspective* 26(1): 45–66.

————. 2019. The Austronesian Homeland and Dispersal. *Annual Review of Linguistics* 5: 417–434.

Boaretto, E, Wu, X., Yuan, J., Bar-Yosef, O., Chu, V., Pan, Y., Liu, K., Cohen, D., Jiao, T., Li, S. et al. 2009. Radiocarbon dating of charcoal and bone collagen associated with early pottery at Yuchanyan Cave, Hunan Province, China. Proceedings of the National Academy of Sciences 106(24): 9595–9600.

Bocquet-Appel, J. P. 2008. Explaining the Neolithic Demographic Transition. In *the Neolithic Demographic Transition and its Consequences.* Edited by J.P. Bocquet-Appel and O. Bar Yosef. Pp. 35–55. New York: Springer.

Booth, T. J. 2019. A Stranger in a Strange Land: A Perspective on Archaeological Response to the Paleogenetic Revolution from an Archaeologist working amongst Paleogeneticists. *World Archaeology* (June 2019).

Bordes, F. 1961. *Typologie du Paleolithique Ancien et Moyen.* Paris: Editions du CNRS.

Boserup, E. 1965. *The Conditions of Agricultural Growth: The Economics of Agrarian Change Under Population Pressure.* Chicago: Aldine.

Bostoen, K., B. Clist, C. Doumenge, R. Grollemund, J-M. Hombert, J. K. Muluwa, and J. Maley. 2015. Middle to Late Holocene Paleoclimatic Change and the Early Bantu Expansion in the Rain Forests of Western Central Africa. *Current Anthropology* 56(3): 354–384.

Botha, R. and C. Knight, editors. 2009. *The Cradle of Language.* Oxford: Oxford University Press.

Bouquiaux, L., ed. 1980. L'expansion bantoue: Actes du Colloque International du Centre National de la Recherche Scientifique, Viviers (France), 4–16 avril 1977. Vol. 2: L'expansion bantoue. Paris: Société des Etudes Linguistiques et Anthropologiques de France.

Bouzouggar, A., L. T. Humphrey, N. Barton, S. A. Parfitt, L. C. Balzan, J.-L. Schwenninger, M. A. El Hajraoui, R. Nespoulet, and S. M. Bello. 2018. 90,000 year-old specialised bone technology in the Aterian Middle Stone Age of North Africa. *PLoS ONE* 13(10): e0202021. https:// doi.org/10.1371/journal. pone.0202021.

Brabant, P. and Gavaud, M. 1985. *Les Sols et les Ressources en Terre du Nord-Cameroun.* Paris: Editions de l'ORSTOM.

Bradley, D. G., D. E. MacHugh, P. Cunnigham, and R. T. Loftus. 1996. Mitochondrial diversity and the origins of African and European Cattle. *Proceedings of the National Academy of Science* 93: 5131–5135.

Brass, M. 2007. Reconsidering the emergence of social complexity in Early Saharan Pastoral Societies. Segrate: *Europe PMC Funders Group Author Manuscript.*

———. 2017. Early North African Cattle Domestication and its Ecological Setting: A Reassessment. *Journal of World Prehistory,* December 2017 [https://doi.org/10 .1007/s10963–017–9112–9].

Braudel, F. 1949. *La Mediterranee et le Monde Mediterraneen a l'epoque de Philippe II.* Paris: Armand Colin.

Bräuer, G. 1992. Africa's place in the evolution of Homo sapiens. In G. Bräuer & F. H. Smith, eds., Continuity or Replacement: Controversies in Homo sapiens Evolution. pp. 83–98. Rotterdam: Balkema.

Breton, G., C. Fortes-Lima and C. M. Schlebusch. 2021. Revisiting the demographic history of Central African populations from a genetic perspective. *Human Population Genetics and Genomics.* https://doi.org/10.47248/hpgg2101010004

Breunig, P. 1996. The 8000–year-old dugout canoe from Dufuna (NE Nigeria). In *Aspects of African Archaeology. Papers from the 10th Congress of the PanAfrican Association for Prehistory and related Studies*. Edited by G. Pwiti and R. Soper. Pp. 461–468. Harare: University of Zimbabwe Publications.

Breunig, P., A. Garba, and I. Waziri. 1992. Recent archaeological surveys in Borno, Northeastern Nigeria. *Nyame Akuma* 37: 10–16.

Breunig, P., A. Ballouche, K. Neumann, Rosing, F. W., H. Thiemeyer, K. P. Wendt, and W. van Neer. 1993. Gajiganna—New data on early settlement and environment in the Chad basin. *Berichte des Sonderforschungsbereichs* 268(2): 51–74.

Breunig, P., K. Neumann, and W. van Neer. 1996. New research on the Holocene settlement and environment of the Chad basin in Nigeria. *The African Archaeological Review* 13: 111–145.

Broom, R. 1938. The Pleistocene anthropoid apes of South Africa. *Nature* 142: 377–379.

Brosch, R., S. V. Gordon, M. Marmiesse, P. Brodin, C. Buchrieser, K. Eiglmeier, T. Garnier, C. Gutierrez, G. Hewinson, K. Kremer, L. M. Parsons, A. S. Pym, S. Samper, D. van Soolingen, and S. T. Cole. 2002. A new evolutionary scenario for the Mycobacterium tuberculosis complex. *Proceedings of the national Academy of Sciences* 99(6): 3684–3889

Brncic, T., Willis, K., Harris, D., Telfer, M., and Bailey, R. 2009. Fire and climate change impacts on lowland forest composition in northern Congo during the last 2580 years from palaeoecological analyses of a seasonally flooded swamp. *The Holocene* 19(1): 79–89. 10.1177/0959683608098954,

Castrì L., Tofanelli S., Garagnani, P., Bini, C., Fosella, X., Pelotti, S., Paoli, G., Pettener, D., Luiselli, D. 2009. mtDNA variability in two Bantu-speaking populations (Shona and Hutu) from Eastern Africa: implications for peopling and migration patterns in sub-Saharan Africa. *American Journal of Physical Anthropology* 140(2): 302–11.

Brucato, N. et al. 2018. The Comoros shows the Earliest Austronesian gene flow into the Swahili corridor. *The American Journal of Human Genetics* 102: 58–68.

Brunet, M. et al. 2002. A new hominid from the Upper Miocene in Chad. *Nature* 418: 145–151.

Buskell, A. 2019. Reciprocal Causation and the Extended Evolutionary Synthesis. *Biological Theory* https://doi.org/10.1007/s13752–019–00325–7.

Camps, G. 1974. *Les Civilisations prehistoriques de l'Afrique du nord et du Sahara.* Doin Editeur, Paris.

———. 1982. Beginnings of pastoralism and cultivation in north-west Africa and the Sahara: Origins of the Berbers. In *Cambridge History of Africa*, edited by J. D. Clark, Vol. 1, pp. 548–623. Cambridge: Cambridge University Press.

Canadi Wargo, M. 2009. *The Bordes-Binford debate: Transatlantic interpretative traditions in Paleolithic archaeology*. PhD thesis. Arlington: University of Texas at Arlington.

Cann, R. L., M. Stoneking, and A. C. Wilson. 1987. Mitochondrial DNA and Human Evolution. *Nature* 325: 31–35.

Carlstein, T. 1982. *Time Resources, Society and Ecology: On the Capacity for Human Interaction in Space and Time.* London: Unwin Hyman.

Cason, A., M. de Garine-Wichatitsky, F. Roger. 2014. Bovine tuberculosis: A double-edge issue at the human/Livestock/wild life interface in Africa. *Empres-Animal Health* 44(2): 10–13.

Cassoli, P. F., and S. Durante. 1974. La fauna del Ti-n-Torha (Acacus, Libia). *Origini* VIII: 159–161.

Castles, S., H. de Haas and M. J. Miller. 2014. *The Age of Migration: International population movements in the Modern world.* 5th edition. New York: Palgrave Macmillan.

Ceolin, A., C. Guardino, M. A. Irimia and G. Longobardi. 2020. Formal Syntax and Deep History. *Frontiers in Psychology* 11: 488871 doi: 10.3389/fpsyg.2020.488871

Cerezo, M., V. Cerny, A. Carracedo, A. Salas. 2011. New Insights into the Lake Chad Basin Population Structure Revealed by High-Throughput Genotyping of Mitochondrial DNA Coding SNPs. *PloS One* 6(4): e18682

Cerny, V., V. Fernandez, M. D. Costa, M. Hayek, C. J. Mulligan, and L. Pereira. 2009. Migration of Chadic speaking pastoralists within Africa based on population structure of Chad basin and Phylogeography of mitochondrial L3f haplogroup. *MBC Evolutionary Biology* 9: 63. doi: 10.1186/1471–2148–9–63.

Chaïr, H., Traore, R. E., Duval, M. F., Rivallan, R., Mukherjee, A., Aboagyem, L. M., et al. 2016. Genetic Diversification and Dispersal of Taro (Colocasia esculenta (L.) Schott). *PLoS ONE* 11(6): e0157712. https://doi.org/10.1371/journal.pone.0157712.

Chandra, M., T. Shrimali, and A. Gupta. 2012. A Survey: Recent Development in Fractals. *Proceedings of the 2012 Fourth International Conference on Computational Intelligence and Communication Networks.* Pp. 251–256. https://doi.org/10.1109/CICN.2012.36.

Chang, C. S., H.-L. Liu, X. Moncadac, A. Seelenfreund, D. Seelenfreunde, and K.-F. Chung. 2015. A holistic picture of Austronesian migrations revealed by phylogeography of Pacific paper mulberry. *Proceedings of the National Academy of Science* 112(44): 13537–13542.

Chayanov, A. V. 1986. *The Theory of Peasant Economy.* Madison: University of Wisconsin Press

Chen, F., Welker, F., Shen, C. et al. 2019. A late Middle Pleistocene Denisovan mandible from the Tibetan Plateau. *Nature* 569: 409–412.

Chetima, M. 2018. Beyond ethnic boundaries: architectural practices and Social identity in the Mandara Highlands, Cameroon. *Cambridge Archaeology Journal* 29(1): 45–63.

Chipunza, K. 1994. *A diachronic analysis of the standing structures of the Hill Complex at Great Zimbabwe.* Uppsala University: Studies in African Archaeology.

Chirikure, S. 2021. *Great Zimbabwe: Reclaiming a 'Confiscated' Past.* London: Routledge.

Chittick, N. H. 1984. *Manda: Excavations at an Island Port on the Kenya Coast.* Nairobi: British Institute in Eastern Africa.

Choudhury, A. et al. 2020. High depth African genomes inform human migration and health. *Nature* 586: 741–748.

Christiansen, M. H. and S. Kirby. 2003. Language evolution: Consensus and controversies. *Trends in Cognitive Sciences* 7(7): 300–307.

Clark, G. 1969. *World Prehistory: A New Outline.* Cambridge: Cambridge University Press.

Clark, J. D., and S. Brandt editors. 1984. *From hunters to farmers: The causes and consequences of food-production in Africa.* University of California Press, Berkeley.

Cleveland, S. D. J. Shaw, S. G. Mfinanga, G. Shirima, R. R. Kazwala, E. Eblate, M. Sharp. 2007. *Mycobacterium bovis* in rural Tanzania: Risk factor for infection in human and cattle population. *Tuberculosis* 87(1): 30–43.

Clist, B. 1989. Archaeology in Gabon. *The African Archaeological Review* 7: 59–95.

Clist, B., E. Cranshof, G. M. de Schryver, D. Herremans, K. Karklins, I. Matonda, F. Steyaert and K. Bostoen. 2015. African-European Contacts in the Kongo Kingdom (Sixteenth-Eighteenth Centuries): New Archaeological Insights from Ngongo Mbata (Lower Congo, DRC). *International Journal of Historical Archaeology* 19: 464–501.

Clist, B., M. Kaumba, I. Matonda and K. Bostoen. 2019. Kitala Ware: A new Early Iron Age Pottery group from the Lower Congo region in Central Africa. *African Archaeological Review* 36: 455–477.

Clist, B. W. Hubau, J. M. Tsibamba, H. Beckman, and K. Bostoen. 2019. The Earliest iron producing communities in the Lower Congo Region of Central Africa: New insights from the Bu, Kindu and Mantsetsi sites. *Azania: Archaeological Research in Africa* 54(2): 221–244.

Clutton-Brock, J. 1993. The spread of domestic animals in Africa. In *The archaeology of Africa: Food, metals and towns,* edited by T. Shaw, P. Sinclair, B. Andah, and A. Okpoko, pp. 61–70. London/New York: Routledge.

———. 1994. The legacy of Iron Age dogs and livestock in 1995 southern Africa. *Azania* 29, 30: 161–167.

———. 1997. The Expansion of domestic animals in Africa. In *Encyclopedia of pre-colonial Africa,* edited by J. O. Vogel, pp. 418–424. Walnut Creek: AltaMira Press.

Coelho M, Sequeira F, Luiselli D, Beleza S, Rocha J. 2009. On the edge of Bantu expansions: mtDNA, Y chromosome and lactase persistence genetic variation in southwestern Angola. *BMC Evolutionary Biology* 21(9): 80.

Connah, G. 1976. The Daima Sequence and the Prehistoric Chronology of the Lake Chad region of Nigeria. *Journal of African History* 17(3): 321–352.

———. 1981. *Three Thousand Years in Africa.* Cambridge: Cambridge University Press.

———. 1984. An archaeological exploration in southern Borno. *The African Archaeological Review* 2: 153–171.

———. 1987. *African Civilizations.* Cambridge: Cambridge University Press.

———. 1996. *Kibiro: the salt of Bunyoro, Past and Present.* London: The British Institute in Eastern Africa.

Connah, G., and Freeth, S.J. 1989. A commodity problem in prehistoric Borno. *Sahara* 2: 7–20.

Corbett, J. 2001. Torsten Hagerstand, Time Geography. CSISS Classics. University of California Santa Barbara. https://escholarship.org/uc/item/2t75b8s

Corvinus, G. 1976. Prehistoric exploration at Hadar, Ethiopia. *Nature* 261: 571–572.

Cremaschi, M., S. Di Lernia, and L. Trombino. 1996. From taming to pastoralism in a drying environment. Site formation processes in the shelters from the Tadrart Acacus massif (Libya, Central Sahara). In *XIII International Congress of Prehistoric and Protohistoric Sciences*, Colloquim VI, pp. 87–106, Forli, Italy.

Crevels, M. and P. Muysken editors 2020. *Language, Dispersal, Diversification and Contact*. Oxford: Oxford University Press.

Crowther, A., L. Lucas, R. Helm, M. Horton, C. Shiptone, H. T. Wright, S. Walshaw, M. Pawlowicz, C. Radimilahy, K. Douka, L. Picornell-Gelabert, D. Q. Fuller, and N. L. Boivin 2015. Ancient crops provide first archaeological signature of the westward Austronesian expansion. *Proceedings of the National Academy of Science* 113(24): 6635–6640.

Currie, T. E., Meade, A., Guillon, M., Mace, R. 2013. Cultural phylogeography of the Bantu Languages of sub-Saharan Africa. *Proceedings of the Royal Society Biology* 280: 20130695. http://dx.doi.org/10.1098/rspb.2013.0695.

Cruciani, F. et al. 2002. A Back Migration from Asia to Sub-Saharan Africa Is Supported by High Resolution Analysis of Human Y-Chromosome Haplotypes. *American Journal of Human Genetics* 70: 1197–1214.

Dalberg, F. editor. 1983. *Woman the gatherer*. New Haven: Yale University Press.

Dalton, G. editor. 1968. *Primitive, Archaic and Modern Economies: Essays of Karl Polanyi*. Garden City: Anchor Books Dambricourt Malassé A et al. 2016. Intentional cut marks on bovid from the Quranwala zone, 2.6 Ma, Siwalik Frontal Range, northwestern India. *Comptes Rendus Palevolution* 15(3–4): 317–339.

Darity Jr., W. A. 1980. The Boserup Theory of Agricultural growth: A model for anthropological Economics. *Journal of Development Economics* 7: 137–157.

Darwin, C. 1859. On the Origin of Species by Means of Natural Selection. London: John Murray.

———. 1871. *The Descent of Man and selection in relation to sex*. London: John Murray.

David, N. 2008. *Performance and Agency: The DGB sites in northern Cameroon*. Oxford. BAR International Series.

David, N., and Sterner, J. 1989. Mandara archaeological project, 1988 - 89. *Nyame Akuma* 32: 5–9.

Decker, J. E., S. D. McKay, M. M. Rolf, J. W. Kim, A. M. Alcala, T. S. Sonstegard, O. Hanotte, A. Gotherstrom, C. M. Seabury, L. Praharani, M. E. Babar, L. C. de Almeida Regitano, M. A. Yildiz, M. P. Heaton, W.-S. Liu, C.-Z. Lei, J. M. Reecy, M. S.-Ur-Rehman, R. D. Schnabel, J. F. Taylor. 2014. Worldwide Patterns of Ancestry, Divergence, and Admixture in Domesticated Cattle. *PLOS Genetics* 10(3) e1004254 (14 pages)

De Fillipo, C.K. Bostoen, M. Stoneking & B. Pakendorf. 2012. Bringing together linguistic and genetic evidence to test the Bantu expansion. *Proceedings of the Royal Society B-Biological Sciences* 279(1741): 3256–3263.

De Foresta, H., D. Schwartz, R. Deschamps and R. Lanfranchi. 1990. Un premier site de metallurgie de l'Age du Fer Ancien (2110 BP) dans le Mayombe Congolais et ses implications sur les dynamiques des ecosystems. *NSI* 7: 10–12.

De Garine-Wichatitsky, A. Caron, R. Kock, R. Tschopp, M. Munyeme, M. Hofmeyr, & A. Michel. 2013. A Review of bovine tuberculosis at the wildlife-Livestock-Human interface in Sub-Saharan Africa. *Epidemiology and Infection* 141: 1342–1356.

De Maret, P. 1997. Savanna States. In *Encyclopedia of Precolonial Africa*. Edited by J.O. Vogel. Pp. 496–501. Walnut Creek: AltaMira Press.

Dejene, S. W., J. M. A. Heitkonig, H. H. T. Prins, F. A. Lemma, D. A. Mekonnen, Z. E. Alemu, T. Z Kelkay, W. F. de Boer. 2016. Risk factors for bovine Tuberculosis in Cattle in Ethiopia. *PLOS One* 11(7): e0159083 1–16.

Denbow, J. R. 1983. Iron Age economics: Herding, wealth and politics along the fringes of the Kalahari Desert during the Early Iron Age (Botswana). Ph.D. thesis, Indiana University.

Deng, G. 2005. *Chinese Maritime Activities and Socioeconomic Development, c. 2100 BC–1900 AD*. London: Greenwood Press.

Deng, Z., H-C. Hung, M. T. Carson, P. Bellwood, S.L. Yang, & H. Lu. 2017. The first discovery of Neolithic rice remains in eastern Taiwan: phytolith evidence from the Chaolaiqiao site. *Archaeological and Anthropological Sciences*. DOI:10.1007/s12520-017-0471-z

Denham, F. R. S., H. Clapperton, and Dr. Oudney. 1828. *Narrative of travels and discoveries in Northern and Central Africa in the years 1822, 1823, and 1824*. London: John Murray.

Denham, T. P., Haberle, S. G., Lentfer, C., Fullagar, R. Field, J. Therin, M. Porch, N. and Winsborough, B. 2003. Origins of agriculture at Kuk Swamp in the Highlands of New-Guinea, *Science* 301: 189–193.

Denham T., S. G. Haberle, and C. Lentfer. 2004. New evidence and interpretations for early agriculture in highland New Guinea. *Antiquity* 78: 839–857.

Denham T, and S. Haberle. 2008. Agricultural emergence and transformation in the Upper Wahgi valley, Papua New Guinea, during the Holocene: theory, method and practice. *The Holocene* 18(3): 481–496.

Denham T., and S. Mooney. 2008. Human–environment interactions in Australia and New Guinea during the Holocene. *The Holocene* 18(3): 365–371.

Denham T., and Barton, H. 2014. Vegeculture: General Principles. In Smith, C. editor, *Encyclopedia of Global Archaeology*. Pp. 7608–7611. New York: Springer.

Desjardin, T., B. Turcq, A.M. Lezine, J. P. Nguetkam, M. Mandeng-Yogo, F. Cetin, and G. Achoundong. 2020. The Origin of the forest-grassland mosaic of central Cameroon: What we learn from the isotopic geochemistry of soil organic matter. *The Holocene* 30(4): 095968362093296.

D'Errico, F. & L. Backwell 2016. Earliest evidence of personal ornaments associated with burial: the *Conus* shells from Border Cave. *Journal of Human Evolution* 93: 91–108.

Détroit, F., Mijares, A.S., Corny, J. et al. 2019. A new species of *Homo* from the Late Pleistocene of the Philippines. *Nature* 568: 181–186.

Dewar, R. E., C. Radimilahy, H. T. Wright, Z. Jacobs, G. O. Kelly, F. Berna. 2013. Stone tools and foraging in northern Madagascar challenge Holocene extinction models. *Proceedings of the National Academy of Science* 110(31): 12583–12588.

Di Lernia, S. 2001. Dismantling Dung: delayed use of food resources among Early Holocene Foragers in the Libyan Sahara. *Journal of Anthropological Archaeology* 20: 408–41.

———. 2006. Building monuments, creating identity: cattle cult as social response to rapid environmental changes in the Holocene Sahara. *Quaternary International* 151: 50–62.

Di Lernia, S., and M. Cremaschi. 1996. Taming barbary sheep: Wild animal management by Early Holocene hunter/gatherers at Uan Afuda (Libyan Sahara). *Nyame Akuma*: 43–54.

Di Lernia, S., and G. Manzi, editors. 2002. *Sand, Stones, and Bones: The Archaeology of death in the Wadi Tanezzuft Valley 5000–2000 BP*. Firenze: All 'Insegna del Giglio.

Di Lernia, S., Tafuri, M. A., Gallinaro, M., Alhaique, F., Balasse, M., et al. 2013. Inside the "African Cattle Complex": Animal Burials in the Holocene Central Sahara. *PLoS ONE* 8(2): e56879. doi: 10.1371/journal.pone.0056879.

DiMucci, A. M. 2015. *An Ancient iron cargo in the Indian Ocean: the Godavay Shipwreck*. MA Thesis: Texas A&M University.

Dreyer, E. L. 2006. *Zheng He: China and the Oceans in the Early Ming, 1405–1433*. London: Longman.

Duda, P., and J. Zrzavy. 2019. Toward a global phylogeny of human population based on genetic and linguistic data. In *Words, Bones, Genes and Tools*. Edited by K. Harvati and G. Jager. Pp. 331–359. DFG Center for Advanced Studies: Tuebingen University.

Dupre, M. C., and B. Pincon. 1997. La Metallurgie du Fer: Technique, Symbolique et Semantique. *Cahiers ORSTOM Sciences Humaines* 31(4): 825–48.

Dunn, M., S. J. Greenhill, S. C. Levinson, and R. D. Gray. 2011. Evolved structure of language shows lineage-specific trends in word-order universals. *Nature*. DOI: 10.1038/nature09923.

Dunne, J., S. di Lernia, M. Chlodnicki, F. Kherbouche, R. P. Evershed. 2018. Timing and pace of dairying inception and animal husbandry practices across Holocene North Africa. *Quaternary International* 471: 147–159.

Earle, T. 1991. The Evolution of Chiefdoms. In *Chiefdoms, Power, Economy, and Ideology*. Edited by T. Earle, pp. 1–15: Cambridge University Press, Cambridge.

Eggert, M. K. H. 2008. the Bantu problem and African archaeology. In A.B. Stahl, ed. *African Archaeology: A Critical Introduction*. Pp. 301–326. Oxford: Blackwell.

Eggert, M. K. H., A. Höhn, S. Kahlheber, C. Meister, K. Neumann and A. Schweizer. 2006. Pits, graves, and grain: Archaeological and archaeobotanical research in southern Cameroon. *Journal of African Archaeology* 4(2): 273–298.

Elredge, N., and S. J. Gould. 1972. Punctuated equilibria: An alternative to phyletic gradualism. In *Models in Paleobiology*. Edited by T. J. M. Schopf. Pp. 82–115. San Francisco: Freeman Cooper.

Essomba, J. M. 1992. *Civilisation du Fer et Societes en Afrique Centrale. Le cas du Cameroon Meridional: Histoire Ancienne et Archeologie*. Paris: L'Harmattan.

Eze-Uzomaka, P. nd. Iron and its influence on the prehistoric site of Lejja (*white paper available as free download, last visited 01/14/2021*).

———. 2009. Iron and its Influence on the Prehistoric Site of Lejja. Paper read at the World of Iron Conference, February 16–20, 2009, University College London: United Kingdom.

Fagundes, N. J. R., Tagliani-Ribeiro, A., Rubicz, R., Tarskaia, L., Crawford, M. H., Slazano F. M., Bonatto, S. L. 2018. How strong was the bottleneck associated to the Peopling of the Americas? New insights from multi-locus sequence data. *Genetics and Molecular Biology* 41(1). https://doi.org/10.1590/1678–4685–gmb-2017–0087

Falconer, H. 1832. Dehra Dun fossil remains. *Journal of the Asiatic Society of Bengal* 1: 249.

Fan, S., D. E. Kelly, M. H. Beltrame, M. E. B. Hansen, S. Mallick, A. Ranciaro, J. Hirbo, S. Thompson, W. Beggs, T. Nyambo, S. A. Omar, D. Wolde Meskel, G. Belay, A. Froment, N. Patterson, D. Reich, and S. A. Tishkoff. 2019. African evolutionary history inferred from whole genome sequence data of 44 indigenous African populations. *Genome Biology* 20(82): 1–14.

Fan, S. et al. 2019. African evolutionary history inferred from whole genome sequence data of 44 indigenous African populations. *Genome Biology* 20: 82 https://doi.org/10.1186/s13059–019–1679–2

Feinman, G., and J. Marcus, editors. 1998. *Archaic States* Santa-Fe: School of American Research Press.

Ferrand, G. 1919. Les K'ouen-Louen et les anciennes navigations inter-oceaniques dans les mers du sud. *Journal Asiatique* 13: 239–333, 431–492, 14: 5–68, 201–241.

———. 1922. L'Empire Sumatranais de Srivijaya. *Journal Asiatique* 20: 1–104.

Ferretti. F., I. Adornetti, A. Chiera, E. Cosentino, S. Nicchiarelli. 2018. Introduction: Origin and Evolution of Language An Interdisciplinary Perspective. *Topoi* 37: 219–234. https://doi.org/10.1007/s11245–018–9560–6.

Filesi, T. 1970. *China and Africa in the Middle Ages*. London: F. Cass.

Finucane, B., K. Manning and M. Toure. 2008. Late Stone Age subsistence in the Tilemsi Valley, Mali: Stable isotope analysis of human and animal remains from the site of Karkarichinkat (KN05) and Karkarichinkat Sud (KS 05). *Journal of Anthropological Archaeology* 27: 82–92.

Fisher, S. E. 2017. Evolution of language: Lessons from the genome. *Psychon Bulletin Review* 24: 34–40.

Flannery, K. 1969. Origins and ecological effects of early domestication in Iran and the Near East. In The domestication and exploitation of plants and animals, edited by P. J. Ucko and G. W. Dimbleby, pp. 73–100. Aldine, Chicago.

Florin, S. A., A. S. Fairbairn, and M. Nango, et al. 2020. The first Australian plant foods at Madjedbebe, 65,000–53,000 years ago. *Nature Communications* 11: 924.

Fong, J. D. M., T. Masunaga and K. Sato. 2015. Assessment of water management on yield component and morphological behavior of rice at post heading stage. *Paddy and Water Environment* 14: 211–220.

Forkl, H. 1983. *Die Beziehungen der zentral-sudanisehen Reiche Bornu, Mandar und Bagirmi sowie Kotoko-staaten zu ihren sudlichen Naehbar unter besonderer Berucksichtigung des Sao-Problems.* Munchen: Minerva Publikation.

———. 1985 *Der Einfluss Bornus, Mandara, Bagirmis, der Kotoko-Staaten und der Jukun- Konfederation auf die Kulturentwicklung ihrer Nachbarn sudlich des Tshadsees.* Munchen: Minerva Publikation.

Fox, J. J. 1995. Austronesian Societies and their Transformations. In *The Austronesians: Historical and Comparative Perspectives.* Edited by P. Bellwood, J. J. Fox, and D. Tryon. 214–228. Canberra: Australian National University.

Fuller, D. Q., N. Boivin, T. Hoogervorst, and R. Allaby. 2011. Across the Indian Ocean: The Prehistoric Movements of Plants and Animals. *Antiquity* 85: 544–558.

Frankenstein, S. and M. Rowlands. 1978. The Internal Structure and Regional Context of Early Iron Age Society in South-Western Germany. *Bulletin of the Institute of Archaeology of London* 15: 73–112.

Galagan, J. E. 2014. Genomic insight into tuberculosis. *Nature Reviews Genetics* 15: 307–320.

Galipaud, J. C., I. Lin Wu and A. Di Piazza. 2014. Un monde sans frontières: la diaspora austronésienne en Asie du Sud-Est et en Océanie. In L. Dousset, B. Glowczewski, and M. Salaun, eds. *Les Sciences Humaines et Sociales dans le Pacifique Sud: Terrains, Questions et Methodes.* Pp. 21–32. Marseille: Pacific-Credo Publications.

Garcin, Y., Deschamps, P., Ménot, G., de Saulieu, G., Schefuß, E., Sebag, D., Dupont, L. M., Oslisly, R., Brademann, B., Mbusnum, K. G., Onana, J.-M., Ako, A. A., Epp, L. S., Tjallingii, R., Strecker, M. R., Brauer, A., Sachse, D. 2018. Early anthropogenic impact on Western Central African rainforests 2,600 y ago. *Proceedings of The National Academy of Science* https://doi.org/10. 1073/pnas.1715336115.

Garnier, T., K. Eiglmeier, J-C. Camus, N. Medina, H. Mansoor, M. Pryor, S. Duthoy, S. Grondin, C. Lacroix, C. Monsempe, S. Simon, B. Harris, R. Atkin, J. Doggett, R. Mayes, L Keating, P. R. Wheeler, J. Parkhill, B. G. Barrell, S. T. Cole, S. V. Gordon, and R. G. Hewinson. 2003. The complete genome sequence of *Mycobacterium bovis*. *Proceedings of the national Academy of Sciences* 100(13): 7877–7882.

Gauthier, A. 1982. Faunal remains excluding fish and general evaluation, prehistoric fauna of Ti-n-Torha (Tadrart Acacus, Libya). *Origini* 11: 87–113.

———. 1987. Prehistoric men and cattle in north Africa: A dearth of data and a surfeit of models. In *Prehistory of Arid North Africa*, edited by A. E. Close, pp. 163–187. Dallas: Southern Methodist University Press.

Gauthier, A., and W. van Neer. 1982. Prehistoric fauna from Ti-n-Torha (Tadrart Acacus, Libya). *Origini* XI: 87–125.

Gebrehiwot, N. Z., E. M. Strucken, H. Aliloo, K. Marshal & J. P. Gibson. 2020 The Patterns of admixture, divergence, and ancestry of African cattle populations determined from genome-wide SNP. *BMC Genomics* 21: 869 [16 pages].

Geggel, L. 2018. Ochre: The world's first red paint. *Live Science.* https://www .livescience.com/64138–ochre-html

Gelabert, P. et al. 2019. Genome-wide data from the Bibi of Bioko Island clarifies the Atlantic fringe of the Bantu dispersal. *BMC Genomics* 20: 179.

Gifford-Gonzales, D. 1998. Early Pastoralists in East Africa: Ecological and Social dimension. *Journal of Anthropological Archaeology* 17: 166–200.

———. 2017. Pastoralism in Sub-saharan Africa: Emergence and ramifications. In *The Oxford Handbook of Zooarchaeology.* Edited by U. Albarella, M. Rizetto, H. Russ, K. Vickers & S. Viner Daniels. doi.10.1093/oxfordhb/9780199686476.

Gould, S. J. 1989. *Wonderful Life: The Burgess Shale and the Nature of History.* New York: W. W. Norton

Greenberg, J. H. 1955. *Studies in African Linguistic Classification.* New Haven: Compass.

———. 2005. Indo-Europeanist practice and American Indianist theory in linguistic classification. In: Croft, W. (Ed.), *Genetic Linguistics: Essays on Theory and Method, by Joseph H. Greenberg.* pp. 153–189. Oxford: Oxford University Press.

Greenhill, S. J., H. Xia, C. F. Caela, H. Schneemann, and L. Bromham. 2018. Population size and the rate of language evolution: A test across Indo-European, Austronesian, and Bantu Languages. *Frontiers in Psychology* 9: 576. doi: 10.3389/fpsyg.2018.00576.

Gronenborn, D. 1998. Archaeological and Ethnohistorical investigations along the southern fringes of Lake Chad 1993–1996. *African Archaeological Review* 15(4): 229–259.

Gronenborn, D., editor. 2011. *Gold, slaves, and ivory. Medieval empires in northern Nigeria.* Catalogue of the exhibition at the Romisch-Germanisches Zentralmuseum 22 September 2011–1 January 2012. Mainz: Romisch-Germanisches Zentralmuseum.

Gronenborn, D., P. Adderley, J. Ameye, A. Banerjee, T. Fenn, G. Liesegang, C. P. Hasse, Y. A. Usman and S. Patcher. 2012. Durbi takusheyi: A High status burial site, Western Central Sudan. *Azania: Archaeological Research in Africa* 47(3): 256–271.

Gumi, B., E. Schelling, S. Berg, R. Fridessa, G. Erenso, W. Mekonnen, E. Hailu, E. Melese, J. Hussein, A. Aseffa, J. Zinstag 2012. Zoonotic transmission of tuberculosis between pastoralists and their livestock in Southwest Ethiopia. *Ecohealth* 9: 139–149.

Guthrie, M. 1967–1971. *Comparative Bantu: Introduction to Comparative linguistics and Prehistory of the Bantu languages* (4 volumes).

Haber, M., M, Mezzavilla, A. Bergström et al. 2016. Chad Genetic Diversity Reveals an African History Marked by Multiple Holocene Eurasian Migrations. *American Journal of Human Genetics* 99(6): 1316–1324.

Habgood, P. J. and N. R. Franklin. 2008. The Revolution that did not arrive: A Review of Pleistocene Sahul. *Journal of Human Evolution* 55(2): 187–222.

Hagerstrand, T. 1970. What about People in Regional Science? *Papers of the Regional Science Association* 24: 6–21.

Haile-Selassie, Y., Suwa, G., and T. D. White. 2004. Late Miocene teeth from Middle Awash, Ethiopia, and early hominid dental evolution. *Science* 303: 1503–1505.

Haile-Selassie, Y., Melollo, S.M., Vazzana, A., Banazzi, S., Tyan, T.M. 2019. A 3.8 million-year-old hominin cranium from Woranso-Mille, Ethiopia. *Nature* 573: 214–221.

Hallaire, A. 1965. *Les monts du Mandara au nord de Mokolo et la plaine de Mora: Étude géographique régionale.* Yaoundé: ORSTOM/IRCAM.

Halstead, P., and J. O'Shea editors. 1989. *Bad Year Economics.* Cambridge: Cambridge University Press.

Hammel, E. A. 2005. Chayanov Revisited: A Model for the Economics of complex kin units. *Proceedings of the National Academy of Sciences* 102(19): 7043–7046.

Han, F., Deng, C., Boeda, E., Hou, Y., Wei, G., Huang, W., Garcia, T., Shao, Q., He, C., Falguieres, C., Voinchet, P., Yin, G. 2017. The earliest evidence of hominid settlement in China: Combined electron spin resonance and uranium series (ESR/U-series) dating of mammalian fossil teeth from Longgupo cave. *Quaternary International* 434: 75–83.

Hanotte, O., D. G. Bradley, J. W. Ochieng, Y. Verjee, E. W. Hill, & J. E. O. Rege. 2002. African pastoralism: Genetic Imprints of origins and migrations. *Science* 296: 336–339.

Harmand, S., Lewis, J., Feibel, C. et al. 2015. 3.3-million-year-old stone tools from Lomekwi 3, West Turkana, Kenya. *Nature* 521, 310–315.

Hart, J. P. 2002. *Darwin and Archaeology.* Boston: Greenwood Publishing Group.

Haskett, D. R. 2014. "Mitochondrial DNA and Human Evolution" (1987), by Rebecca Louise Cann, Mark Stoneking, and Allan Charles Wilson https://embryo .asu.edu/pages/mitochondrial-dna-and-human-evolution

Hassan, F. 1985. A radiocarbon chronology of neolithic and predynastic sites in Upper Egypt and the Delta. *The African Archaeological Review* 3: 95–116.

Heather, P. J. 2005. *The Fall of the Roman Empire: A New History of Rome and the Barbarians.* Oxford: Oxford University Press.

Heine, B., H. Hoff, & R. Vossen 1977. Neuere Ergebnisse zur Territorialgeschichte des Bantu. In W. J.G. Möhlig, F. Rottland, & B. Heine, eds. 1976. *Zur Sprachgeschichte und ethnohistorie in Afrika: Neue Beiträge afrikanistischer Forschungen.* Pp. 57–72: Berlin, Reimer.

Hellenthal, G., G. B. J. Busby, G. Band, J. F. Wilson, C. Capelli, D. Falush and S. Myers. 2014. A Genetic Atlas of Human Admixture History *Science* 343 (6172), 747–751. DOI: 10.1126/science.1243518

Henshilwood, C. S., F. d'Errico, K. van Niekerk, Y. Coquinot, Z. Jacobs, S. E. Lauritzen, M. Menu, R. Garcia-Moreno. 2011. A 100,000–year old Ochre processing workshop at Blombos Cave, South Africa. *Science* 334: 219–222.

Henshilwood, C. S., F. d'Errico, K. van Niekerk, L. Dayet, A. Queffelec and L. Pollarolo. 2018. An Abstract drawing from the 73000 year old levels at Blombos Cave, South Africa. *Nature* 562: 115–118.

Herries, A. I. R., Martin, J. M., Leece, A. B., Adams et al. 2020. Contemporaneity of *australopithecus, paranthropus*, and early *homo erectus* in South Africa. Science, 368(6486), [eaaw7293]. https://doi.org/10.1126/science.

Hershkovitz, I., H. D. Donoghue, D. E. Minnikin, G. S. Besra, O. Y-C. Lee, A. M. Gernaey, E. Galili, V. Eshed, C. L. Greenblatt, E. Lemma, G. K. Bar-Gal, M. Spigelman, N. Ahmed. 2008. Detection and Molecular Characterization of 9000–Year-Old Mycobacterium tuberculosis from a Neolithic Settlement in the Eastern Mediterranean. *PLoS ONE, 3* (10) DOI: 10.1371/journal.pone.0003426

Hershkovitz, I. et al. 2018. The Earliest modern humans outside Africa. *Science* 359: 456–459.

Hiatt, L. 1996. *Arguments about Aborigines: Australia and the evolution of social anthropology.* Cambridge: Cambridge University Press.

Higgs, E. S. 1967. Domestic animals. In *The Haua Fteah (Cyrenaica) and the Stone Age of the south-east Mediterranean,* edited by C. B. M. McBurney, pp. 313–319. Cambridge: Cambridge University Press.

———. 1979. Exploitation patterns. In *Economie pastorale preagricaole en Algerie Orientale: le Neolithique de Tradition Capsienne*, edited by C. Roubet, pp. 412–413. Paris: Editions du CNRS.

Higham, C. 2013. Hunter-Gatherers in Southeast Asia from Prehistory to the Present. *Human Biology* 85(1–3): 21–44.

———. 2017. The Prehistoric House: A Missing factor in Southeast Asia. In *New Perspectives in Southeast Asian and Pacific Prehistory*. Edited by P. J. Piper, H. Matsumura, and D. Bulbeck. pp. Canberra: Australian National University. Pressfiles.anu.edu.au/downloads/press/n2320/html/ch15.xhtml.

Hohn, A., P. Breunig, D. Gronenborn, K. Neumann. 2020. After the flood and with people—Late Holocene changes of the woody vegetation in southwestern Chad Basin, Nigeria. *Quaternary International* https://doi.org/10.1016/j.quaint.2020.11.04.

Holl, A. 1985. Subsistence patterns of the Dhar Tichitt Neolithic, Mauretania. *African Archaeological Review* 3: 151–162.

———. 1986. *Economie et societe Neolithique du Dhar Tichitt (Mauritanie).* Paris: Editions Recherche sur les Civilisations.

———. 1988a. *Houlouf I: Archéologie des Sociétés Protohistoriques du Nord-Cameroun,* Oxford: British Archaeological Reports.

———. 1988b. Transition du Néolithique à l'Age du Fer dans la plaine péritehadi-enne: le cas de Mdaga. In *Le Milieu et les Hommes: Recherches Comparatives et Historiques dans le Bassin du Lac Tchad.* edited by D. Barreteau and H. Tourneux. Editions de l'ORSTOM, pp. 81–110: Paris.

———. 1993a. Transition from Late Stone Age to Iron Age in the Sudano-Sahelian zone: A case study from the perichadian plain. In *The Archaeology of Africa: Food, Metals and Towns.* Edited by T. Shaw, P. Sinclair, B. Andah and A. Okpoko. pp. 330–343: London and New York: Routledge:

———. 1993b. Community interaction and settlement patterning in Northern Cameroon. In *Spatial Boundaries and Social Dynamics: Case Studies from Food-producing Societies.* Edited by A. Holl and T. E. Levy, pp. 39–61: Ann Arbor: International Monographs in Prehistory.

———. 1994. The Cemetery of Houlouf in Northern Cameroon (AD 1500–1600): Fragments of a past social system. *African Archaeological Review* 12: 133–170.

―――. 1995. Pathways to elderhood: Research on past pastoral iconography, the paintings from Tikadiouine (Tassili-n-Ajjer). *Origini* XVIII: 69–113.

―――. 1996. Genesis of Central Chadic Polities. In *Aspects of African Archaeology*, edited by G. Pwiti & R. Soper: pp. 581–591. Harare: University of Zimbabwe Publications.

―――. 1998a. The Dawn of African Pastoralisms: An Introductory Note. *Journal of Anthropological Archaeology* 17: 81–96.

―――. 1998b. Livestock Husbandry, Pastoralisms, and Territoriality: The West African Record. *Journal of Anthropological Archaeology* 17: 143–165

―――. 2000. *The Diwan Revisited: Literacy, State formation and the Rise of Kanuri Domination (AD 1200–1600)*. London/New York: Kegan Paul.

―――. 2001. 500 Years in the Cameroons: Making Sense of the Archaeological Record. In *West Africa during the Atlantic Slave Trade: Archaeological Perspectives* edited by C. R. DeCorse, pp. 152–178. London, New York: Leicester University Press.

―――. 2002. *The Land of Houlouf: Genesis of a Chadic Chiefdom (1900 BC–1800 AD)*. Ann Arbor: Memoirs of the University of Michigan Museum of Anthropology.

―――. 2003. *Ethnoarchaeology of Shuwa-Arab*. Lanham: Lexington Books.

―――. 2004a. *Saharan Rock Art: Archaeology of Tassilian Pastoralist Iconography*. Walnut Creek: AltaMira Press.

―――. 2004b. *Holocene Saharans: An Anthropological Perspective*. New York/London: Continuum Publishing Group.

―――. 2005. The archaeology of Africa. In D. L. Hardesty, editor, *Archaeology, Volume II.* Pp. 21–65. Oxford: UNESCO-EOLSS.

―――. 2009. West African early metallurgies: New Evidence and old orthodoxy. *Journal of World Prehistory*. 22 (4): 415–438.

―――. 2013. Grass, Water, Salt, Copper, and Others: Pastoralists' Territorial Strategies in Central Sudan. *Archaeological Papers of the American Anthropological Association*. 22: 39–53.

―――. 2015a. L'expansion bantoue. Dynamiques des populations et dynamiques environnementales. In Baussant M. et al. (dir.), *Migrations humaines et mises en récit mémorielles.* p. 93–116. Nanterre: Presses universitaires de Paris-Ouest,.

―――. 2015b. *Africa: The Archaeological Background*. Yaoundé: Editions du CERDOTOLA.

―――. 2017. L'Expansion Bantoue: Une Nouvelle Synthese. In D. Garcia and H. Le Bras eds. *Archeologie des Migrations*. Pp 225–236. Paris: La Decouverte/Inrap.

―――. 2018. Diffusion de l'Agriculture et de l'elevage en Afrique. In *Une Histoire des Civilisations.* Edited by J. P. Demoule, D. Garcia and A. Schnapp.pp. 213–218. Paris: La Decouverte / Inrap.

―――. 2020a. China and East Africa Ancient Ties and Contemporary Flows: A Critical Appraisal. In Kusimba, C.M., T.Q Zhu and P. Kiura eds *Ancient Ties, Contemporary Flows Between China and Africa*. Pp. 259–265. Lanham: Lexington Books.

―――. 2020b. The Origins of African Metallurgies. *Oxford Research Encyclopedia: Anthropology*. DOI: 10.1093/acrefore/9780190854584.013.63 T

————. 2020c. Dark Side Archaeology: Climate Change and Mid-Holocene Saharan Pastoral Adaptation. *African Archaeological Rev*iew 37: 491–495. https://doi.org /10.1007/s10437–020–09406–6

Holl, A., T. E. Levy, Cl. Lechevalier et A. Bridault. 1991. Of Mounds, Cattle and Men: Archaeology and Ethnoarchaeology in the Houlouf Region (Northern Cameroon). *West African Journal of Archaeology* 29: 7–36.

Horton, M., H. W. Brown, N. Mudida. 1996. *Shanga: The Archaeology of a Muslim Trading Community on the Coast of East Africa.* Nairobi: British Institute in Eastern Africa.

Horton, M., D. Nurse, F. Topan, W. E. van den Hoonard. 2011. East Africa: Persian relations with the lands of the East African Coast, particularly Somalia, Kenya and Tanzania. *Encyclopedia Iranica* VII(6): 640–644.

Hu, C., M. Henderson, J. Huang, S. Xie, Y. Sun, R. R. Johnson. 2008. Quantification of Holocene Asian Monsoon rainfall from spatially separated cave records. *Earth and Planetary Science Letters* 266(3–4): 221–232.

Hublin, J. J., A. Benncer, S. E. Bailey, S. E. Freidline, S. Neubauer, M. M. Skinner, I. Bergmann, A. Le Cabec, S. Benazzi, K. Harvati & P. Gunz. 2017. New fossils from Jebel Irhoud, Morocco and the pan-African origin of Homo sapiens. *Nature* 546: 286.

Huffman, T. N. 1986. Iron Age settlement patterns and the origins of class distinction in southern Africa. In *Advances in world archaeology*, edited by F. Wendorf and A. E. Close, Vol. 5, pp. 291–338. Academic Press, New York.

————. 1996. *Snakes and Crocodiles: Power and Symbolism in Ancient Zimbabwe*. Johannesburg: Witwatersrand University Press.

————. 2007. A Handbook to the Iron Age: The Archaeology of Pre-Colonial Farming Societies in Southern Africa. Pietermaritzburg. University of KwaZulu-Natal Press,

Huffman, T. N. and S. Woodborne 2020. AMS dates and the Chronology of Great Zimbabwe. *Journal of African Archaeology* 18: 86–108.

Hung, H.-C. 2019. History and Current Debates of Archaeology in Island Southeast Asia. In *Encyclopedia of Global Archaeology*. Edited by C. Smith. Springer Nature Switzerland https://doi.org/10.1007/978–3–319–51726–1_3373–1

Hung, H.-C. and C. Zhang. 2019. The Origins, Expansion, and Decline of early hunter- gatherers along south China coast. In *Prehistoric Maritime Cultures and Seafaring in East-Asia: The Archaeology of Asia-Pacific Navigation I.* Edited by C. Wu and B. V. Rolett. Pp. 53–79. Singapore: Springer Nature.

Ibrahim, S., S. I. B. Cadmus, J. U. Umoh, I. Ajogi, U. M. Farouk, U. B. Abubakar & A. E. Kudi. 2012. Tuberculosis in Humans and Cattle in Jigawa State, Nigeria: Risk factors analysis. *Veterinary Medicine International* 865924 (5 pages).

Inlamea, O. F., P. Soares, C. Y. Ikuta, M. B. Heinemann, S. J. Acha, A. Machada, J. S. F. Neto, M. Correa-Neves, & T. Rito. 2020. Evolutionary analysis of Mycobacterium bovis genotypes across Africa suggests co-evolution with livestock and humans. *PLOS Neglected Disease* (March 2: 2020: 1–16 pages).

Inskeep, R. R. 1997. Southern and eastern Africa: History of archaeology. In Encyclopedia of precolonial Africa, edited by J. O. Vogel, pp. 75–84. Walnut Creek: AltaMira Press.

Isaac, G. L. 1981 Stone Age visiting cards: approaches to the study of early land-use patterns. In *Pattern of the past*. Edited by I. Hodder, G. Ll. Isaac and N. Hammond. pp. 131–55. Cambridge: Cambridge University Press.

Janson, T. 2011. *The History of Languages*. Oxford: Oxford University Press

Jasdanwalla, F. 2011. "African Settlers on the West Coast of India: The Sidi Elite of Janjira." *African and Asian Studies* 10: 41–58.

Jiao, T. 2007. *The Neolithic of Southeast China: Cultural Transformation and Regional Interaction on the Coast*. New York: Cambria Press.

Johanson, D. C., and M. Taieb. 1976. Plio-Pleistocene hominid discoveries in Hadar, Ethiopia. *Nature* 260: 293–297.

Johanson, D. C., White, T. D., Coppens, Y. 1978. A New species of the genus *Australopithecus* (Primates » Hominidae) from the Pliocene of Eastern Africa. *Kirtandia* 28: 2–14.

Johanson, D. C., and M. E. Edey. 1981. *Lucy: The Beginnings of Humanking*. Granada: Saint Albans.

Johnston, H. H. H. 1886. *The Kilma-Njaro Expedition: A Record of Scientific Exploration in Eastern Equatorial Africa.* London: K. Paul, Trench & Co.

———. 1919. *A Comparative Study of the Bantu and Semi-Bantu Languages*. Oxford: Clarendon Press.

Jousse, H. 2004. A new contribution to the history of pastoralism in West Africa. *Journal of African Archaeology* 2: 187–201.

Juwayeyi, Y. M. 1993. Iron Age settlement and subsistence patterns in southern Malawi. In *The archaeology of Africa: Food, metals and towns,* edited by T. Shaw, P. Sinclair, B. Andah, and A. Okpoko, pp. 391–398. London/New York: Routledge.

Kahn, J. G. 2014. Household Archaeology and House Societies in the Hawaiian archipelago. *Journal of Pacific Archaeology* 5(2): 18–29.

Kappelman, J. 2018. An early hominin arrival in Asia. *Nature* 559: 480–481.

Kelly, M. C. S. 2017. Early Pottery in Island Southeast Asia. In *Handbook of East and Southeast Asian Archaeology*. Edited by J. Habu, P. N. Lape and J. W. Olsen. Pp. 397–418. New York: Springer.

Kemunto, N., Mogoa, E., Osoro, E., Bitek, A., Njenga, M. K., & Thumbi, S. M. 2018. Zoonotic disease research in East Africa. *BMC Infectious Disease* 18: 545.

Kench, P. S., R. F. McLean, S. D. Owen, E. Ryan, K. M. Morgan, L. Ke, X. Wang and K. Roy. 2020. Climate-forced sea-level lowstands in the Indian Ocean during the last two millennia. *Nature Geoscience* 13: 61–64.

Kennedy, H. 2007. *The Great Arab Conquests: How the Spread of Islam Changed the World we live in*. Boston: Da Capo Press.

Kennedy, K. A. R., and R. L. Ciochon. 1999. A canine tooth from the Siwaliks: first recorded discovery of a fossil ape? *Human Evolution* 14(3): 231–253.

Kim, J., O. Hanotte, O. A. Mwai, T. Dessie, S. Bashir, B. Diallo, M. Agaba, K. Kim, W. Kwak, S. Sung, M. Seo1, H. Jeong, T Kwon, M. Taye, K-D. Song, D. Lim, S. Cho, H.-J. Lee, D. Yoon, S. J. Oh, S. Kemp, H.-K. Lee and H. Kim. 2017. The genome landscape of indigenous African cattle. *Genome Biology* 18: 34

Kinahan, J. 1993. The rise and fall of nomadic pastoralism in the central Namib desert. In *The archaeology of Africa: Food, metals and towns,* edited by T. Shaw, P. Sinclair, B. Andah, and A. Okpoko, pp. 372–385. London/New York: Routledge.

———. 1994. A new archaeological perspective on nomadic pastoralist expansion in South-western Africa. *Azania* 29, 30: 211–226.

Kirch, P. V. 1982. The impact of prehistoric polynesians on the Hawai ecosystem. *Pacific Science* 36(1): 1–14.

Kiyaga-Mulindwa, D. 1993. The Iron Age peoples of east-central Botswana. In *The archaeology of Africa: Food, metals and towns,* edited by T. Shaw, P. Sinclair, B. Andah, and A. Okpoko, pp. 386– 390. London/New York: Routledge.

Ko, A. M. S, Chung-Yu Chen, Qiaomei Fu, F. Delfin, Mingkun Li, Hung-Lin Chiu, M. Stoneking, and Ying-Chin Ko. 2014. Early Austronesians: Into and Out of Taiwan. *American Journal of Human Genetics* 94: 426–436.

Koch, R. 1882. Die Atiologie des Tuberculose. *Berliner Klinischen Wochenschrift* 15: 221–230.

Krigbaum, J. 2003. Neolithic subsistence patterns in Northern Borneo reconstructed with stable carbon isotopes of enamel. *Journal of Anthropological Archaeology* 22: 292–304.

Kristof, N. D. 1999. "1492: The prequel." The New York Times, 6 June 1999.

Krzyzaniak, L. 1978. New light on early food-production in the central Sudan. *Journal of African History* 19: 159–172.

———. 1991 Early farming in the middle Nile basin: Recent discoveries at Kadero (Central Sudan). *Antiquity* 65: 515–532.

Kuhnert, H., H. Kuhlmann, M. Mohtadi, H. Meggers, K. H. Baumann and J. Patzold. 2014. Holocene tropical Western Indian Ocean surface temperatures in covariation with climatic changes in the Indonesian region. *Paleoceanography* 29: 423–437.

Kusimba, C. M. 1999. *The Rise and Fall of Swahili States*. Walnut Creek: AltaMira Press.

Kusimba, C. M., T. Q Zhu, and P. Kiura, editors. 2020. *Ancient Ties, Contemporary Flows Between China and Africa*. Lanham: Lexington Books.

Laland, K. N., T. Uller, M.W. Feldman, K. Sterelny, G. B. Muller, A Moczek, E. Jablonka and J. Odling-Smee. 2015. The Extended Evolutionary Synthesis: Its Structure, Assumptions and Predictions. *Proceedings of the Royal Society, Biology* 282: 1019.

Lander, F., and T. Russell. 2018. The archaeological evidence for the appearance of pastoralism and farming in Southern Africa. *PloS One.* https://doi.org/10.1371/journal.pone.0198941.

Lange, D. 1977. *Le diwan des sultans du (Kanem)-Bornu: Chronologie et histoire d'un royaume africain de la fi n du 10e siècle jusqu'à 1808*. Studien zur Kulterkunde. Wiesbaden: Franz Steiner Verlag.

———. 1987. *A Sudanic Chronicle: The Borno Expeditions of Idris Alauma (1564–1576)*. Studien zur Kulturkunde 86. Weisbaden: Franz Steiner Verlag.

Lartet, E. 1837. Note sur les ossements fossiles des terrains tertiaires de Simorre, de Sansan, etc., dans le department du Gers: et sur la découverte récente d'une mâchoire de singe fossile. *Comptes Rendus de l'Académie de Sciences* 4: 85–93.

Lawler, A. 2018. Scarred bird bones reveal early settlement on Madagascar. *Science* 361(6407): 1059.

Leakey, L. S. 1959. A New fossil from Olduvai. *Nature* 184: 491–494.

Leakey, M. G., Feibel, C. S., McDougall, I., Walker, A. 1995. New four-million-year-old hominid species from Kanapio and Allia Bay, Kenya. *Nature* 376: 565–571.

Leakey, M. G., Spoor, F., Brown, F. H., Gathogo, P. N., Kiarie, C., Leaky, L. N., McDougall, I. 2001. New hominin genus from eastern Africa shows diverse middle Pliocene lineages. *Nature* 410: 433–440.

Lebeuf, A. M. D. 1969. *Les Principautés Kotoko: Essai sur le Caractère Saeré de l'Autorité*. Paris: Editions du CNRS.

Lebeuf, J. P. 1969. *Carte Archéologique des Abords du Lac Tchad.* Paris: Editions du C.N.R.S.

———. 1981. *Supplément à la Carte Archéologique des Abords du Lac Tchad.* Paris: Editions du CNRS.

Lebeuf, J. P., and A. Lebeuf. 1977. *Les Arts Sao.* Paris: Editions du Chene.

Lebeuf, J. P., A. M. D. Lebeuf, Fr. Treinen-Claustre, and J. Courtin. 1980. *Le Gisement Sao de Mdaga.* Paris: Société d'Ethnographie.

Lee, R. B. and I. DeVore, editors. 1976. *Kalahari Hunter-gatherers.* Cambridge, Mass. Harvard University Press.

Le Quellec, L. 1993. *Symbolisme et Art Rupestre au Sahara.* Paris: L'Harmattan.

Letouzey, R. 1985. *Notice de la Carte Phytogéographique du Cameroun au 1: 500 000.* Toulouse: Institut de la Carte Internationale de la Végétation.

Levtzion, N., and J. F. P. Hopkins. 1981. *Corpus of Early Arabic Sources for West African History.* Cambridge: Cambridge University Press.

Levathes, L. 1997. *When China Ruled the Seas: The Treasure Fleet of the Dragon Throne, 1405–1433.* Oxford: Oxford University Press.

Lewin, R. 1992. *Complexity: Life at the Edge of Chaos.* Macmillan, New York.

Lézine, A. M, A. F. C. Holl, C. Assi-Khaudjis, J. Lebamba, L. Février, A. Vincens & E. Sultan. 2013. Central African forest, human populations and climate during the Holocène. *Comptes Rendus de l'Académie des Sciences—Géosciences* 345: 327–335.

Li, A. 2005. African Studies in China in the twentieth century: A historical survey. *African Studies Review* 48(1) 59–87.

———. 2015. Contact between China and Africa before Vasco da Gama: Archaeology, Document, and Historiography. *World History Studies* 2(1): 34–59.

———. 2020. *China and Africa in the Global context: Encounter, Policy, Cooperation and Migration.* Cape Town: Africa Century Editions.

Li, S., C. Schlebusch and M. Jakobson. 2014. Genetic variation reveals large scale population expansion and migration during the expansion of Bantu speaking people. *Proceedings of the Royal Society, Biology* 281: 21141448.

Li, X. 2017. *China in Africa: In Zheng He's Footsteps.* Cape-Town: Human Science Research Council Press.

Li, Z., L. Doyon, H. Fang, R. Ledevin, A. Queffelec, E. Raguin, et al. 2020. A Paleolithic bird figurine from the Lingjing site, Henan, China. *PLoS ONE* 15(6): e0233370. https://doi.org/ 10.1371/journal.pone.0233370.

Liebert, H. 2011. Alexander the Great and the History of Globalization. *Review of Politics* 73(4): 533–560. Doi: 10.17/S0034670511003639.

Liesegang, G. 2009. Selma (8th Century BC), Takusheyi (13th/14th Century AD) and Surame (16th/17th Century AD), research on the rise of the Iron Age, the states of Katsina, Gobir and Kebbi, "fossilized" urbanism in northern Nigeria 1990–1994 and the impact of paradigms. In *Festschrift Ulrich Braukamper*. Edited by A. Dohrman, D. Bustorf and N. Poissonnier, 317–340. Munster: Lit Verlag.

Lihoreau, M. 1993. *Poteries Prehistoriques Sahariennes.* Paris: Karthala.

Lipson, M. et al. 2020. Ancient West Africa Foragers in the context of African population History. *Nature* 577: 665–672.

Lipson, M., Ribot, I., Mallick, S. et al. 2020. Ancient West African foragers in the context of African population history. *Nature* 577: 665–670.

Lim, J., J. Y. Lee, S. S. Hong, S. Park, E. Lee, S. Yi. 2019. Holocene coastal environmental change and ENSO-driven hydroclimatic variability in East Asia. *Quaternary Science Reviews* 220: 75–96.

Lin, H. L., and R. Scaglion. 2019. Austronesian Speakers and Hereditary Leadership in the Pacific. *Anthropological Forum* 29(3): 267–283.

Linne, von C. [1735] 2015. *Systema Naturae*. Warsaw: Andesite Press.

Liu, F. and Z. Feng. 2012. A Dramatic climatic transition at 4000 Cal yr BP and its cultural responses in Chinese cultural domain. *The Holocene* 22(10): 1181–1197

Liu, W., Martinón-Torres, M., Cai, Y. et al. 2015. The earliest unequivocally modern humans in southern China. *Nature* 526: 696–699.

Loiseau, C., F. Menardo, A. Aseffa, E. Hailu, B. Gumi, G. Ameni, S. Berg, L. Rigouts, S. Robbe—Austerman, J. Zinsstag, S. Gagneux, & D. Brites. 2020. An African origin for *Mycobacterium bovis*. *Evolution, Medicine and Public Health* 2020: 49–59.

Lombard, M., M. Jakobson and C. Schlebusch. 2018. Ancient Human DNA: How sequencing the genome of a boy from Ballito Bay changed Human History. *South Africa Journal of Science* 114(1–2) art#a0253

Lubec, G., J. Holaubek, C. Feld, B. Lubek, E. Strouhal. 1993. Use of Silk in Ancient Egypt. *Nature* 362 (6415): 25.

Lobell, J. A. 2012. New Life for the Lion Man. *Archaeology* 65(2). https://archive .archaeology.org/1203/.

Loewe, M. and E. L. Shaughnessy. 1999. *The Cambridge History of Ancient China: From the Origins of Civilization to 221 BC*. Cambridge: Cambridge University Press.

Lombard, M., M. Jakobson and C. Schlebusch. 2018. Ancient Human DNA: How sequencing the genome of a boy from Ballito Bay changed Human History. *South Africa Journal of Science* 114(1–2): art#a0253.

Lopez, S., L. van Dorp and G. Hellenthal. 2016. Human dispersal out of Africa: A long lasting debate. *Evolutionary Bioinformatics* 11: 57–68.

Lorente-Galdos, B., Lao, O., Serra-Vidal, G. et al. 2019. Whole-genome sequence analysis of a Pan African set of samples reveals archaic gene flow from an extinct basal population of modern humans into sub-Saharan populations. *Genome Biology* 20(77) https://doi.org/10.1186/s13059-019-1684-5.

Lovejoy, C. O., Suwa, G., Simpson, S. W., Matternes, J. H., White, T. D. 2009. The great divides: *Ardipithecus ramidus* reveals the postcrania of our last common ancestor with African apes. *Science* 326: 100–106.

Lucassen, J., and Lucassen, L. 2009. The mobility transition revisited, 1500–1900: What the Case of Europe can offer to global history. *Journal of Global History* 4(3): 347–377. Doi: 10.1017/S174002280999012X.

Lupo, K. D., C. A. Kiahtipes, D. N. Schmidt, J. P. Ndanga, D. C. Young, & B. Simiti. 2018. An Elusive record exposed: Radiocarbon chronology of Late Holocene Human settlement in the Northern Congo basin, Central African Republic. *Azania: archaeological Research in Africa* 53(2): 209–227.

Lyell, C. [1830] 1998. *Principles of Geology*. London: Penguin Classics.

MacDonald, K. C. 1998. Before the empire of Ghana: pastoralism and the origins of cultural complexity in the Sahel. In *Transformations in Africa*, edited by G. Connah: pp. 71–103. London: Leicester University Press.

MacEachern, S. 1993. Selling the iron for their shackles: Wandala-Montagnards interaction in Northern Cameroon. *Journal of African History* 34: 247–270.

———. 1996. Iron Age beginnings north of the Mandara Mountains, Cameroon Nigeria. In G. Pwiti and R. Soper eds. *Aspects of African Archaeology*. Pp. 489–496. Harare: University of Zimbabwe Press.

———. 2012a. Prehistory and Early History of the Mandara Mountains and surrounding Plains. In N. David editor *Metals in Mandara Mountains Society and Culture*. Pp. 27–66. Trenton: Africa World Press.

MacEachern, S. 2012b. Wandala and DGB sites: Political centralisation and its alternative north of the Mandara Mountains, Cameroon. *Azania: Archaeological Research in Africa* 47(3): 271–287.

Maggs, T. 1994. The early Iron Age in the extreme south: Some patterns and problems. *Azania* 29, 30: 171–178.

Maley, J. 1981. *Etudes Palynologiques dans le Bassin du Tchad et Paléoclimatologie dans l'Afrique Nord-Tropicale de 30 000 ans à l'Epoque Actuelle*. Paris: Editions de l'ORSTOM.

———. 2001. La destruction catastrophique des forêts d'Afrique c. il y a 2500 ans exerce encore une influence majeure sur la répartition actuelle des formations végétales. *Systematics and Geography of Plants* 71: 777–796.

———. 2012. The fragmentation of the African rain forests during the third millennium BP: palaeoenvironmental data and palaeoclimatic framework. Comparison with another previous event during the LGM. Poster au Colloque *"Impact d'une crise environnementale majeure sur les espèces, les populations et les communautés: la fragmentation de la forêt africaine à la fin de l'Holocène."* Paris, 1–2 Mars.

Maley, J. & Brenac, P. 1998. Vegetation dynamics in the Forests of West Cameroon during the last 28,000 years BP. *Rev. Palaeobotany & Palynology* 99: 157–187.

Maley, J., P. Giresse, C. Doumenge, et C. Favier. 2012. "Central Africa" Comment on Intensifying Weathering and Land Use in Iron Age. *Science* 337: 1040.

Mandelbrot, B. B. 1982. *The Fractal Geometry of Nature.* San Francisco. W. H. Freeman and Company.

Martínez Sánchez, R. M., Vera Rodríguez, J.C ., Peña-Chocarro, L. et al. 2018a. The Middle Neolithic of Morocco's North-Western Atlantic Strip: New Evidence from the El-Khil Caves (Tangier). *African Archaeological Review* 35: 417–442. https:// doi.org/10.1007/s10437-018-9310-6.

Martínez-Sánchez, R. M., Vera-Rodríguez, J. C., G. Pérez-Jordà, L. Peña-Chocarro, Y. Bokbot. 2018b. The beginning of the Neolithic in northwestern Morocco. *Quaternary International* 470: 485–496.

Martinon-Torres, M. et al. 2021. Earliest known human burial in Africa. *Nature* 593: 95–100.

Matisoo-Smith, E. A. 2015. Tracking Austronesian expansion into the Pacific via the paper Mulberry plant. *Proceedings of the National Academy of Science* 112(44): 13432-3.

Matute, D. R. 2013. The role of founder effects on the evolution of reproductive isolation. *Journal of Evolutionary Biology* 26: 2299–2311.

Mc Burney, C. B. M. 1967. *The Haua Fteah (Cyrenaica) and the Stone Age of the south-east Mediterranean.* Cambridge: Cambridge University Press.

McColl, H. et al. 2018. The Prehistoric Peopling of Southeast Asia. *Science* 361: 88–92.

McDaniel C. J., D. M. Cardwell, R.B. Moeller, and G. C. Gray. 2014. Humans and Cattle: A Review of Bovine Zoonoses. *Vector-Borne and Zoonotic Diseases* 14(1): 1–19.

McIntosh, S. K. & R. J. McIntosh. 1980. *Prehistoric Investigations in the Region of Jenne, Mali.* Oxford: British Archaeological Reports.

McIntosh, S. K. editor. 1994. *Excavations at Jenne-jeno, Hambarketolo, and Kaniana (Inland Niger Delta Mali), the 1981 Season.* Berkeley: University of California Press.

McIntosh, R. J. 1998. *The peoples of the Middle Niger.* Oxford: Blackwell.

McGrew, W. C. 1992. *Chimpanzee Material Culture: Implications for Human Evolution.* Cambridge: Cambridge University Press.

Meinhof, C. F. M. 1906. *Grundzüge einer Vergleichenden Grammatik des Bantusprachen.* Berlin: Reimer.

Mohammadou, E. 1982. *Le Royaume du Wandala ou Mandara au 19ᵉ siecle.* Tokyo: Institute for the study of languages and culture of Asia and Africa.

Momigliano, P., H. Jokinen, A. Fraimont, A. B. Florin, A. Norkko and J. Merila. 2017. Extraordinarily rapid speciation in a marine fish. *Proceedings of the National Academy of Science* 114(23) 67074-79.

Montano, V. G. Ferri, V. Mercari, C. Batini, O. Anyaele, G. Destro-bisol, & D. Cosmas. 2011. The Bantu expansion revisited: A new analysis of Y chromosome variation in Central Western Africa. *Molecular Ecology* 20: 2693 – 08.

Mori, F. 1965. *Tadrart Acacus.* Torino: Einaudi.

Morin-Rivat, J., A. Biwole, A. P. Gorel, J. Vleminckx, J. F. Gillet, N. Bourland, O. J. Hardy, A. Livingstone-Smith, K. Dainou, L. Dedry, H. Beckman & J. L. Doucet. 2016. High spatial resolution of Late Holocene human activities in the moist forest of Central Africa using soil charcoal and charred botanical remains. *The Holocene* 1–14.

Morin-Rivat, J., A. Fayolle, C. Favier, L. Bremond, S. Gourlet-Fleury, N. Bayol, P. Lejeune, H. Beechman. 2016. Present-day central Africa forest is legacy of the 19th century human history. *elife* 6: e20347: 1–18.

Mounier, A., C. Nous and A. Balzeau. 2020. Paleoneurology and the emergence of language. *BMSAP* 32: 147–157.

Muller, B., M. Hilty, S. Berg, M. Carmen Garcia-Pelayo, et al. 2009. African 1, an Epidemiologically Important Clonal Complex of *Mycobacterium bovis* dominant in Mali, Nigeria, Cameroon, and Chad. *Journal of Bacteriology* 191(6): 1951–1960. doi: 10.1128/JB.01590–08

Muller, G. B. 2017. Why and extended evolutionary synthesis is necessary. *Interface Focus* 7: 15.

Mulligan, C. J., and E. J. F. Szathmary. 2017. The Peopling of the Americas and the Origins of the Beringian Occupation Model. *American Journal of Physical Anthropology* 162(3): 403–408.

Munoz-Moreno, M. de L. and M. H. Crawford editors. 2021. *Human Migration.* Oxford: Oxford University Press.

Murray, J. K., R. A. Benitez and M. J. O'Brien. 2020. The Extended evolutionary synthesis and Human origins: Archaeological Perspectives. *Evolutionary Anthropology* 1–4.

Muzzolini, A. 1995. *Les Images Rupestres du Sahara.* Toulouse.

Mwai, O., O. Hannotte, Y. J. Kwon & S. Cho. 2015. African indigenous cattle: Unique genetic resource in a rapidly changing world. *Asian Australasian Journal of Animal Science* 28(7): 911–921.

Nachtigal, G. 1987. *Sahara and Sudan (Vol III): The Chad basin and Bagirmi.* Translated and annotated by A. G. B. Fisher and H. J. Fisher. London: C. Hurst.

Ndukum, J. A., A. C. Kudi, G. Bradley, I. N. Anyangwe, S. Fon-Tebug & J. Tchomboue. 2010. Prevalence of Bovine tuberculosis in abattoirs of the littoral and western Highlands regions of Cameroons: A cause for public health concern. *Veterinary Research International* article ID 495015 (8 pages).

Neige, P. 2015. The Phenomenon of Evolutionary Radiation. In *Events of Increased Biodiversity.* Edited by P. Neige. Pp. 47–64. New York: Elsevier.

Neumann, K. 1995. Archaeobotany and Late Holocene vegetation history in Burkina Faso and Nigeria. *Abstracts: 10th Congress of the Pan-African Association for Prehistory and Related Studies.* Harare: p. 29.

Neumann, K. et al. 2012. Comment on "Intensifying Weathering and Land Use in Iron Age Central Africa." *Science* 337, 1040.

O'Brien, M. J. 1996 editor. 1996. *Evolutionary Archaeology.* Salt Lake City: Utah University Press.

O'Brien, M. J., and R. L. Lyman. 2000. *Applying Evolutionary Archaeology: A Systematic Approach.* New York: Kluwer Academic/Plenum.

O'Brien, P. K., editor. 1999. *Oxford Atlas of World History.* Oxford: Oxford University Press.

O'Connor, S. 2015. Rethinking the Neolithic in Island Southeast Asia, with particular reference to the Archaeology of Timor-Leste and Sulawesi. *Archipel: Etudes Interdisciplinaires sur le Monde Insulindien* 90: 15–47.

Orlova, M, and E. Schurr. 2017. Human genomics of Mycobacterium tuberculosis infection and disease. *Current Genetic and Medical Report* 5(3): 125–131.

Oujaa, A., Arnaud, J., Bardey-Vaillant, M. et al. 2017. The Fossil Human from Rabat-Kébibat (Morocco): Comparative Study of the Cranial and Mandibular Fragments. *African Archaeological Review* 34: 511–523.

Padilla-Iglesias C, Gjesfjeld E, Vinicius L. 2020. Geographical and social isolation drive the evolution of Austronesian languages. *PLoS ONE* 15(12): e0243171.

Pakendorf, B., K. Bostoen & C. de Fillippo. 2011. Molecular perspectives on the Bantu expansion: A synthesis. *Language Dynamics and Change* 1: 50–88.

Pantuliano, S. and S. Pavanello. 2009 Taking drought into account: Addressing chronic vulnerability among pastoralists in the Horn of Africa. *HPG Policy Brief 35*. London: Overseas Development Institute.

Paris, F. 1984. *La region d'In Gall-Teggida-n-Tesemt (Niger) III: Les sepultures du Neolithique final a l'Islam*. Niamey: Etudes Nigeriennes 50.

———. 1992. Chin Tafidet, Village Neolithique. *Journal des Africanistes* 62: 35–53.

Park, J., J. Park, S. Yi, J. C. Kim, E. Lee and J. Choi. 2019. Abrupt Holocene climate shifts in coastal East Asia, including the 8.2ka, 4.2 ka and 2.8 ka BP events and societal response of the Korean peninsula. *Scientific Reports. Nature Communications* 9: 10806.

Parsons, K. J. 2016. Adaptive Radiations: Insights From Evo-Devo. In *Encyclopedia of Evolutionary Biology*. Edited by Richard M. Kliman, pp. 37–45. New York: Academic Press.

Pelejero, C., M. Kienast, L. Wang, J. O. Grimaldi. 1999. The Flooding of Sundaland during The last deglaciation: Imprints in hemipelagic sediments from Southern China Sea. *Earth and Planetary Science Letters* 17(4): 661–671.

Peñailillo, J., G. Olivares, X. Moncada, C. Payacán, C.-S. Chang, K.-F. Chung, P. J. Matthews, et al. 2016. Sex distribution of paper mulberry (*Broussonetia papyrifera*) in the Pacific. *PLoS ONE* 11: e0161148. *People's Daily*, April 2, 1993. *People's Daily Online*, August 26, 2007.

Peregrine, P. N. 1996. Archaeology and World-Systems theory. *Sociological Inquiry* 66(4): 486–495.

Pérez-Pardal, L., A. Sánchez-Gracia, I. Álvarez, A. Traoré, J. B. S. Ferraz, I. Fernández, V. Costa, S. Chen, M. Tapio, R. J. C. Cantet, A. Patel, R. H. Meadow, F. B. Marshall, A. Beja-Pereira, and F. Goyache. 2018. Legacies of domestication, trade and herder mobility shape extant male zebu cattle diversity in South Asia and Africa. *Scientific Reports* 8: 18027. Doi: 10.1038/s41598-018-36444-7.

Perreault, C., and S. Mathew. 2012. Dating the origin of language using phonemic diversity. *PLoS One* 7(4): e35289. doi: 10.1371/journal.pone.0035289.

Perrier, X. et al. 2011. Multidisciplinary Perspectives on Bananas (*Musa* spp) Domestication. *Proceedings of National Academy of Sciences*. www.pnas.org/cgi/doi/10.1073/pnas.1102001108.

Peter, B. M., and M. Slatkin. 2015 The effective founder effect in a spatially expand-ing population. *Evolution* 69(3): 721–734.

Phelps, L. N., O. Broennimann, K. Manning, A. Timpson, H. Jousse, G. Mariethoz, D. A. Fordham, T. M. Shanahan, B. A. S. Davis, and A. Guisan. 2019. Reconstruction the climate niche breadth of land use for animal production during the African Holocene. *Global Ecology and Biogeography*: 1–21.

Phillipson, D. W. 1993. The antiquity of cultivation and herding in Ethiopia. In *The archaeology of Africa: Food, metals and towns*, edited by T. Shaw, P. Sinclair, B. Andah, and A. Okpoko, pp. 344–357. London/New York: Routledge.

———. 2010. *African Archaeology*. Cambridge: Cambridge University Press.

Pickford, M. and Senut, B. 2001. 'Millennium ancestor,' a 6–million-year-old bipedal hominid from Kenya. *South African Journal of Science* 97(1–2): 22.

Picq, P. 2010. *Il etait une fois la Paleoanthropologie*. Paris: Odile Jacob.

Pierron, D. et al. 2017. Genomic landscape of Human diversity across Madagascar. *Proceedings of the National Academy of Science* Early edition 1–9. www.pnas.org /cgi/doi /10.1073/pnas.1704906114

Pigliucci, M. 2007. Do we need an extended evolutionary synthesis? *Evolution* 61(12): 2743–2749.

Pigliucci, M., and G. B. Muller. 2010. Elements of an Extended Evolutionary Synthesis. In *Evolution—The Extended Synthesis*. Edited by M. Pigliucci and G. B. Muller. Pp. 3–17. Boston: MIT Press.

Pipek, O. A., A. Medgyes-Horváth, L. Dobos, J. Stéger, J. Szalai-Gindl, D. Visontai, R. S. Kaas, M. Koopmans, R. S. Hendriksen, F. M. Aarestrup, and I. Csabai 2019. Worldwide human mitochondrial haplogroup distribution from urban sewage. *Nature: Scientific Reports* 9: 11624.

Pikirayi, I. 2001. *The Zimbabwe Culture: Origins and decline of Southern Zambezian States*. Walnut Creek: AltaMira Press.

———. 2017. Globalization and the Archaic State in Southern Africa. *Journal of Southern Africa Studies* 43: 879–893.

Plaza, S., Salas, A., Calafell, F., Corte-Real, F., Bertranpetit, J., Carracedo, A., Comas, D. 2004. Insights into the western Bantu dispersal: mtDNA lineage analysis in Angola. *Human Genetics* 115(5): 439–47.

Plug, I. 1997. Early Iron Age Buffalo hunters on the Kadzi River, Zimbabwe. *African Archaeological Review* 14: 85–105.

Plug, I., and E. A. Voigt. 1985. Archaeozoological studies of Iron Age Communities in Southern Africa. In *Advances in World Archaeology*, edited by F. Wendorf and A. E. Close, Vol. 4, pp. 189–238. New York: Academic Press.

Polanyi, K., C. M. Arensburg and H. W. Pearson editors. 1957. *Trade and Market in Early Empires: Economies in History and Theory.* Glencoe: Free Press and Falcon Wing Press.

Popovic, A. 1999. *The Revolt of African Slaves in Iraq in the 3rd / 9th Century*. Princeton: Markus Wiener.

Popper, K. 2002. *Conjectures and Refutations: The Growth of Scientific Knowledge*. London: Routledge.

Prendergast, M. E., Buckley, M., Crowther, A., Frantz, L., Eager, H., Lebrasseur, O., et al. 2017. Reconstructing Asian faunal introductions to eastern Africa from multi-proxy biomolecular and archaeological datasets. *PLoS ONE* 12(8): e0182565.

Prendergast, M. E., M. Lipson, E. A. Sawchuk et al. 2019. Ancient DNA reveals a multistep spread of the first herders into sub-Saharan Africa. *Science* 365 (6448) Doi: 10.1126/Science.aaw6275

Prentiss, A. M. editor. 2009. *Macroevolution in Human Prehistory*. New York: Springer.

———. 2019. *Handbook of Evolutionary Research in Archaeology*. New York: Springer.

Preston, S. D., and F. B. M. de Waal. 2002. Empathy: Its ultimate and proximate bases. *Behavioral and Brain Sciences* 25: 1–72.

Price, M. 2016. Study reveals culprit behind Piltdown Man, one of the Science's most famous hoaxes. https://www.sciencemag.org/news/2016/08

Prigogine, I. 1977. Time, Structure, and Fluctuations. Lecture. Universite Libre de Bruxelles.

Prigogine, I., and I. Stengers. 1984. *Order out of chaos: Man's new dialogue with nature*. New York: Bantam New Age Books.

Pringle, H. 2009. Seeking Africa's First Iron Men. *Science* 323: 200–202.

Prinsloo, L. C., N. Wood, M. Loubser, S. M. C. Verryn, and S. Tiley. 2005. Re-dating of celadon shards excavated on Mapungubwe Hill, a 13th century Iron Age site in South Africa, using Raman spectroscopy, XRF and XRD *Journal of Raman Spectroscopy* 36(8): 806–816.

Pulselli, R. M., G. C. Magnoli, N. Marchettini, and E. Tiezzi. 2004. Dissipative structures, Complexity and Strange attractors. In *Design and Nature II*. M. W. Collins and C. A. Brebbia editors. Pp. 381–387. Johannesburg: WIT Press.

Pwiti, G. 1994. Early farming communities of the middle Zambezi valley. *Azania* 29, 30: 202–208.

———. 1996. Continuity and change. *Studies in African Archaeology* 13. Uppsala University.

Quintana-Murci, L. et al. 2008. Maternal traces of deep common ancestry ans asymmetric gene flow between pygmy hunter-gatherers and Bantu speaking farmers. *Proceedings of the National Academy of Science* 105(5): 1596–1601.

Ranciaro, A., M. C. Campbell, J. B. Hirbo, W. Y. Ko, A. Froment, P. Anagnostou, M. J. Kotze, M. Ibrahim, T. Nyambo, S. A. Omar, & S. A. Tishkoff. 2014. Genetic origins of lactase persistence and the spread of Pastoralism in Africa. *The American Journal of Human Genetics* 34: 496–510.

Rapp, J. 1984. *Quelques Aspects des Civilisations Néolithiques et Post-néolithiques à l'Extrême Nord du Cameroun: étude des décors céramiques et essai de chronologie* PhD thesis. University of Bordeaux I.

Rasolofo-Razanamparany, V., D. Ménard, T. Rasolonavalona, H. Ramarokoto, F. Rakotomanana, G. Aurégan, V. Vincent, S. Chanteau. 1999. Prevalence of Mycobacterium bovis in human pulmonary and extra-pulmonary tuberculosis in Madagascar. *International Journal of Tuberculosis and Lung Disease* 3(7): 632–634.

Regueiro, M., S. Mirabal, H. Lacau, J. L. Caeiro, R. L. Garcia-Bertrand, R. J. Herrera. 2008. Austronesian genetic signature in East African Madagascar and Polynesia. *Journal of Human Genetics* 53: 106–120.

Reid, A. 1997. Lacustrine States. In *Encyclopedia of Precolonial Africa*. Edited by J. O. Vogel. Pp: 501–507. Walnut Creek: AltaMira Press.

Renfrew, C. A. 1975. Trade as Action at a Distance: Questions of integration and communication. In *Ancient Civilizations and Trade*. Edited by Sabloff, J. A. and C.C. Lamberg-Karlovsky. Pp. 3–59. School of American Research Book. Albuquerque: University of New Mexico Press.

Reyna, S. P. 1990. *Wars without End: The Political Economy of a Precolonial African State.* Hanover: University Press of New England.

Richards, C. L., and M. Pigliucci. 2021. Epigenetic inheritance: A decade into the Extended evolutionary synthesis. *Paradigmi* 38(3): 463–494.

Rightmire, G. P. 1998. Human evolution in the Middle Pleistocene: The role of *Homo heidelbergensis*. *Evolutionary Anthropology* 6: 218–227.

Roberts, C. A. 2015. Old World tuberculosis: Evidence from Human remains with a view of current research and future prospects. *Tuberculosis* 95(1): 117–121.

Robertshaw, P. 1993. The beginning of food production in southwestern Kenya. In *The archaeology of Africa: Food, metals and towns*, edited by T. Shaw, P. Sinclair, B. Andah, and A. Okpoko, pp. 358–371. London/New York: Routledge.

———. 1999. Seeking and Keeping Power in Bunyoro-Kitara, Uganda. In *Beyond Chiefdoms: Pathways to Complexity in Africa*. Edited by S. K. McIntosh. Pp: 124–135. Cambridge: Cambridge University Press.

———. 2003. Explaining the Origins of the State in East Africa. In *East African Archaeology: Foragers, Potters, Smiths, and Traders*. Edited by C. M. Kusimba and S. B. Kusimba. Pp. 145–166. Philadelphia: The University of Pennsylvania Museum of Archaeology and Anthropology.

———. 2021. Archaeology of Early Pastoralism in East Africa. Oxford Research Encyclopedia: African History. https://doi.org/10.1093/acrefore/97801902777734 .013.1045

Roebroeks, W., M. J. Sier, T. K. Nielsen, D. de Loecker, J. Maria Pares, C. E. S. Arps, and H. J. Mucher. 2012. Use of red Ochre by Early Neandertals. *Proceedings of the National Academy of Science* 109(6): 1889–94.

Rolett, B. V., Z. Guo and T. Jiao. 2007. Geological sourcing of volcanic stone adzes from Neolithic sites in southeast China. *Asian Perspectives* 46(2): 275–297.

Rosenberg, K. 2002. A Late Pleistocene Human skeleton from Liujiang, China suggests regional population variation in sexual dimorphism in the human pelvis. *Variability and Evolution* 10: 5–17.

Rotstein, A. 1970. Karl Polanyi's Concept of Non-Market Trade. *The Journal of Economic History* 30(1): 117–126.

Roubet, C. 1979. *Economie pastorale preagricole en Algerie Orientale: le Neolithique de Tradition Capsienne*. Paris: Editions du CNRS.

Sabloff, J. A., and C. C. Lamberg-Karlovsky eds. 1975. *Ancient Civilizations and Trade*. School of American Research Book. Albuquerque: University of New Mexico Press.

Sahlins, M. D. 1972. *Stone age economics: The first affluent societies.* New York: Routledge.

Sahnouni, M., J. P. Pares, M. Duval, I. Caceres, Z. Harichane, J. V. D Made, A A. Perz-Gonzales, S. Abdessadok, N. Kandi, A. Derradji, M. Medig, K. Boullagharif, S. Semaw. 2018. 1.9–million- and 2.4—million-year-old artifacts and stone tool-cutmarked bones from Ain Boucherit, Algeria. *Science* 362: 1297–1301

Salazar-García D.C., García-Puchol O. 2017. Current Thoughts on the Neolithisation Process of the Western Mediterranean. In: García-Puchol O., Salazar-García D. (eds) *Times of Neolithic Transition along the Western Mediterranean.* Fundamental Issues in Archaeology. Springer, Cham. https://doi.org/10.1007/978–3–319–52939 –4_1

Salman, M. D., & Steneroden, K. 2015. Important public health zoonoses through cattle. In A. Sing (Ed.), *Zoonoses: Infections affecting humans and animals* pp. 3–23. Dordrecht: Springer Science.

Samkange, A., B. Mushonga, D. Mudimba, B. A. Chiwone, M. Jago, E. Kandiwa, A. S. Bishi, & U. Molini. 2019. African Swine fever outbreak at a farm in Central Namibia. *Case Reports in Veterinarian Medicine* Volume 2019 Article ID 3619593 (6 pages).

Sauer, C. O. 1952. *Agricultural Origins and Their Dispersals.* New York: American Geographical Society.

Scardia, G., Parenti, F., Miggins, D., Gerdes, A., Araujo, A. & Neves, W. 2019. Chronologic constraints on hominin dispersal outside Africa since 2.48 Ma from the Zarqa Valley, Jordan. *Quaternary Science Review* 219: 1–19.

Scardia, G., W. A. Neves, I. Tattersall and L. Blumrich 2020. What kind of hominid left Africa first? *Evolutionary Anthropology* 2020: 1–6.

Scerri, E. M. L., N. A. Drake, R. Jennings, H. S. Groucutt. 2014. Earliest evidence for the structure of Homo sapiens populations in Africa. *Quaternary Science Reviews* 101: 206–207.

Schlebusch, C. M., and M. Jakobson. 2018. Tales of Human migrations, Admixture and selection in Africa. *Anuual Review of Genomics and Human Genetics* 19: 405–428.

Schlebusch, C. M. et al. 2017. Southern African ancient genomes estimates modern human divergence to 350,000 to 260,000 years ago. *Science* 358: 652–655.

Schmidt, P. R. 2006. *Historical Archaeology in Africa: Representation, Social Memory and Oral Traditions.* Walnut Creek: AltaMira Press

Schwartz, G. M. 2017. The archaeological study of sacrifice. *Annual Review of Anthropology* 46: 223–240.

Seidensticker, D., W. Hubau, D. Verschuren, C. Fortes-Lima, P. de Maret, C. M. Schlebusch and K. Bostoen. 2021. Population collapse in Congo from 400 CE urges reassessment of the Bantu Expansion. *Science Advances* 7: eabd8352, 1–13.

Sekand, E. H. 2013. Networks and Social Cohesion in ancient Indian Ocean trade: Geography, Ethnicity and Religion. *Journal of Global History* 8: 373–390.

Sengupta, D. et al. 2020. Genetic structure and complex demographis history of South African Bantu speakers. *BioR$_x$iv*, doi: https://doi.org/10.1101/2020.08.11.243840

Senut, B., and M. Pickford. 2001. The geological and faunal context of Late Miocene hominid remains from Lukeino, Kenya. *Comptes Rendus de l'Academie des Sciences, Series IIA - Earth and Planetary Science* 332 (2): 145–152.

Senut, B., M. Pickford, D. Gommery, P. Mein, K. Cheboi, Y. Coppens. 2001. First hominid from the Miocene (Lukeino Formation, Kenya). *Comptes Rendus de l'Academie des Sciences, Series IIA - Earth and Planetary Science* 332 (2): 137–144.

Servant, M. and Servant-Vildary, S. 1980. L'environnement quaternaire du bassin du Tehad. In *The Sahara and the Nile*. Edited by M.A.J. Williams and H. Faure. A.A. Balkema, pp. 133–162. Rotterdam.

Shennan, S. 2018. The First Westward expansion of Farming. In *The First Farmers of Europe: An Evolutionary Perspective*. Pp. 55–78. Cambridge: Cambridge University Press.

Sherratt, A. 1981. Plough and pastoralism: aspects of the secondary products revolution. In *Pattern of the Past: Studies in honour of David Clarke*. Edited by I Hodder, G Isaac and N. Hammond. Pp. 261–305. Cambridge: Cambridge University Press.

Sichewo, P. R., C. V. Kelen, S. Thys, A. L. Michel. 2020. Risk practices for bovine tuberculosis transmission to cattle and livestock farming communities living at Wildlife-Livestock-human interface in Northern KwaZulu Natal, South Africa. *PLOS One Neglected Tropical Diseases.* March 30, 1–18.

Sinclair, P. J. J., I. Pikirayi, G. Pwiti, and R. Soper. 1993. Urban Trajectories on the Zimbabwe Plateau. In *The Archaeology of Africa: Food, Metals and Towns*. Edited by T. Shaw, P. Sinclair, B. Andah, and A. Okpoko. Pp. 705–731. New York/London: Routledge.

Sinclair, P., J. M. F. Morais, L. Adamowicz, and R. T. Duarte 1993. A perspective on archaeological research in Mozambique. In *The archaeology of Africa: Food, metals and towns*, edited by T. Shaw, P. Sinclair, B. Andah, and A. Okpoko, pp. 409– 431. New York/London: Routledge.

Shriner, D. and C. N. Rotimi. 2018. Genetic History of Chad. *American Journal of Physical Anthropology* 167: (4): 804–812. doi: 10.1002/ajpa.23711

Skoglund, P., C. Posth, K. Sirak, M. Spriggs, F. Valentin, S. Bedford, G. Clark, et al. 2016. Genomic Insights into the Peopling of the Southwest Pacific." *Nature* 538 (7626): 510–513.

Skoglund, P., et al. 2017. Reconstructing Prehistoric African Population Structure. *Cell* 171: 59–71.

Smith, A. B. 1992. Pastoralism in Africa: Origins and development ecology. London: Hurst.

———. 1997. Southern African pastoralists. In *Encyclopedia of precolonial Africa*, edited by J. O. Vogel, pp. 210–213. Walnut Creek: AltaMira Press.

———. 1998. Keeping People on the Periphery: The Ideology of Social Hierarchies between Hunters and Herders. *Journal of Anthropological Archaeology* 17(2): 201–215.

Smith, F. H., Falsetti, A. B., Donnelly, S. 1989. Modern human origins. *Yearbook of Physical Anthropology* 32: 35–68.

Smith, T., M. P. Tafforeau, D. J. Reid, R. Grun, S. Eggins, M. Boutakiout, and J.-J. Hublin. 2007. Earliest evidence of modern human life history in North African early *Homo sapiens*. *Proceedings of the National Academy of Science* 104 (15): 6128–6133 www.pnas.org cgi doi: 10.1073 pnas.0700747104.

Smith, C. M., L. Gabora and W. Gardner-O'Keraney. 2018. The Extended Evolutionary Synthesis paved the way for a theory of Cultural Evolution. *Cliodynamics* 9(2): 84–107.

Soares, P. A., et al. 2016. Resolving the ancestry of Austronesian-speaking populations. *Human Genetics* 135: 309–326.

Speidel, L., L. Cassidy, R. W. Davies, G. Hellenthal, P. Skoglund, and S. R. Myers. 2021. Inferring Population Histories for Ancient genomes using genome-wide genealogies. *bioRxiv 1–56.* doi: https://doi.org/10.1101/2021.02.17.431573

Spriggs, M., and D. Reich. 2020. An ancient DNA Pacific journey: A case study of collaboration between archaeologists and geneticists, *World Archaeology*, DOI:10.1080/00438243.2019.1733069

Stahl, A. B. 1985. Reinvestigation of Kintampo 6 rock shelter, Ghana: Implications for the nature of culture change. *The African Archaeological Review* 3: 117–150.

———. 1993. Intensification in the west African Late Stone Age: A view from central Ghana. In *The archaeology of Africa: Food, metals and towns*, edited by T. Shaw, P. Sinclair, B. Andah, and A. Okpoko, pp. 261–273. London/New York: Routledge.

Stiner, M. C. 2001. Thirty years on the "Broad Spectrum Revolution" and Paleolithic Demography. *Proceedings of the National Academy of Science* 98(13): 6993–6996

Stock, F., and D. Gifford-Gonzales. 2013. Genetics and African Cattle domestication. *African Archaeological Review* 30: 51–72.

Stringer, C., and P. Andrews. 2005. *The Complete World of Human Evolution*. London: Thames and Hudson

Stringer, C., and J. Galway-Whitman. 2018. When did Modern Humans leave Africa? *Science* 359: 389–390.

Subrahmanyam, S. 2001. Written on Water: designs and Dynamics in the Portuguese *Estado da India*. In *Empires: Perspectives from Archaeology and History*. Edited by Alcock, S. E., T. N. D'Altroy, K. D. Morrison, and C. M. Sinopoli. Pp. 42– 69. Cambridge: Cambridge University Press.

Sun, J., L. Ying-Xiang, M. Peng-Cheng, Y. Shi, C. Hui-Zhen, F. Zhi-Quan, D. Xiao-Hua, R. Kai, W. Chuan-Chao, C. Gang, W. Lan-Hai. 2021. Shared paternal ancestry of Han, Tai-Kadai-speaking, and Austronesian-speaking populations as revealed by the high-resolution phylogeny of O1a-M119 and distribution of its sub-lineages within China. *American Journal of Physical Anthropology* 1–15. DOI: 10.1002/ajpa.24240

Sutton, J. E. G., 1979. Towards a less orthodox history of Hausaland. *Journal of African History* 20: 179–201.

———. 2010. Hausa as a process in time and space. In *Being and becoming Hausa: Interdisciplinary Perspectives*. Edited by A. Haour and B. Rossi, 279–299. Leiden: Brill.

Szalay, J. 2916. Piltdown Man: Infamous Fake Fossil. https://www.livescience.com /56327–piltdown-man-hoax.html

Szczepanski, K. 2019. "Indian Ocean Trade Routes." thoughtco.com/indian-ocean-trade-routes195514.

Talib, Y., and F. Samir. 1988. The African Diaspora in Asia. In M. El Fasi and I. Hrbek, editors, *General History of Africa III: Africa from the Seventh to the Eleventh Century*. Pp. 704–733. Oxford/Berkeley/Paris: Heinemann, California University Press, and UNESCO.

Telster, P. A., editor 1994. *Evolutionary Archaeology: Methodological Issues*. Tucson: University of Arizona Press.

Thomas, M. G., Stumpf, M. P. H. and Harke, H. 2006. Evidence for an Apartheid-like social structure in Early Anglo-Saxon England. *Proceedings Biological Sciences, the Royal Society* 273(1601): 2651–2657.

Ting, J. 2005. The Egalitarian architecture of the Iban longhouse. In *Celebration— Proceedings of the 22nd Annual Conference of the Society of Architectural Historians, Australia and New Zealand*. Edited by Leach, A. and G. Matthewson. Napier.

Tishkoff, S., Reed, F., Ranciaro, A. et al. 2007. Convergent adaptation of human lactase persistence in Africa and Europe. *Nature Genetics* 39: 31–40. https://doi.org/10.1038/ng1946

Tomley, F. M. and M. W. Shirley. 2009. Livestock infectious diseases and zoonoses. *Philosophical Transactions of the Royal Society- Biology* 364: 2637–2642.

Toth, N., and Schick, K. 2005. "African origins." In *The Human Past: World Prehistory and the Development of Human Societies*. Edited by C. Scarre, 46–83. London: Thames and Hudson.

———. 2009. The Oldowan: The Tool Making of Eearly Hominins and Chimpanzees. *Annual Review of Anthropology* 38: 289–305.

Trimingham, J. S. 1962. *A history of Islam in West Africa.* London: Oxford University Press.

Tsang, C. 1992. *Archaeology of the P'eng-hu Islands*. Taipei: Institute of History and Philology, Academia Sinica, Special Publication 95

Tsofact, J. B. 2006. (De)nominations et constructions identitaires au Cameroun. *Cahiers de Sociolinguistique* 11: 101–115.

Vansina, J. 1980. Bantu in the Crystal Ball II. *History in Africa* 7: 293–325

———. 1983. Review of *L'Expansion Bantoue* by Luc Bouquiaux. *The International Journal of African Historical Studies* 16(1): 127–131.

———. 1984. Western bantu expansion. *Journal of African History* 25: 129–145.

———. 1990. *Paths in the Rainforests: Toward a History of Political Tradition in Equatorial Africa*. Madison: University of Wisconsin Press.

———. 1995. New linguistic evidence and the Bantu Expansion. *Journal of African History* 36: 173–195.

Vermeersch, P. M., E. Paulissen, S. Stokes, C. Charlier, P. Van Peer, C. Stringer & W. Lindsay. 1998. A Middle paleolithic burial burial of a modern human at Taramsa Hill, Egypt. *Antiquity* 72: 475–84.

Vicente, M., and C. M. Schlebusch. 2020. African population history: An Ancient DNA perspective. *Current Opinion in Genetics and Development* 62: 8–15.

Vignaud, P. et al. 2002. Geology and paleontology of the Upper Miocene Toros-Menalla hominid locality, Chad. *Nature* 418: 152–155.

Villmoare, B., W. H. Kimbel, C. Seyoum, C. J. Campisano, E. N. DiMaggio, J. Rowan, D. R. Braun, J R. Arrowsmith, & K. E. Reed. 2015. Early *Homo* at 2.8 Ma from Ledi-Geraru, Afar, Ethiopia. *Science* 347(6228): 1352–1355.

Vincent, J. F. 1991. *Prince Montagnards du Nord-Cameroun: Les Mofu Diamare et le pouvoir Politique*. Paris: L'Harmattan.

Vincens, A., D. Schwartz, H. Elenga, I. Reynaud-Farrera, A. Alexandre, J. Bertaux, A. Mariotti, L. Martin, J. D. Meunier, F. Nguetsop, M. Servant, S. Servant-Vildary, and D. Wirrman. 1999. Forest response to climate chnage in Atlantic Africa during the last 4000 years BP and inheritance on the modern landscapes. *Journal of Biogeography* 26: 879–885.

Vincens, A., G. Buchet, M. servant, ECOFIT Mbalang collaborators 2010. Vegetation response to the "African Humid Period" termination in Central Cameroon (7°N): new pollen insight from Lake Mbalang. *Climate of the Past* 6: 2577–2606.

Vita-Finzi, C., and Higgs, E. S. 1970. Prehistoric Economy in the Mount Carmel Area of Palestine: Site Catchment Analysis. *Proceedings of the Prehistoric Society* 36: 1–37.

Viviano, F. 2005. "China's Great Armada." *National Geographic*, 208(1): 28–53, July.

Vleminckx, J., J. Morin-Rivat, A. B. Biwole, K. Dainou, J. F. Gillet, J. L. Doucet, T. Drouet, & O. J. Hardy. 2014. Soil charcoal to assess the impacts of past human disturbances on tropical forests. *PloS One* 9(11): e108121

Waldrop, M. M. 1992. *Complexity: The Emerging Science at the Edge of Order and Chaos*. New York: Touchstone Book.

Wallerstein, I. 1976. *The Modern World System: Capitalist agriculture and the Origins of the European World-Economy in the 16th century*. New York: Academic Press.

———. 2004. *World-Systems Analysis: An Introduction*. Durham: Duke University Press.

Walker, A. C., Leakey, R. E., Harris, J. M., & Brown, F. H. 1986. 2.5 Myr *Australopithecus bosei* from west of Lake Turkana, Kenya. *Nature* 322: 517–522.

Wang, C-C. et al. 2021. Genomic Insights into the Formation of Human Populations in East Asia. *Nature* https://doi. org/10.1038/s41586–021–03336–2.

Wang, K. et al. 2020. Ancient genomes reveal complex patterns of population movement, interaction and replacement in Sub-saharan Africa. *Science Advances* 6: 1–14.

Wendorf, F.. and R. Schild. 1998. Nabta Playa and its place in Northeastern African Prehistory. *Journal of Anthropological Archaeology* 17: 97–123.

Wendorf, F., R. Schild, and Associates 2001. *Holocene Settlement of the Egyptian Sahara: Volume I: The Archaeology of Nabta Playa*. New York: Springer.

Western, D., and V. Finch. 1986. Cattle and Pastoralism: Survival and Production in Arid Lands *Human Ecology* 14(1): 77–94.

Wetterstrom, W. 1993. Foraging and farming in Egypt: The transition from hunting and gathering to horticulture in the Nile valley. In The archaeology of Africa: Food, metals and towns, edited by T. Shaw, P. Sinclair, B. Andah, and A. Okpoko, pp. 165–226. London/New York: Routledge.

Witas, H. W., H. D. Donoghue, D. Kubiak, M. Lewandowska, J. J. Gladykowska-Rzeczcka. 2015. Molecular studies on ancient M. tuberculosis and M. leprae: Methods of pathogens and host DNA analysis. *European Journal of Clinical Microbiology and Infectious Diseases* 34: 1733–49.

White, T. D. 2003. Paleoanthropology: Early hominids- Diversity or Distorsion? *Science* 299: 1994.

White, T. D., Suwa, G., Asfaw, B. 1994. Australopithecus ramidus, a new species of early hominid from Aramis, Ethiopia. *Nature* 371: 306–312.

White, T. D., Asfaw, B., Beyene, Y., Haile-Selassie, Y. Lovejoy, C.O., Suwa, G., Woldegabriel, G. 2009. *Ardipithecus ramidus* and the paleobiology of early hominids. *Science* 326: 75–86.

Whiteley, P. M., X. Ming and W. C. Wheeler. 2018. Revising the Bantu tree. *Cladistics* (2018): 1–20.

Wolpoff, M. H. and R. Caspari. 1997. *Race and Human Evolution*. New York: Simon & Schuster.

Wolpoff, M. H., J. Hawks, B. Senut, M. Pickford and J. Ahern. 2006. An Ape or *the* Ape: is the Toumai TM 266 cranium a hominid? *PaleoAnthropology* 2006: 36–50.

Wood, B., and M. Collard. 1999. The changing face of genus Homo. *Evolutionary Anthropology* 8: 195–207.

Wotzka, H. P. 2006. Record of activity: Radiocarbon and the structure of Iron Age settlement in Central Africa. In *Grundlegungen: Beitrage zur europaischen und afrikanischen Archaologie fur Manfred K. Eggert*. Edited by H. P. Wotzka. Pp. 271–289. Tubingen: Franke.

Wright, H. T. 1998. Uruk States in Southwestern Iran. In *Archaic States*, edited by G. Feinman and J. Marcus, pp. 173–198. Santa Fe: School of American research Press.

Wrigley, C. 1960. Speculations on the economic prehistory of Africa. *Journal of African History* 1(2): 189–203.

———. 1962. Linguistic clues to African History. *Journal of African History* 7: 293–325.

Wu, L., C. Zhu, C. Zhang, C. Ma, X. Wang, F. Li, B. Li and K. Li. 2014. Impact of Holocene climate change on the Prehistoric cultures of Zhejiang region, East China. *Journal of Geographical Science* 24: 669–688.

Wu, X., Zhang, C., Goldberg, P., Cohen, D., Pan, Y., Arpin, T., Bar-Yosef, O. 2012. Early Pottery at 20,000 Years Ago in Xianrendong Cave, China. *Science* 336: 1696–1700.

Xin, W., B. T. Fuller, P. Zhang, S. Hu, Y. Hu and X. Shang. 2018. Millet manuring as a driving force for the Late Neolithic agricultural expansion of north China. *Nature Scientific Reports* 8(5552): 1–9. |DOI: 10.1038/s41598–018–23315–4

Xu, S., I. Pugach, M. Stoneking, M. Kayser, Li Jin and the HUGO Pan-Asian SNP Consortium. 2012. Genetic Dating indicates that Asian-Papuan admixture through Eastern Indonesia corresponds to the Austronesian Expansion. *Proceedings of the National Academy of Sciences* 109(12): 4574–4579.

Yang, X., H. J. Barton, Z. Wan, Q. Li, Z. Ma, M. Li, D. Zhang, and J. Wu. 2013. Sago type palms were important plant food prior to rice in southern subtropical China. *PloS One* 8(5): 63148.

Yang, X., Q. Chen, Y. Ma, Z. Li, H.-C. Hung, Q. Zhang, Z. Jin, S. Liu, Z. Zhou, X. Fu. 2018. New Radiocarbon and archaeobotanic evidence reveal the timing and route of southward dispersal of rice farming in South China. *Science Bulletin* 63: 1495–1501.

Zangato, E., and A. F. C. Holl. 2010. On the Iron Front: New Evidence from North Central Africa. *Journal of African Archaeology* 8(1): 1–17.

Zeder, M. A. 2012. The Broad-Spectrum Revolution at 40: Resource diversity, Intensification, and an Alternative to optimal Foraging explanations. *Journal of Anthropological Archaeology* 31: 241–264.

Zeltner, J. C. 1980. *Pages d'Histoire du Kanem: Pays Tchadien,* Paris: L'Harmattan.

Zhang, C., and Hung, H. C. 2008. The Neolithic of Southern China: Origin, development, and dispersal. *Asian Perspectives* 47(2): 299–329.

Zink, A. R., W. Grabner, U. Reischl, H. Wolf &A. G. Nerlich. 2003. Molecular study on human tuberculosis in three geographically distinct and time delineated populations from Ancient Egypt. *Epidemiology and Infection* 130 (2): 239–249.

Zhu, Z., Dennell, R., Huang, W., et al. 2018. Hominin occupation of the Chinese loess plateau since about 2.1 million years ago. *Nature* 559: 608–612.

Glossary

Adaptive radiation: Adaptive radiation is the evolutionary process through which an organism differentiates into variants that adapt and successfully colonize new environments

aDNA: Ancient DNA refers to DNA extracted from biological samples of paleontological, archaeological, and historical origins

Admixture: In population genetics, admixture refers to the combination of genetic material between individuals and populations.

Ardipithecines: Ardipithecines are a genus of extinct early hominids consisting of four species with occasional bipedalism that lived in East and North-Central Africa between 7 and 4.1 million years ago.

Australopithecines: The Australopithecines consist of any of various extinct hominids (*Australopithecus* and *Paranthropus*) that lived in southern, eastern, and north-central Africa between 2 and 4 million years ago. They include gracile and robust forms with relatively small brains, bipedal locomotion, and near-human dentition.

Austronesian: Austronesian refers to a group of about 1,200 languages spread from Hawaii and Easter Island in the east to Madagascar in the west, New Zealand in the south, and the islands of Southeast Asia in the north.

Bantu: Bantu refers to groups of languages from the Niger-Congo family spoken in Central, Eastern, and Southern Africa.

BCE/CE: Before Common Era, previously known as Before Christ (BC) / Common Era, previously known as Anno Domini (AD)

Carrying capacity: Carrying capacity generally expressed in term of total population of total biomass refers to the maximum population an area can sustain without ecological environmental degradation

Chadic: Chadic is a group of languages from the Afro-Asiatic family spoken in north-central and West Africa, essentially in the Chad basin.

Extended evolutionary synthesis: As used in theoretical biology, the extended evolutionary synthesis (EES) is a broad and plural interpretative framework encompassing different approaches. It is geared to understand evolution based on empirical and theoretical findings of current studies such as heredity and evolutionary developmental biology.

Founder effect: The founder effect is the reduced genetic diversity resulting from the separation of a small colonizing group from a larger initial population

Fractal: Driven by recursion, fractals are images of dynamic systems, never-ending patterns created by repetition at different scales of a simple process over and over in an ongoing feedback loop.

Genomics: Genomics is the study of the genetic makeup of organisms

Gradualism: Gradualism is the theoretical conception of biological evolution according to which organisms' morphological changes occur in small cumulative steps

Inheritance: As used in biology, inheritance is the transmission of genes from parents to offspring.

Introgression: In biology introgression refers to the gradual transfer of gene from one organism to the gene pool of another.

Mendelian genetics: Mendelian genetics is simply the theory of genetic inheritance.

Modern synthesis: The modern synthesis, also called neo-Darwinism, combined Mendelian genetics with Darwin's natural selection to frame a more comprehensive evolutionary theory.

Natural selection: Natural selection is a process through which organisms with traits enhancing their better adaptation to an environment will survive and reproduce, while those unable to adapt are eliminated.

Neo-Darwinism: Neo-Darwinism is the fusion of Darwin's natural selection and Mendelian genetics.

Phoneme: A phoneme is the smallest basic distinctive unit of speech sound of any language

Punctuated equilibrium: Punctuated equilibrium is an evolutionary process made of long periods of stability in an organism's characteristics and short periods of rapid change

Uniformitarianism: Uniformitarianism is a geological theory popularized in the nineteenth century by Charles Lyell in his *Principles of Geology*. It states that the processes and forces observable at the earth surface today are the same that have shaped present-day landforms over long time scales.

Variation: In biology, variation that can be either genetic (genotypic) or environmentally derived (phenotypic), refers to any difference between cells, individual organisms, or groups of organisms of any species.

Index

Abang Minko, 155
Abbasid, 87;
    Caliphate, 88;
    Dynasty, 164
Abydos, 198
Achaemenid, 7, 87
Acheulean, 35
Adamawa, 149, 155
Aden, Gulf, 87
Admixture, 2, 6, 27, 45, 46, 48, 50,
    73, 74, 83–84, 143–46, 158, 162,
    175–77, 188
Adrar Bous, 184, 200
Adrar-n-Ifogha, 124, 185
Afade, 97–98, 120
Afghanistan, 7
Africa, ix, 1, 2, 8, 13–14, 17, 19–20,
    25–28, 37–43, 45–50, 53, 56, 59–60,
    62, 86, 88–90, 93, 95, 103, 106,
    114, 130, 134–35, 141–43, 148, 157,
    163, 169–71, 174–77, 179, 185, 193,
    195–96, 198, 204–5, 207–8;
        Central, 2, 13, 20–21, 23–24, 68,
            134, 139–41, 143, 145–46,
            148–51, 154–55, 157–58, 160,
            195, 197, 208;
        East, 1, 9, 13, 20–21, 23–24,
            26–28, 34–36, 39, 41, 50,
            60, 82, 84, 89–91, 103–5,

134–35, 137, 139, 141,
    144–48, 150–51, 154, 158,
    161–63, 175, 187–88, 194–95,
    197, 205, 208;
    Horn of, 42, 134;
    North, 7, 8, 27–28, 35, 41–43,
        105, 122, 129, 134, 171, 174–
        75, 182, 195, 205, 207–8;
    Northeast, 2, 90, 163, 176–77,
        188, 192, 196;
    South 8, 9, 18, 20–21, 23–25,
        27–28, 37, 41, 43, 54–56, 90,
        134–36, 139, 143–46, 151,
        154, 161–63, 165, 168, 171,
        189, 191–92, 195;
    Southeast, 148;
    Sub-Saharan, 133, 144–46;
    West, 125, 134–35, 139, 143, 148,
        151, 175, 184, 186, 188, 192,
        195, 197, 205, 207–8
Afroasiatic, 1, 50, 188, 205, 207
Ahaggar, 179, 181, 184
Aihdab, 90
Air, Mountains, 171, 181
Alawma, Idriss King, 125
Algeria, 9, 35, 54, 182–84, 186, 197
Alph, 97, 120
Amachita, 119
Ambolisatra, 84

About the Author

Augustin F. C. Holl (PhD 1983, Paris-1: Pantheon-Sorbonne, Habilitation 1994, Paris X-Nanterre) is now Distinguished University Professor and Director of the Africa Research Center at Xiamen University (Fujian, P.R. China). He was successively professor of anthropology at the University of California, San Diego; curator at the Museum of Anthropology, professor of anthropology, and professor of Afro-American and African studies at the University of Michigan, Ann Arbor (USA); professor and vice president for international relations at Paris Nanterre University (France); and deputy director at the Institute of Humanities and Social Science (CNRS, Paris, France). He has conducted fieldwork in the Negev Desert (Israel), Dhar Tichitt (Mauretanian Sahara), Mouhoun Bend (Burkina Faso), Houlouf region (Cameroon), and at the Senegambian Megaliths and Saloum Shell-middens (Senegal). He has published fifteen books, including The *Diwan Revisited* (2000), *Ancient African Metallurgy* (2000, with M. S. Bisson, S. T. Childs, and P. De Barros), *The Land of Houlouf* (2002), *Holocene Saharans* (2004), *Ethnoarchaeology of Shuwa-Arab Settlements* (2003), *Saharan Rock Art* (2004), *West African Early Towns* (2006), *Africa: The Archaeological Background* (2015) and *Megaliths, Cultural Landscape and the Production of Ancestors* (2017).

www.ingramcontent.com/pod-product-compliance
Lightning Source LLC
Chambersburg PA
CBHW022304280326
41932CB00010B/982